Lewis Trondheim   Stéphane Oiry

MAGGY GARRISSON

First published in English in 2019
by SelfMadeHero
139–141 Pancras Road
London NW1 1UN
www.selfmadehero.com

Words by Lewis Trondheim
Art by Stéphane Oiry
Translated from the French edition by Emma Wilson

Publishing Director: Emma Hayley
Sales & Marketing Manager: Sam Humphrey
Editorial & Production Manager: Guillaume Rater
Designer: Txabi Jones
UK Publicist: Paul Smith
With thanks to: Dan Lockwood and Edward Gauvin

First published in French by Dupuis as
Maggy Garrisson 1 – Fais un sourire, Maggy
© DUPUIS 2014, by Trondheim, Oiry
Maggy Garrisson 2 – L'homme qui est entré dans mon lit
© DUPUIS 2015, by Trondheim, Oiry
Maggy Garrisson 3 – Je ne voulais pas que ça finisse comme ça
© DUPUIS 2016, by Trondheim, Oiry
www.dupuis.com
All rights reserved

A CIP record for this book is available from the British Library

ISBN: 978-1-910593-64-6

10 9 8 7 6 5 4 3 2 1

Printed and bound in Slovenia

Lewis Trondheim   Stéphane Oiry

MAGGY GARRISSON

SELF MADE HERO

1. GIVE US A SMILE, MAGGY

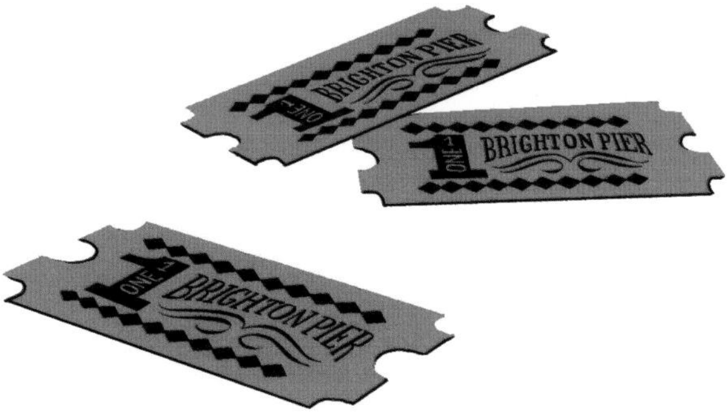
ONE 1 BRIGHTON PIER
ONE 1 BRIGHTON PIER
ONE 1 BRIGHTON PIER

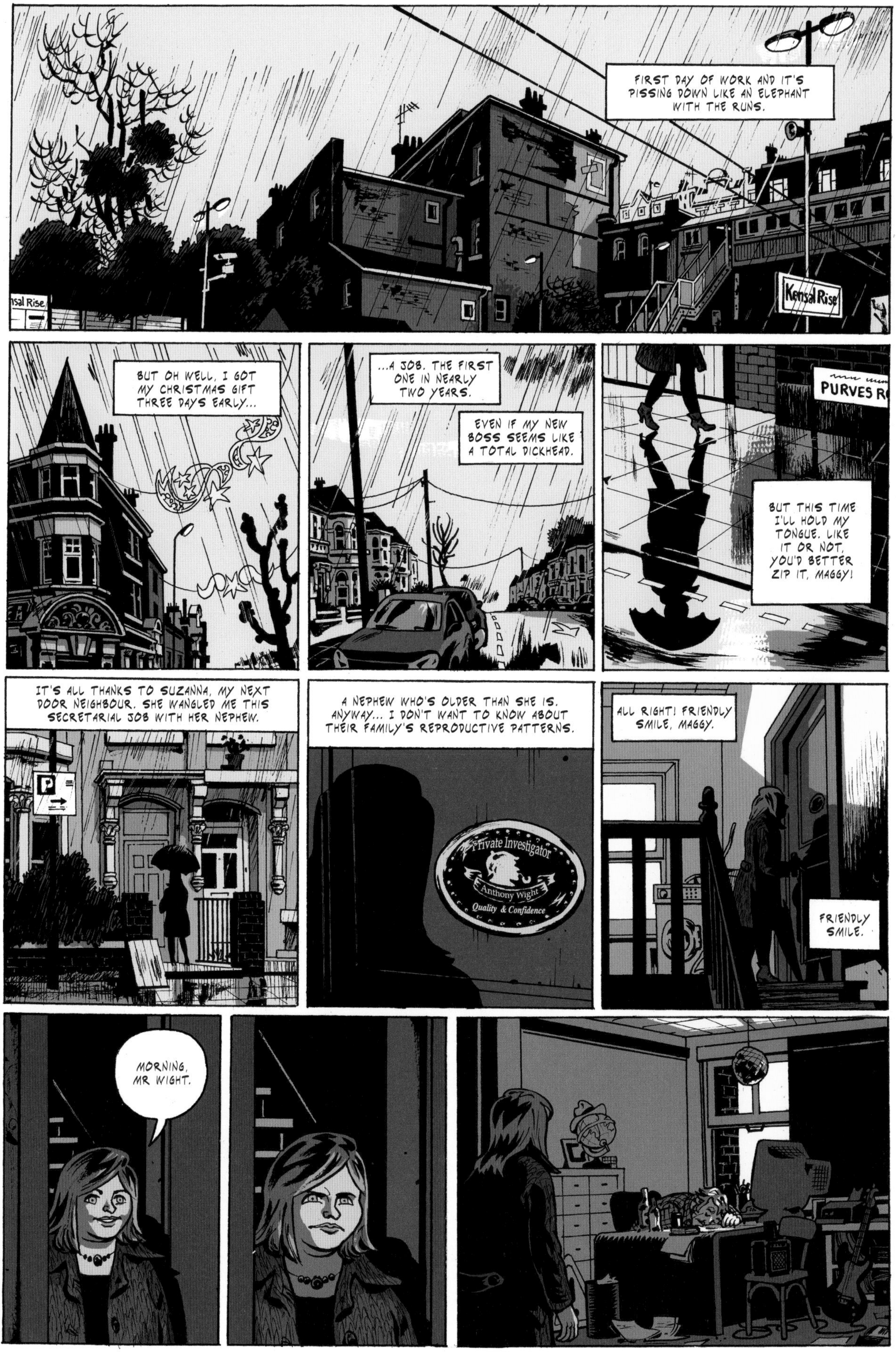

FIRST DAY OF WORK AND IT'S PISSING DOWN LIKE AN ELEPHANT WITH THE RUNS.
Kensal Rise
BUT OH WELL, I GOT MY CHRISTMAS GIFT THREE DAYS EARLY...
...A JOB. THE FIRST ONE IN NEARLY TWO YEARS.
EVEN IF MY NEW BOSS SEEMS LIKE A TOTAL DICKHEAD.
PURVES R
BUT THIS TIME I'LL HOLD MY TONGUE. LIKE IT OR NOT, YOU'D BETTER ZIP IT, MAGGY!
IT'S ALL THANKS TO SUZANNA, MY NEXT DOOR NEIGHBOUR. SHE WANGLED ME THIS SECRETARIAL JOB WITH HER NEPHEW.
A NEPHEW WHO'S OLDER THAN SHE IS. ANYWAY... I DON'T WANT TO KNOW ABOUT THEIR FAMILY'S REPRODUCTIVE PATTERNS.
Private Investigator
Anthony Wight
Quality & Confidence
ALL RIGHT! FRIENDLY SMILE, MAGGY.
FRIENDLY SMILE.
MORNING, MR WIGHT.

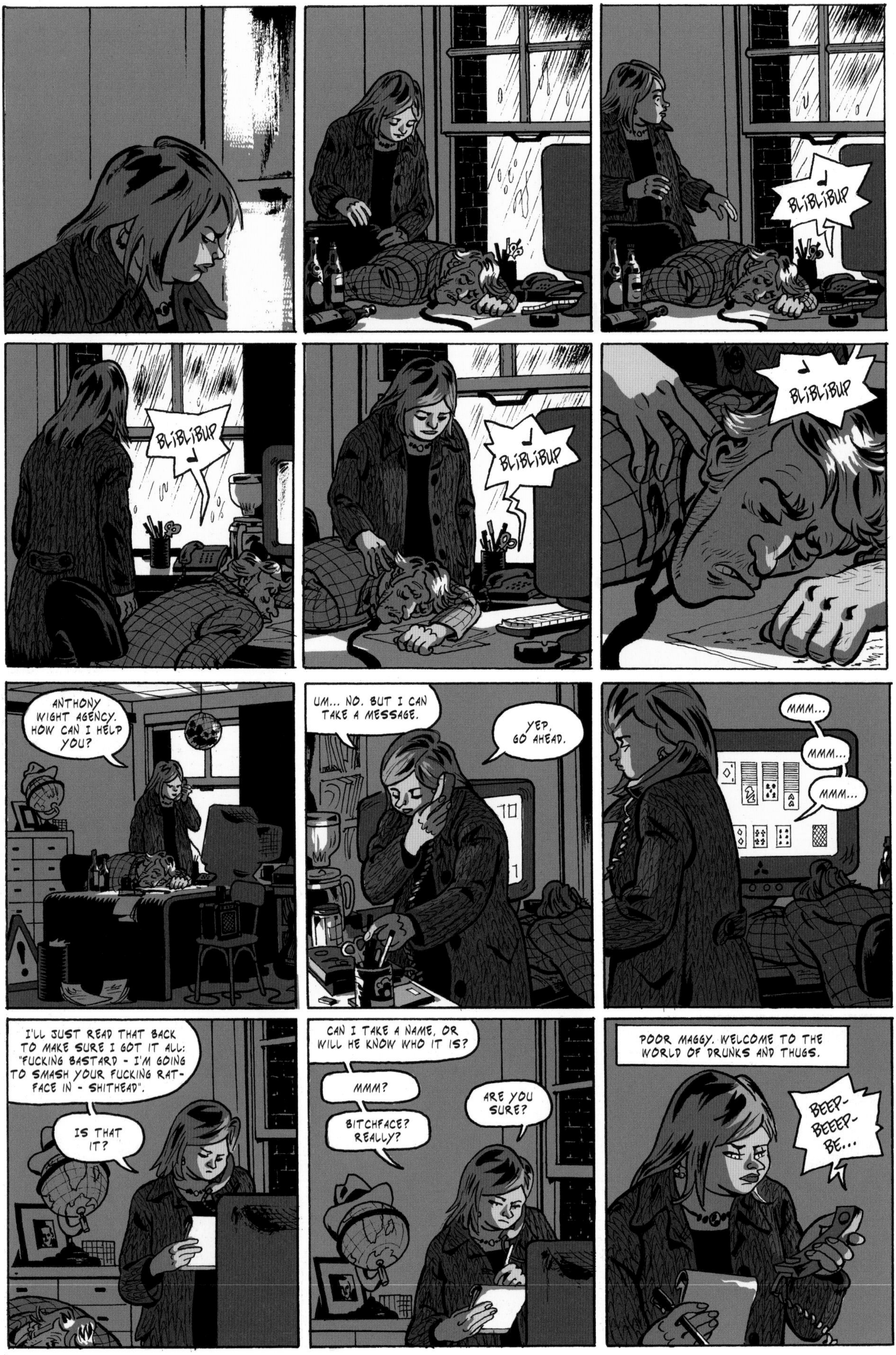
BLIBLIBUP
BLIBLIBUP
BLIBLIBUP
BLIBLIBUP
ANTHONY WIGHT AGENCY. HOW CAN I HELP YOU?
UM... NO. BUT I CAN TAKE A MESSAGE.
YEP, GO AHEAD.
MMM...
MMM...
MMM...
I'LL JUST READ THAT BACK TO MAKE SURE I GOT IT ALL: "FUCKING BASTARD - I'M GOING TO SMASH YOUR FUCKING RAT-FACE IN - SHITHEAD".
IS THAT IT?
CAN I TAKE A NAME, OR WILL HE KNOW WHO IT IS?
MMM?
BITCHFACE? REALLY?
ARE YOU SURE?
POOR MAGGY. WELCOME TO THE WORLD OF DRUNKS AND THUGS.
BEEP-BEEEP-BE...

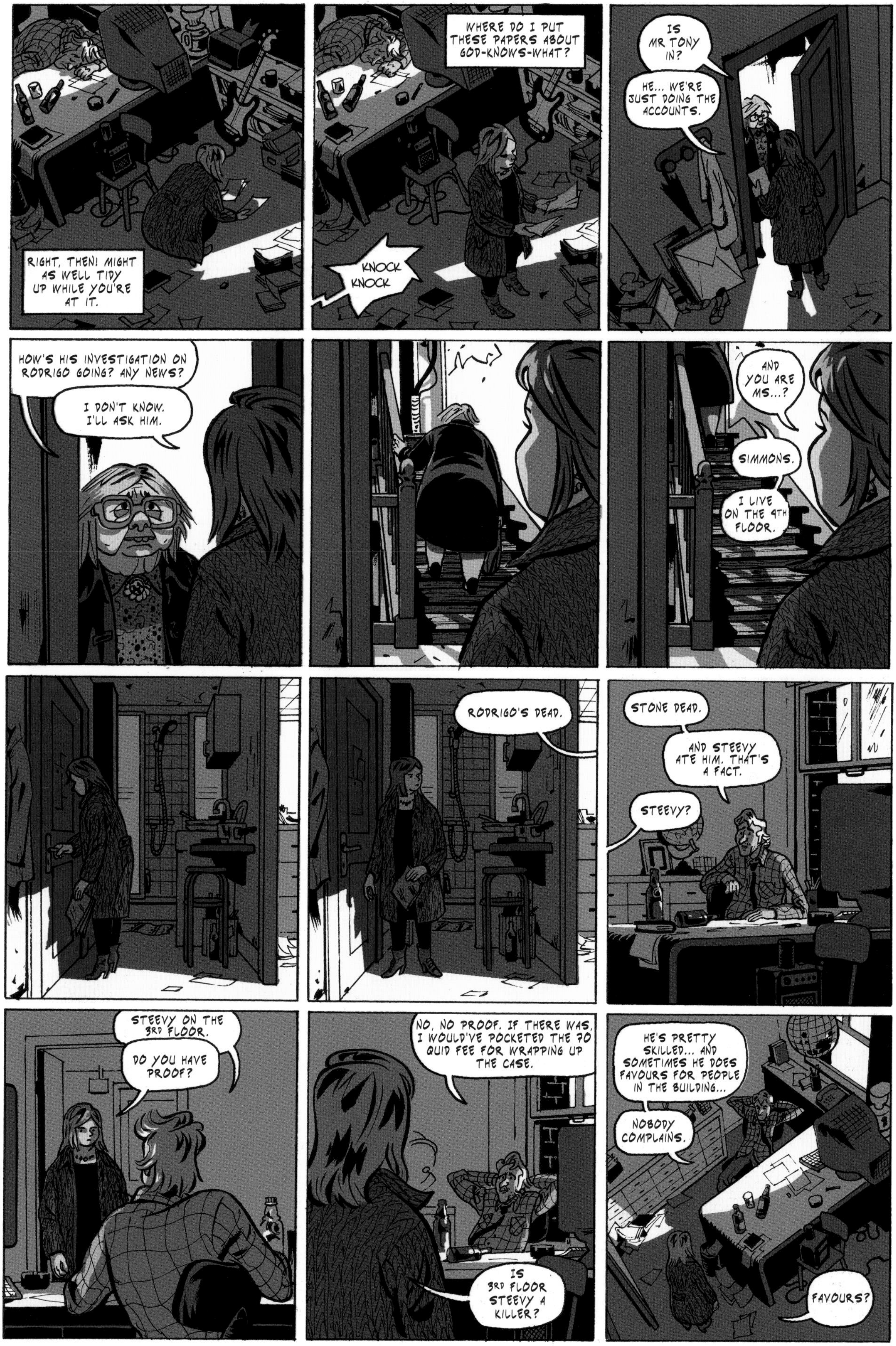
RIGHT, THEN! MIGHT AS WELL TIDY UP WHILE YOU'RE AT IT.
WHERE DO I PUT THESE PAPERS ABOUT GOD-KNOWS-WHAT?
KNOCK KNOCK
IS MR TONY IN?
HE... WE'RE JUST DOING THE ACCOUNTS.
HOW'S HIS INVESTIGATION ON RODRIGO GOING? ANY NEWS?
I DON'T KNOW. I'LL ASK HIM.
AND YOU ARE MS...?
SIMMONS.
I LIVE ON THE 4TH FLOOR.
RODRIGO'S DEAD.
STONE DEAD.
AND STEEVY ATE HIM. THAT'S A FACT.
STEEVY?
STEEVY ON THE 3RD FLOOR.
DO YOU HAVE PROOF?
NO, NO PROOF. IF THERE WAS, I WOULD'VE POCKETED THE 70 QUID FEE FOR WRAPPING UP THE CASE.
IS 3RD FLOOR STEEVY A KILLER?
HE'S PRETTY SKILLED... AND SOMETIMES HE DOES FAVOURS FOR PEOPLE IN THE BUILDING...
NOBODY COMPLAINS.
FAVOURS?

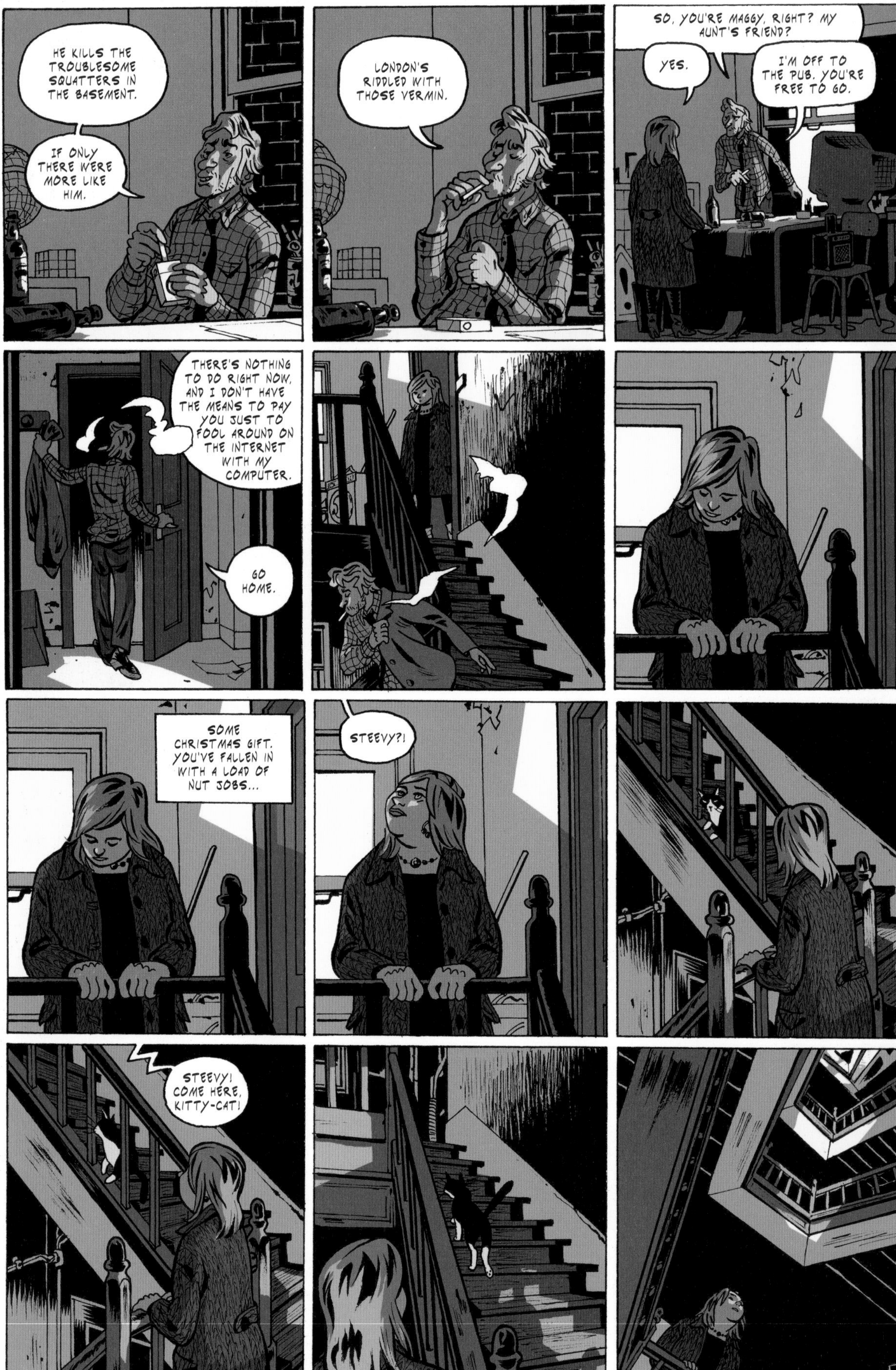
HE KILLS THE TROUBLESOME SQUATTERS IN THE BASEMENT.
IF ONLY THERE WERE MORE LIKE HIM.
LONDON'S RIDDLED WITH THOSE VERMIN.
SO, YOU'RE MAGGY, RIGHT? MY AUNT'S FRIEND?
YES.
I'M OFF TO THE PUB. YOU'RE FREE TO GO.
THERE'S NOTHING TO DO RIGHT NOW, AND I DON'T HAVE THE MEANS TO PAY YOU JUST TO FOOL AROUND ON THE INTERNET WITH MY COMPUTER.
GO HOME.
SOME CHRISTMAS GIFT. YOU'VE FALLEN IN WITH A LOAD OF NUT JOBS...
STEEVY?!
STEEVY! COME HERE, KITTY-CAT!

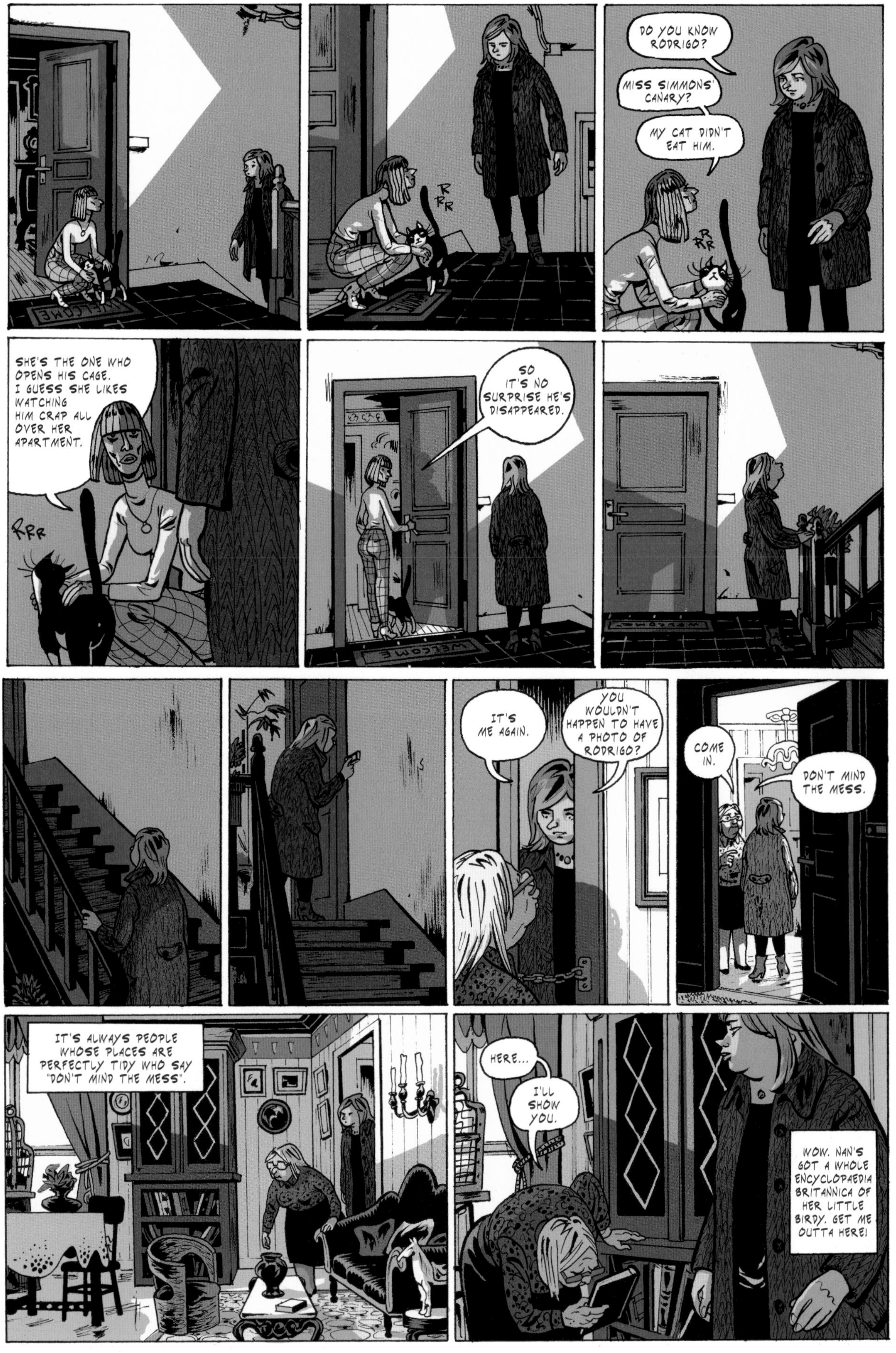
DO YOU KNOW RODRIGO?
MISS SIMMONS' CANARY?
MY CAT DIDN'T EAT HIM.
SHE'S THE ONE WHO OPENS HIS CAGE. I GUESS SHE LIKES WATCHING HIM CRAP ALL OVER HER APARTMENT.
SO IT'S NO SURPRISE HE'S DISAPPEARED.
IT'S ME AGAIN.
YOU WOULDN'T HAPPEN TO HAVE A PHOTO OF RODRIGO?
COME IN.
DON'T MIND THE MESS.
IT'S ALWAYS PEOPLE WHOSE PLACES ARE PERFECTLY TIDY WHO SAY "DON'T MIND THE MESS".
HERE...
I'LL SHOW YOU.
WOW. NAN'S GOT A WHOLE ENCYCLOPAEDIA BRITANNICA OF HER LITTLE BIRDY. GET ME OUTTA HERE!

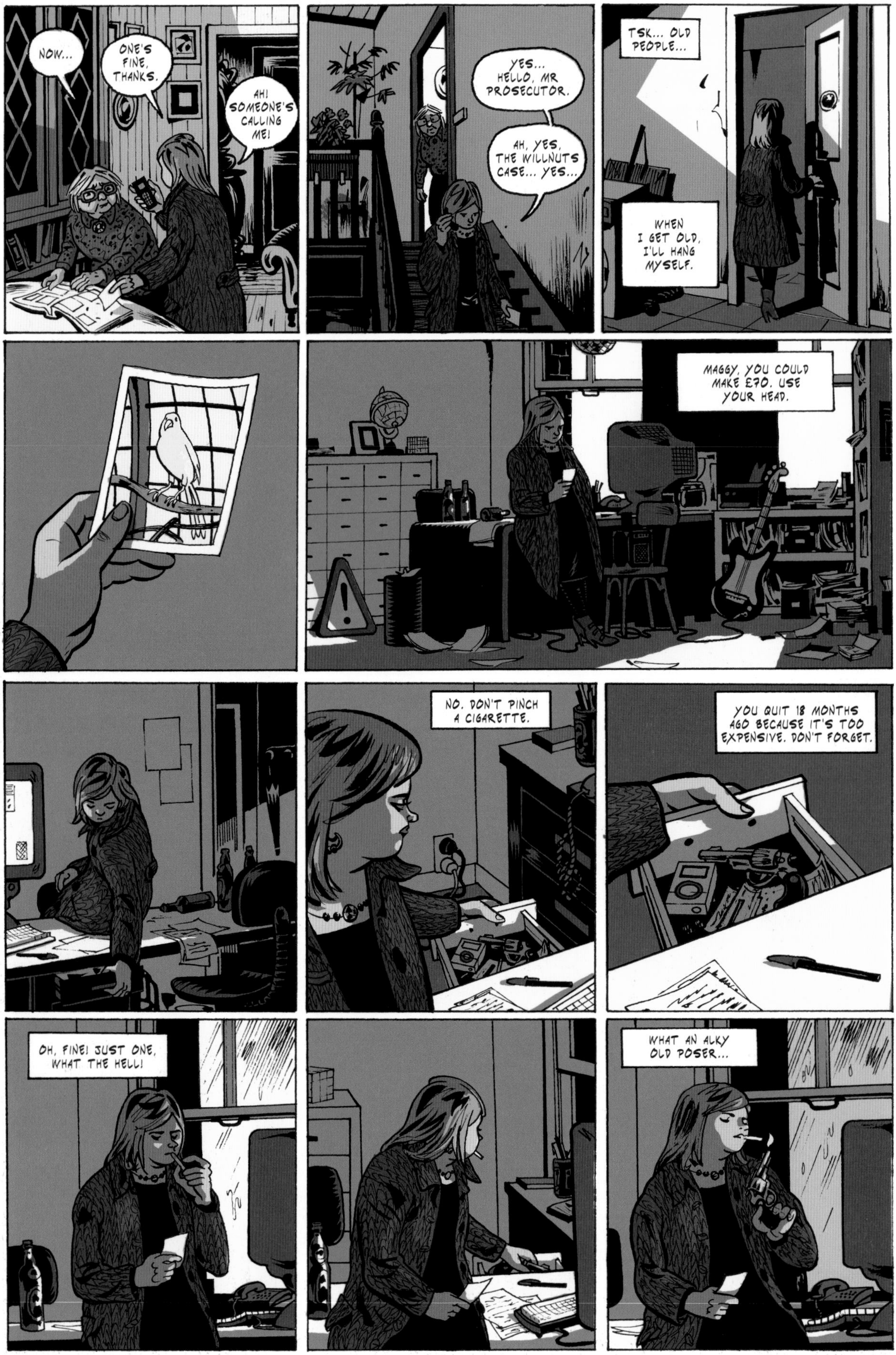
NOW...
ONE'S FINE, THANKS.
AH! SOMEONE'S CALLING ME!
YES... HELLO, MR PROSECUTOR.
AH, YES, THE WILLNUTS CASE... YES...
TSK... OLD PEOPLE...
WHEN I GET OLD, I'LL HANG MYSELF.
MAGGY, YOU COULD MAKE £70. USE YOUR HEAD.
NO. DON'T PINCH A CIGARETTE.
YOU QUIT 18 MONTHS AGO BECAUSE IT'S TOO EXPENSIVE. DON'T FORGET.
OH, FINE! JUST ONE, WHAT THE HELL!
WHAT AN ALKY OLD POSER...

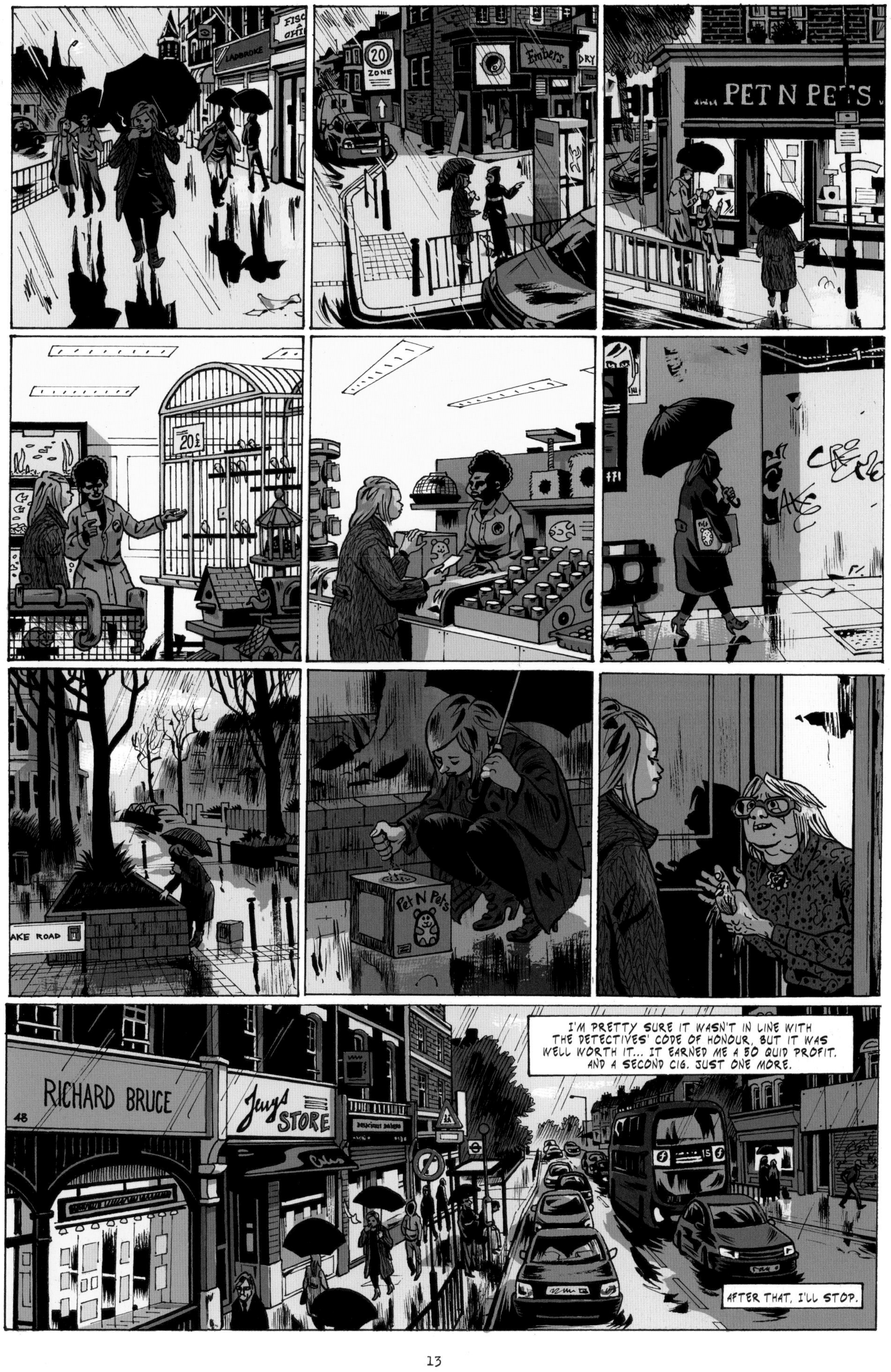
LADBROKE
20
ZONE
Embers
PET N PETS
20£
Pet N Pets
AKE ROAD
RICHARD BRUCE
48
STORE
I'M PRETTY SURE IT WASN'T IN LINE WITH THE DETECTIVES' CODE OF HONOUR, BUT IT WAS WELL WORTH IT... IT EARNED ME A 50 QUID PROFIT. AND A SECOND CIG. JUST ONE MORE.
AFTER THAT, I'LL STOP.

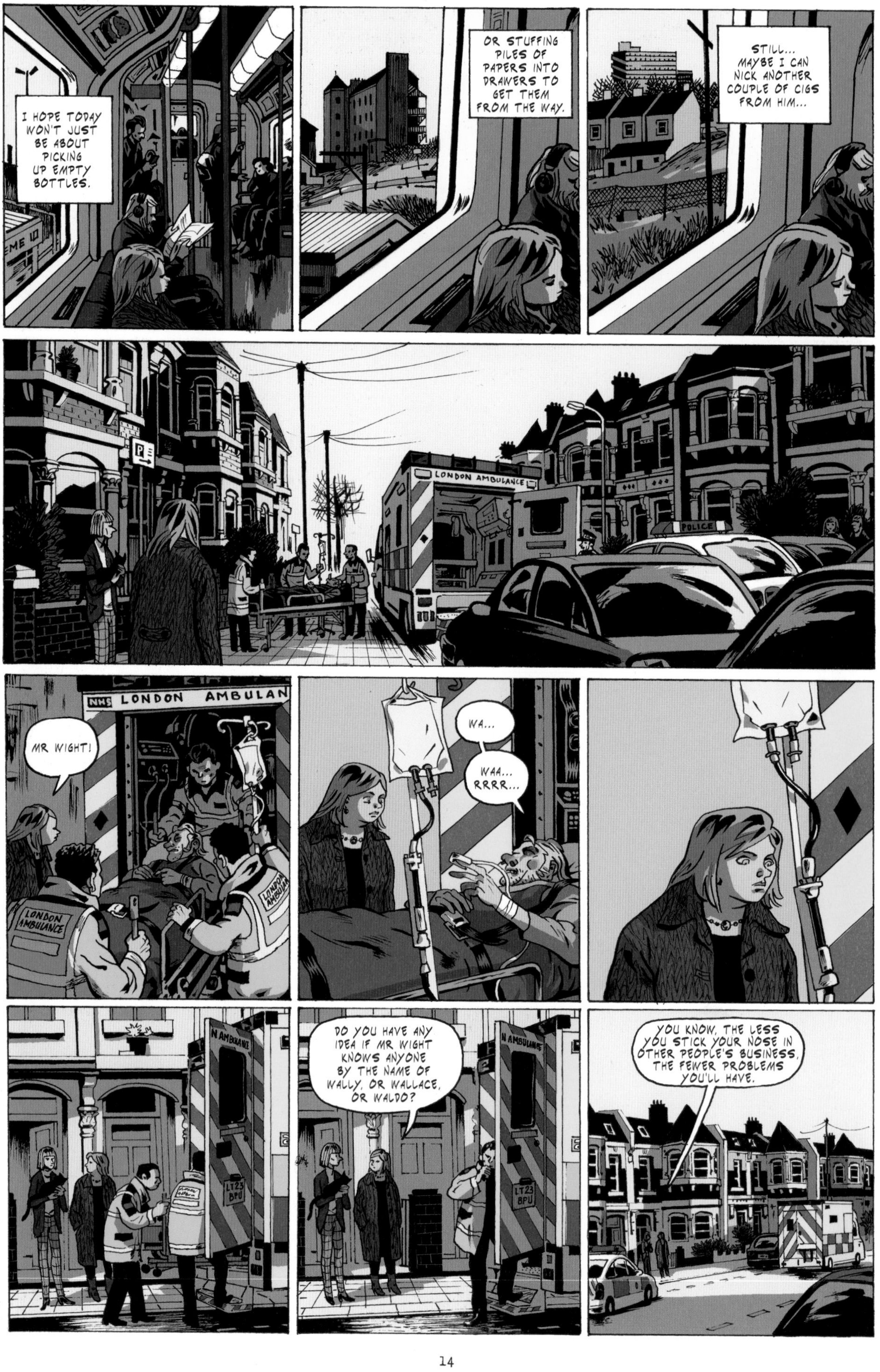
I HOPE TODAY WON'T JUST BE ABOUT PICKING UP EMPTY BOTTLES.
OR STUFFING PILES OF PAPERS INTO DRAWERS TO GET THEM FROM THE WAY.
STILL... MAYBE I CAN NICK ANOTHER COUPLE OF CIGS FROM HIM...
LONDON AMBULANCE
POLICE
NHS LONDON AMBULAN
MR WIGHT!
LONDON AMBULANCE
WA...
WAA... RRRR...
DO YOU HAVE ANY IDEA IF MR WIGHT KNOWS ANYONE BY THE NAME OF WALLY, OR WALLACE, OR WALDO?
YOU KNOW, THE LESS YOU STICK YOUR NOSE IN OTHER PEOPLE'S BUSINESS, THE FEWER PROBLEMS YOU'LL HAVE.

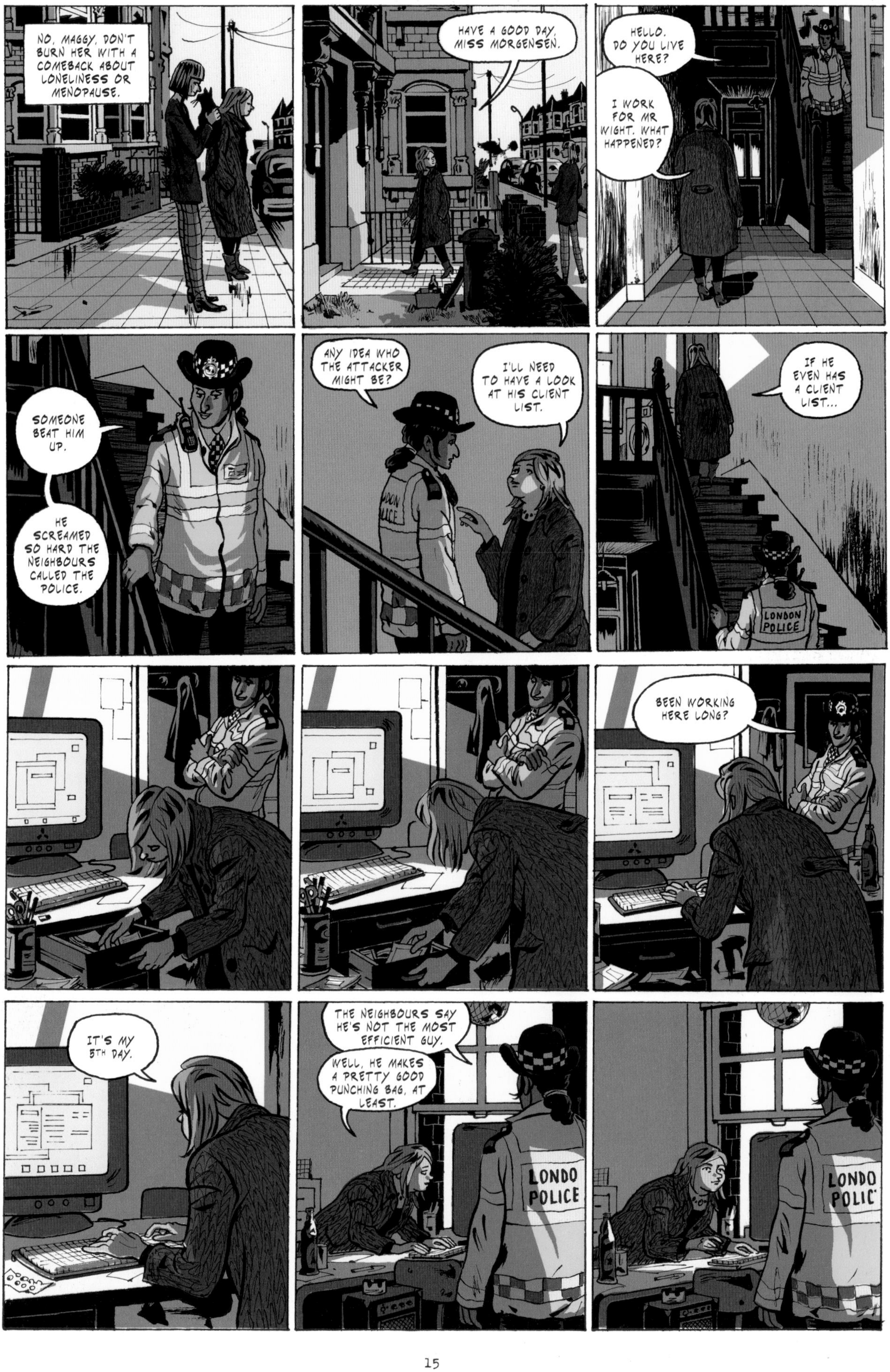

NO, MAGGY, DON'T BURN HER WITH A COMEBACK ABOUT LONELINESS OR MENOPAUSE.
HAVE A GOOD DAY, MISS MORGENSEN.
HELLO. DO YOU LIVE HERE?
I WORK FOR MR WIGHT. WHAT HAPPENED?
SOMEONE BEAT HIM UP.
HE SCREAMED SO HARD THE NEIGHBOURS CALLED THE POLICE.
ANY IDEA WHO THE ATTACKER MIGHT BE?
I'LL NEED TO HAVE A LOOK AT HIS CLIENT LIST.
IF HE EVEN HAS A CLIENT LIST...
LONDON POLICE
BEEN WORKING HERE LONG?
IT'S MY 5TH DAY.
THE NEIGHBOURS SAY HE'S NOT THE MOST EFFICIENT GUY.
WELL, HE MAKES A PRETTY GOOD PUNCHING BAG, AT LEAST.
LONDO POLICE
LONDO POLIC

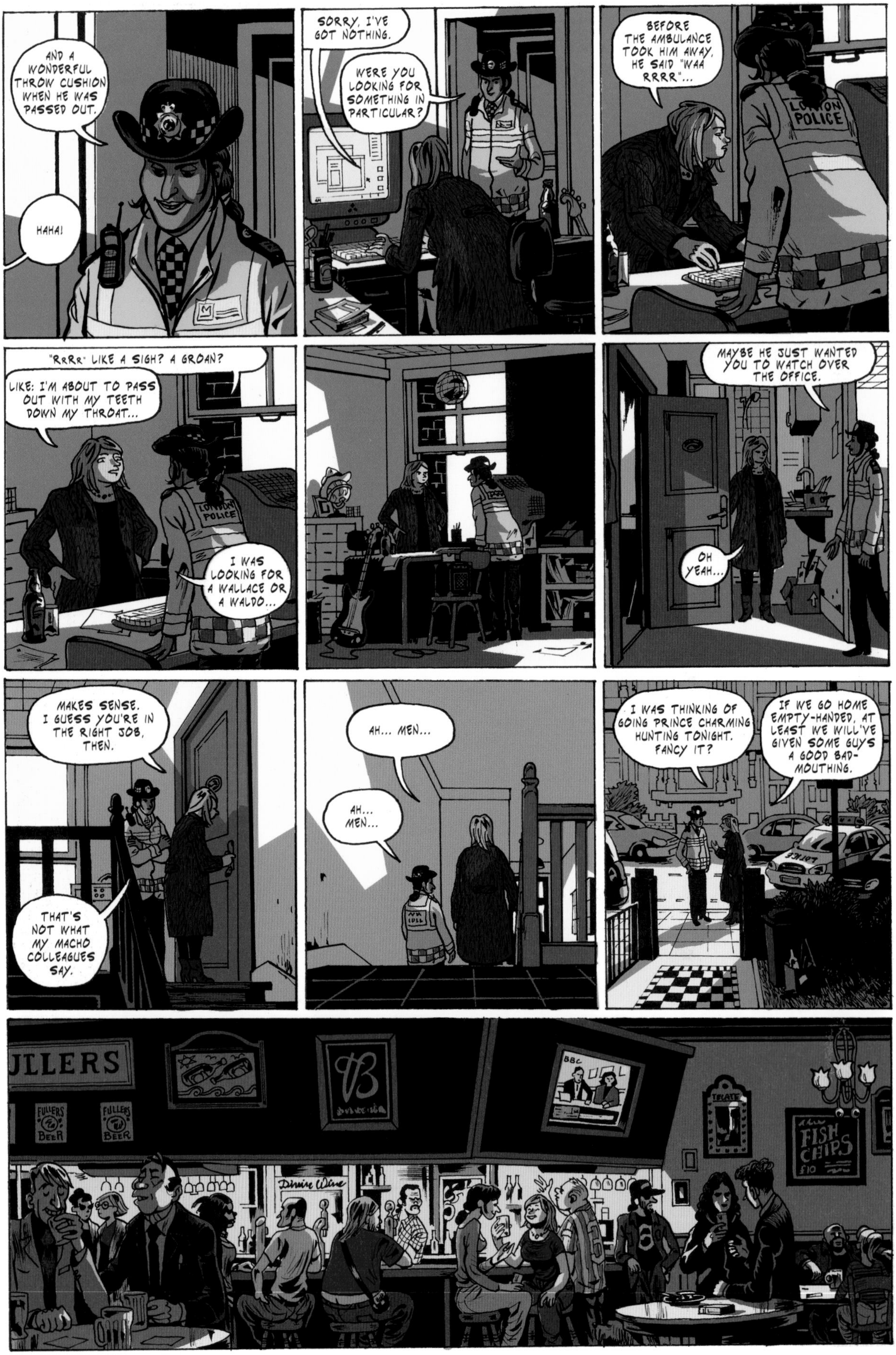
AND A WONDERFUL THROW CUSHION WHEN HE WAS PASSED OUT.
HAHA!
SORRY, I'VE GOT NOTHING.
WERE YOU LOOKING FOR SOMETHING IN PARTICULAR?
BEFORE THE AMBULANCE TOOK HIM AWAY, HE SAID "WAA RRRR"...
POLICE
"RRRR" LIKE A SIGH? A GROAN?
LIKE: I'M ABOUT TO PASS OUT WITH MY TEETH DOWN MY THROAT...
I WAS LOOKING FOR A WALLACE OR A WALDO...
MAYBE HE JUST WANTED YOU TO WATCH OVER THE OFFICE.
OH YEAH...
MAKES SENSE. I GUESS YOU'RE IN THE RIGHT JOB, THEN.
THAT'S NOT WHAT MY MACHO COLLEAGUES SAY.
AH... MEN...
AH... MEN...
I WAS THINKING OF GOING PRINCE CHARMING HUNTING TONIGHT. FANCY IT?
IF WE GO HOME EMPTY-HANDED, AT LEAST WE WILL'VE GIVEN SOME GUYS A GOOD BAD-MOUTHING.
ULLERS
FULLERS BEER
FULLERS BEER
BBC
FISH CHIPS
£10

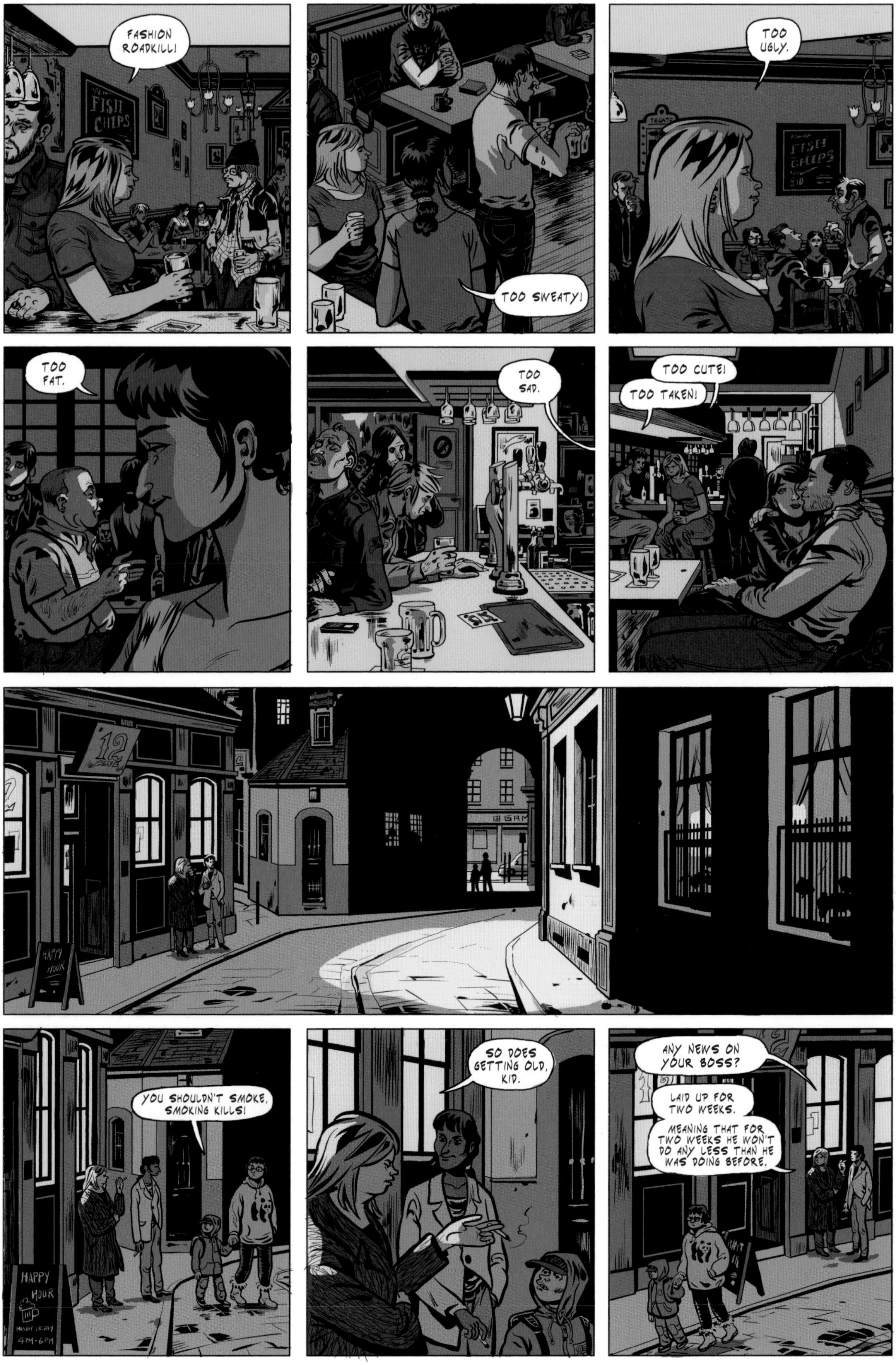
FASHION ROADKILL!
FISH CHIPS
TOO SWEATY!
TOO UGLY.
FISH CHIPS
TOO FAT.
TOO SAD.
TOO CUTE!
TOO TAKEN!
HAPPY HOUR
YOU SHOULDN'T SMOKE. SMOKING KILLS!
HAPPY HOUR
SO DOES GETTING OLD, KID.
ANY NEWS ON YOUR BOSS?
LAID UP FOR TWO WEEKS.
MEANING THAT FOR TWO WEEKS HE WON'T DO ANY LESS THAN HE WAS DOING BEFORE.

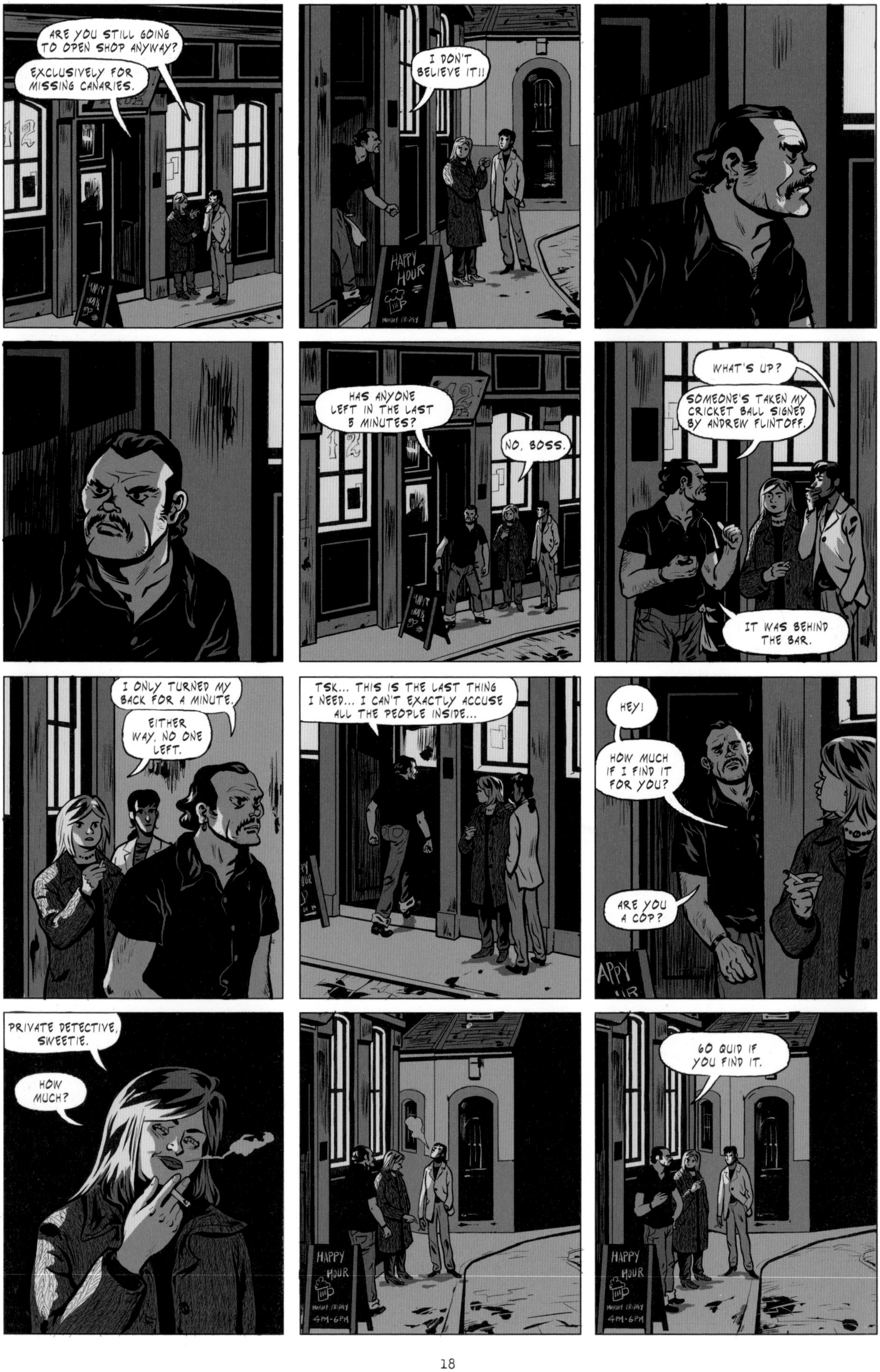
ARE YOU STILL GOING TO OPEN SHOP ANYWAY?
EXCLUSIVELY FOR MISSING CANARIES.
I DON'T BELIEVE IT!!
HAPPY HOUR
HAS ANYONE LEFT IN THE LAST 5 MINUTES?
NO, BOSS.
WHAT'S UP?
SOMEONE'S TAKEN MY CRICKET BALL SIGNED BY ANDREW FLINTOFF.
IT WAS BEHIND THE BAR.
I ONLY TURNED MY BACK FOR A MINUTE.
EITHER WAY, NO ONE LEFT.
TSK... THIS IS THE LAST THING I NEED... I CAN'T EXACTLY ACCUSE ALL THE PEOPLE INSIDE...
HEY!
HOW MUCH IF I FIND IT FOR YOU?
ARE YOU A COP?
PRIVATE DETECTIVE, SWEETIE.
HOW MUCH?
HAPPY HOUR
4PM-6PM
60 QUID IF YOU FIND IT.
HAPPY HOUR
4PM-6PM

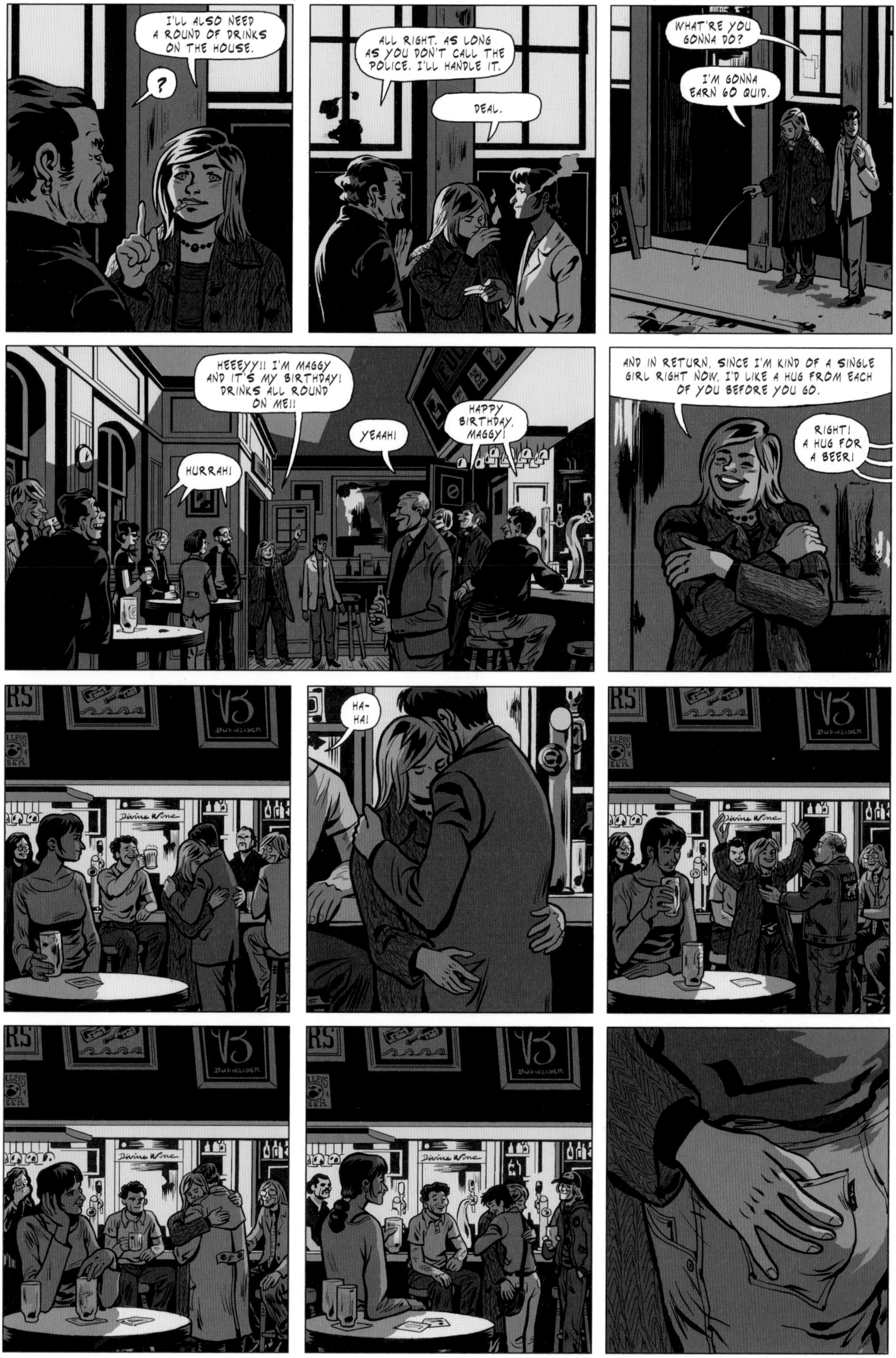
I'LL ALSO NEED A ROUND OF DRINKS ON THE HOUSE.
?
ALL RIGHT. AS LONG AS YOU DON'T CALL THE POLICE. I'LL HANDLE IT.
DEAL.
WHAT'RE YOU GONNA DO?
I'M GONNA EARN 60 QUID.
HEEEYY!! I'M MAGGY AND IT'S MY BIRTHDAY! DRINKS ALL ROUND ON ME!!
HURRAH!
YEAAH!
HAPPY BIRTHDAY, MAGGY!
AND IN RETURN, SINCE I'M KIND OF A SINGLE GIRL RIGHT NOW, I'D LIKE A HUG FROM EACH OF YOU BEFORE YOU GO.
RIGHT! A HUG FOR A BEER!
HA-HA!
Divine Wine
BUDWEISER

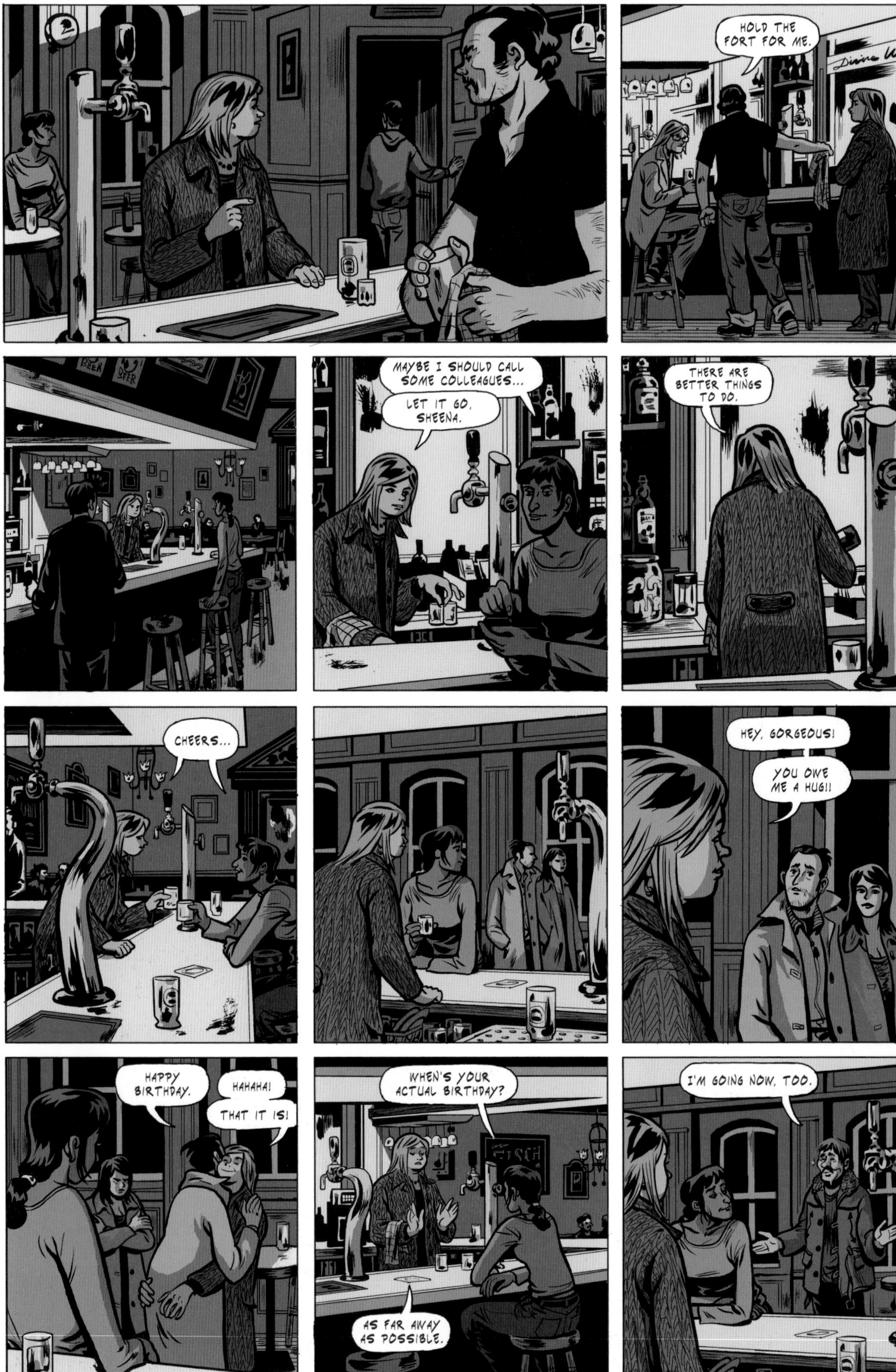
HOLD THE FORT FOR ME.
MAYBE I SHOULD CALL SOME COLLEAGUES...
LET IT GO, SHEENA.
THERE ARE BETTER THINGS TO DO.
CHEERS...
HEY, GORGEOUS!
YOU OWE ME A HUG!!
HAPPY BIRTHDAY.
HAHAHA!
THAT IT IS!
WHEN'S YOUR ACTUAL BIRTHDAY?
AS FAR AWAY AS POSSIBLE.
I'M GOING NOW, TOO.

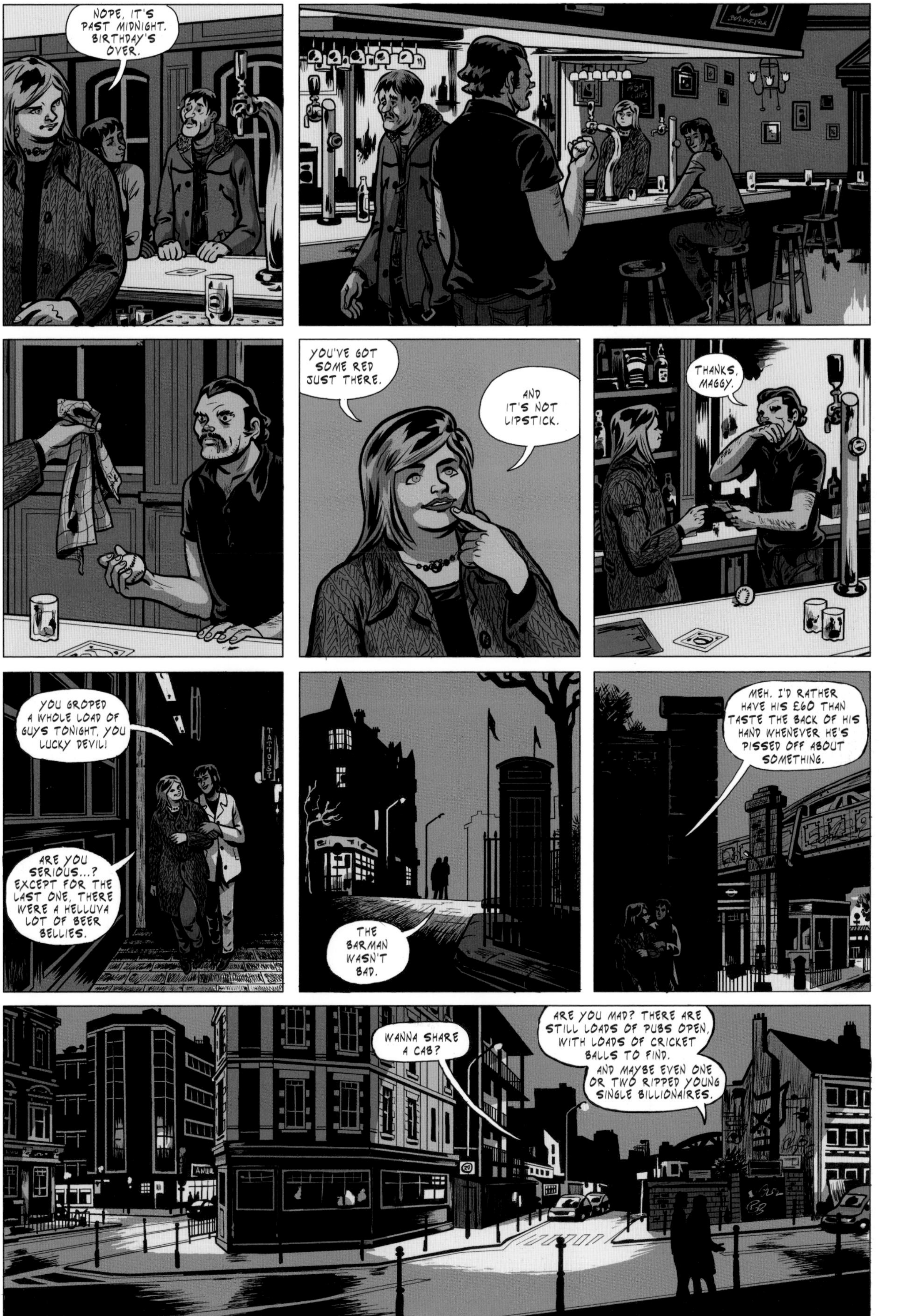
NOPE, IT'S PAST MIDNIGHT. BIRTHDAY'S OVER.
YOU'VE GOT SOME RED JUST THERE.
AND IT'S NOT LIPSTICK.
THANKS, MAGGY.
YOU GROPED A WHOLE LOAD OF GUYS TONIGHT, YOU LUCKY DEVIL!
ARE YOU SERIOUS...? EXCEPT FOR THE LAST ONE, THERE WERE A HELLUVA LOT OF BEER BELLIES.
THE BARMAN WASN'T BAD.
MEH. I'D RATHER HAVE HIS £60 THAN TASTE THE BACK OF HIS HAND WHENEVER HE'S PISSED OFF ABOUT SOMETHING.
WANNA SHARE A CAB?
ARE YOU MAD? THERE ARE STILL LOADS OF PUBS OPEN, WITH LOADS OF CRICKET BALLS TO FIND.
AND MAYBE EVEN ONE OR TWO RIPPED YOUNG SINGLE BILLIONAIRES.

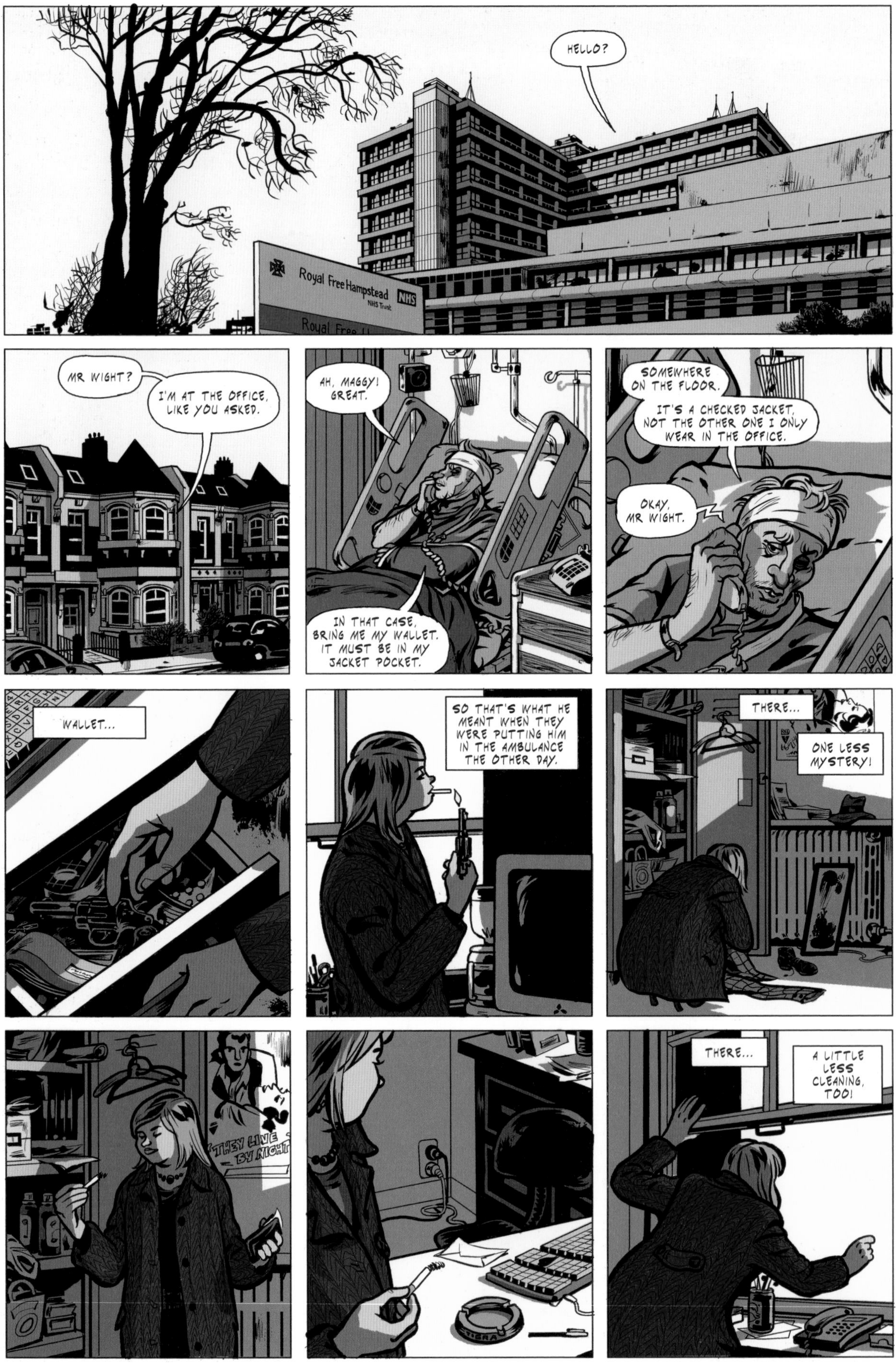
Royal Free Hampstead NHS Trust
NHS
HELLO?
MR WIGHT?
I'M AT THE OFFICE, LIKE YOU ASKED.
AH, MAGGY! GREAT.
IN THAT CASE, BRING ME MY WALLET. IT MUST BE IN MY JACKET POCKET.
SOMEWHERE ON THE FLOOR.
IT'S A CHECKED JACKET, NOT THE OTHER ONE I ONLY WEAR IN THE OFFICE.
OKAY, MR WIGHT.
WALLET...
SO THAT'S WHAT HE MEANT WHEN THEY WERE PUTTING HIM IN THE AMBULANCE THE OTHER DAY.
THERE...
ONE LESS MYSTERY!
THEY LIVE BY NIGHT
THERE...
A LITTLE LESS CLEANING, TOO!

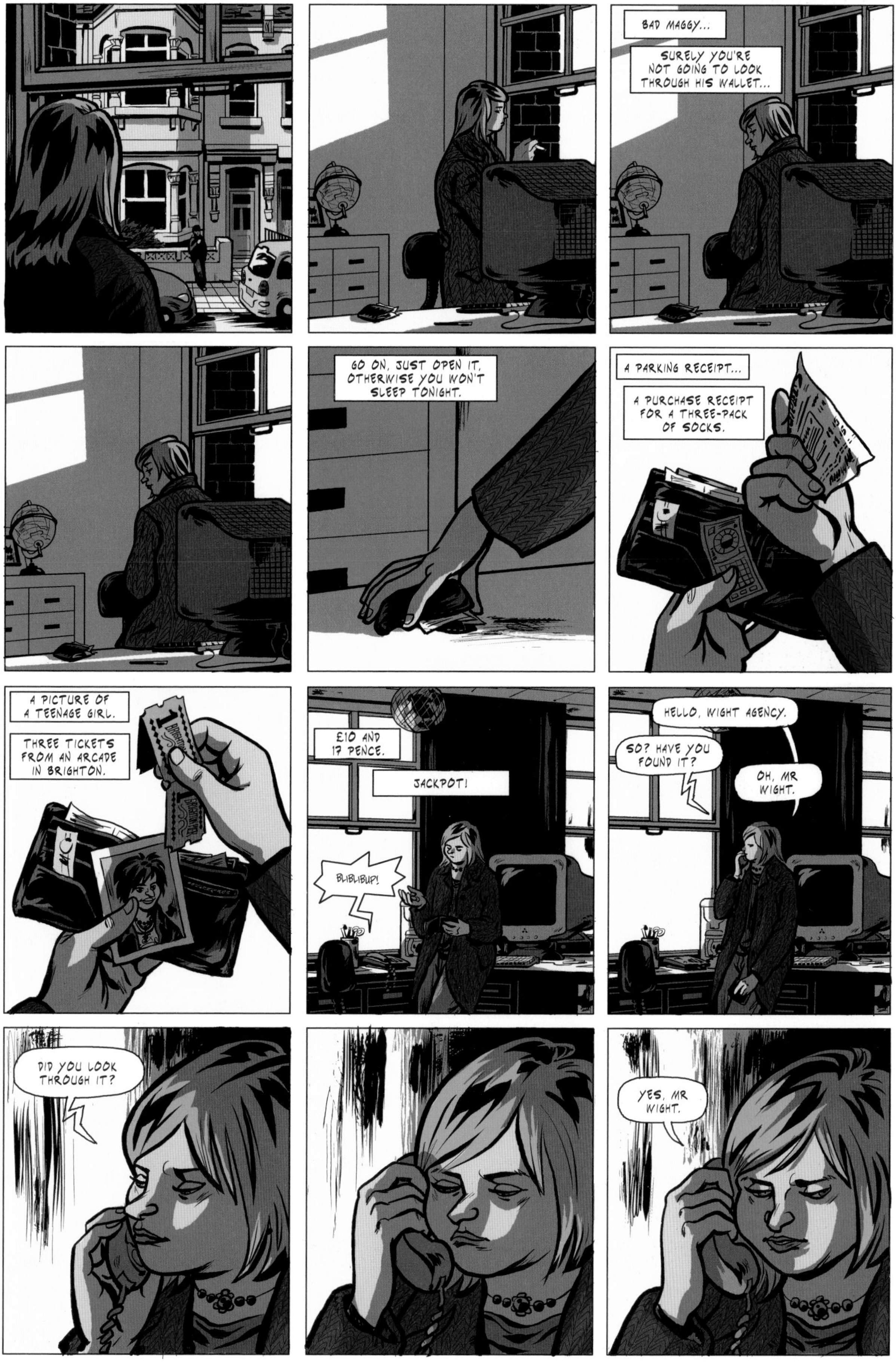
BAD MAGGY...
SURELY YOU'RE NOT GOING TO LOOK THROUGH HIS WALLET...
GO ON, JUST OPEN IT, OTHERWISE YOU WON'T SLEEP TONIGHT.
A PARKING RECEIPT...
A PURCHASE RECEIPT FOR A THREE-PACK OF SOCKS.
A PICTURE OF A TEENAGE GIRL.
THREE TICKETS FROM AN ARCADE IN BRIGHTON.
£10 AND 17 PENCE.
JACKPOT!
BLIBLIBUP!
HELLO, WIGHT AGENCY.
SO? HAVE YOU FOUND IT?
OH, MR WIGHT.
DID YOU LOOK THROUGH IT?
YES, MR WIGHT.

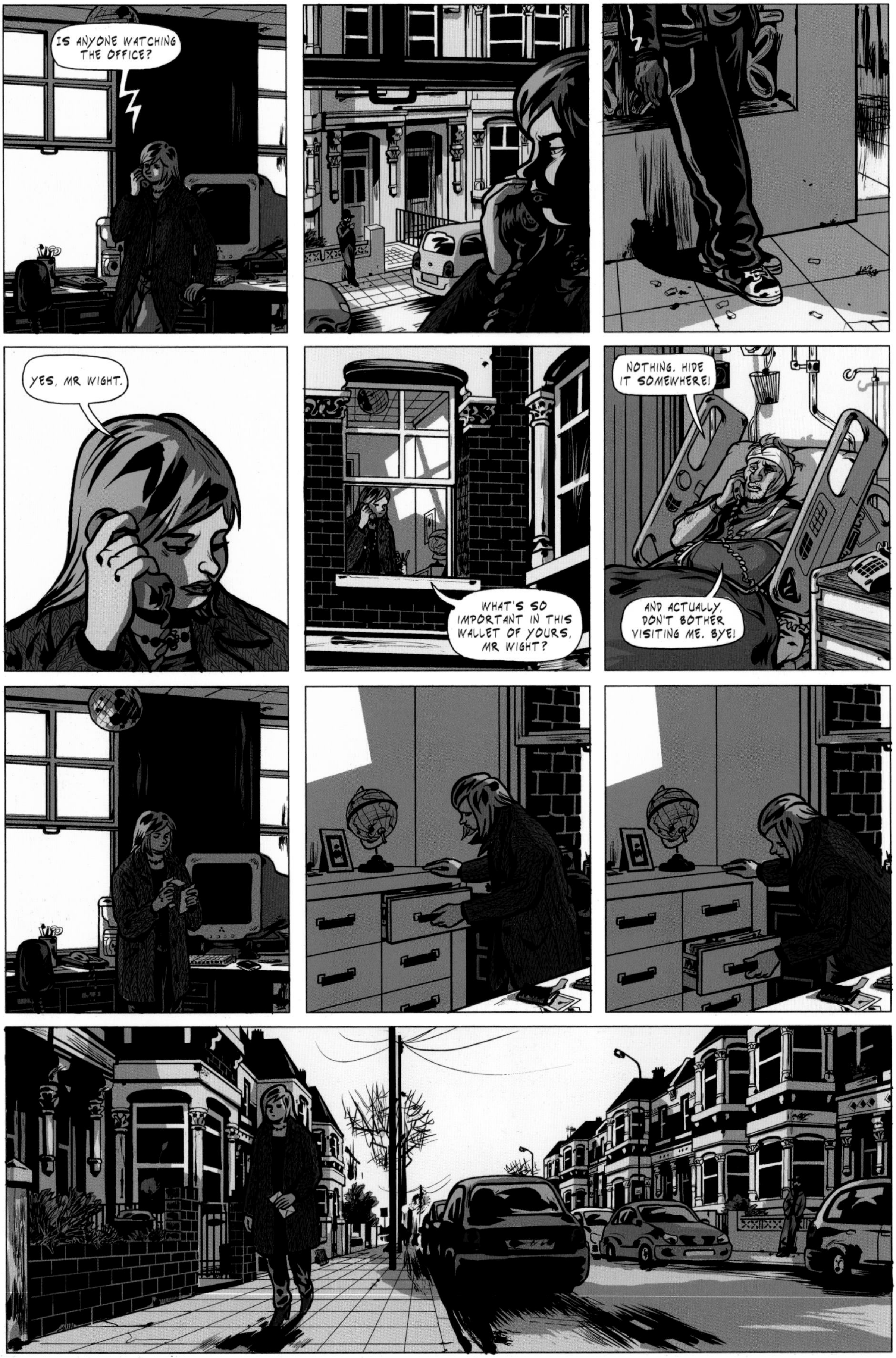
IS ANYONE WATCHING THE OFFICE?
YES, MR WIGHT.
WHAT'S SO IMPORTANT IN THIS WALLET OF YOURS, MR WIGHT?
NOTHING. HIDE IT SOMEWHERE!
AND ACTUALLY, DON'T BOTHER VISITING ME. BYE!

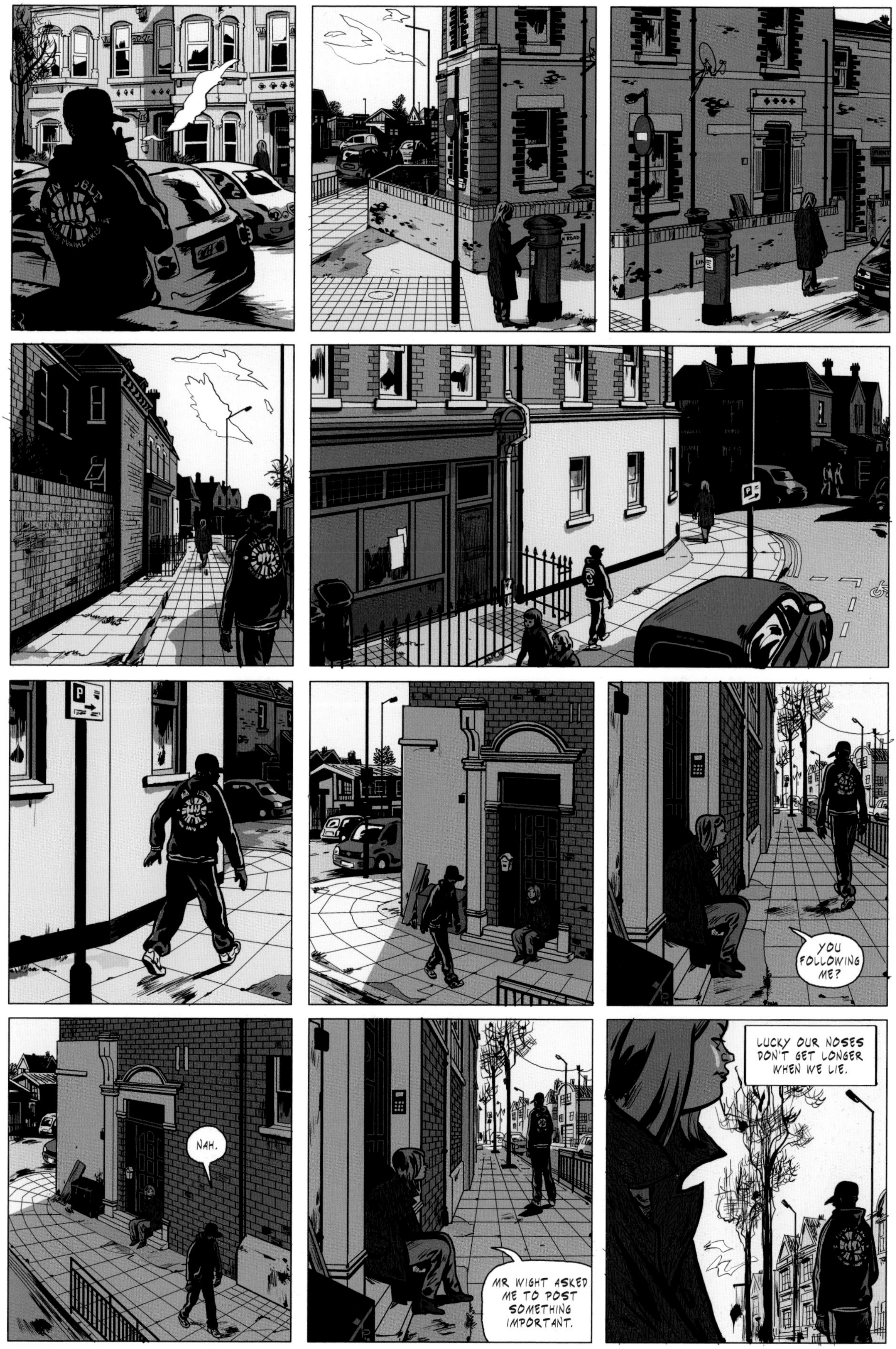
YOU FOLLOWING ME?
NAH.
MR WIGHT ASKED ME TO POST SOMETHING IMPORTANT.
LUCKY OUR NOSES DON'T GET LONGER WHEN WE LIE.

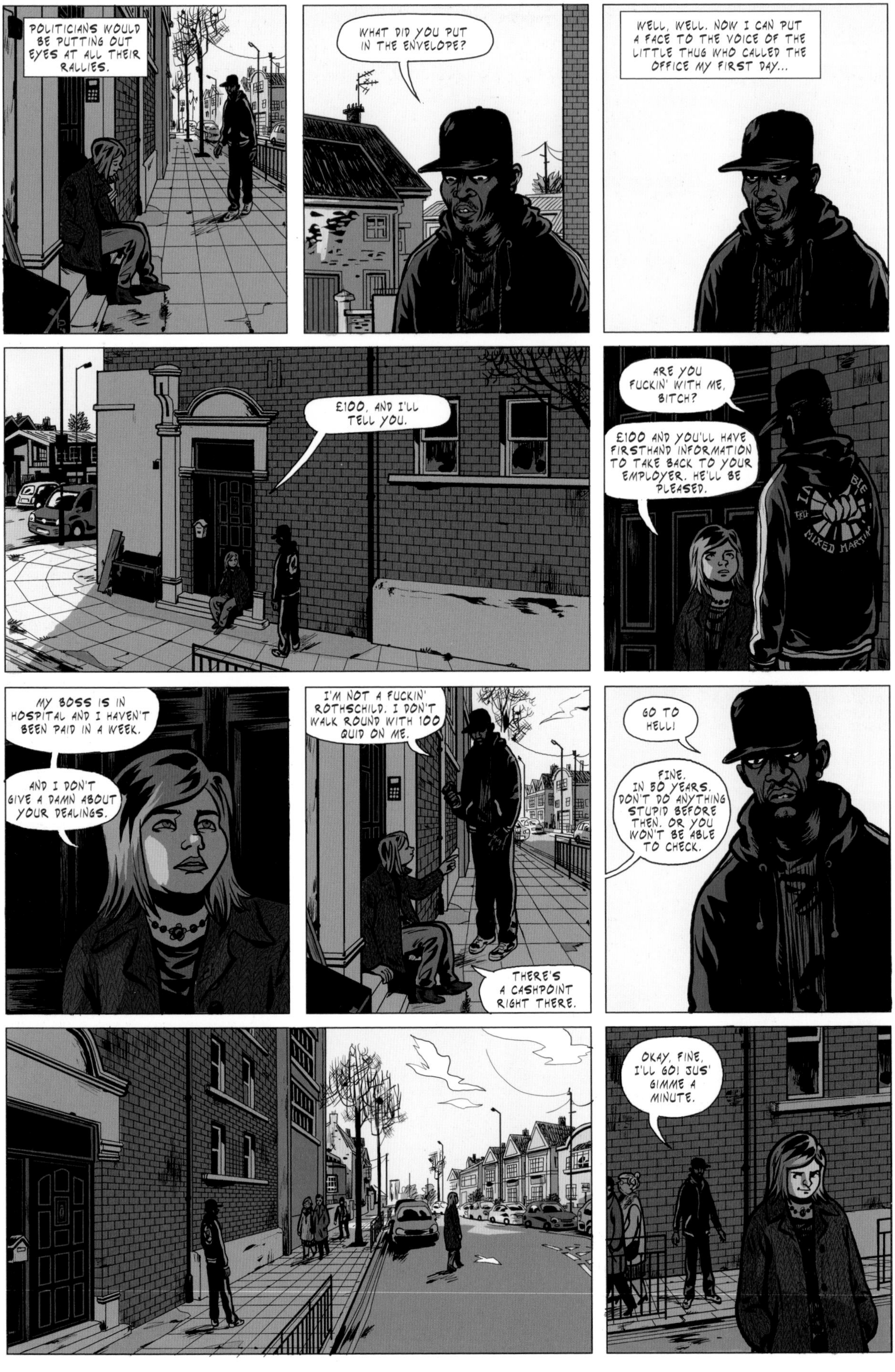

POLITICIANS WOULD BE PUTTING OUT EYES AT ALL THEIR RALLIES.
WHAT DID YOU PUT IN THE ENVELOPE?
WELL, WELL. NOW I CAN PUT A FACE TO THE VOICE OF THE LITTLE THUG WHO CALLED THE OFFICE MY FIRST DAY...
£100, AND I'LL TELL YOU.
ARE YOU FUCKIN' WITH ME, BITCH?
£100 AND YOU'LL HAVE FIRSTHAND INFORMATION TO TAKE BACK TO YOUR EMPLOYER. HE'LL BE PLEASED.
MIXED MARTIA
MY BOSS IS IN HOSPITAL AND I HAVEN'T BEEN PAID IN A WEEK.
AND I DON'T GIVE A DAMN ABOUT YOUR DEALINGS.
I'M NOT A FUCKIN' ROTHSCHILD. I DON'T WALK ROUND WITH 100 QUID ON ME.
THERE'S A CASHPOINT RIGHT THERE.
GO TO HELL!
FINE. IN 50 YEARS. DON'T DO ANYTHING STUPID BEFORE THEN. OR YOU WON'T BE ABLE TO CHECK.
OKAY, FINE, I'LL GO! JUS' GIMME A MINUTE.

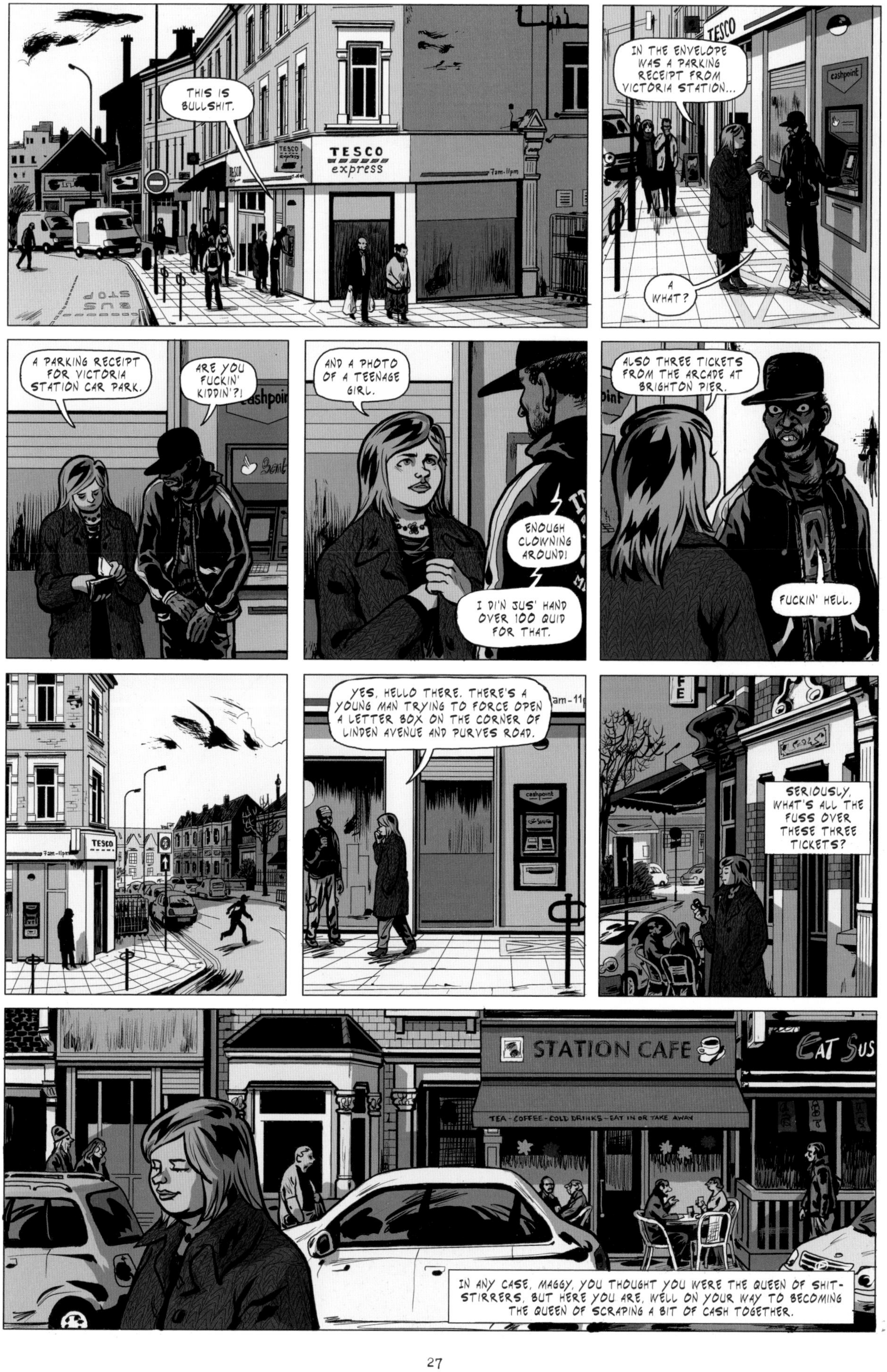
THIS IS BULLSHIT.
TESCO express
7am-11pm
BUS STOP
IN THE ENVELOPE WAS A PARKING RECEIPT FROM VICTORIA STATION...
A WHAT?
A PARKING RECEIPT FOR VICTORIA STATION CAR PARK.
ARE YOU FUCKIN' KIDDIN'?!
AND A PHOTO OF A TEENAGE GIRL.
ENOUGH CLOWNING AROUND!
I DI'N JUS' HAND OVER 100 QUID FOR THAT.
ALSO THREE TICKETS FROM THE ARCADE AT BRIGHTON PIER.
FUCKIN' HELL.
YES, HELLO THERE. THERE'S A YOUNG MAN TRYING TO FORCE OPEN A LETTER BOX ON THE CORNER OF LINDEN AVENUE AND PURVES ROAD.
SERIOUSLY, WHAT'S ALL THE FUSS OVER THESE THREE TICKETS?
STATION CAFE
TEA - COFFEE - COLD DRINKS - EAT IN OR TAKE AWAY
IN ANY CASE, MAGGY, YOU THOUGHT YOU WERE THE QUEEN OF SHIT-STIRRERS, BUT HERE YOU ARE, WELL ON YOUR WAY TO BECOMING THE QUEEN OF SCRAPING A BIT OF CASH TOGETHER.

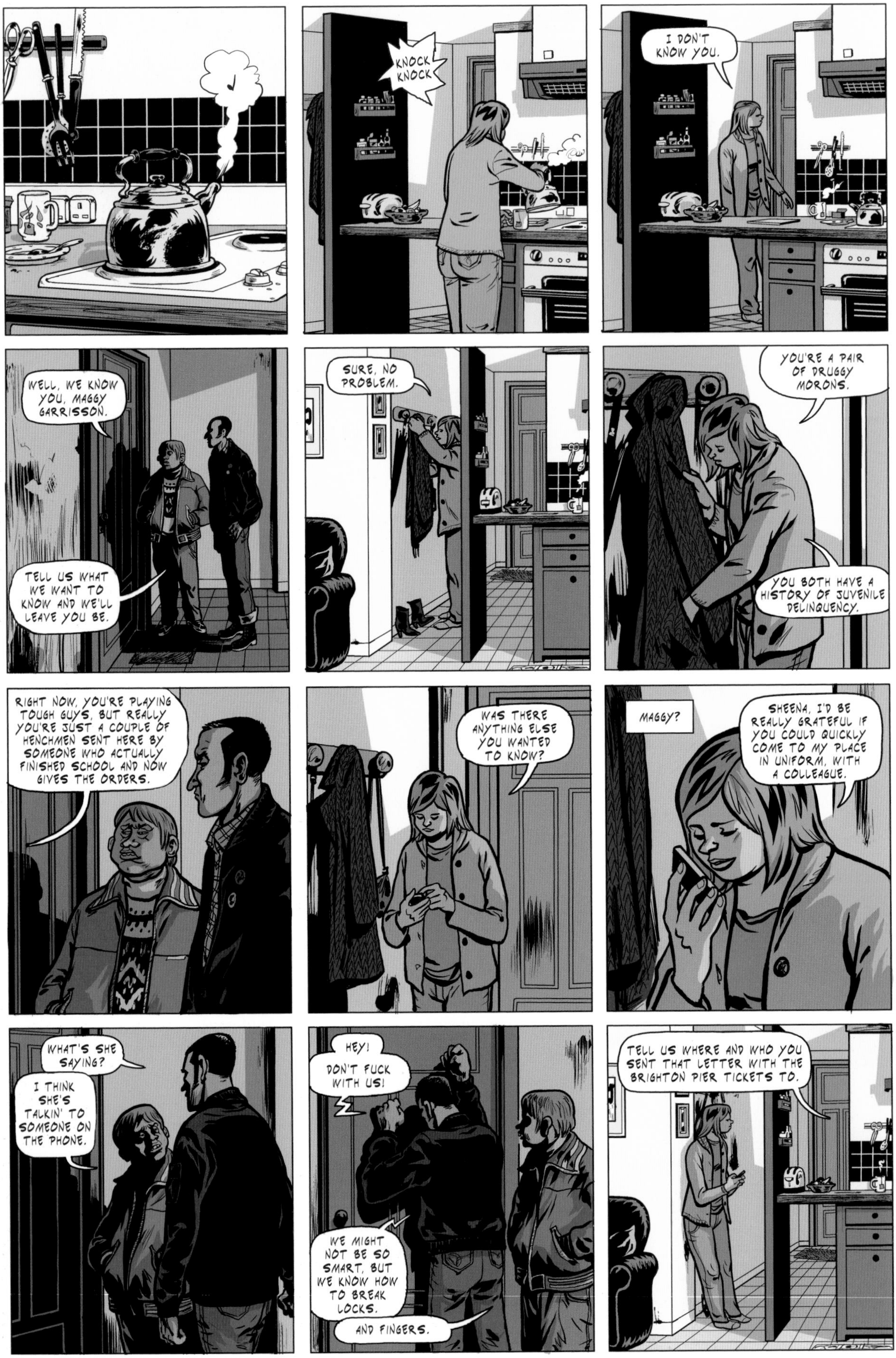
KNOCK KNOCK
I DON'T KNOW YOU.
WELL, WE KNOW YOU, MAGGY GARRISSON.
TELL US WHAT WE WANT TO KNOW AND WE'LL LEAVE YOU BE.
SURE, NO PROBLEM.
YOU'RE A PAIR OF DRUGGY MORONS.
YOU BOTH HAVE A HISTORY OF JUVENILE DELINQUENCY.
RIGHT NOW, YOU'RE PLAYING TOUGH GUYS, BUT REALLY YOU'RE JUST A COUPLE OF HENCHMEN SENT HERE BY SOMEONE WHO ACTUALLY FINISHED SCHOOL AND NOW GIVES THE ORDERS.
WAS THERE ANYTHING ELSE YOU WANTED TO KNOW?
MAGGY?
SHEENA, I'D BE REALLY GRATEFUL IF YOU COULD QUICKLY COME TO MY PLACE IN UNIFORM, WITH A COLLEAGUE.
WHAT'S SHE SAYING?
I THINK SHE'S TALKIN' TO SOMEONE ON THE PHONE.
HEY!
DON'T FUCK WITH US!
WE MIGHT NOT BE SO SMART, BUT WE KNOW HOW TO BREAK LOCKS.
AND FINGERS.
TELL US WHERE AND WHO YOU SENT THAT LETTER WITH THE BRIGHTON PIER TICKETS TO.

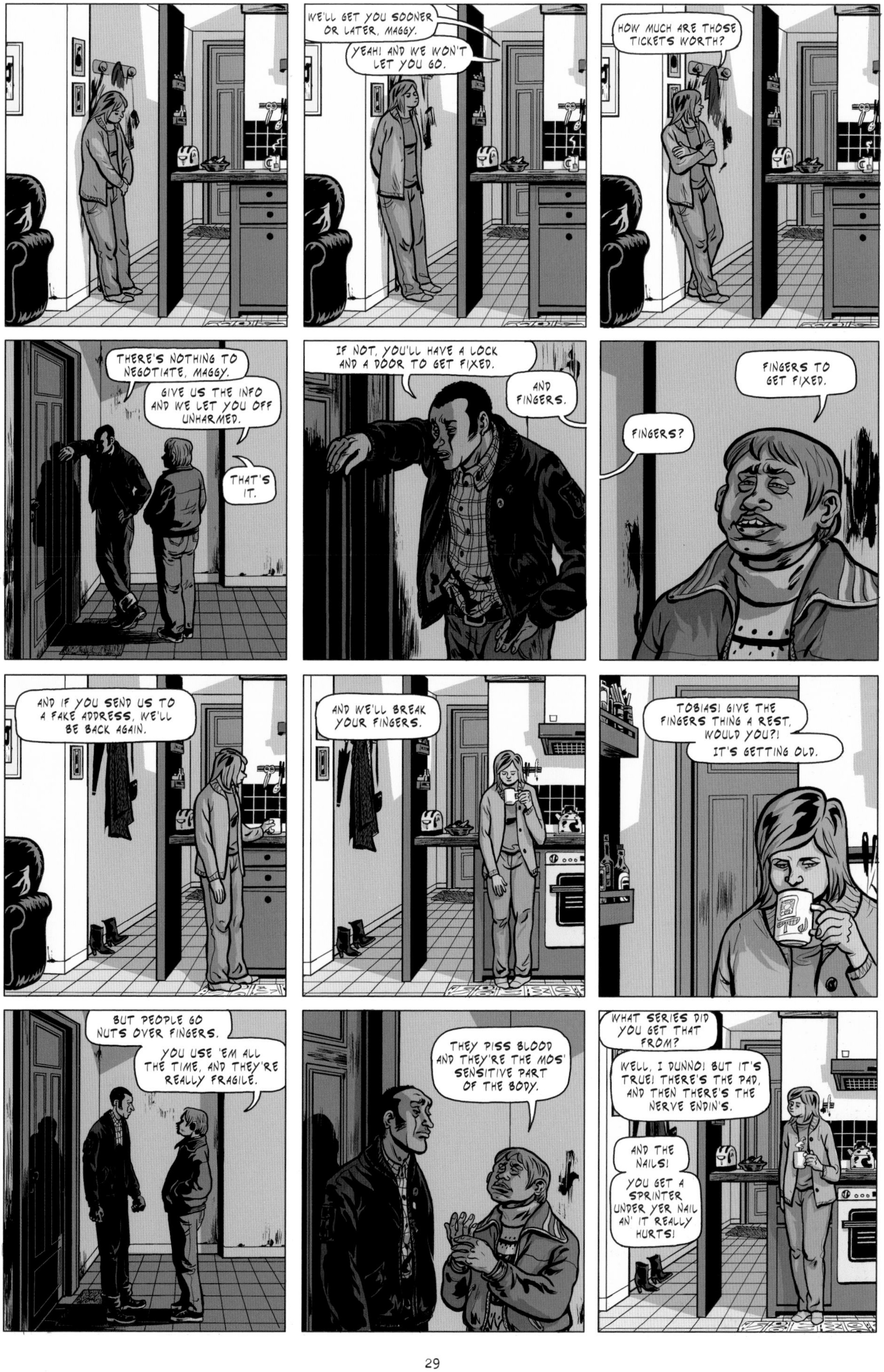
WE'LL GET YOU SOONER OR LATER, MAGGY.
YEAH! AND WE WON'T LET YOU GO.
HOW MUCH ARE THOSE TICKETS WORTH?
THERE'S NOTHING TO NEGOTIATE, MAGGY.
GIVE US THE INFO AND WE LET YOU OFF UNHARMED.
THAT'S IT.
IF NOT, YOU'LL HAVE A LOCK AND A DOOR TO GET FIXED.
AND FINGERS.
FINGERS?
FINGERS TO GET FIXED.
AND IF YOU SEND US TO A FAKE ADDRESS, WE'LL BE BACK AGAIN.
AND WE'LL BREAK YOUR FINGERS.
TOBIAS! GIVE THE FINGERS THING A REST, WOULD YOU?!
IT'S GETTING OLD.
BUT PEOPLE GO NUTS OVER FINGERS.
YOU USE 'EM ALL THE TIME, AND THEY'RE REALLY FRAGILE.
THEY PISS BLOOD AND THEY'RE THE MOS' SENSITIVE PART OF THE BODY.
WHAT SERIES DID YOU GET THAT FROM?
WELL, I DUNNO! BUT IT'S TRUE! THERE'S THE PAD, AND THEN THERE'S THE NERVE ENDIN'S.
AND THE NAILS!
YOU GET A SPRINTER UNDER YER NAIL AN' IT REALLY HURTS!

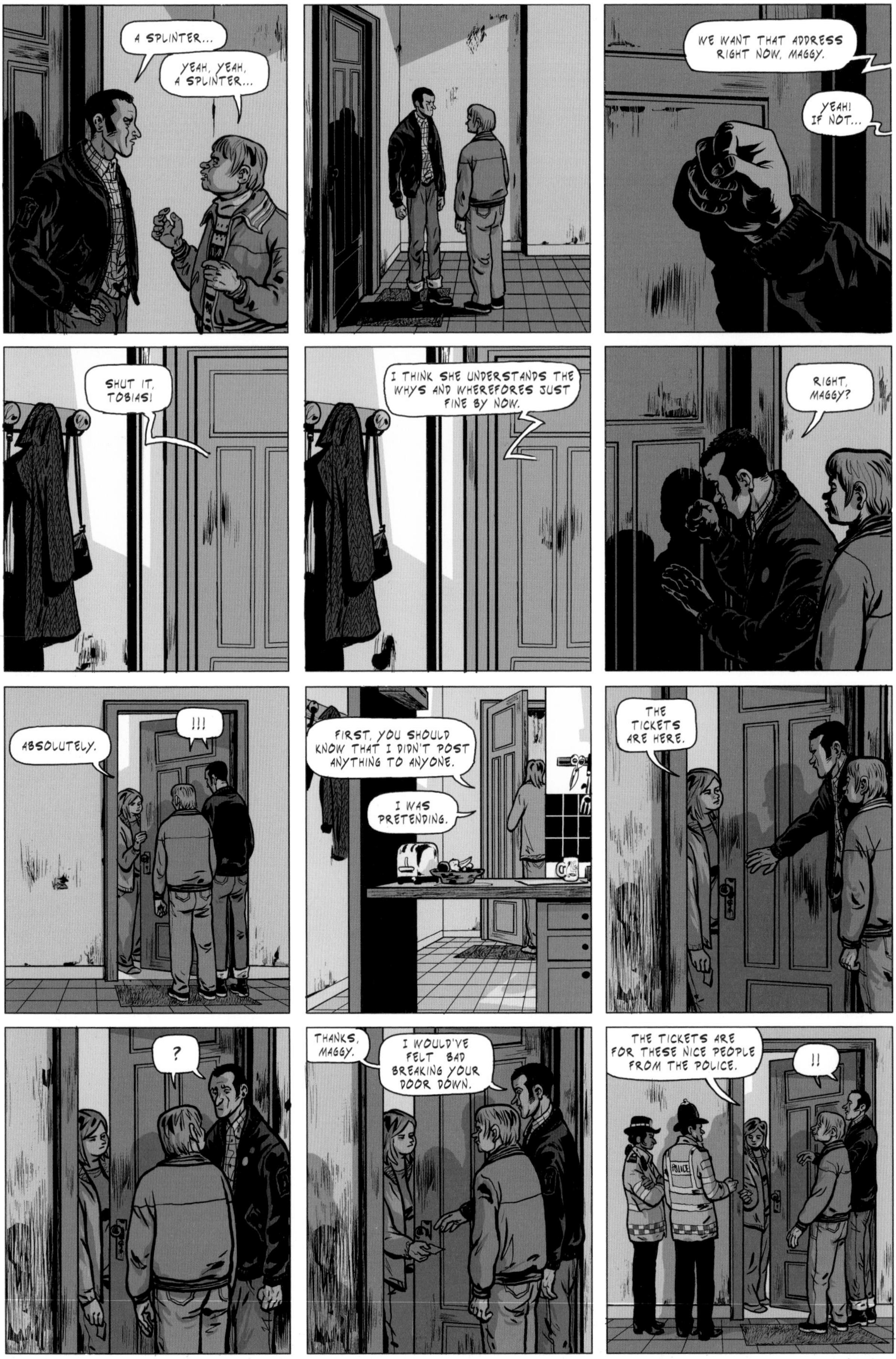

A SPLINTER...
YEAH, YEAH, A SPLINTER...
WE WANT THAT ADDRESS RIGHT NOW, MAGGY.
YEAH! IF NOT...
SHUT IT, TOBIAS!
I THINK SHE UNDERSTANDS THE WHYS AND WHEREFORES JUST FINE BY NOW.
RIGHT, MAGGY?
ABSOLUTELY.
!!!
FIRST, YOU SHOULD KNOW THAT I DIDN'T POST ANYTHING TO ANYONE.
I WAS PRETENDING.
THE TICKETS ARE HERE.
?
THANKS, MAGGY.
I WOULD'VE FELT BAD BREAKING YOUR DOOR DOWN.
THE TICKETS ARE FOR THESE NICE PEOPLE FROM THE POLICE.
!!
POLICE

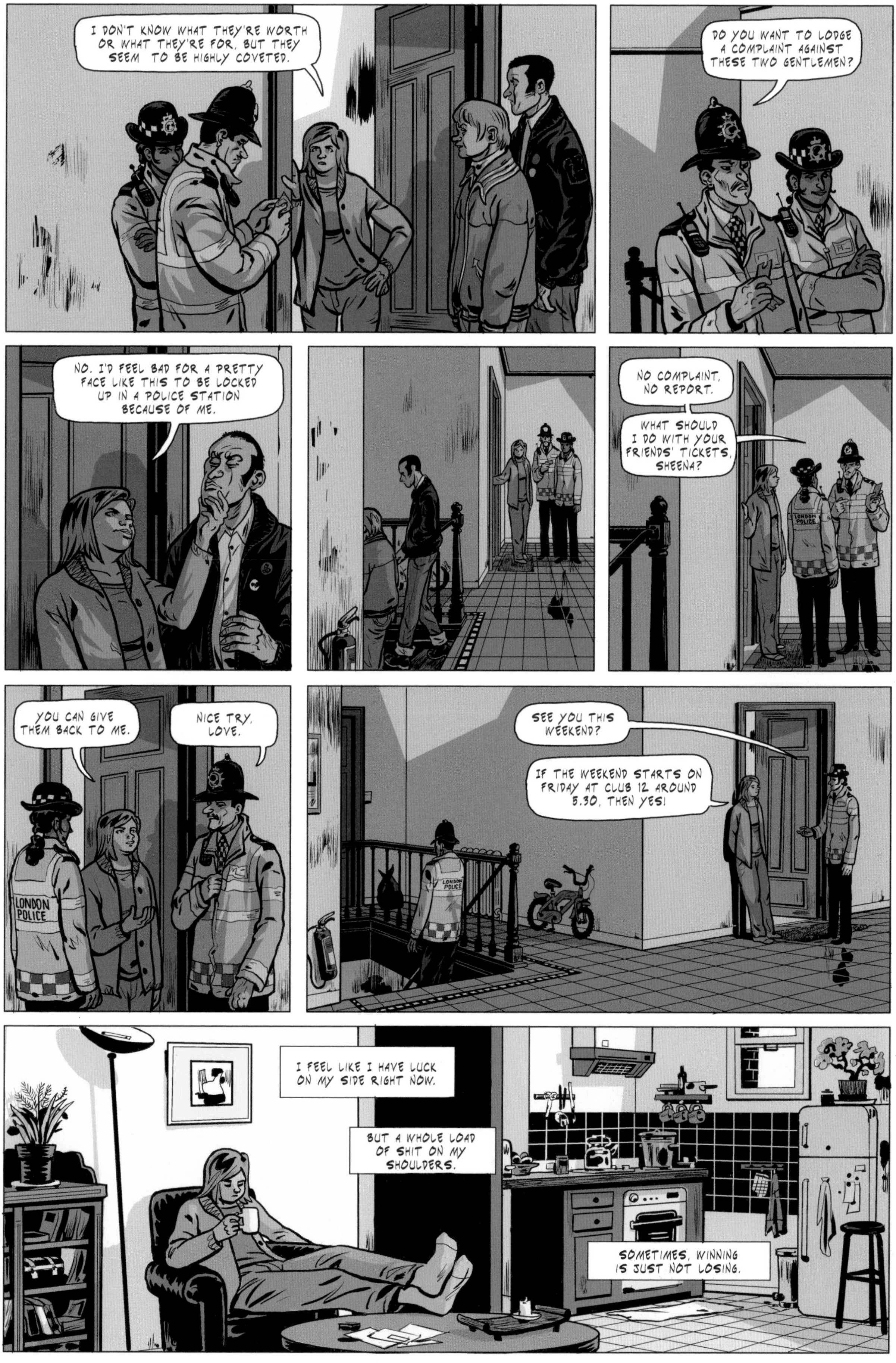
I DON'T KNOW WHAT THEY'RE WORTH OR WHAT THEY'RE FOR, BUT THEY SEEM TO BE HIGHLY COVETED.
DO YOU WANT TO LODGE A COMPLAINT AGAINST THESE TWO GENTLEMEN?
NO. I'D FEEL BAD FOR A PRETTY FACE LIKE THIS TO BE LOCKED UP IN A POLICE STATION BECAUSE OF ME.
NO COMPLAINT, NO REPORT.
WHAT SHOULD I DO WITH YOUR FRIENDS' TICKETS, SHEENA?
LONDON POLICE
YOU CAN GIVE THEM BACK TO ME.
NICE TRY, LOVE.
LONDON POLICE
SEE YOU THIS WEEKEND?
IF THE WEEKEND STARTS ON FRIDAY AT CLUB 12 AROUND 5.30, THEN YES!
LONDON POLICE
I FEEL LIKE I HAVE LUCK ON MY SIDE RIGHT NOW.
BUT A WHOLE LOAD OF SHIT ON MY SHOULDERS.
SOMETIMES, WINNING IS JUST NOT LOSING.

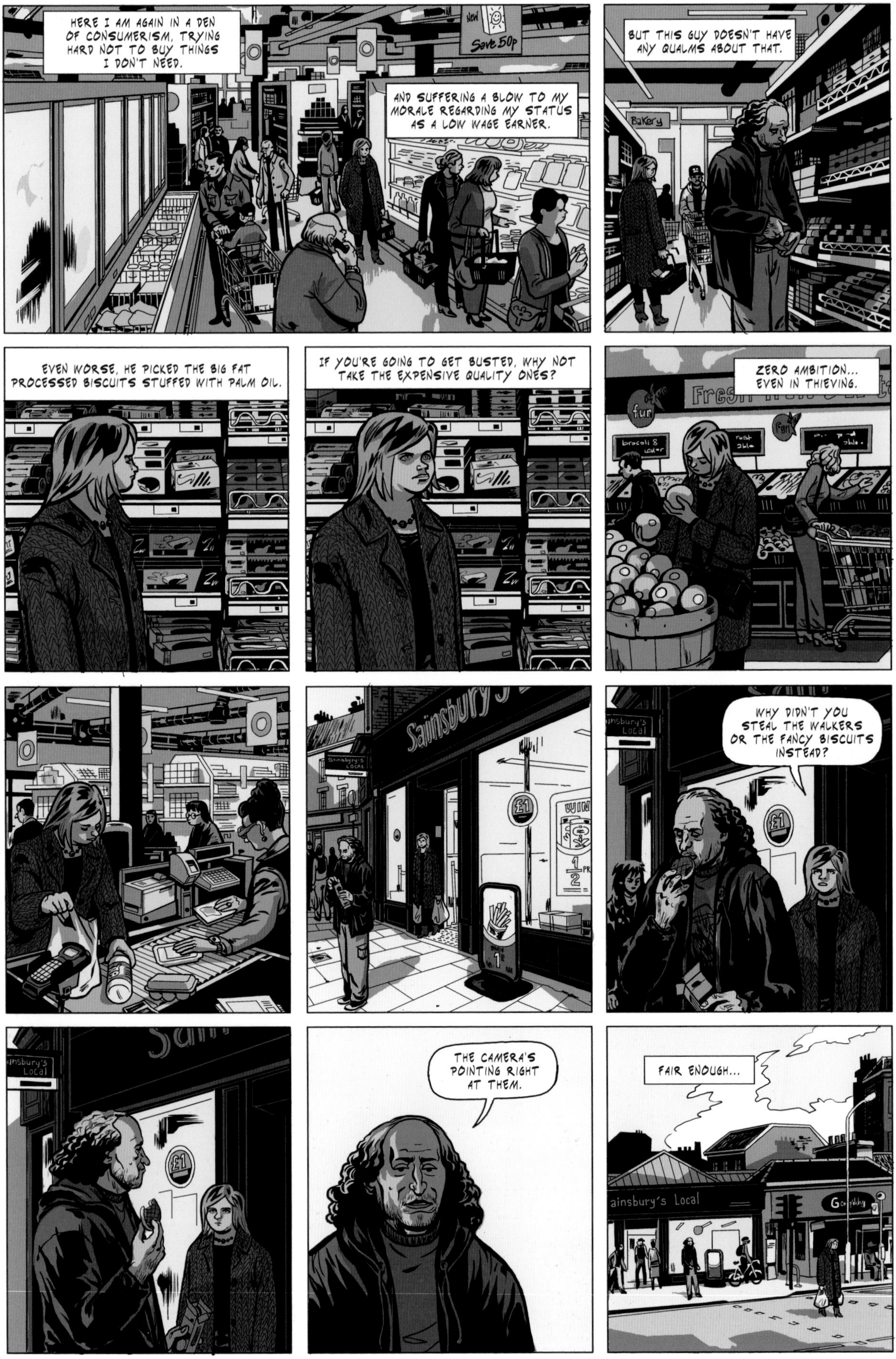
HERE I AM AGAIN IN A DEN OF CONSUMERISM, TRYING HARD NOT TO BUY THINGS I DON'T NEED.
New
Save 50p
AND SUFFERING A BLOW TO MY MORALE REGARDING MY STATUS AS A LOW WAGE EARNER.
BUT THIS GUY DOESN'T HAVE ANY QUALMS ABOUT THAT.
Bakery
EVEN WORSE, HE PICKED THE BIG FAT PROCESSED BISCUITS STUFFED WITH PALM OIL.
IF YOU'RE GOING TO GET BUSTED, WHY NOT TAKE THE EXPENSIVE QUALITY ONES?
ZERO AMBITION... EVEN IN THIEVING.
Sainsbury's
Sainsbury's Local
£1
WHY DIDN'T YOU STEAL THE WALKERS OR THE FANCY BISCUITS INSTEAD?
THE CAMERA'S POINTING RIGHT AT THEM.
FAIR ENOUGH...

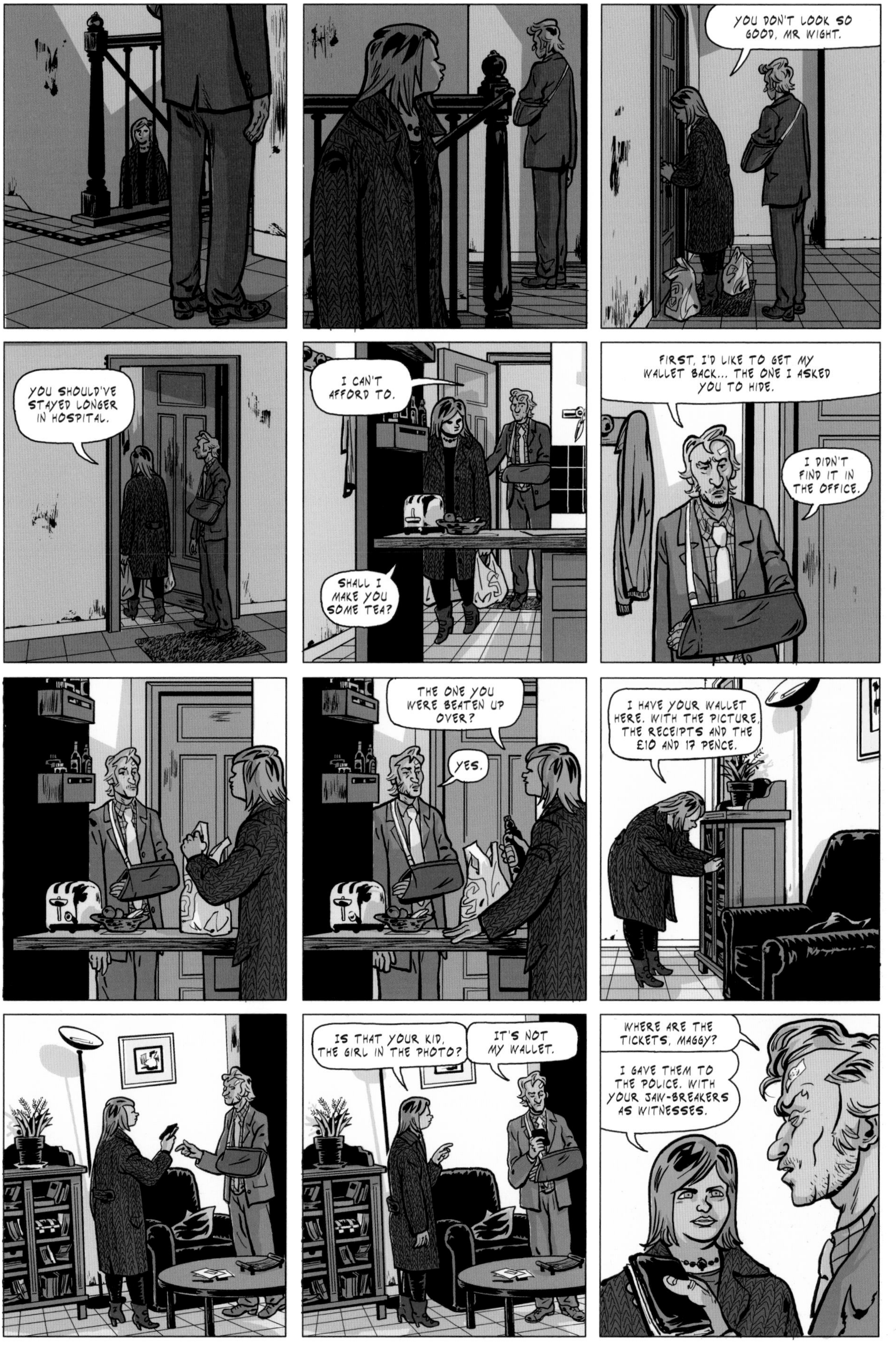
YOU DON'T LOOK SO GOOD, MR WIGHT.
YOU SHOULD'VE STAYED LONGER IN HOSPITAL.
I CAN'T AFFORD TO.
SHALL I MAKE YOU SOME TEA?
FIRST, I'D LIKE TO GET MY WALLET BACK... THE ONE I ASKED YOU TO HIDE.
I DIDN'T FIND IT IN THE OFFICE.
THE ONE YOU WERE BEATEN UP OVER?
YES.
I HAVE YOUR WALLET HERE. WITH THE PICTURE, THE RECEIPTS AND THE £10 AND 17 PENCE.
IS THAT YOUR KID, THE GIRL IN THE PHOTO?
IT'S NOT MY WALLET.
WHERE ARE THE TICKETS, MAGGY?
I GAVE THEM TO THE POLICE. WITH YOUR JAW-BREAKERS AS WITNESSES.

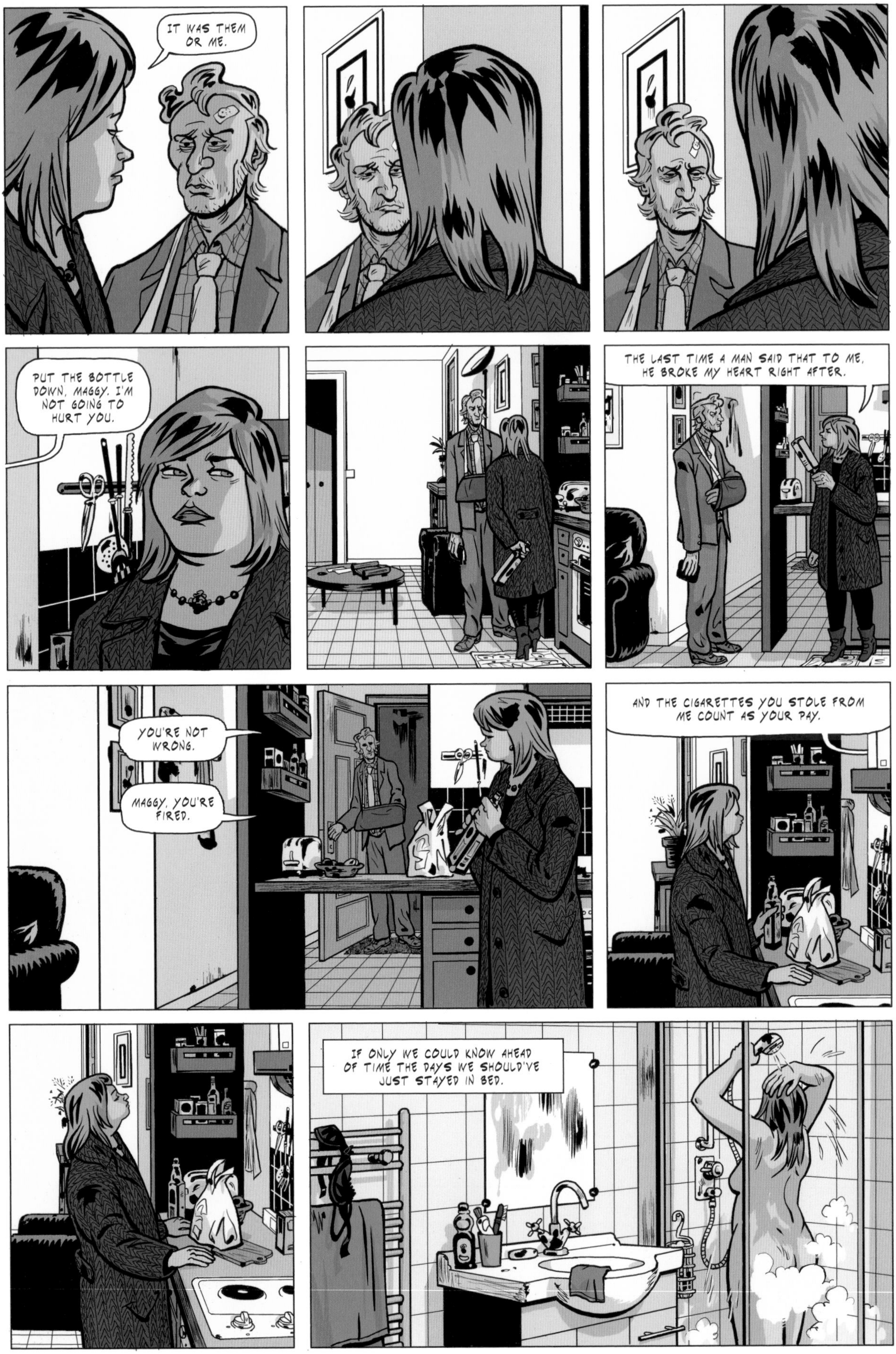

IT WAS THEM OR ME.
PUT THE BOTTLE DOWN, MAGGY. I'M NOT GOING TO HURT YOU.
THE LAST TIME A MAN SAID THAT TO ME, HE BROKE MY HEART RIGHT AFTER.
YOU'RE NOT WRONG.
MAGGY, YOU'RE FIRED.
AND THE CIGARETTES YOU STOLE FROM ME COUNT AS YOUR PAY.
IF ONLY WE COULD KNOW AHEAD OF TIME THE DAYS WE SHOULD'VE JUST STAYED IN BED.

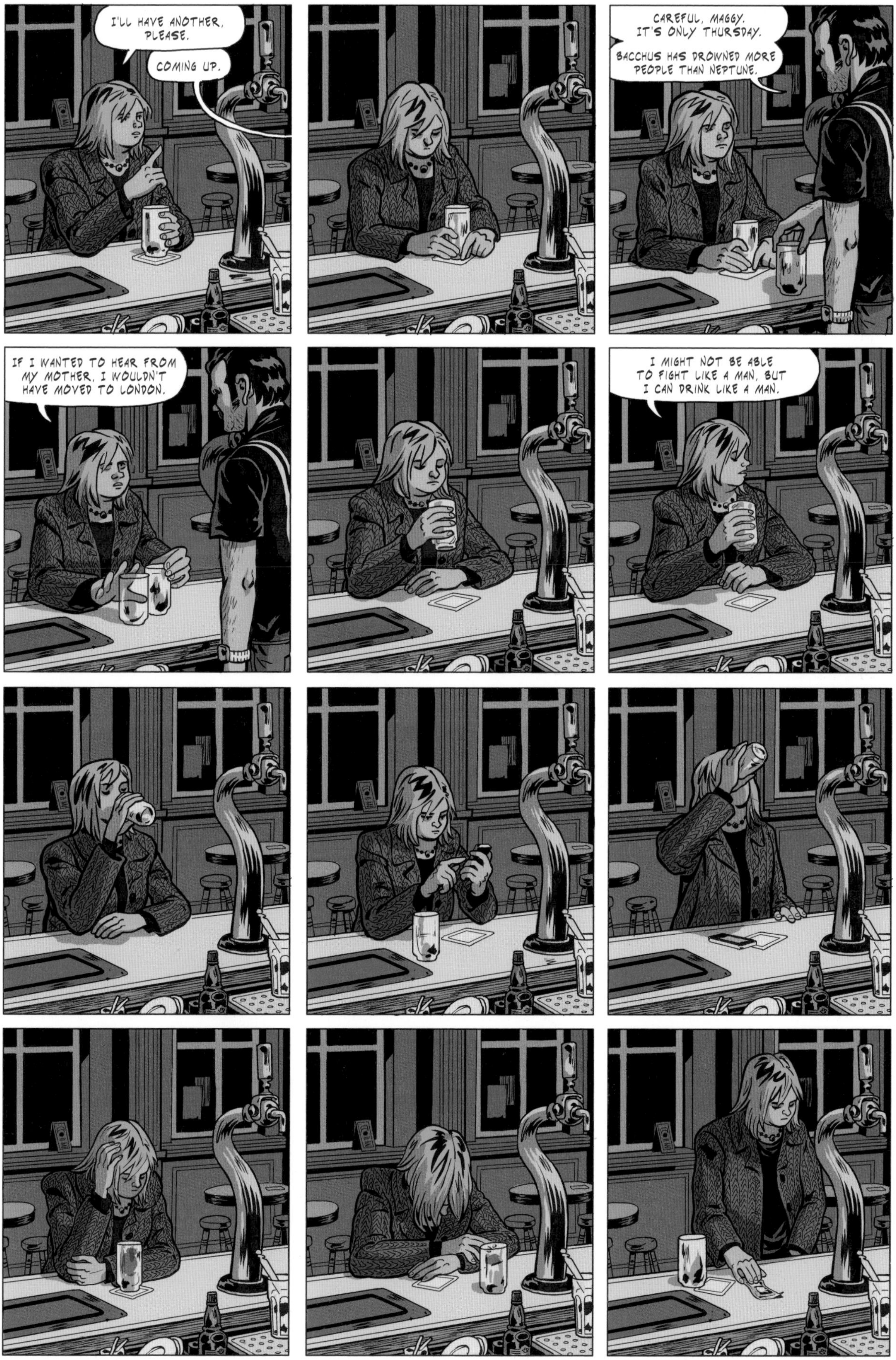
I'LL HAVE ANOTHER, PLEASE.
COMING UP.
CAREFUL, MAGGY. IT'S ONLY THURSDAY.
BACCHUS HAS DROWNED MORE PEOPLE THAN NEPTUNE.
IF I WANTED TO HEAR FROM MY MOTHER, I WOULDN'T HAVE MOVED TO LONDON.
I MIGHT NOT BE ABLE TO FIGHT LIKE A MAN, BUT I CAN DRINK LIKE A MAN.

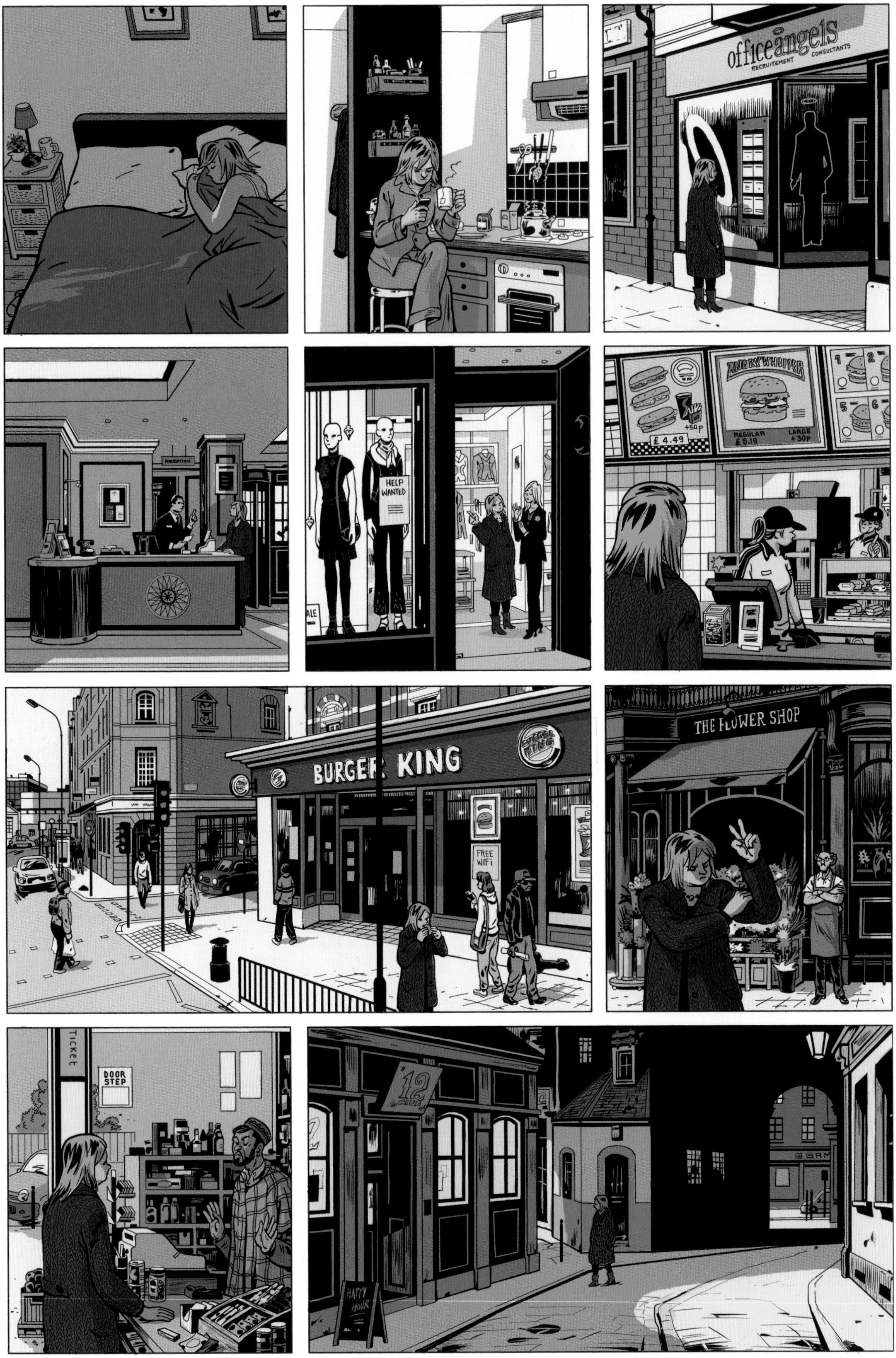
officeangels
RECRUITMENT CONSULTANTS
HELP WANTED
ANGRY WHOPPER
£ 4.49
+50p
REGULAR £ 5.19
LARGE +30p
BURGER KING
FREE WIFI
THE FLOWER SHOP
Ticket
DOOR STEP
HAPPY HOUR

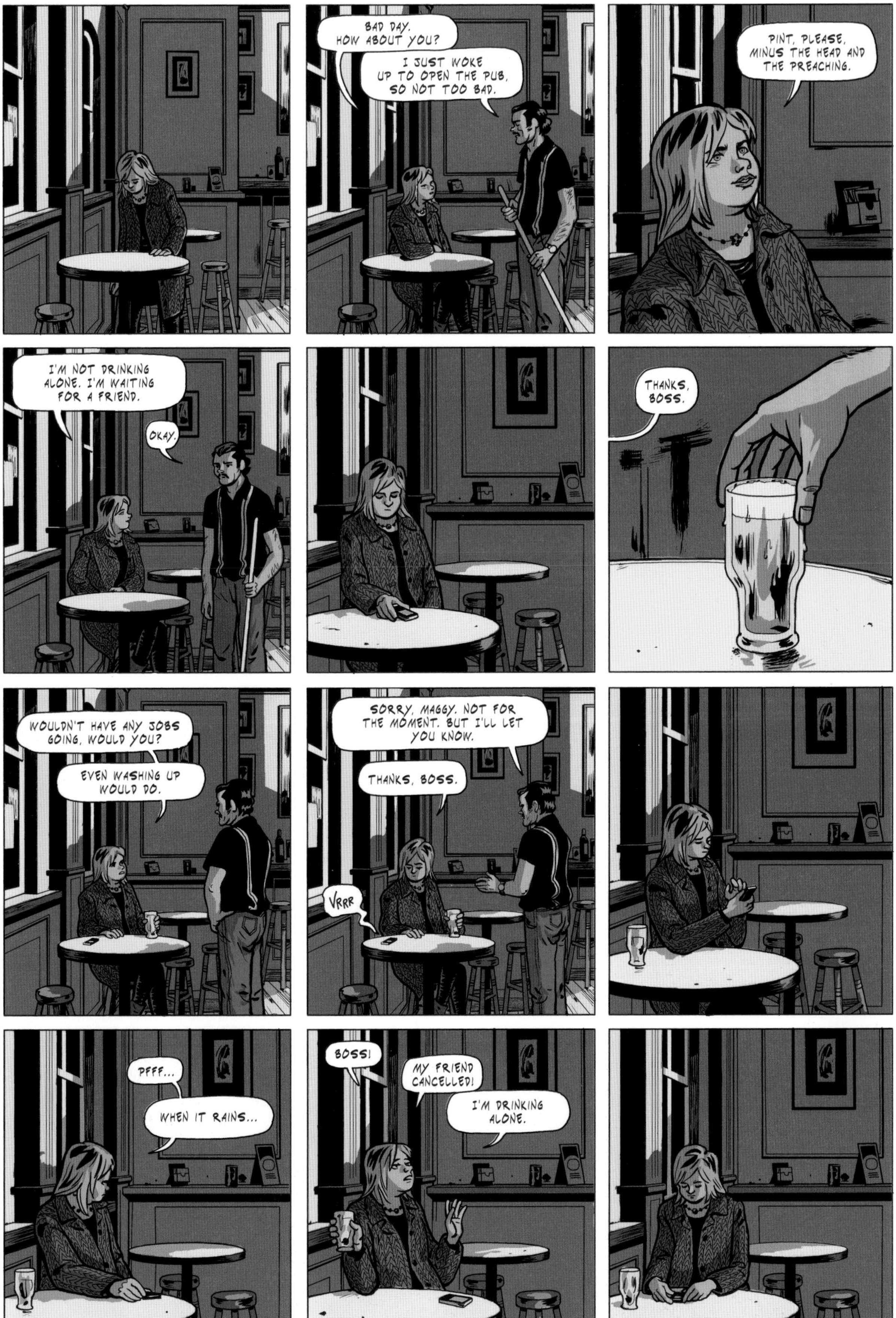
BAD DAY. HOW ABOUT YOU?
I JUST WOKE UP TO OPEN THE PUB, SO NOT TOO BAD.
PINT, PLEASE, MINUS THE HEAD AND THE PREACHING.
I'M NOT DRINKING ALONE. I'M WAITING FOR A FRIEND.
OKAY.
THANKS, BOSS.
WOULDN'T HAVE ANY JOBS GOING, WOULD YOU?
EVEN WASHING UP WOULD DO.
SORRY, MAGGY. NOT FOR THE MOMENT. BUT I'LL LET YOU KNOW.
THANKS, BOSS.
VRRR
PFFF...
WHEN IT RAINS...
BOSS!
MY FRIEND CANCELLED!
I'M DRINKING ALONE.

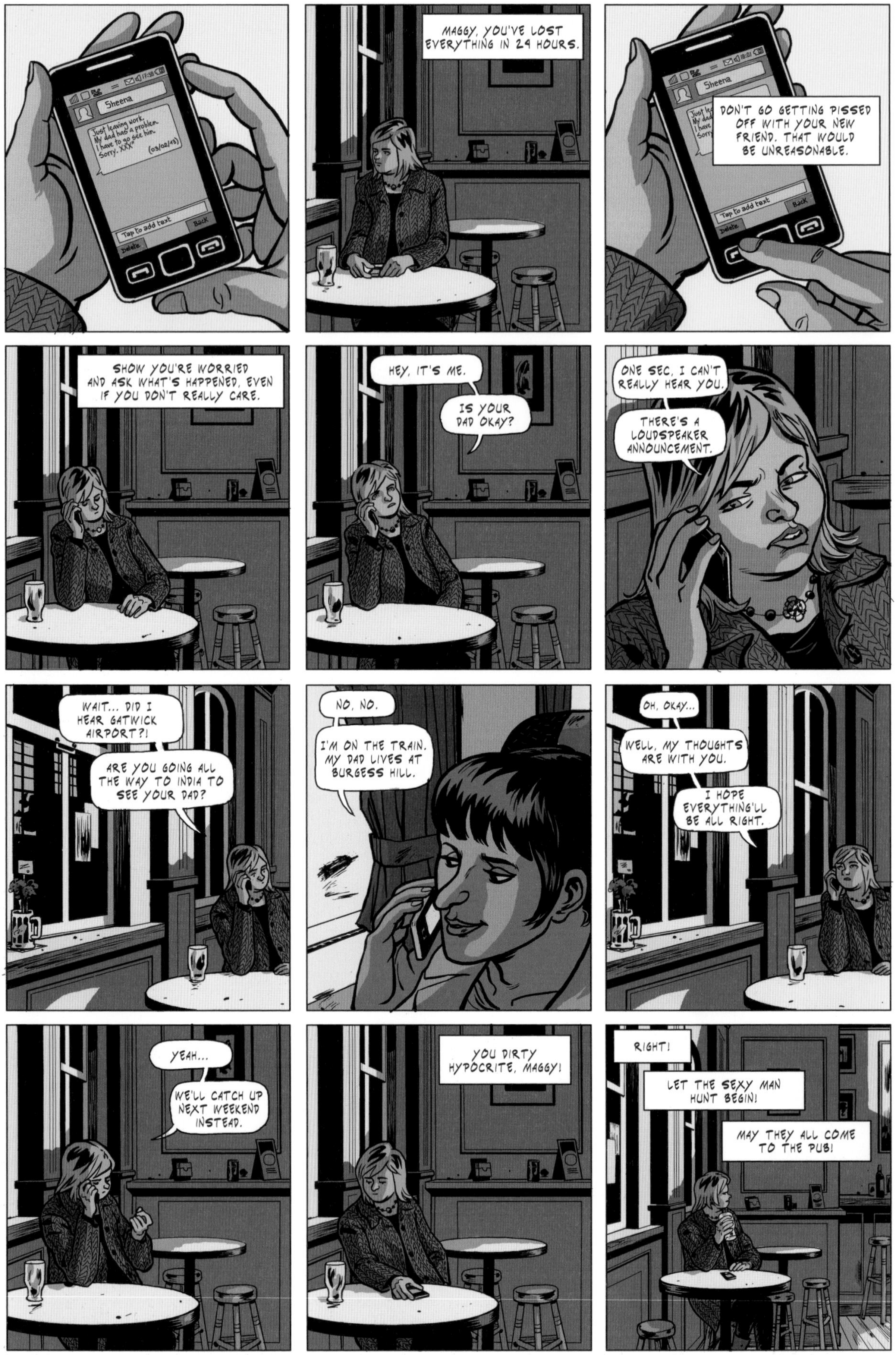
Sheena
Just leaving work. My dad has a problem. I have to go see him. Sorry. XXX" (03/02/13)
Tap to add text
Back
Delete
MAGGY, YOU'VE LOST EVERYTHING IN 24 HOURS.
DON'T GO GETTING PISSED OFF WITH YOUR NEW FRIEND. THAT WOULD BE UNREASONABLE.
SHOW YOU'RE WORRIED AND ASK WHAT'S HAPPENED, EVEN IF YOU DON'T REALLY CARE.
HEY, IT'S ME.
IS YOUR DAD OKAY?
ONE SEC, I CAN'T REALLY HEAR YOU.
THERE'S A LOUDSPEAKER ANNOUNCEMENT.
WAIT... DID I HEAR GATWICK AIRPORT?!
ARE YOU GOING ALL THE WAY TO INDIA TO SEE YOUR DAD?
NO, NO.
I'M ON THE TRAIN. MY DAD LIVES AT BURGESS HILL.
OH, OKAY...
WELL, MY THOUGHTS ARE WITH YOU.
I HOPE EVERYTHING'LL BE ALL RIGHT.
YEAH...
WE'LL CATCH UP NEXT WEEKEND INSTEAD.
YOU DIRTY HYPOCRITE, MAGGY!
RIGHT!
LET THE SEXY MAN HUNT BEGIN!
MAY THEY ALL COME TO THE PUB!

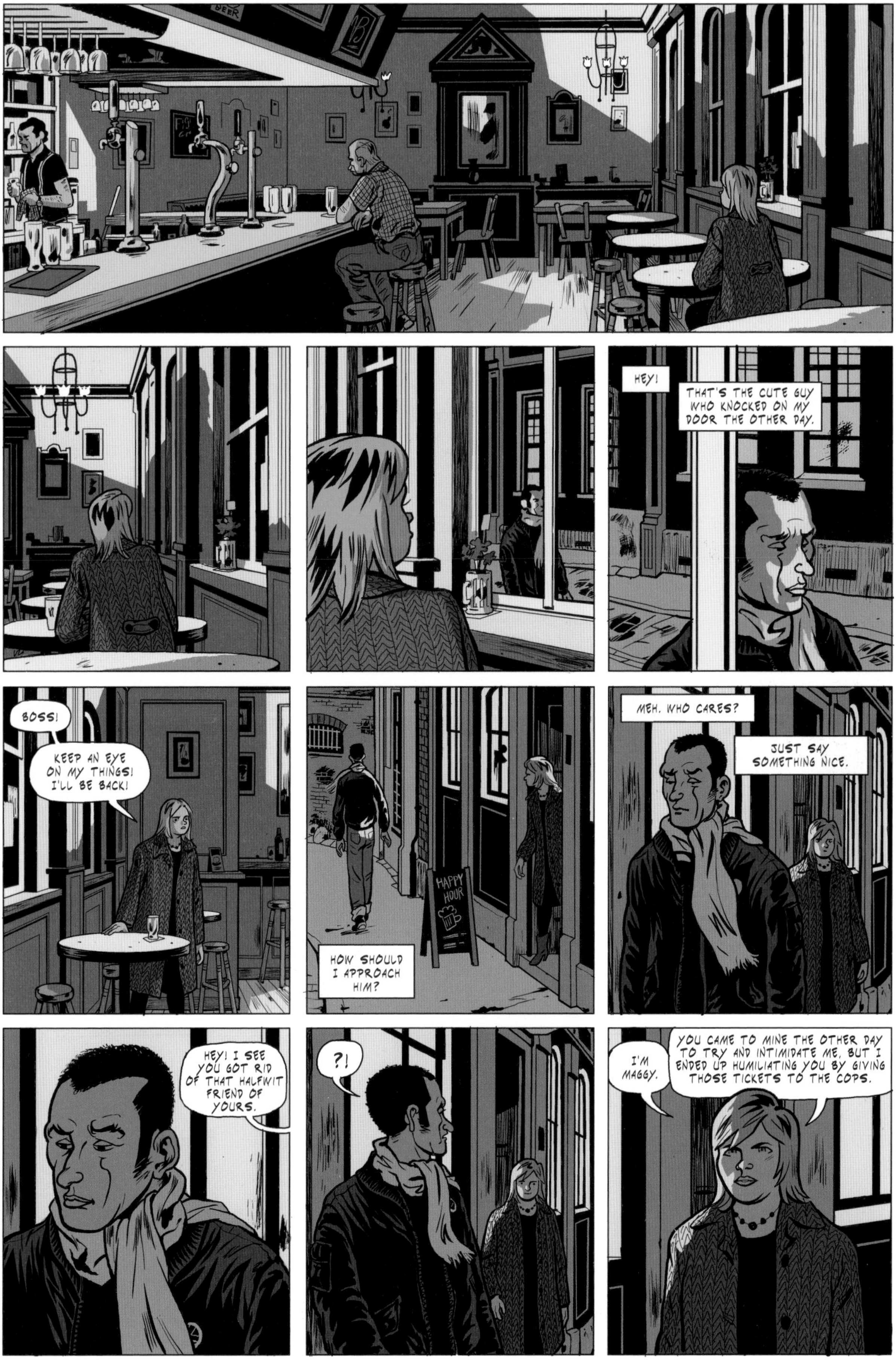
BEER
HAPPY HOUR
HEY!
THAT'S THE CUTE GUY WHO KNOCKED ON MY DOOR THE OTHER DAY.
BOSS!
KEEP AN EYE ON MY THINGS! I'LL BE BACK!
HOW SHOULD I APPROACH HIM?
MEH. WHO CARES?
JUST SAY SOMETHING NICE.
HEY! I SEE YOU GOT RID OF THAT HALFWIT FRIEND OF YOURS.
?!
I'M MAGGY.
YOU CAME TO MINE THE OTHER DAY TO TRY AND INTIMIDATE ME, BUT I ENDED UP HUMILIATING YOU BY GIVING THOSE TICKETS TO THE COPS.

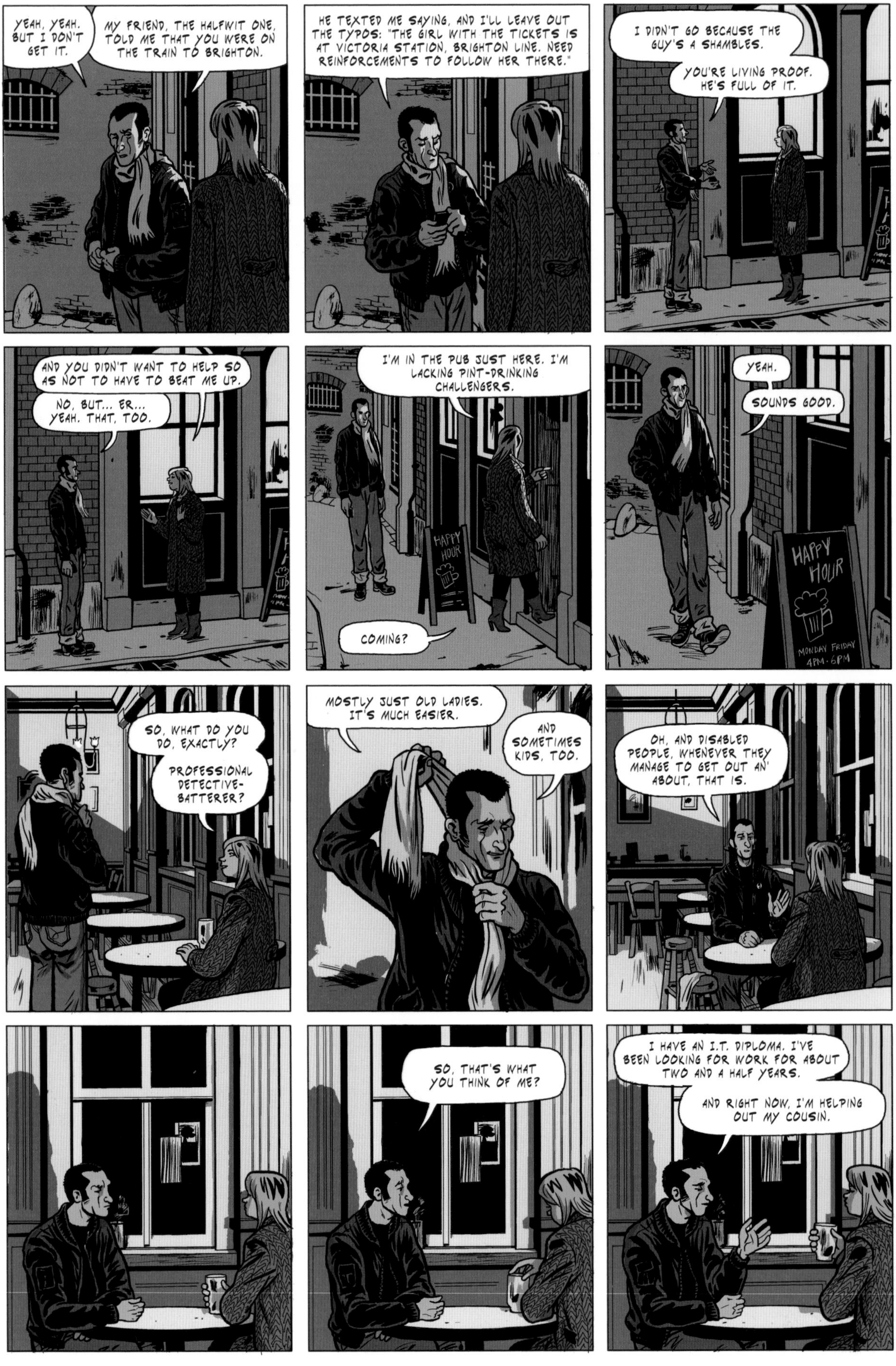
YEAH, YEAH. BUT I DON'T GET IT.
MY FRIEND, THE HALFWIT ONE, TOLD ME THAT YOU WERE ON THE TRAIN TO BRIGHTON.
HE TEXTED ME SAYING, AND I'LL LEAVE OUT THE TYPOS: "THE GIRL WITH THE TICKETS IS AT VICTORIA STATION, BRIGHTON LINE. NEED REINFORCEMENTS TO FOLLOW HER THERE."
I DIDN'T GO BECAUSE THE GUY'S A SHAMBLES.
YOU'RE LIVING PROOF. HE'S FULL OF IT.
AND YOU DIDN'T WANT TO HELP SO AS NOT TO HAVE TO BEAT ME UP.
NO, BUT... ER... YEAH. THAT, TOO.
I'M IN THE PUB JUST HERE. I'M LACKING PINT-DRINKING CHALLENGERS.
HAPPY HOUR
COMING?
YEAH.
SOUNDS GOOD.
HAPPY HOUR
MONDAY FRIDAY 4PM-6PM
SO, WHAT DO YOU DO, EXACTLY?
PROFESSIONAL DETECTIVE-BATTERER?
MOSTLY JUST OLD LADIES. IT'S MUCH EASIER.
AND SOMETIMES KIDS, TOO.
OH, AND DISABLED PEOPLE, WHENEVER THEY MANAGE TO GET OUT AN' ABOUT, THAT IS.
SO, THAT'S WHAT YOU THINK OF ME?
I HAVE AN I.T. DIPLOMA. I'VE BEEN LOOKING FOR WORK FOR ABOUT TWO AND A HALF YEARS.
AND RIGHT NOW, I'M HELPING OUT MY COUSIN.

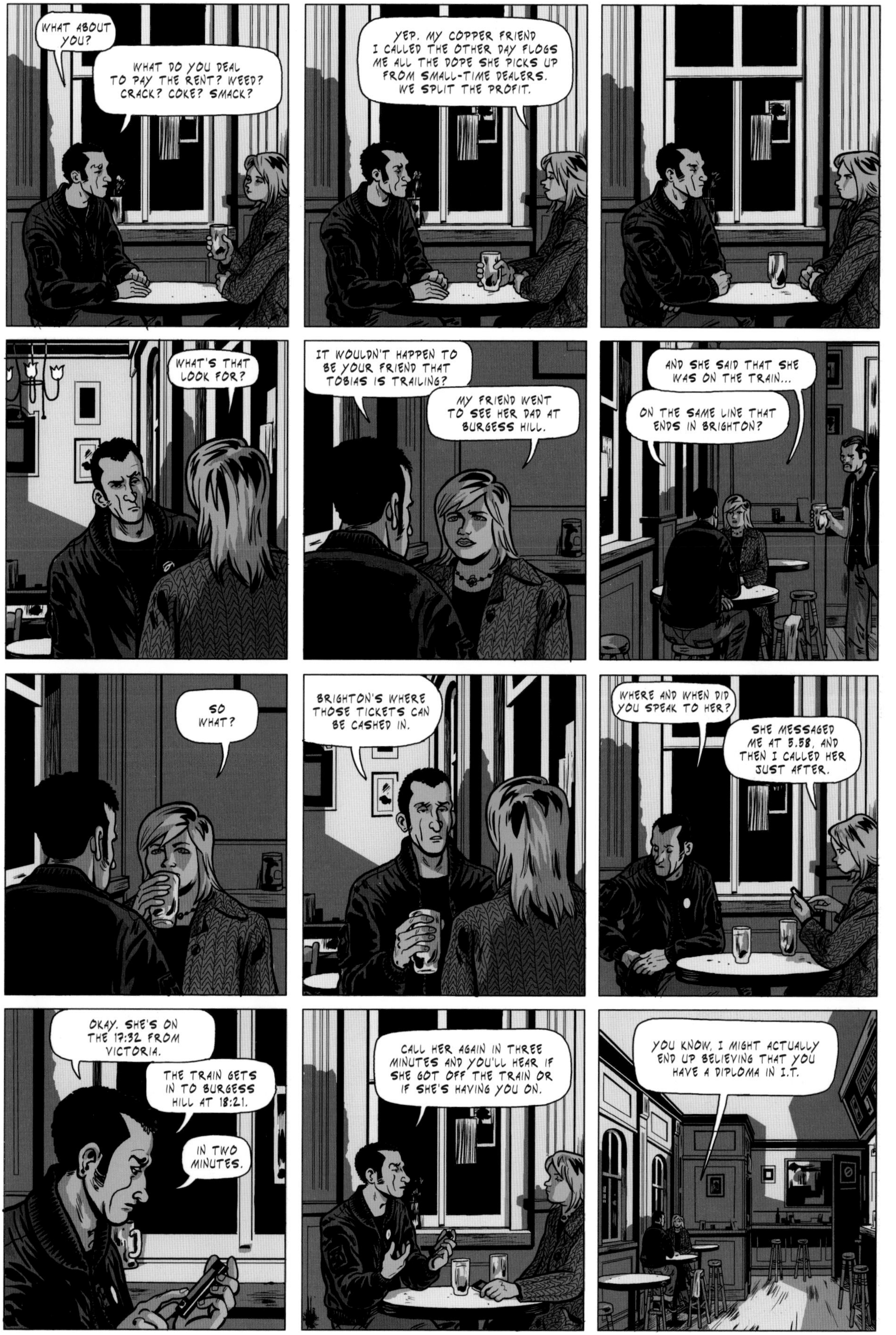
WHAT ABOUT YOU?
WHAT DO YOU DEAL TO PAY THE RENT? WEED? CRACK? COKE? SMACK?
YEP. MY COPPER FRIEND I CALLED THE OTHER DAY FLOGS ME ALL THE DOPE SHE PICKS UP FROM SMALL-TIME DEALERS. WE SPLIT THE PROFIT.
WHAT'S THAT LOOK FOR?
IT WOULDN'T HAPPEN TO BE YOUR FRIEND THAT TOBIAS IS TRAILING?
MY FRIEND WENT TO SEE HER DAD AT BURGESS HILL.
AND SHE SAID THAT SHE WAS ON THE TRAIN...
ON THE SAME LINE THAT ENDS IN BRIGHTON?
SO WHAT?
BRIGHTON'S WHERE THOSE TICKETS CAN BE CASHED IN.
WHERE AND WHEN DID YOU SPEAK TO HER?
SHE MESSAGED ME AT 5.58, AND THEN I CALLED HER JUST AFTER.
OKAY. SHE'S ON THE 17:32 FROM VICTORIA.
THE TRAIN GETS IN TO BURGESS HILL AT 18:21.
IN TWO MINUTES.
CALL HER AGAIN IN THREE MINUTES AND YOU'LL HEAR IF SHE GOT OFF THE TRAIN OR IF SHE'S HAVING YOU ON.
YOU KNOW, I MIGHT ACTUALLY END UP BELIEVING THAT YOU HAVE A DIPLOMA IN I.T.

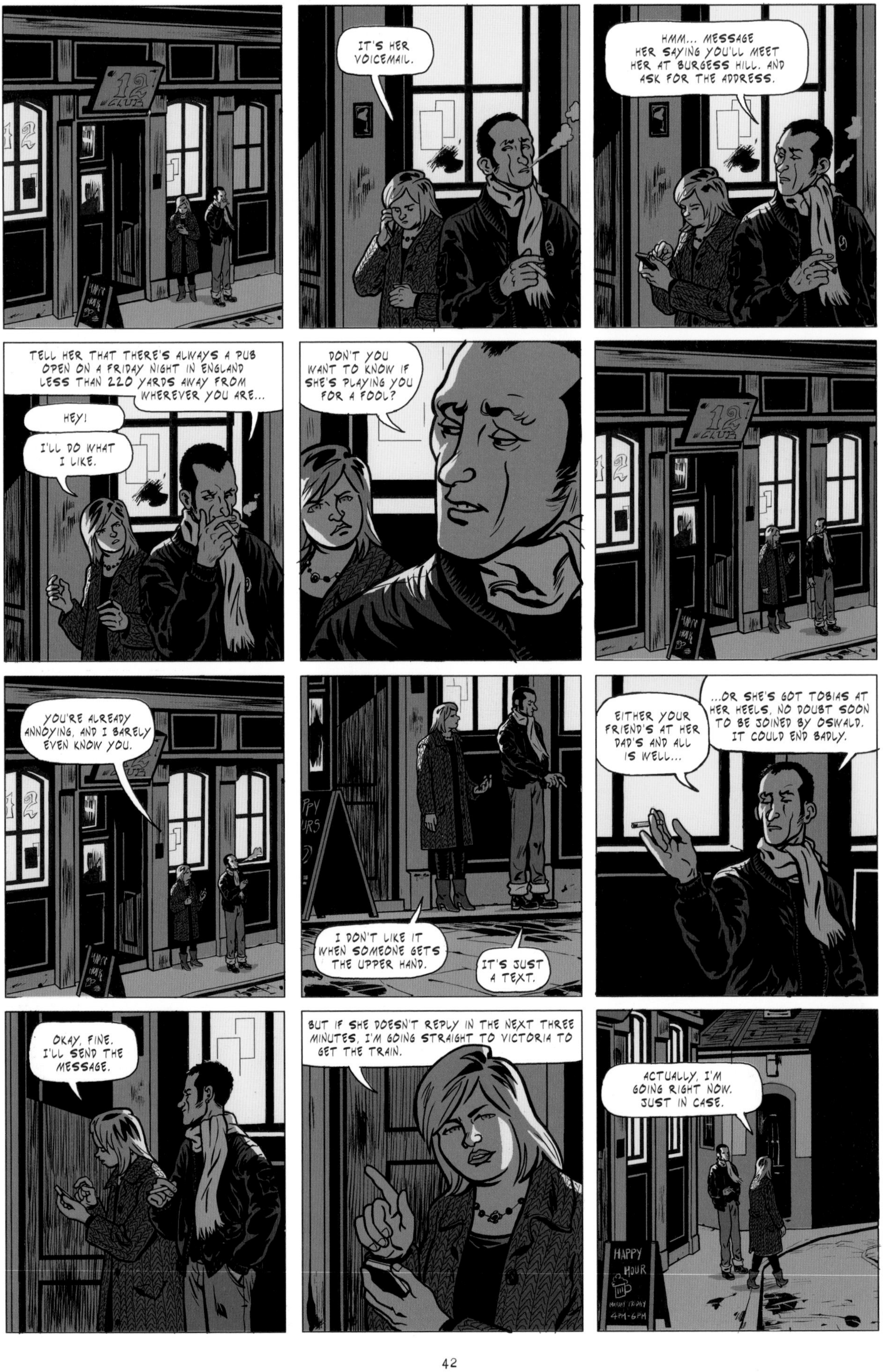

IT'S HER VOICEMAIL.
HMM... MESSAGE HER SAYING YOU'LL MEET HER AT BURGESS HILL. AND ASK FOR THE ADDRESS.
TELL HER THAT THERE'S ALWAYS A PUB OPEN ON A FRIDAY NIGHT IN ENGLAND LESS THAN 220 YARDS AWAY FROM WHEREVER YOU ARE...
HEY!
I'LL DO WHAT I LIKE.
DON'T YOU WANT TO KNOW IF SHE'S PLAYING YOU FOR A FOOL?
YOU'RE ALREADY ANNOYING, AND I BARELY EVEN KNOW YOU.
I DON'T LIKE IT WHEN SOMEONE GETS THE UPPER HAND.
IT'S JUST A TEXT.
EITHER YOUR FRIEND'S AT HER DAD'S AND ALL IS WELL...
...OR SHE'S GOT TOBIAS AT HER HEELS, NO DOUBT SOON TO BE JOINED BY OSWALD. IT COULD END BADLY.
OKAY, FINE. I'LL SEND THE MESSAGE.
BUT IF SHE DOESN'T REPLY IN THE NEXT THREE MINUTES, I'M GOING STRAIGHT TO VICTORIA TO GET THE TRAIN.
ACTUALLY, I'M GOING RIGHT NOW. JUST IN CASE.
HAPPY HOUR
4PM-6PM

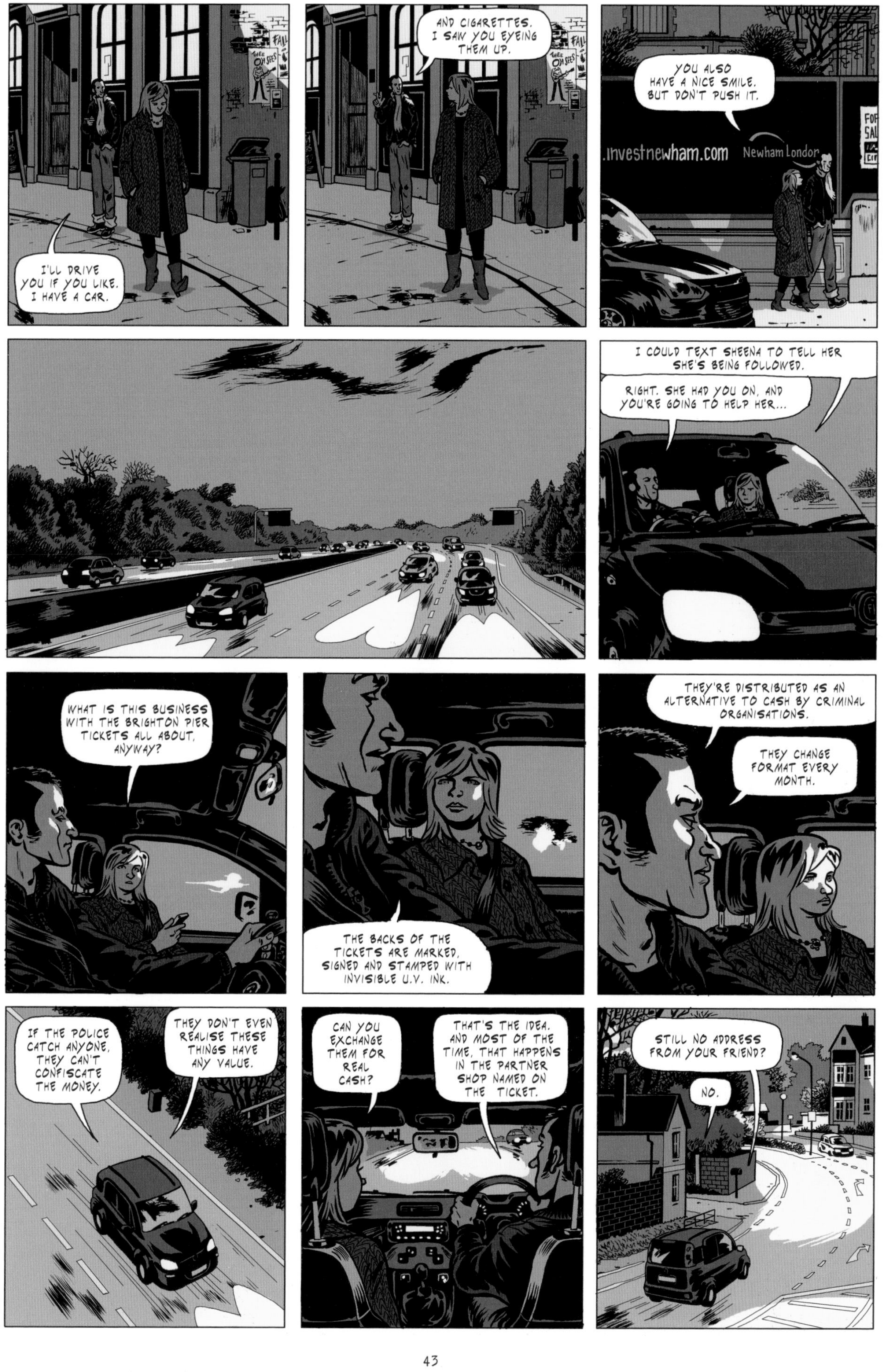

I'LL DRIVE YOU IF YOU LIKE. I HAVE A CAR.
AND CIGARETTES. I SAW YOU EYEING THEM UP.
YOU ALSO HAVE A NICE SMILE. BUT DON'T PUSH IT.
.investnewham.com
Newham London
I COULD TEXT SHEENA TO TELL HER SHE'S BEING FOLLOWED.
RIGHT. SHE HAD YOU ON, AND YOU'RE GOING TO HELP HER...
WHAT IS THIS BUSINESS WITH THE BRIGHTON PIER TICKETS ALL ABOUT, ANYWAY?
THE BACKS OF THE TICKETS ARE MARKED, SIGNED AND STAMPED WITH INVISIBLE U.V. INK.
THEY'RE DISTRIBUTED AS AN ALTERNATIVE TO CASH BY CRIMINAL ORGANISATIONS.
THEY CHANGE FORMAT EVERY MONTH.
IF THE POLICE CATCH ANYONE, THEY CAN'T CONFISCATE THE MONEY.
THEY DON'T EVEN REALISE THESE THINGS HAVE ANY VALUE.
CAN YOU EXCHANGE THEM FOR REAL CASH?
THAT'S THE IDEA. AND MOST OF THE TIME, THAT HAPPENS IN THE PARTNER SHOP NAMED ON THE TICKET.
STILL NO ADDRESS FROM YOUR FRIEND?
NO.

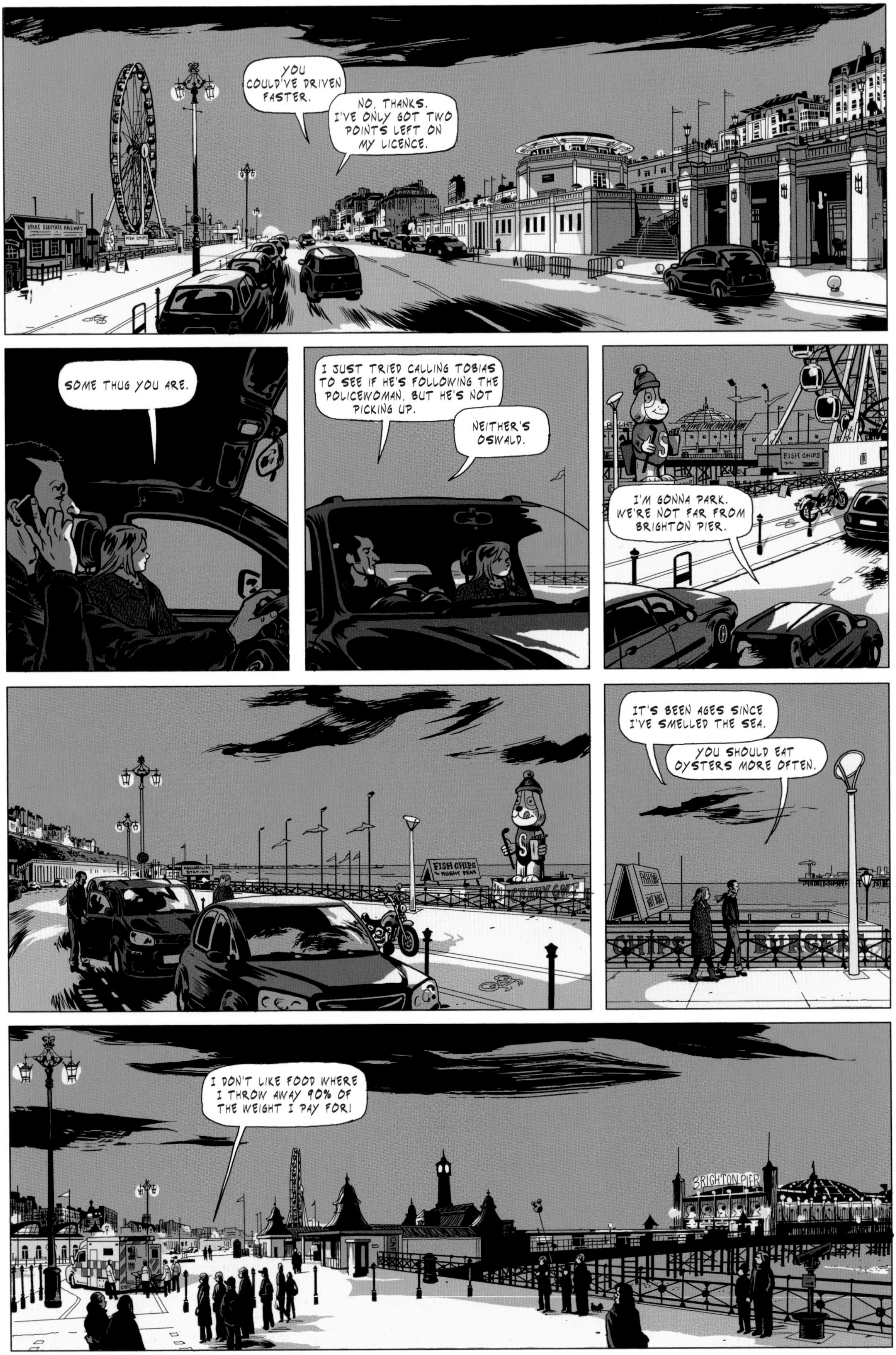

YOU COULD'VE DRIVEN FASTER.
NO, THANKS. I'VE ONLY GOT TWO POINTS LEFT ON MY LICENCE.
SOME THUG YOU ARE.
I JUST TRIED CALLING TOBIAS TO SEE IF HE'S FOLLOWING THE POLICEWOMAN, BUT HE'S NOT PICKING UP.
NEITHER'S OSWALD.
I'M GONNA PARK. WE'RE NOT FAR FROM BRIGHTON PIER.
FISH CHIPS
IT'S BEEN AGES SINCE I'VE SMELLED THE SEA.
YOU SHOULD EAT OYSTERS MORE OFTEN.
I DON'T LIKE FOOD WHERE I THROW AWAY 90% OF THE WEIGHT I PAY FOR!
BRIGHTON PIER

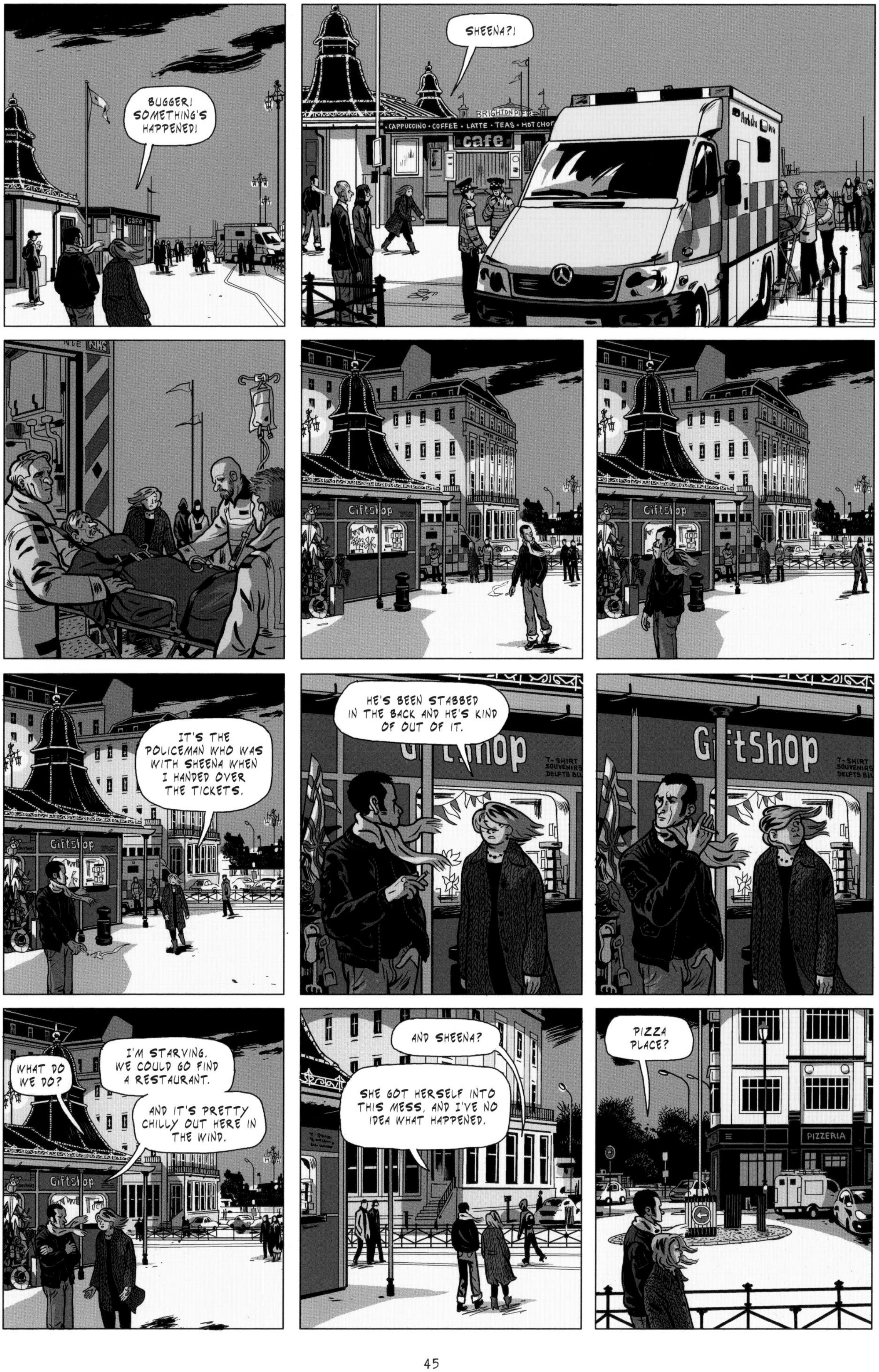

BUGGER! SOMETHING'S HAPPENED!
SHEENA?!
CAPPUCCINO • COFFEE • LATTE • TEAS • HOT CHOC
cafe
BRIGHTON PIER
Giftshop
IT'S THE POLICEMAN WHO WAS WITH SHEENA WHEN I HANDED OVER THE TICKETS.
HE'S BEEN STABBED IN THE BACK AND HE'S KIND OF OUT OF IT.
GiftShop
T-SHIRT SOUVENIRS
WHAT DO WE DO?
I'M STARVING. WE COULD GO FIND A RESTAURANT.
AND IT'S PRETTY CHILLY OUT HERE IN THE WIND.
AND SHEENA?
SHE GOT HERSELF INTO THIS MESS, AND I'VE NO IDEA WHAT HAPPENED.
PIZZA PLACE?
PIZZERIA

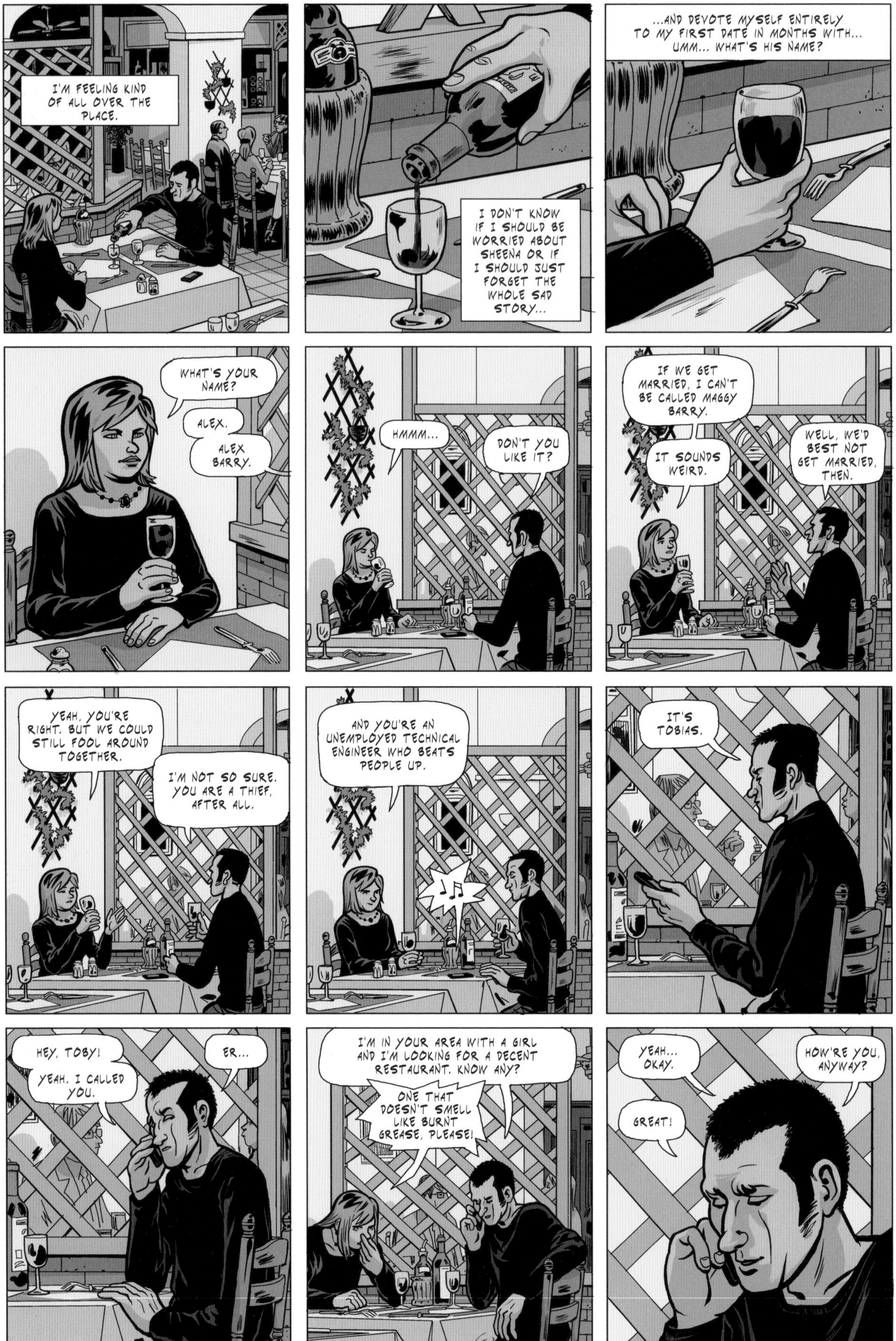
I'M FEELING KIND OF ALL OVER THE PLACE.
I DON'T KNOW IF I SHOULD BE WORRIED ABOUT SHEENA OR IF I SHOULD JUST FORGET THE WHOLE SAD STORY...
...AND DEVOTE MYSELF ENTIRELY TO MY FIRST DATE IN MONTHS WITH... UMM... WHAT'S HIS NAME?
WHAT'S YOUR NAME?
ALEX.
ALEX BARRY.
HMMM...
DON'T YOU LIKE IT?
IF WE GET MARRIED, I CAN'T BE CALLED MAGGY BARRY.
IT SOUNDS WEIRD.
WELL, WE'D BEST NOT GET MARRIED, THEN.
YEAH, YOU'RE RIGHT. BUT WE COULD STILL FOOL AROUND TOGETHER.
I'M NOT SO SURE. YOU ARE A THIEF, AFTER ALL.
AND YOU'RE AN UNEMPLOYED TECHNICAL ENGINEER WHO BEATS PEOPLE UP.
IT'S TOBIAS.
HEY, TOBY!
YEAH. I CALLED YOU.
ER...
I'M IN YOUR AREA WITH A GIRL AND I'M LOOKING FOR A DECENT RESTAURANT. KNOW ANY?
ONE THAT DOESN'T SMELL LIKE BURNT GREASE, PLEASE!
YEAH... OKAY.
GREAT!
HOW'RE YOU, ANYWAY?

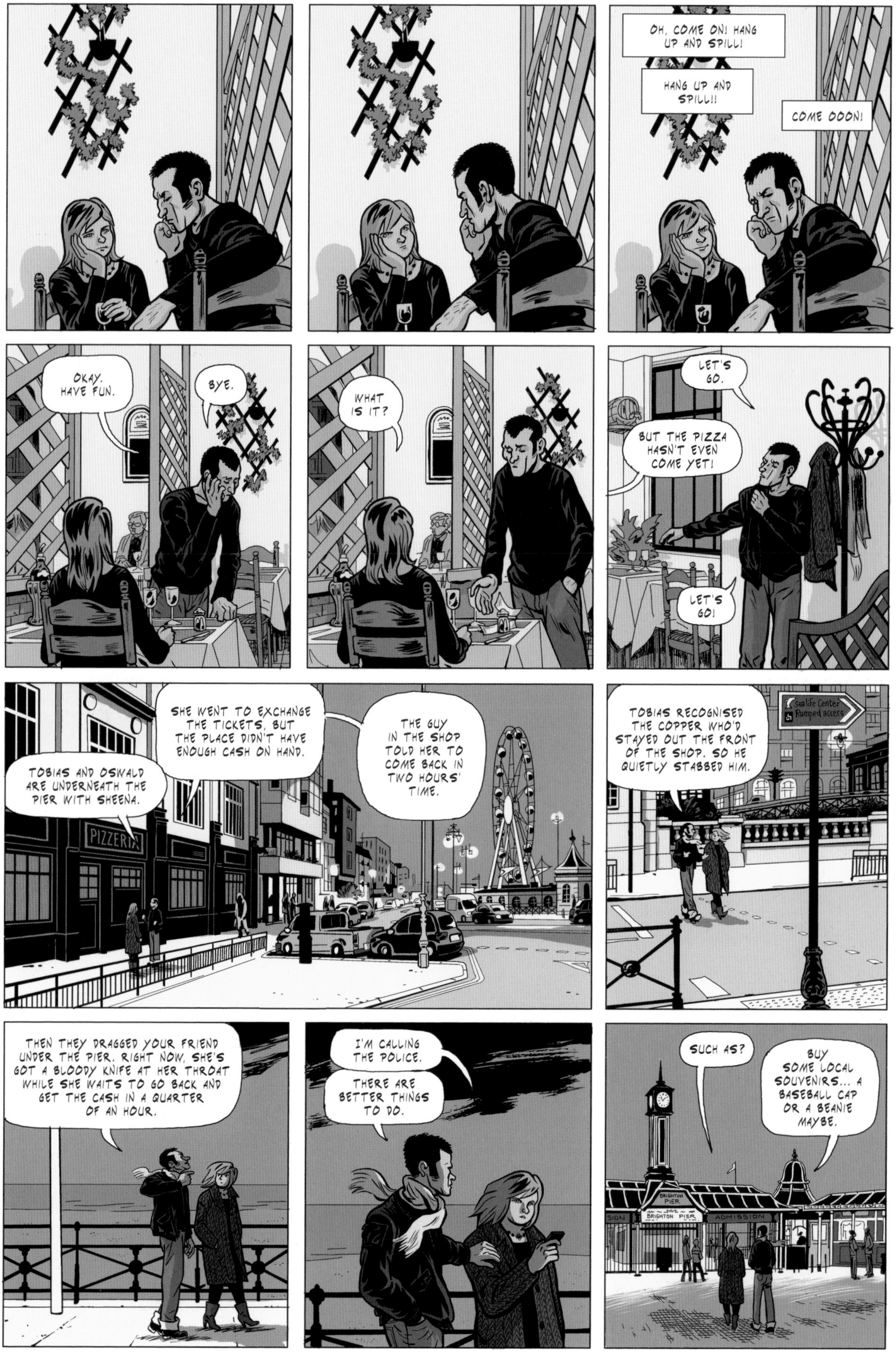
OH, COME ON! HANG UP AND SPILL!
HANG UP AND SPILL!!
COME OOON!
OKAY. HAVE FUN.
BYE.
WHAT IS IT?
LET'S GO.
BUT THE PIZZA HASN'T EVEN COME YET!
LET'S GO!
TOBIAS AND OSWALD ARE UNDERNEATH THE PIER WITH SHEENA.
SHE WENT TO EXCHANGE THE TICKETS, BUT THE PLACE DIDN'T HAVE ENOUGH CASH ON HAND.
THE GUY IN THE SHOP TOLD HER TO COME BACK IN TWO HOURS' TIME.
PIZZERIA
TOBIAS RECOGNISED THE COPPER WHO'D STAYED OUT THE FRONT OF THE SHOP. SO HE QUIETLY STABBED HIM.
Sea life Center
Ramped access
THEN THEY DRAGGED YOUR FRIEND UNDER THE PIER. RIGHT NOW, SHE'S GOT A BLOODY KNIFE AT HER THROAT WHILE SHE WAITS TO GO BACK AND GET THE CASH IN A QUARTER OF AN HOUR.
I'M CALLING THE POLICE.
THERE ARE BETTER THINGS TO DO.
SUCH AS?
BUY SOME LOCAL SOUVENIRS... A BASEBALL CAP OR A BEANIE MAYBE.
BRIGHTON PIER
BRIGHTON PIER
ADMISSION

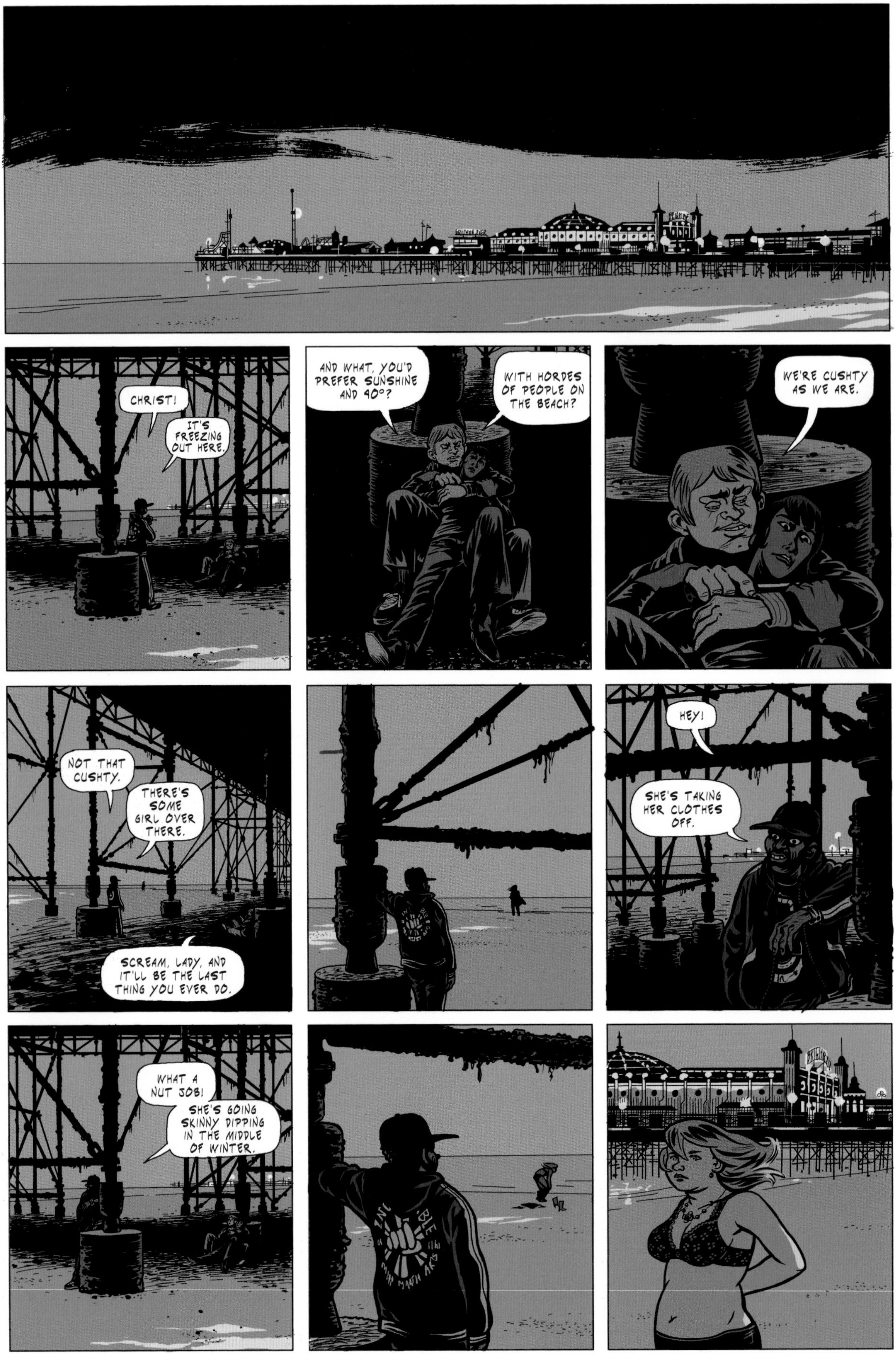
CHRIST!
IT'S FREEZING OUT HERE.
AND WHAT, YOU'D PREFER SUNSHINE AND 40°?
WITH HORDES OF PEOPLE ON THE BEACH?
WE'RE CUSHTY AS WE ARE.
NOT THAT CUSHTY.
THERE'S SOME GIRL OVER THERE.
SCREAM, LADY, AND IT'LL BE THE LAST THING YOU EVER DO.
HEY!
SHE'S TAKING HER CLOTHES OFF.
WHAT A NUT JOB!
SHE'S GOING SKINNY DIPPING IN THE MIDDLE OF WINTER.

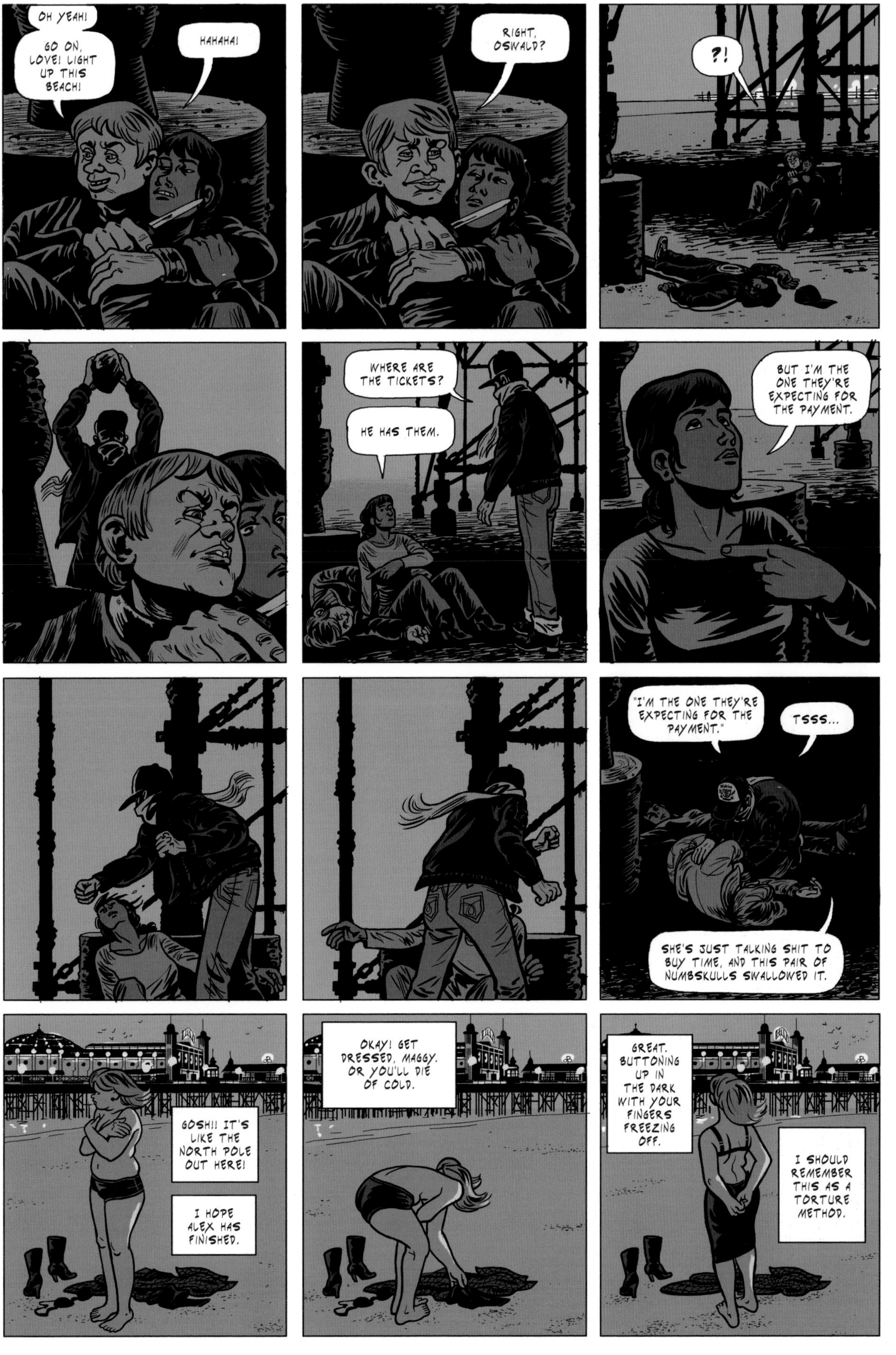
OH YEAH!
GO ON, LOVE! LIGHT UP THIS BEACH!
HAHAHA!
RIGHT, OSWALD?
?!
WHERE ARE THE TICKETS?
HE HAS THEM.
BUT I'M THE ONE THEY'RE EXPECTING FOR THE PAYMENT.
"I'M THE ONE THEY'RE EXPECTING FOR THE PAYMENT."
TSSS...
SHE'S JUST TALKING SHIT TO BUY TIME, AND THIS PAIR OF NUMBSKULLS SWALLOWED IT.
GOSH!! IT'S LIKE THE NORTH POLE OUT HERE!
I HOPE ALEX HAS FINISHED.
OKAY! GET DRESSED, MAGGY. OR YOU'LL DIE OF COLD.
GREAT. BUTTONING UP IN THE DARK WITH YOUR FINGERS FREEZING OFF.
I SHOULD REMEMBER THIS AS A TORTURE METHOD.

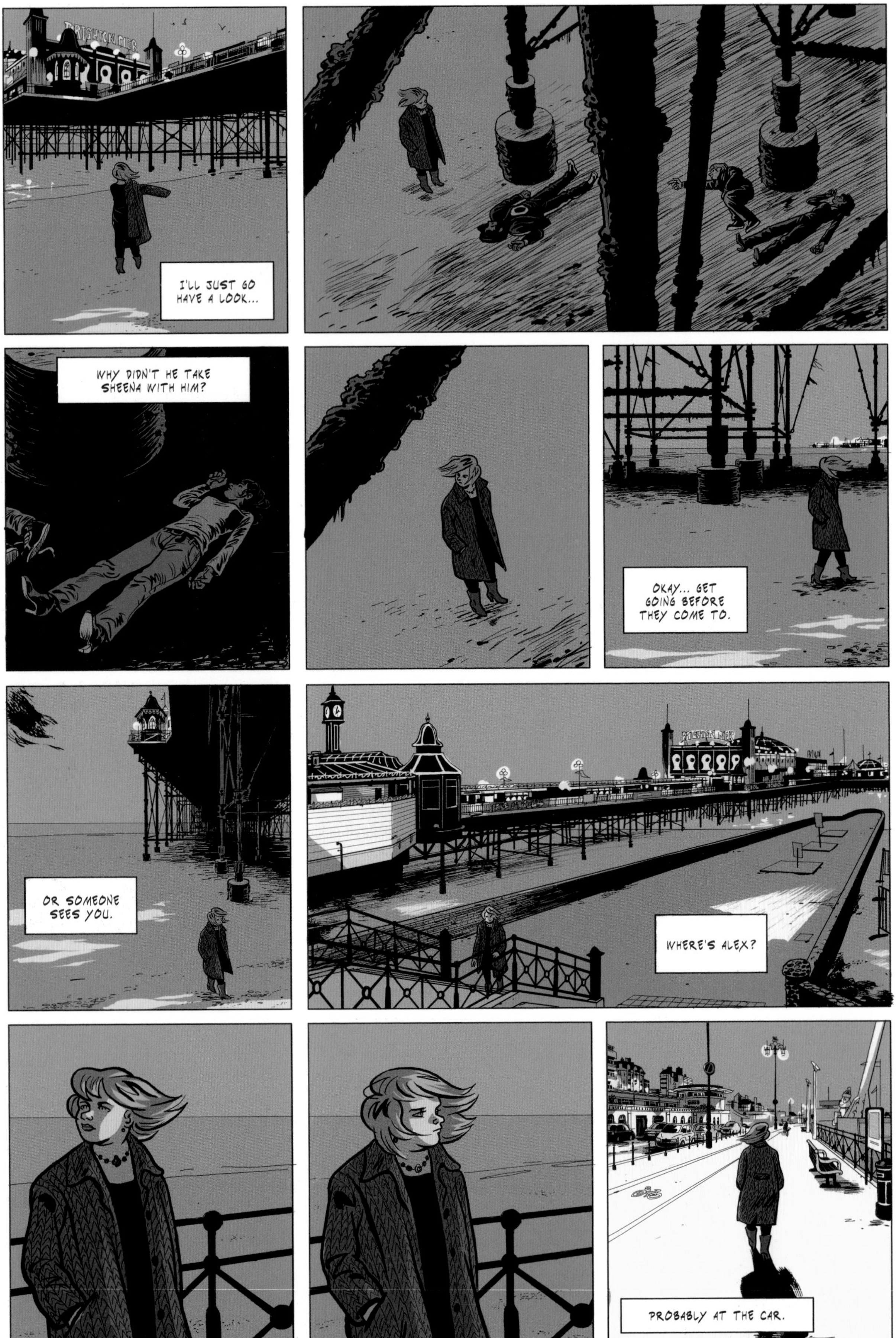
I'LL JUST GO HAVE A LOOK...
WHY DIDN'T HE TAKE SHEENA WITH HIM?
OKAY... GET GOING BEFORE THEY COME TO.
OR SOMEONE SEES YOU.
WHERE'S ALEX?
PROBABLY AT THE CAR.

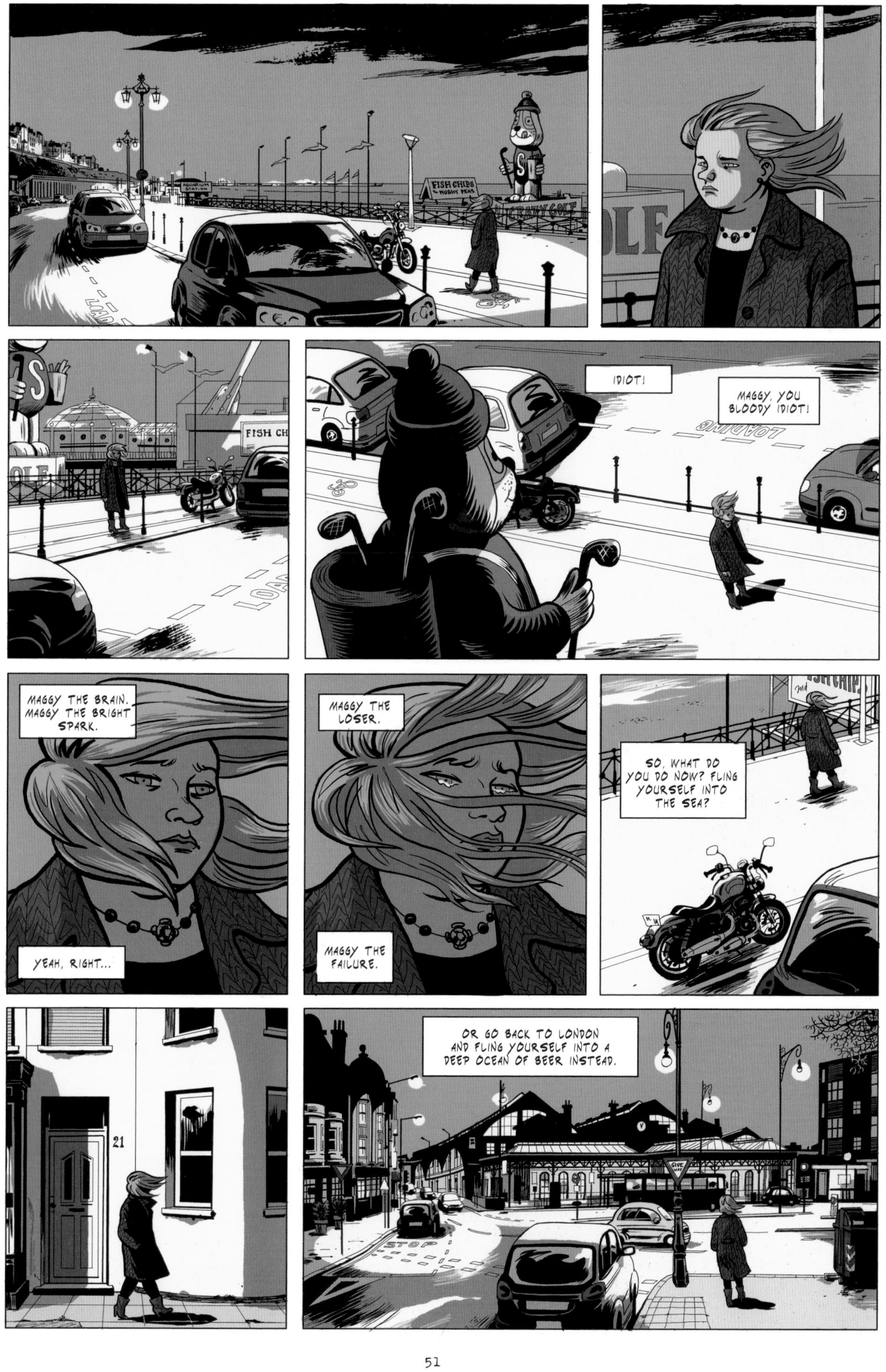
FISH CHIPS & MUSHY PEAS
CRAZY GOLF
AQUARIUM STATION
LOADING
IDIOT!
MAGGY, YOU BLOODY IDIOT!
MAGGY THE BRAIN. MAGGY THE BRIGHT SPARK.
YEAH, RIGHT...
MAGGY THE LOSER.
MAGGY THE FAILURE.
SO, WHAT DO YOU DO NOW? FLING YOURSELF INTO THE SEA?
21
OR GO BACK TO LONDON AND FLING YOURSELF INTO A DEEP OCEAN OF BEER INSTEAD.
STOP
GIVE WAY

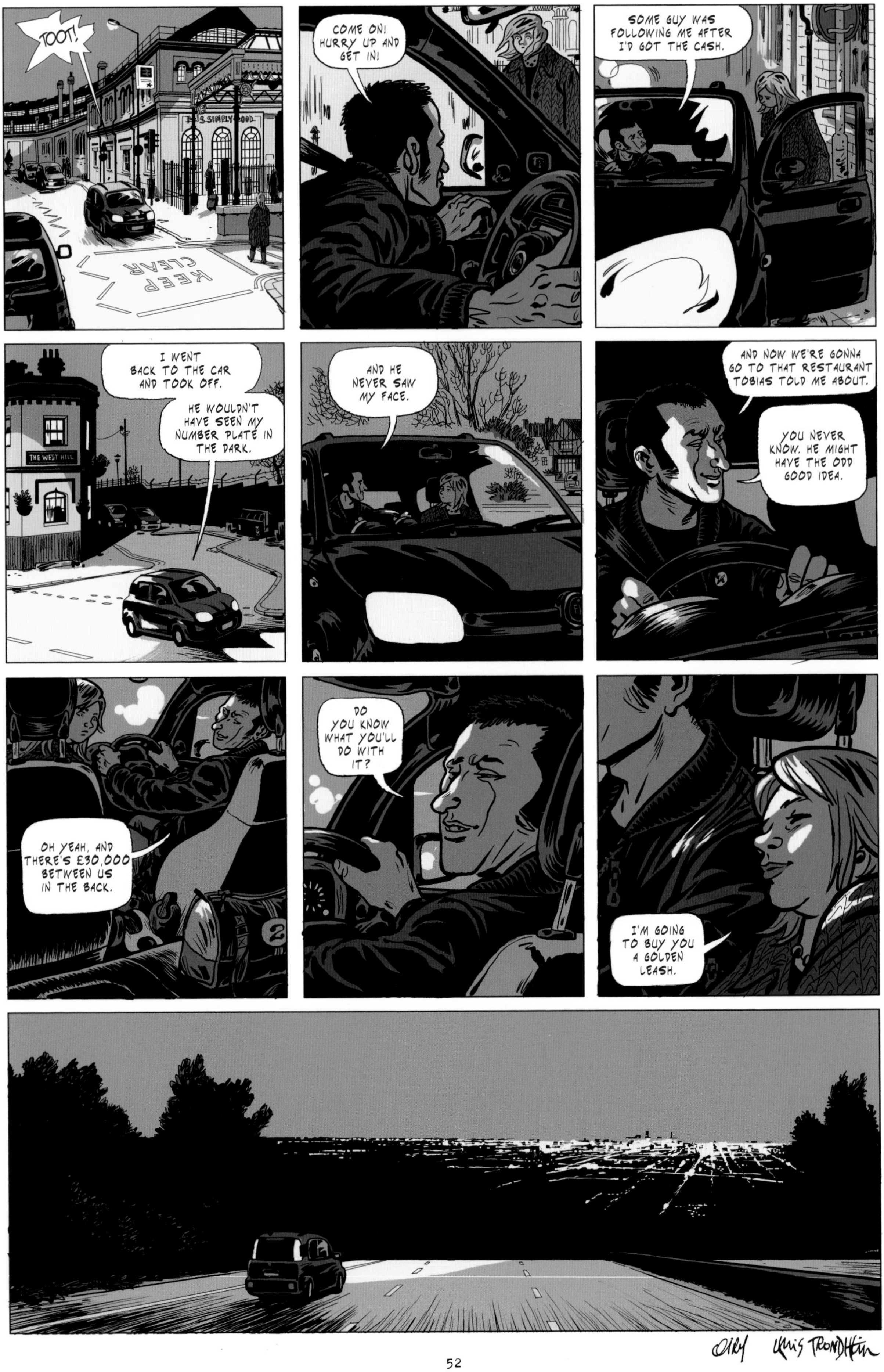
TOOT!
KEEP CLEAR
COME ON! HURRY UP AND GET IN!
SOME GUY WAS FOLLOWING ME AFTER I'D GOT THE CASH.
THE WEST HILL
I WENT BACK TO THE CAR AND TOOK OFF.
HE WOULDN'T HAVE SEEN MY NUMBER PLATE IN THE DARK.
AND HE NEVER SAW MY FACE.
AND NOW WE'RE GONNA GO TO THAT RESTAURANT TOBIAS TOLD ME ABOUT.
YOU NEVER KNOW. HE MIGHT HAVE THE ODD GOOD IDEA.
OH YEAH, AND THERE'S £30,000 BETWEEN US IN THE BACK.
DO YOU KNOW WHAT YOU'LL DO WITH IT?
I'M GOING TO BUY YOU A GOLDEN LEASH.

2. THE MAN IN MY BED

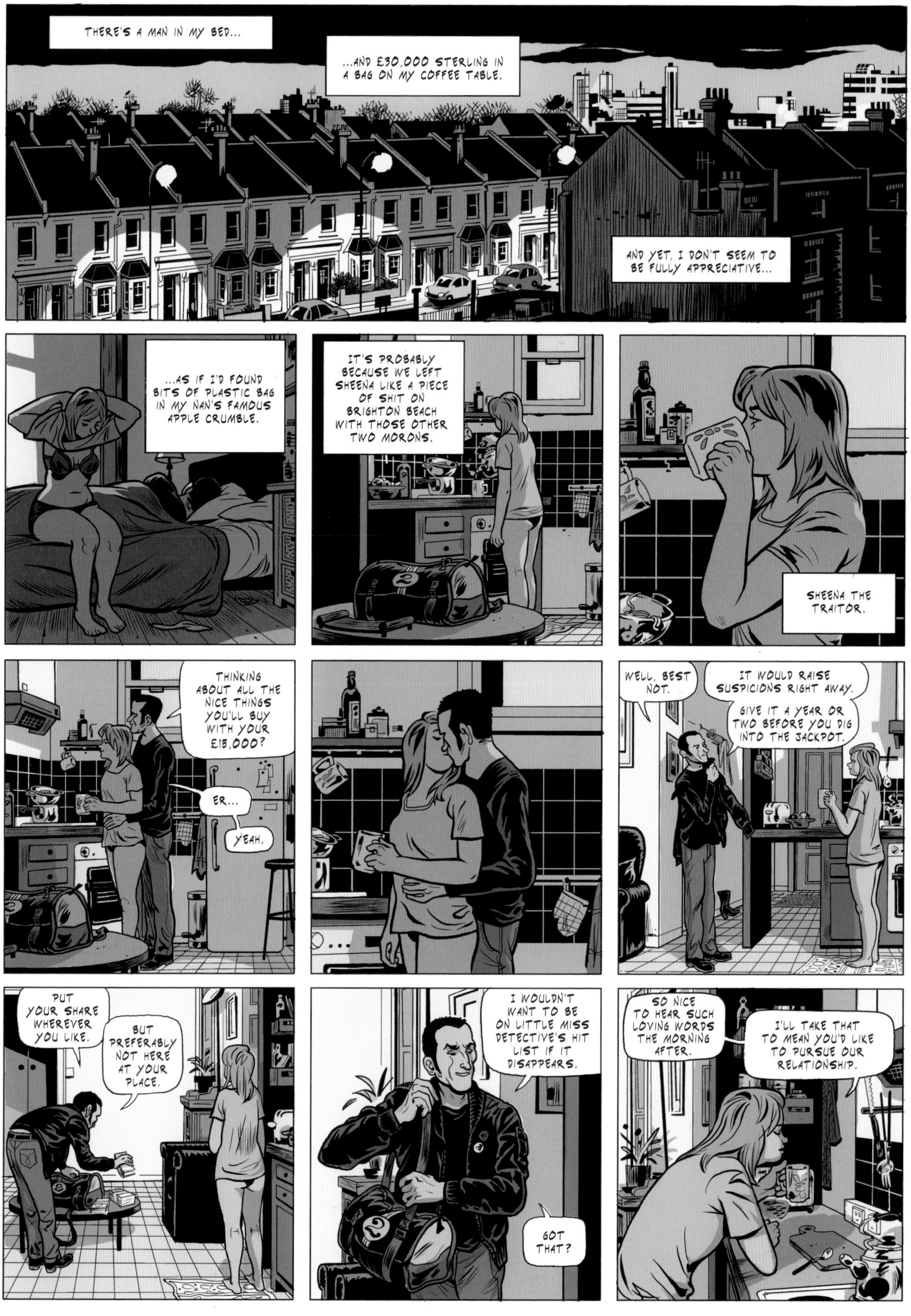
THERE'S A MAN IN MY BED...
...AND £30,000 STERLING IN A BAG ON MY COFFEE TABLE.
AND YET, I DON'T SEEM TO BE FULLY APPRECIATIVE...
...AS IF I'D FOUND BITS OF PLASTIC BAG IN MY NAN'S FAMOUS APPLE CRUMBLE.
IT'S PROBABLY BECAUSE WE LEFT SHEENA LIKE A PIECE OF SHIT ON BRIGHTON BEACH WITH THOSE OTHER TWO MORONS.
SHEENA THE TRAITOR.
THINKING ABOUT ALL THE NICE THINGS YOU'LL BUY WITH YOUR £15,000?
ER...
YEAH.
WELL, BEST NOT.
IT WOULD RAISE SUSPICIONS RIGHT AWAY.
GIVE IT A YEAR OR TWO BEFORE YOU DIG INTO THE JACKPOT.
PUT YOUR SHARE WHEREVER YOU LIKE.
BUT PREFERABLY NOT HERE AT YOUR PLACE.
I WOULDN'T WANT TO BE ON LITTLE MISS DETECTIVE'S HIT LIST IF IT DISAPPEARS.
GOT THAT?
SO NICE TO HEAR SUCH LOVING WORDS THE MORNING AFTER.
I'LL TAKE THAT TO MEAN YOU'D LIKE TO PURSUE OUR RELATIONSHIP.

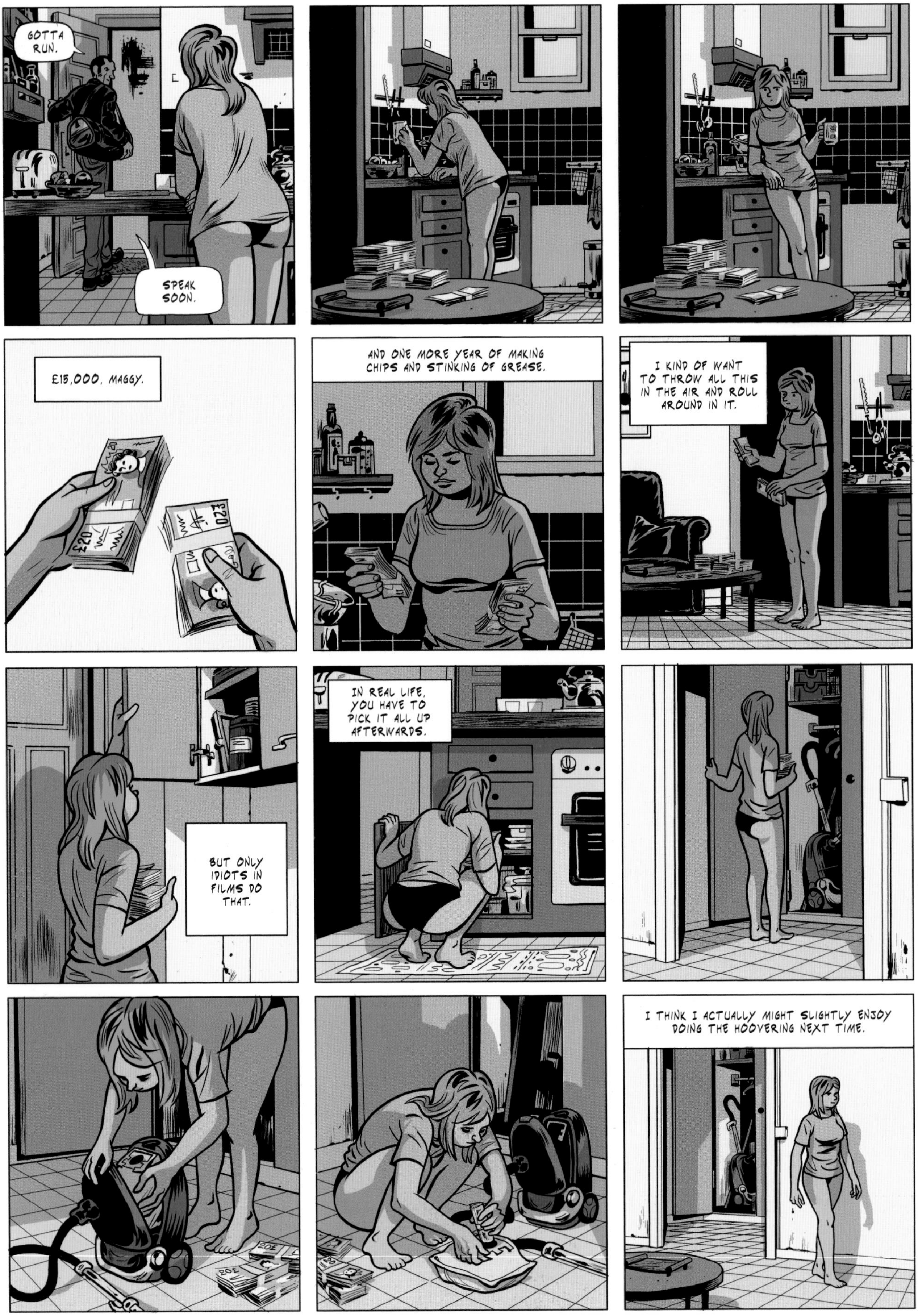

GOTTA RUN.
SPEAK SOON.
£15,000, MAGGY.
AND ONE MORE YEAR OF MAKING CHIPS AND STINKING OF GREASE.
I KIND OF WANT TO THROW ALL THIS IN THE AIR AND ROLL AROUND IN IT.
BUT ONLY IDIOTS IN FILMS DO THAT.
IN REAL LIFE, YOU HAVE TO PICK IT ALL UP AFTERWARDS.
I THINK I ACTUALLY MIGHT SLIGHTLY ENJOY DOING THE HOOVERING NEXT TIME.

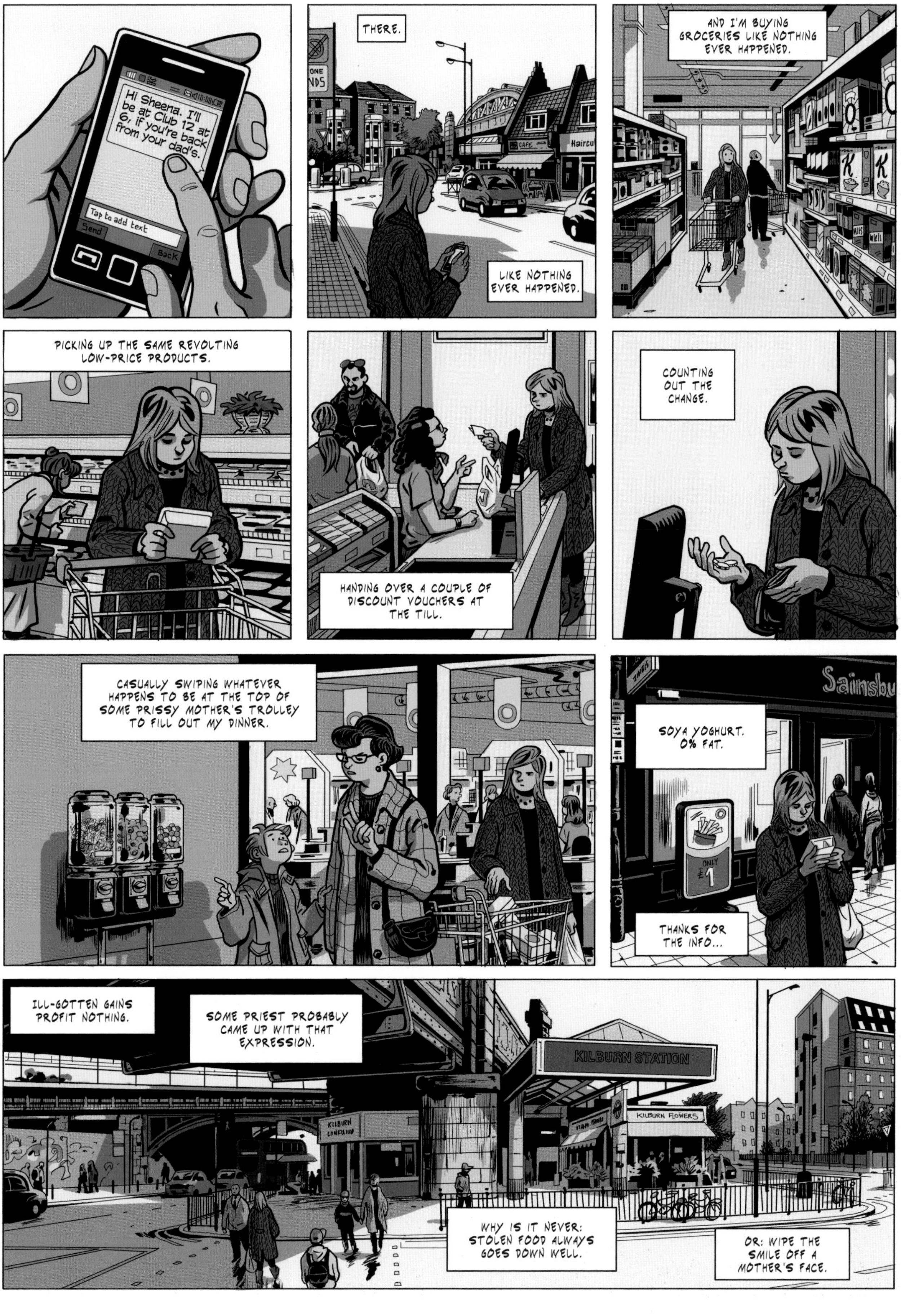

Hi Sheena. I'll be at Club 12 at 6, if you're back from your dad's.
Tap to add text
Send
Back
THERE.
LIKE NOTHING EVER HAPPENED.
AND I'M BUYING GROCERIES LIKE NOTHING EVER HAPPENED.
PICKING UP THE SAME REVOLTING LOW-PRICE PRODUCTS.
HANDING OVER A COUPLE OF DISCOUNT VOUCHERS AT THE TILL.
COUNTING OUT THE CHANGE.
CASUALLY SWIPING WHATEVER HAPPENS TO BE AT THE TOP OF SOME PRISSY MOTHER'S TROLLEY TO FILL OUT MY DINNER.
SOYA YOGHURT. 0% FAT.
THANKS FOR THE INFO...
ILL-GOTTEN GAINS PROFIT NOTHING.
SOME PRIEST PROBABLY CAME UP WITH THAT EXPRESSION.
KILBURN STATION
KILBURN FLOWERS
WHY IS IT NEVER: STOLEN FOOD ALWAYS GOES DOWN WELL.
OR: WIPE THE SMILE OFF A MOTHER'S FACE.

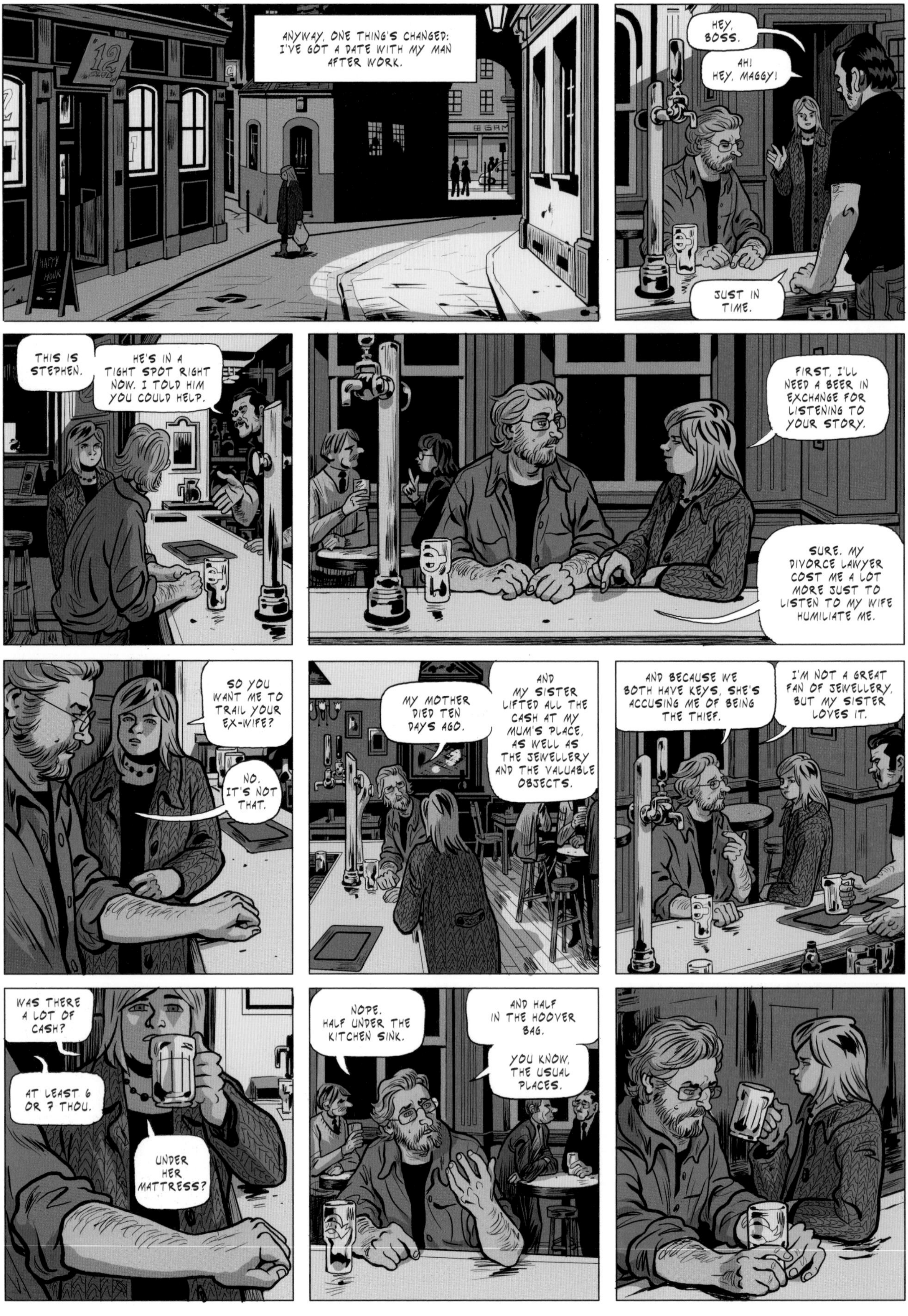
ANYWAY, ONE THING'S CHANGED: I'VE GOT A DATE WITH MY MAN AFTER WORK.
12
HAPPY HOUR
HEY, BOSS.
AH! HEY, MAGGY!
JUST IN TIME.
THIS IS STEPHEN.
HE'S IN A TIGHT SPOT RIGHT NOW. I TOLD HIM YOU COULD HELP.
FIRST, I'LL NEED A BEER IN EXCHANGE FOR LISTENING TO YOUR STORY.
SURE. MY DIVORCE LAWYER COST ME A LOT MORE JUST TO LISTEN TO MY WIFE HUMILIATE ME.
SO YOU WANT ME TO TRAIL YOUR EX-WIFE?
NO. IT'S NOT THAT.
MY MOTHER DIED TEN DAYS AGO.
AND MY SISTER LIFTED ALL THE CASH AT MY MUM'S PLACE, AS WELL AS THE JEWELLERY AND THE VALUABLE OBJECTS.
AND BECAUSE WE BOTH HAVE KEYS, SHE'S ACCUSING ME OF BEING THE THIEF.
I'M NOT A GREAT FAN OF JEWELLERY, BUT MY SISTER LOVES IT.
WAS THERE A LOT OF CASH?
AT LEAST 6 OR 7 THOU.
UNDER HER MATTRESS?
NOPE. HALF UNDER THE KITCHEN SINK.
AND HALF IN THE HOOVER BAG.
YOU KNOW, THE USUAL PLACES.

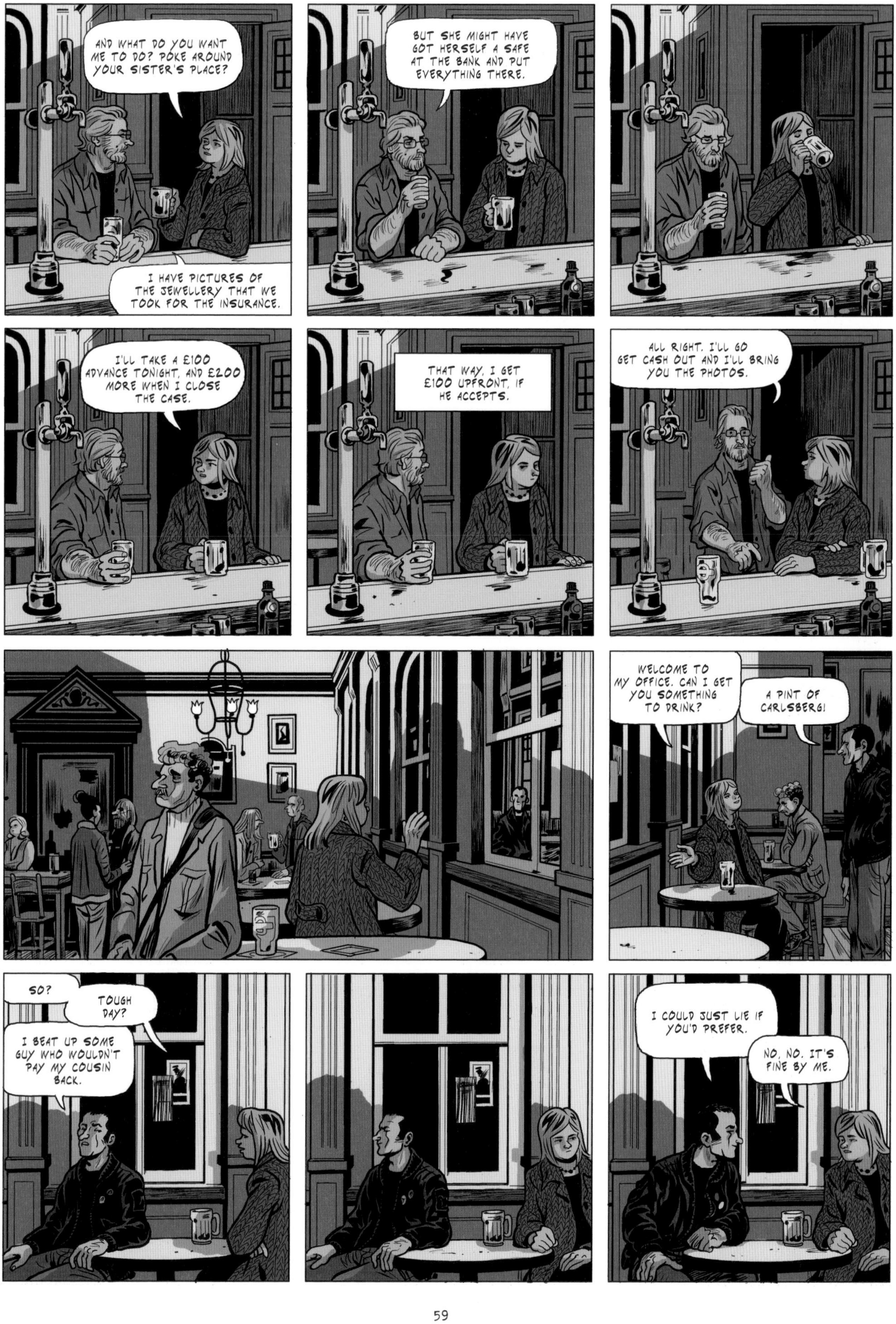

AND WHAT DO YOU WANT ME TO DO? POKE AROUND YOUR SISTER'S PLACE?
I HAVE PICTURES OF THE JEWELLERY THAT WE TOOK FOR THE INSURANCE.
BUT SHE MIGHT HAVE GOT HERSELF A SAFE AT THE BANK AND PUT EVERYTHING THERE.
I'LL TAKE A £100 ADVANCE TONIGHT, AND £200 MORE WHEN I CLOSE THE CASE.
THAT WAY, I GET £100 UPFRONT, IF HE ACCEPTS.
ALL RIGHT. I'LL GO GET CASH OUT AND I'LL BRING YOU THE PHOTOS.
WELCOME TO MY OFFICE. CAN I GET YOU SOMETHING TO DRINK?
A PINT OF CARLSBERG!
SO?
TOUGH DAY?
I BEAT UP SOME GUY WHO WOULDN'T PAY MY COUSIN BACK.
I COULD JUST LIE IF YOU'D PREFER.
NO, NO. IT'S FINE BY ME.

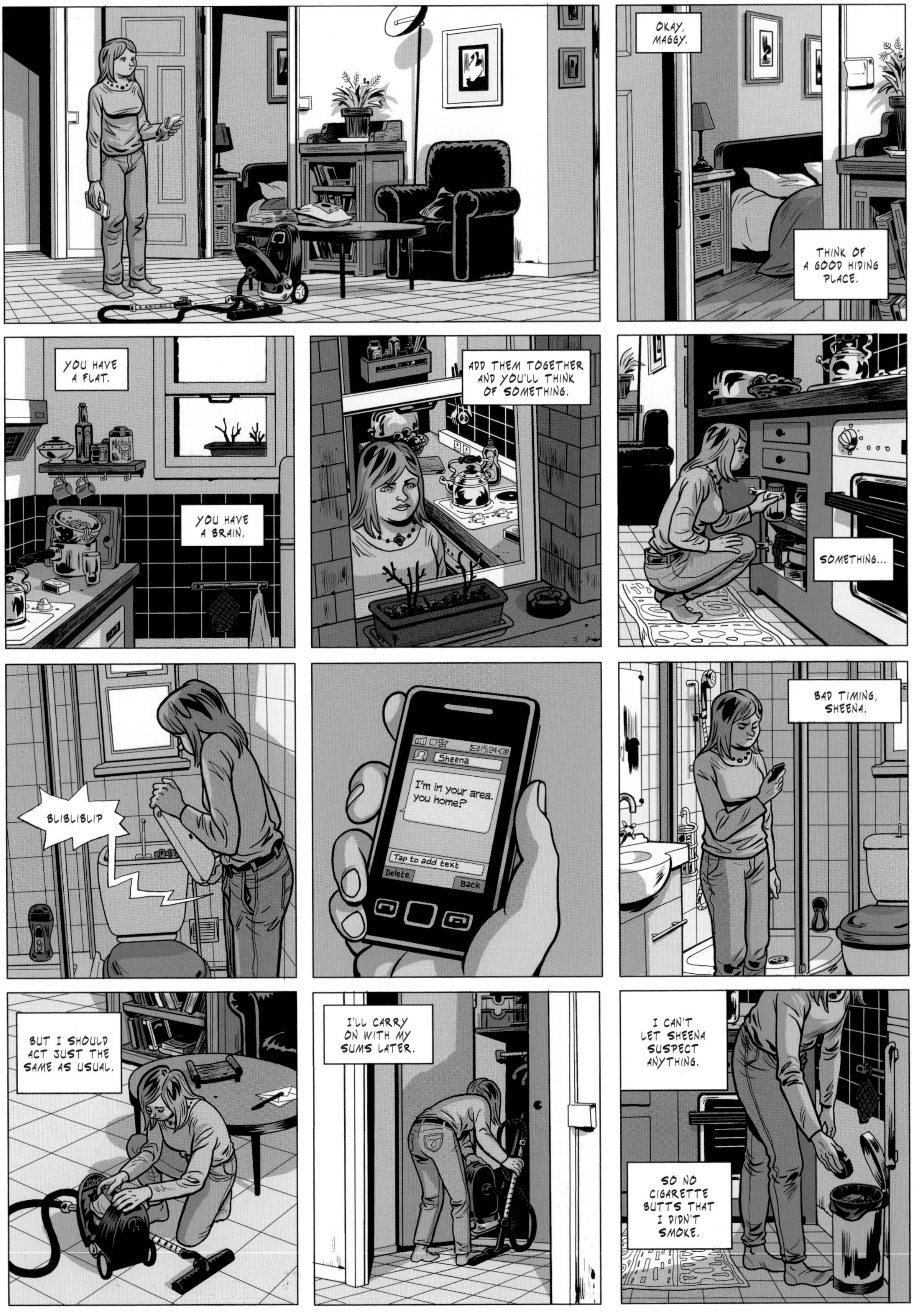
OKAY, MAGGY.
THINK OF A GOOD HIDING PLACE.
YOU HAVE A FLAT.
YOU HAVE A BRAIN.
ADD THEM TOGETHER AND YOU'LL THINK OF SOMETHING.
SOMETHING...
BLIBLIBLIP
Sheena
I'm in your area. you home?
Tap to add text
Delete
Back
BAD TIMING, SHEENA.
BUT I SHOULD ACT JUST THE SAME AS USUAL.
I'LL CARRY ON WITH MY SUMS LATER.
I CAN'T LET SHEENA SUSPECT ANYTHING.
SO NO CIGARETTE BUTTS THAT I DIDN'T SMOKE.

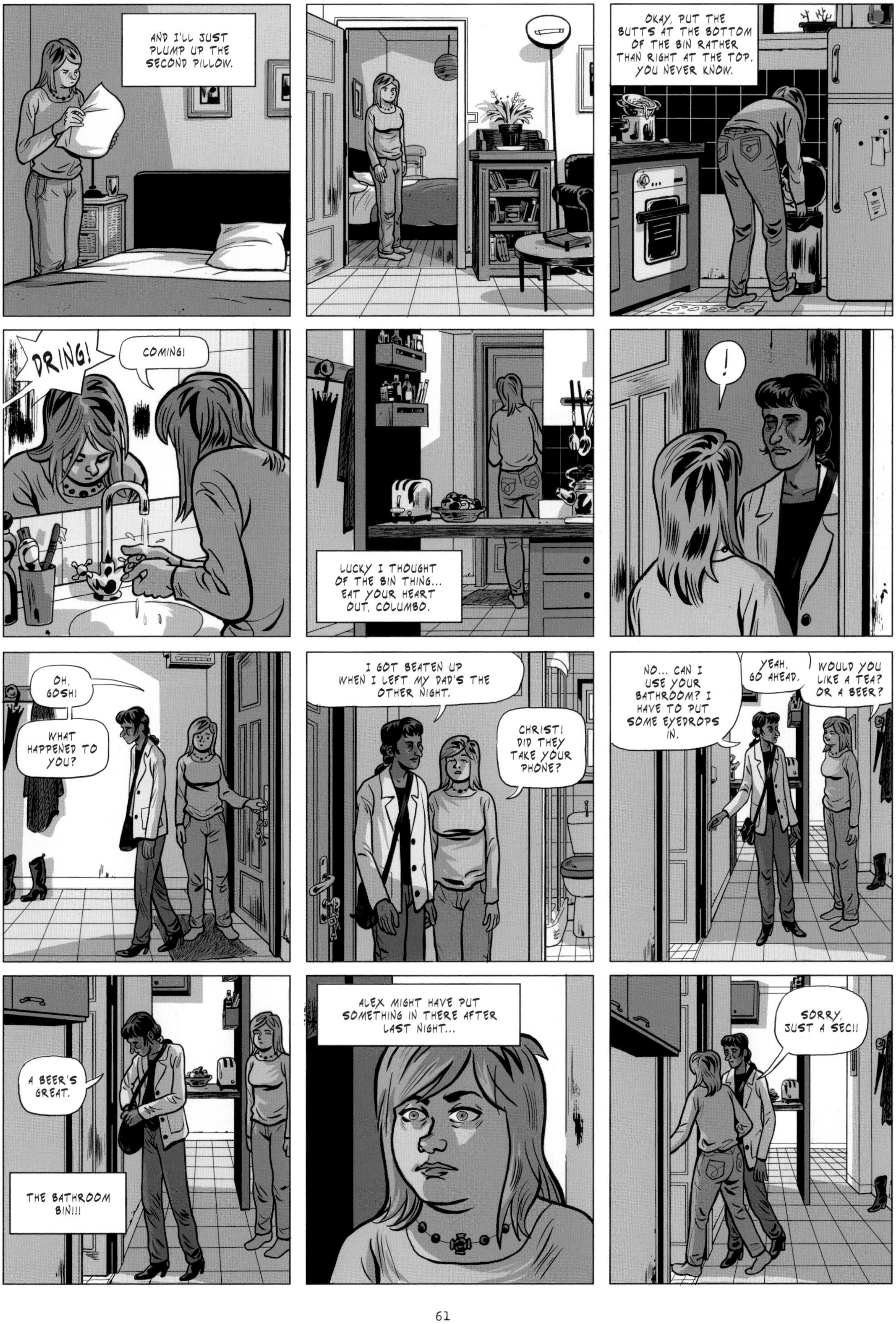
AND I'LL JUST PLUMP UP THE SECOND PILLOW.
OKAY, PUT THE BUTTS AT THE BOTTOM OF THE BIN RATHER THAN RIGHT AT THE TOP. YOU NEVER KNOW.
DRING!
COMING!
LUCKY I THOUGHT OF THE BIN THING... EAT YOUR HEART OUT, COLUMBO.
!
OH, GOSH!
WHAT HAPPENED TO YOU?
I GOT BEATEN UP WHEN I LEFT MY DAD'S THE OTHER NIGHT.
CHRIST! DID THEY TAKE YOUR PHONE?
NO... CAN I USE YOUR BATHROOM? I HAVE TO PUT SOME EYEDROPS IN.
YEAH, GO AHEAD.
WOULD YOU LIKE A TEA? OR A BEER?
A BEER'S GREAT.
THE BATHROOM BIN!!!
ALEX MIGHT HAVE PUT SOMETHING IN THERE AFTER LAST NIGHT...
SORRY, JUST A SEC!!

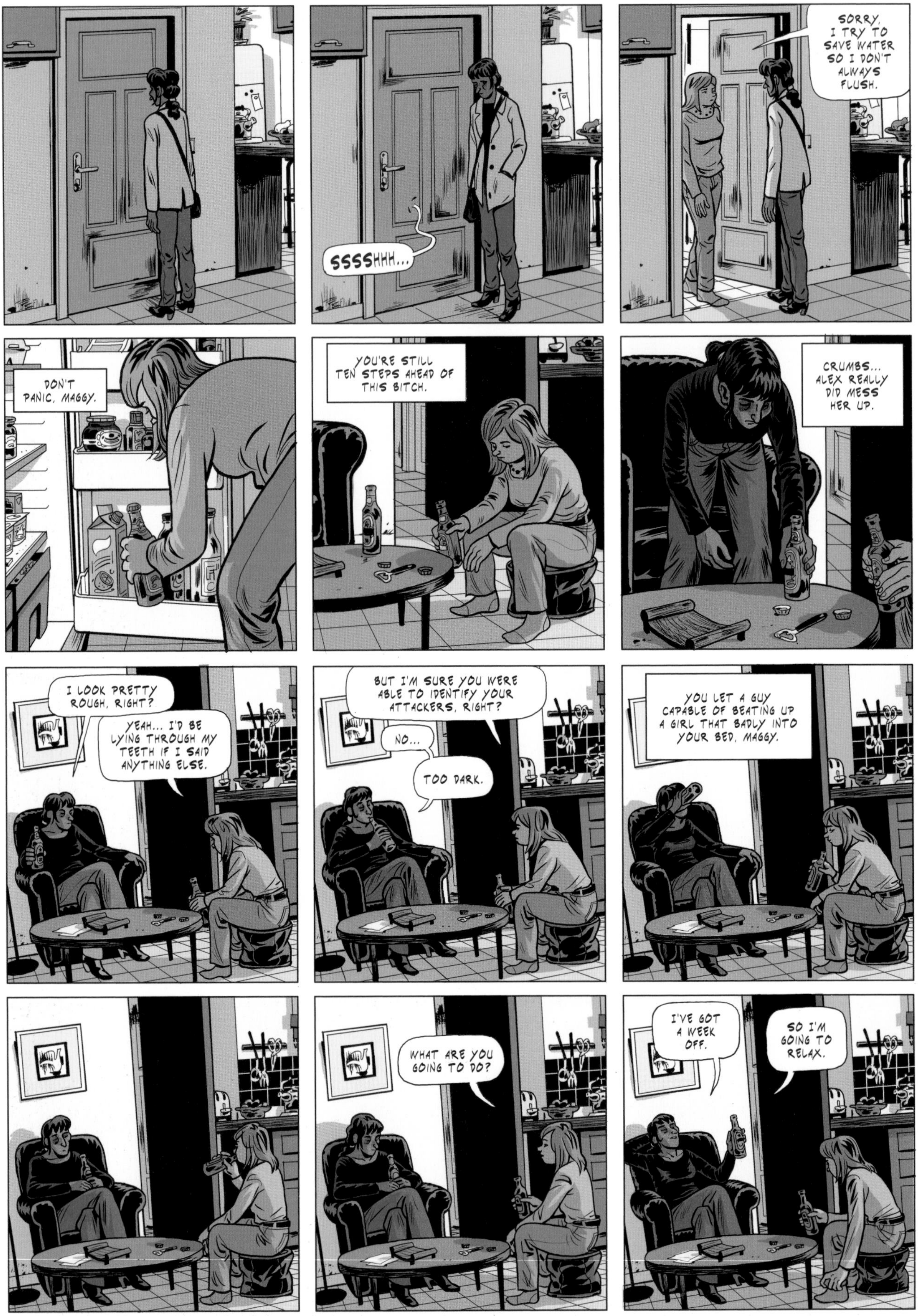
SSSSHHH...
SORRY, I TRY TO SAVE WATER SO I DON'T ALWAYS FLUSH.
DON'T PANIC, MAGGY.
YOU'RE STILL TEN STEPS AHEAD OF THIS BITCH.
CRUMBS... ALEX REALLY DID MESS HER UP.
I LOOK PRETTY ROUGH, RIGHT?
YEAH... I'D BE LYING THROUGH MY TEETH IF I SAID ANYTHING ELSE.
BUT I'M SURE YOU WERE ABLE TO IDENTIFY YOUR ATTACKERS, RIGHT?
NO...
TOO DARK.
YOU LET A GUY CAPABLE OF BEATING UP A GIRL THAT BADLY INTO YOUR BED, MAGGY.
WHAT ARE YOU GOING TO DO?
I'VE GOT A WEEK OFF.
SO I'M GOING TO RELAX.

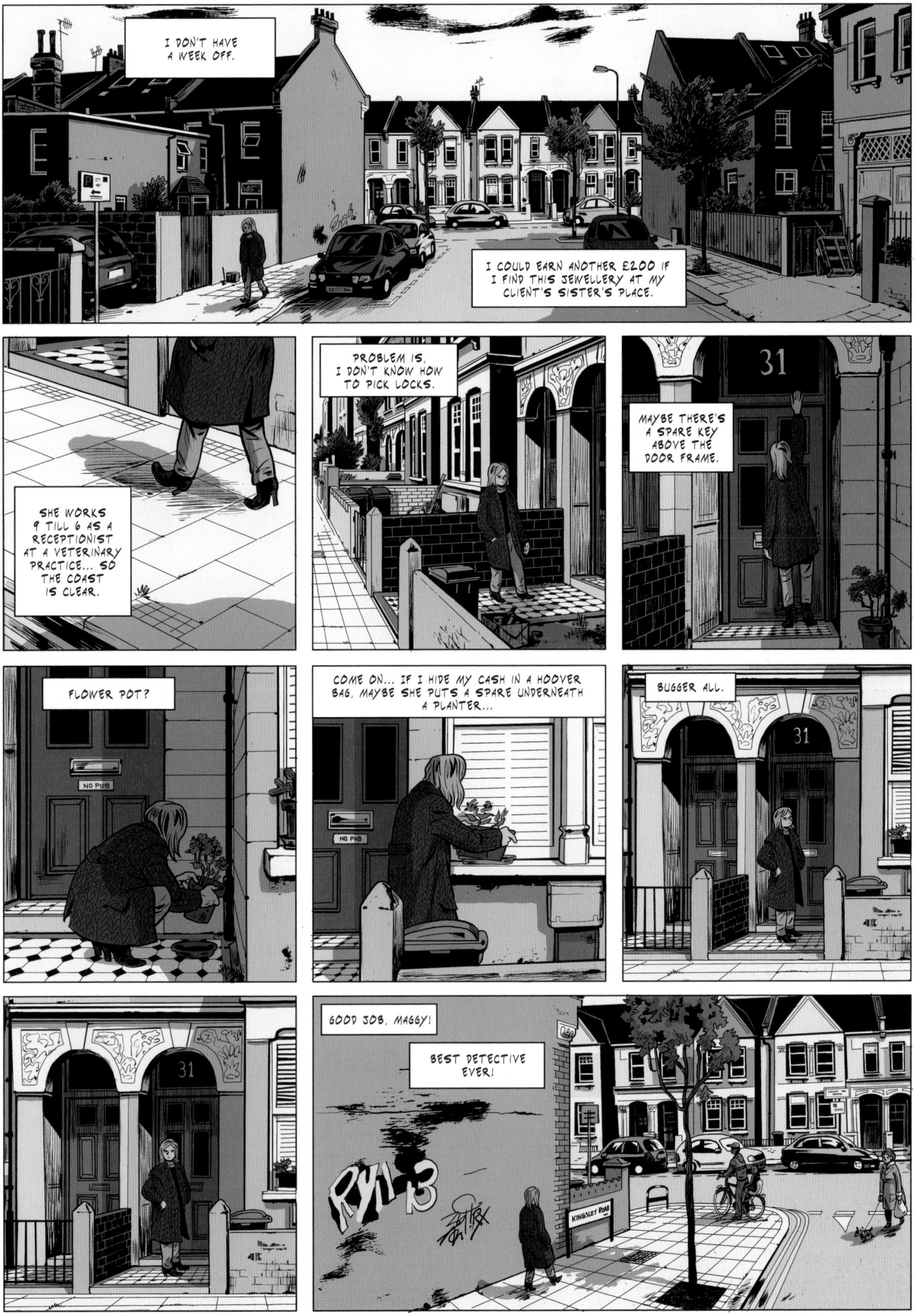
I DON'T HAVE A WEEK OFF.
I COULD EARN ANOTHER £200 IF I FIND THIS JEWELLERY AT MY CLIENT'S SISTER'S PLACE.
SHE WORKS 9 TILL 6 AS A RECEPTIONIST AT A VETERINARY PRACTICE... SO THE COAST IS CLEAR.
PROBLEM IS, I DON'T KNOW HOW TO PICK LOCKS.
31
MAYBE THERE'S A SPARE KEY ABOVE THE DOOR FRAME.
FLOWER POT?
NO PUB
COME ON... IF I HIDE MY CASH IN A HOOVER BAG, MAYBE SHE PUTS A SPARE UNDERNEATH A PLANTER...
NO PUB
BUGGER ALL.
31
31
GOOD JOB, MAGGY!
BEST DETECTIVE EVER!
KINGSLEY ROAD

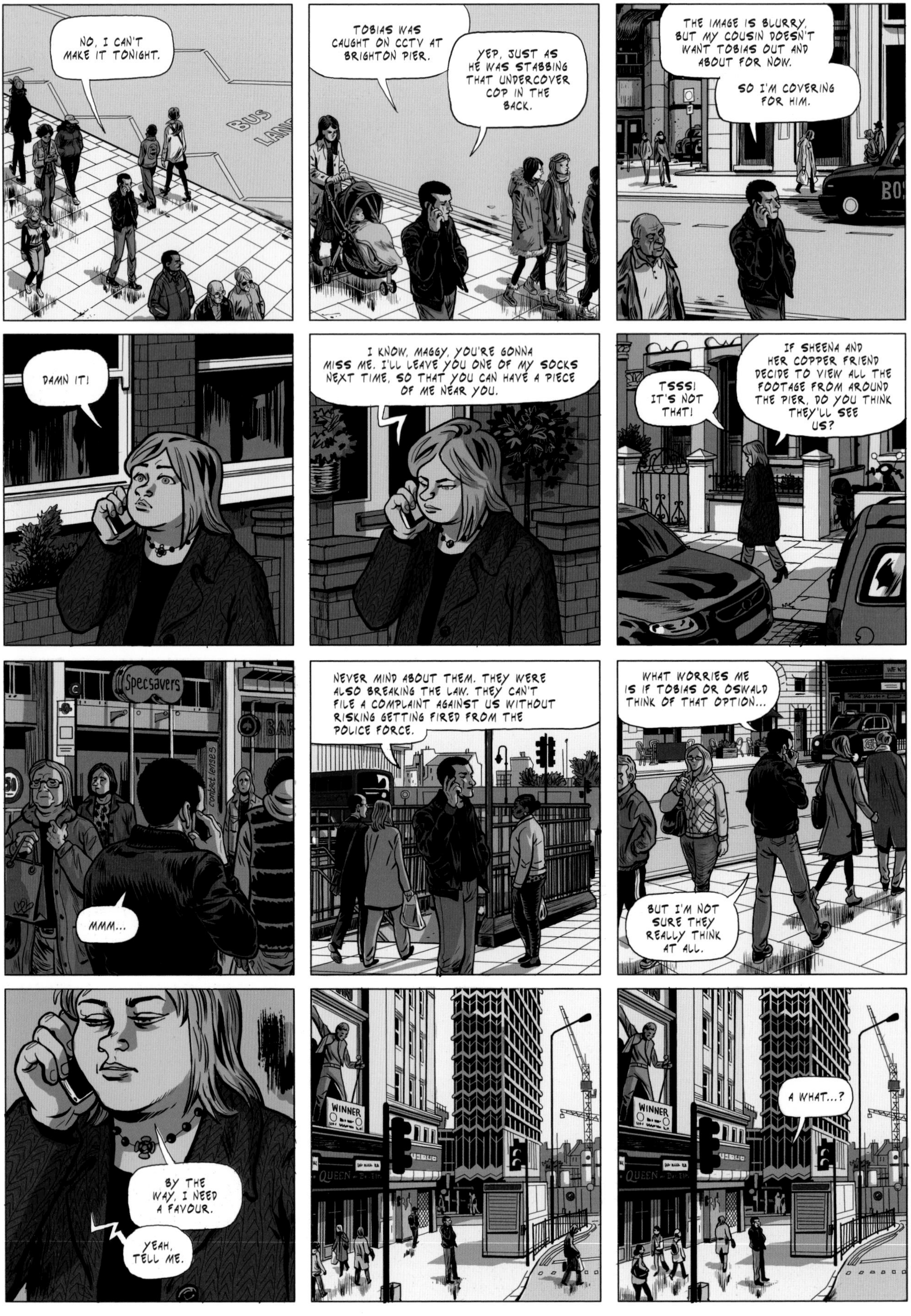
NO, I CAN'T MAKE IT TONIGHT.
BUS LANE
TOBIAS WAS CAUGHT ON CCTV AT BRIGHTON PIER.
YEP, JUST AS HE WAS STABBING THAT UNDERCOVER COP IN THE BACK.
THE IMAGE IS BLURRY, BUT MY COUSIN DOESN'T WANT TOBIAS OUT AND ABOUT FOR NOW.
SO I'M COVERING FOR HIM.
DAMN IT!
I KNOW, MAGGY, YOU'RE GONNA MISS ME. I'LL LEAVE YOU ONE OF MY SOCKS NEXT TIME, SO THAT YOU CAN HAVE A PIECE OF ME NEAR YOU.
TSSS! IT'S NOT THAT!
IF SHEENA AND HER COPPER FRIEND DECIDE TO VIEW ALL THE FOOTAGE FROM AROUND THE PIER, DO YOU THINK THEY'LL SEE US?
Specsavers
contact lenses
MMM...
NEVER MIND ABOUT THEM. THEY WERE ALSO BREAKING THE LAW. THEY CAN'T FILE A COMPLAINT AGAINST US WITHOUT RISKING GETTING FIRED FROM THE POLICE FORCE.
WHAT WORRIES ME IS IF TOBIAS OR OSWALD THINK OF THAT OPTION...
BUT I'M NOT SURE THEY REALLY THINK AT ALL.
BY THE WAY, I NEED A FAVOUR.
YEAH, TELL ME.
WINNER
QUEEN
A WHAT...?

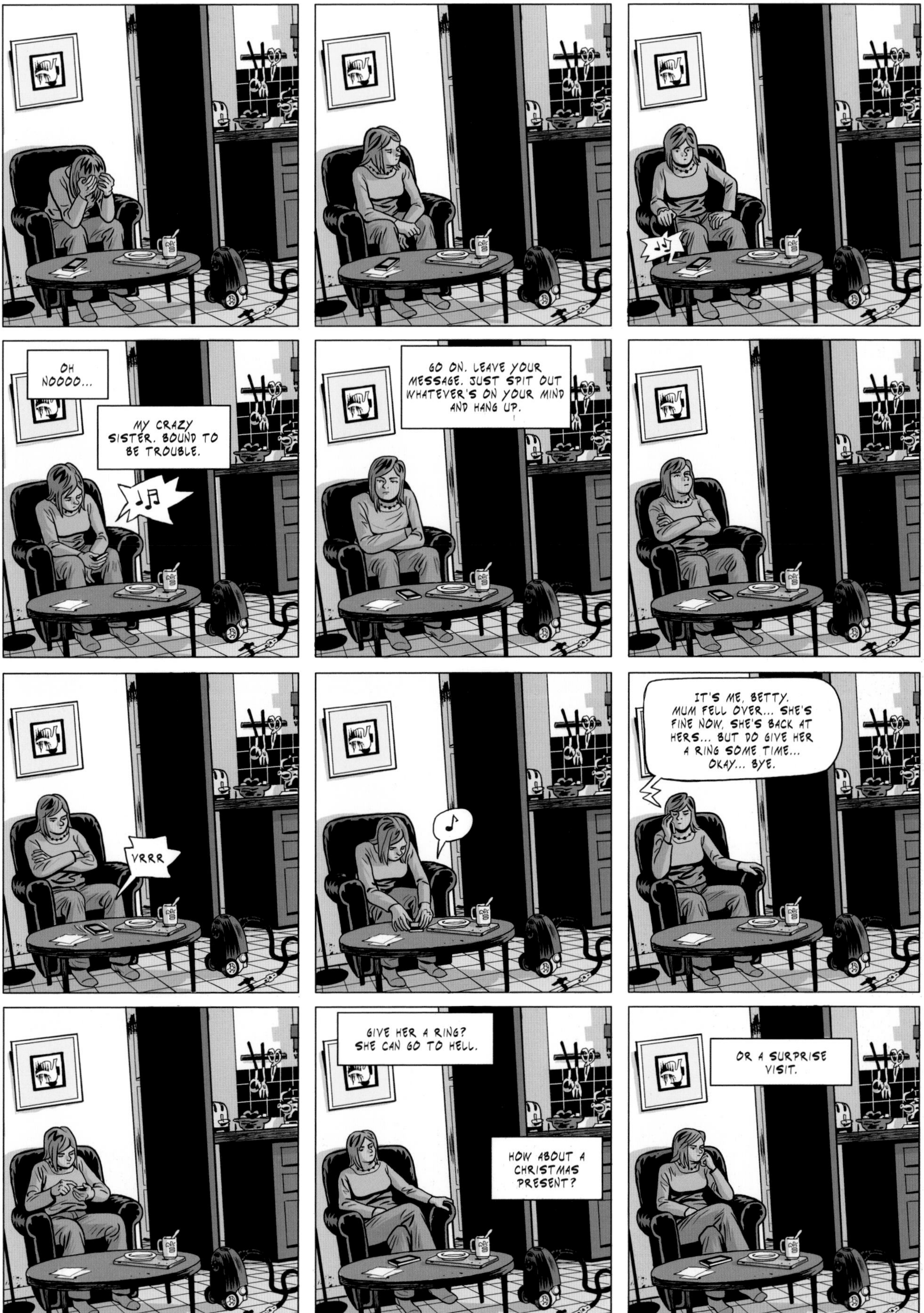
OH NOOOO...
MY CRAZY SISTER. BOUND TO BE TROUBLE.
GO ON. LEAVE YOUR MESSAGE. JUST SPIT OUT WHATEVER'S ON YOUR MIND AND HANG UP.
VRRR
IT'S ME, BETTY. MUM FELL OVER... SHE'S FINE NOW, SHE'S BACK AT HERS... BUT DO GIVE HER A RING SOME TIME... OKAY... BYE.
GIVE HER A RING? SHE CAN GO TO HELL.
HOW ABOUT A CHRISTMAS PRESENT?
OR A SURPRISE VISIT.

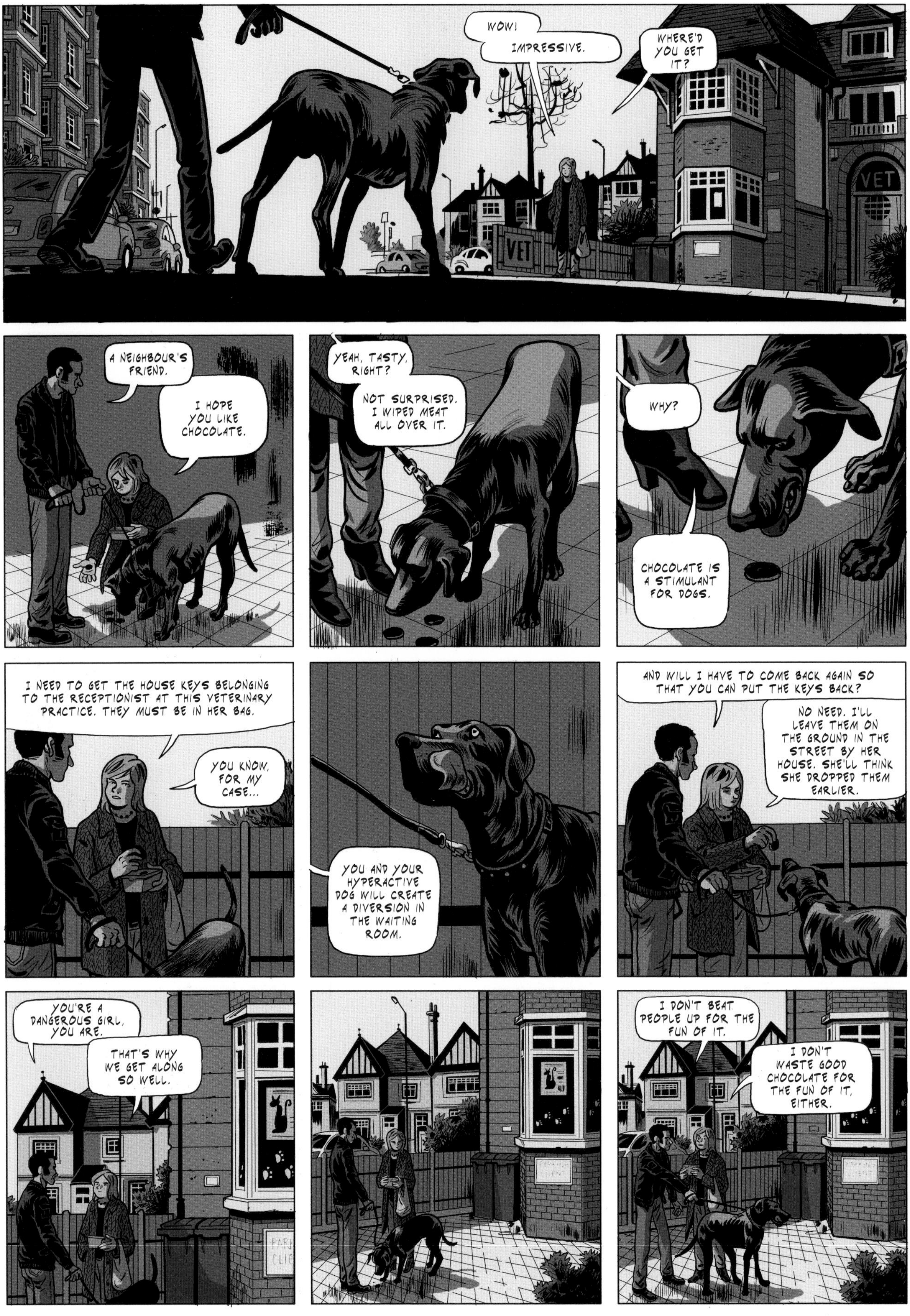

WOW!
IMPRESSIVE.
WHERE'D YOU GET IT?
VET
VET
A NEIGHBOUR'S FRIEND.
I HOPE YOU LIKE CHOCOLATE.
YEAH, TASTY, RIGHT?
NOT SURPRISED. I WIPED MEAT ALL OVER IT.
WHY?
CHOCOLATE IS A STIMULANT FOR DOGS.
I NEED TO GET THE HOUSE KEYS BELONGING TO THE RECEPTIONIST AT THIS VETERINARY PRACTICE. THEY MUST BE IN HER BAG.
YOU KNOW, FOR MY CASE...
YOU AND YOUR HYPERACTIVE DOG WILL CREATE A DIVERSION IN THE WAITING ROOM.
AND WILL I HAVE TO COME BACK AGAIN SO THAT YOU CAN PUT THE KEYS BACK?
NO NEED. I'LL LEAVE THEM ON THE GROUND IN THE STREET BY HER HOUSE. SHE'LL THINK SHE DROPPED THEM EARLIER.
YOU'RE A DANGEROUS GIRL, YOU ARE.
THAT'S WHY WE GET ALONG SO WELL.
I DON'T BEAT PEOPLE UP FOR THE FUN OF IT.
I DON'T WASTE GOOD CHOCOLATE FOR THE FUN OF IT, EITHER.

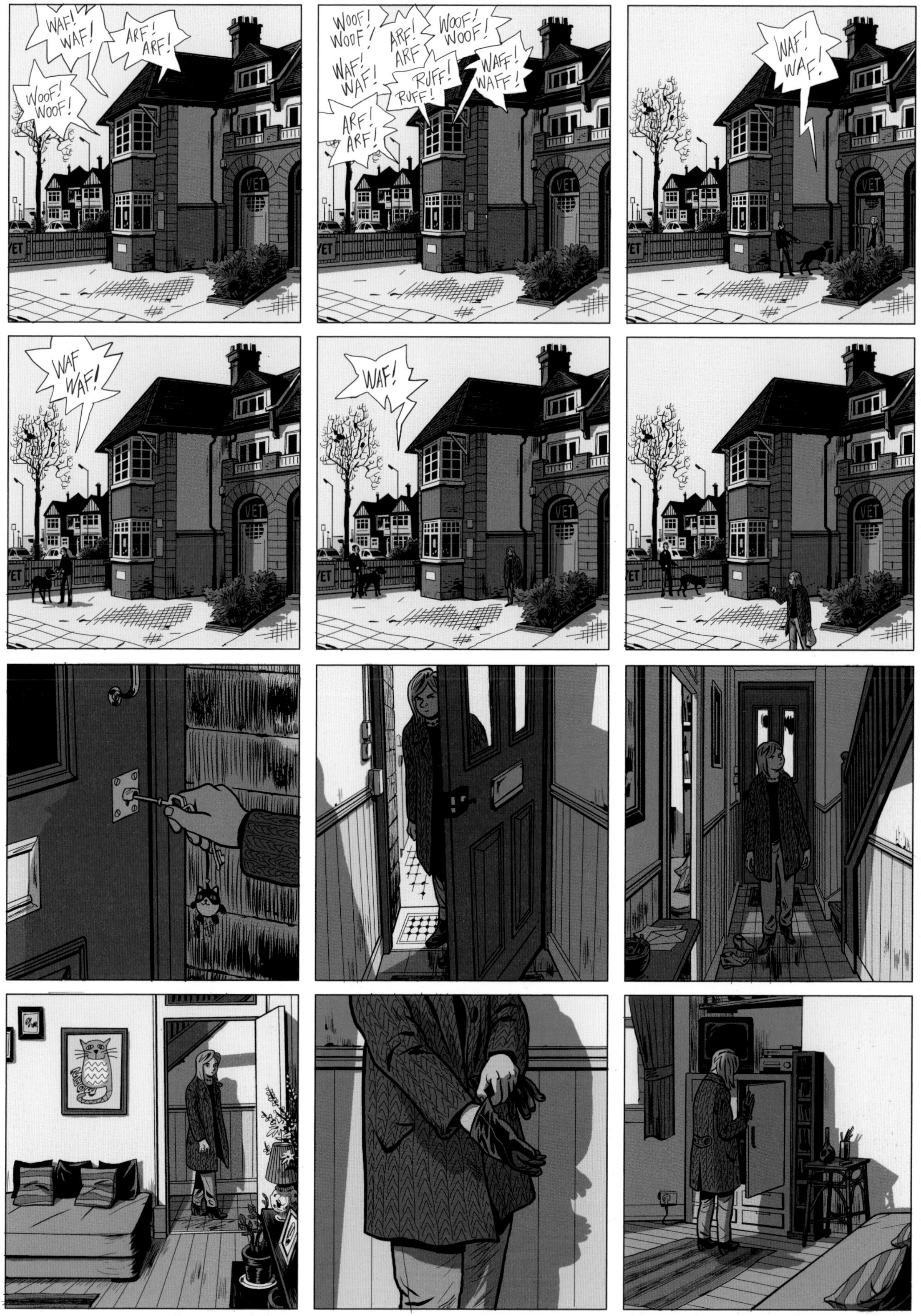

WAF! WAF!
ARF! ARF!
WOOF! WOOF!
WOOF! WOOF!
WAF! WAF!
ARF! ARF!
WOOF! WOOF!
RUFF! RUFF!
WAFF! WAFF!
ARF! ARF!
WAF! WAF!
WAF WAF!
WAF!

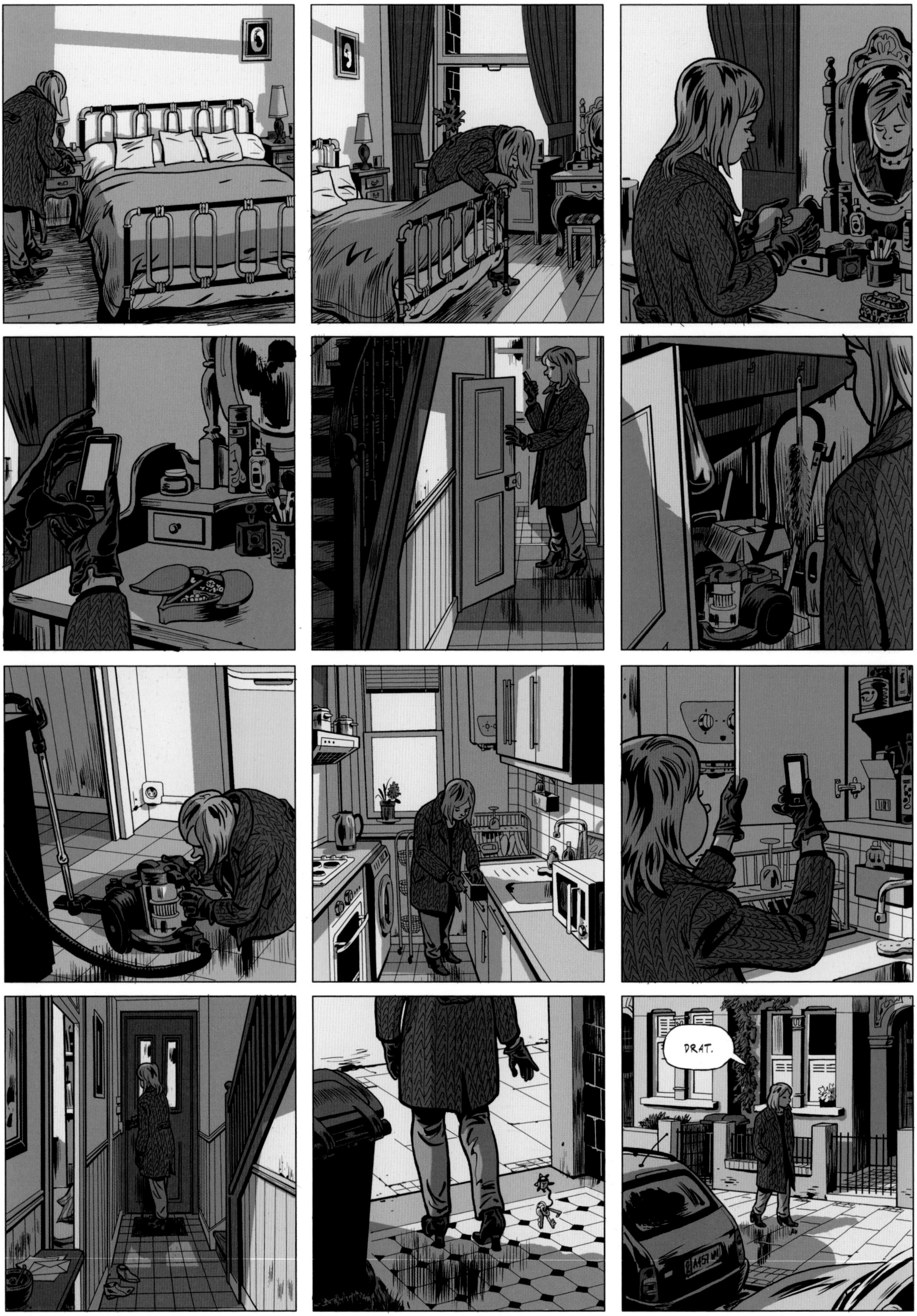
DRAT.

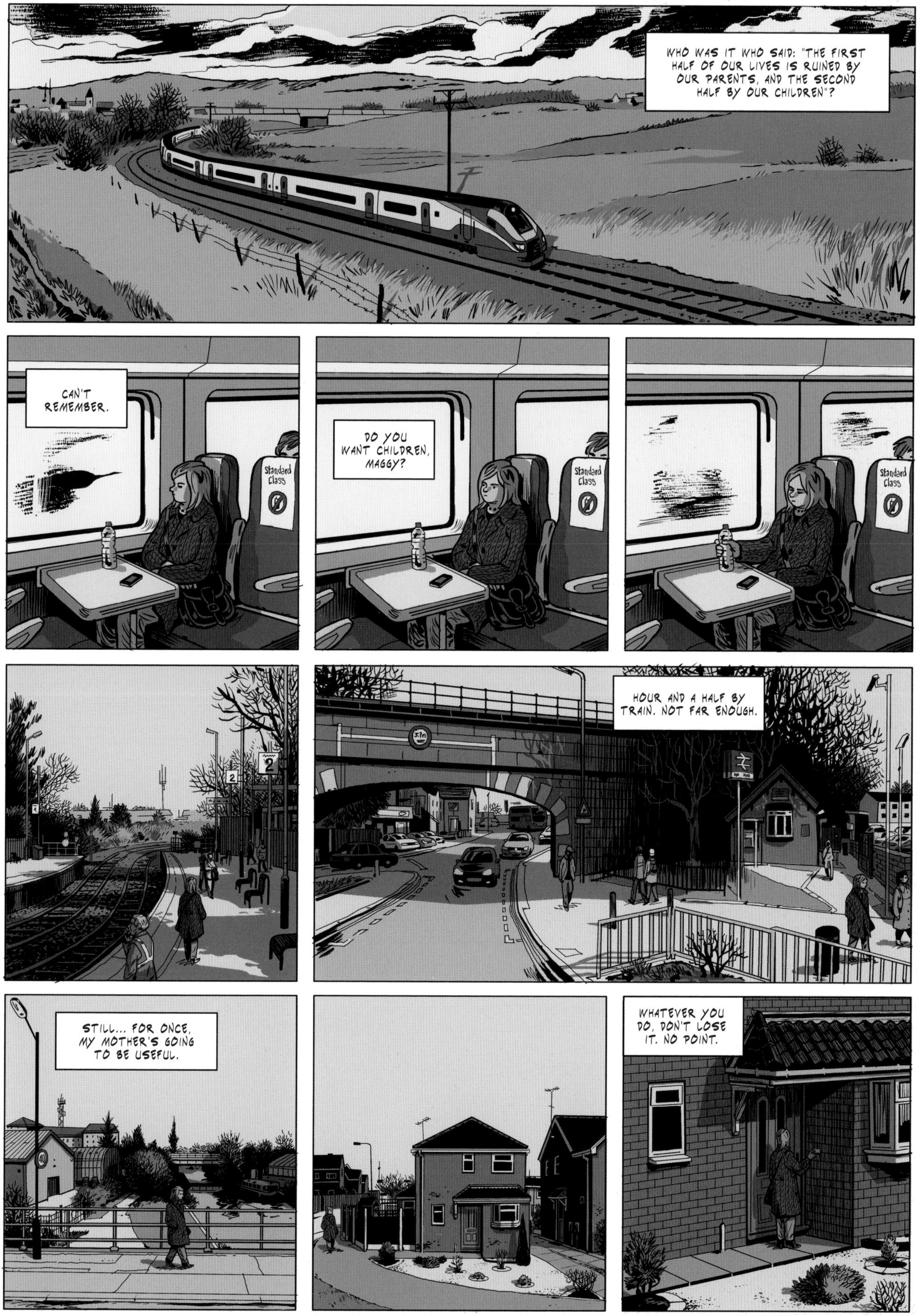
WHO WAS IT WHO SAID: "THE FIRST HALF OF OUR LIVES IS RUINED BY OUR PARENTS, AND THE SECOND HALF BY OUR CHILDREN"?
CAN'T REMEMBER.
Standard Class
DO YOU WANT CHILDREN, MAGGY?
Standard Class
Standard Class
2
2
HOUR AND A HALF BY TRAIN. NOT FAR ENOUGH.
STILL... FOR ONCE, MY MOTHER'S GOING TO BE USEFUL.
40
WHATEVER YOU DO, DON'T LOSE IT. NO POINT.

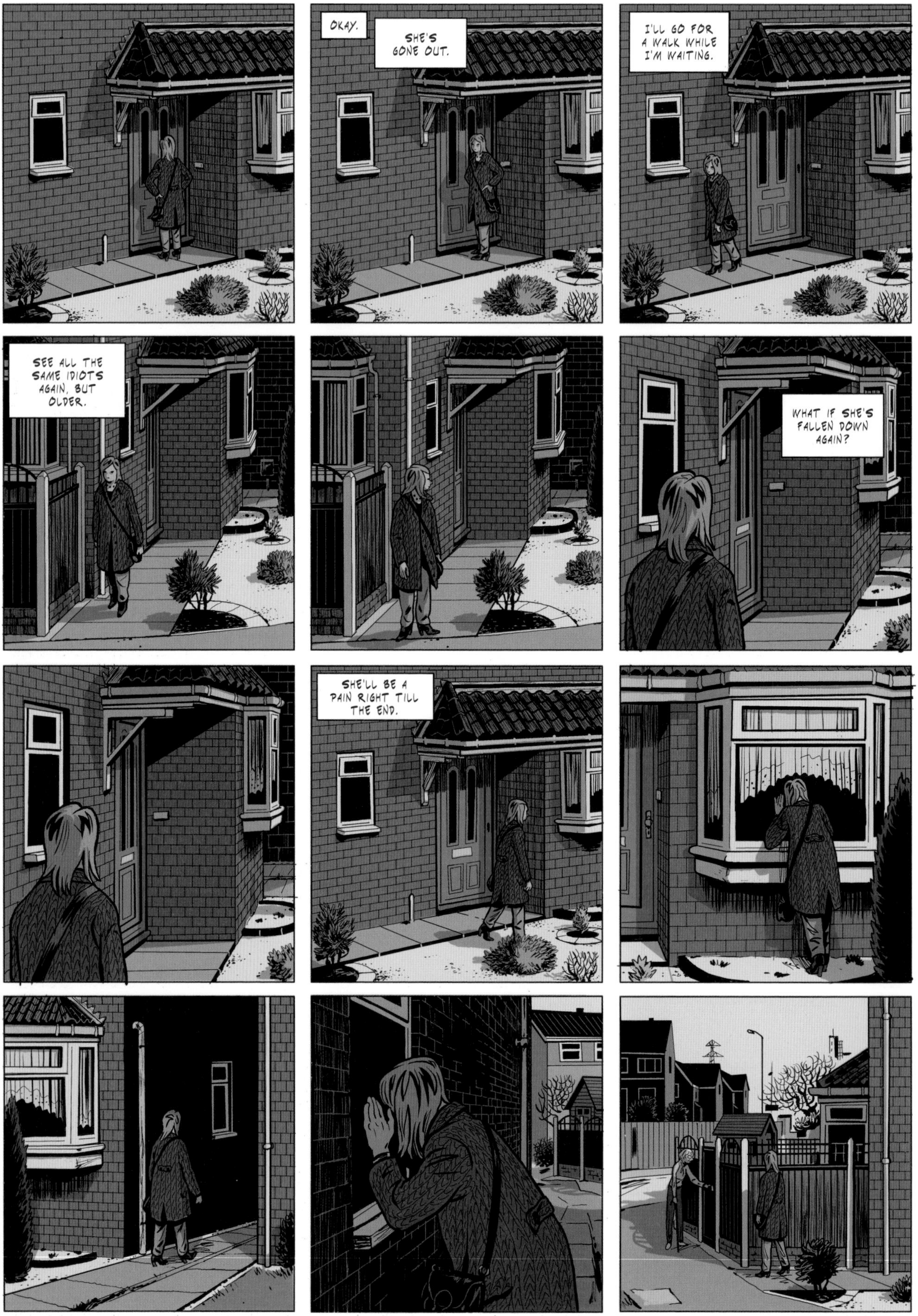
OKAY.
SHE'S GONE OUT.
I'LL GO FOR A WALK WHILE I'M WAITING.
SEE ALL THE SAME IDIOTS AGAIN, BUT OLDER.
WHAT IF SHE'S FALLEN DOWN AGAIN?
SHE'LL BE A PAIN RIGHT TILL THE END.

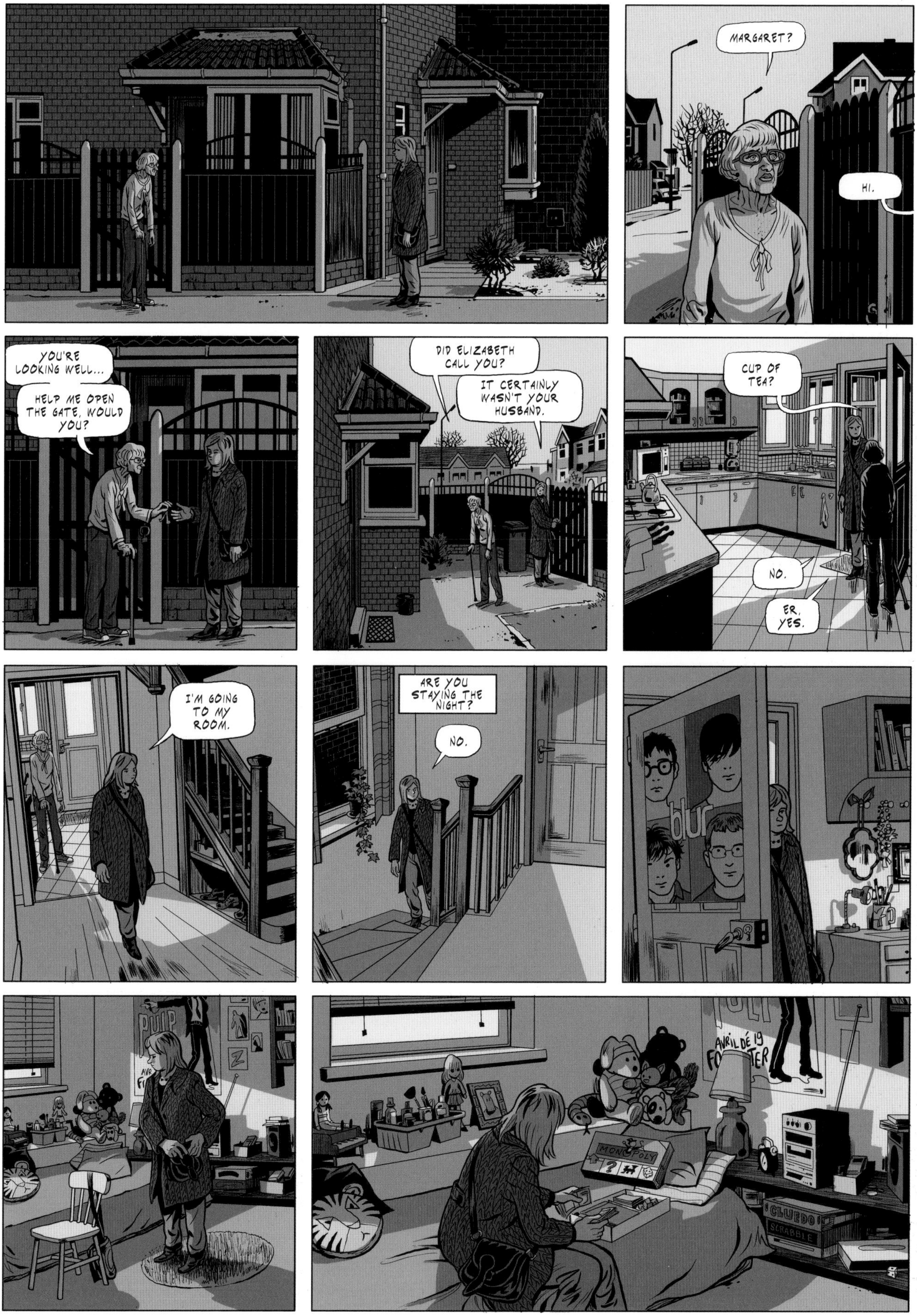
MARGARET?
HI.
YOU'RE LOOKING WELL...
HELP ME OPEN THE GATE, WOULD YOU?
DID ELIZABETH CALL YOU?
IT CERTAINLY WASN'T YOUR HUSBAND.
CUP OF TEA?
NO.
ER, YES.
I'M GOING TO MY ROOM.
ARE YOU STAYING THE NIGHT?
NO.
blur
PULP
MONOPOLY
CLUEDO
SCRABBLE

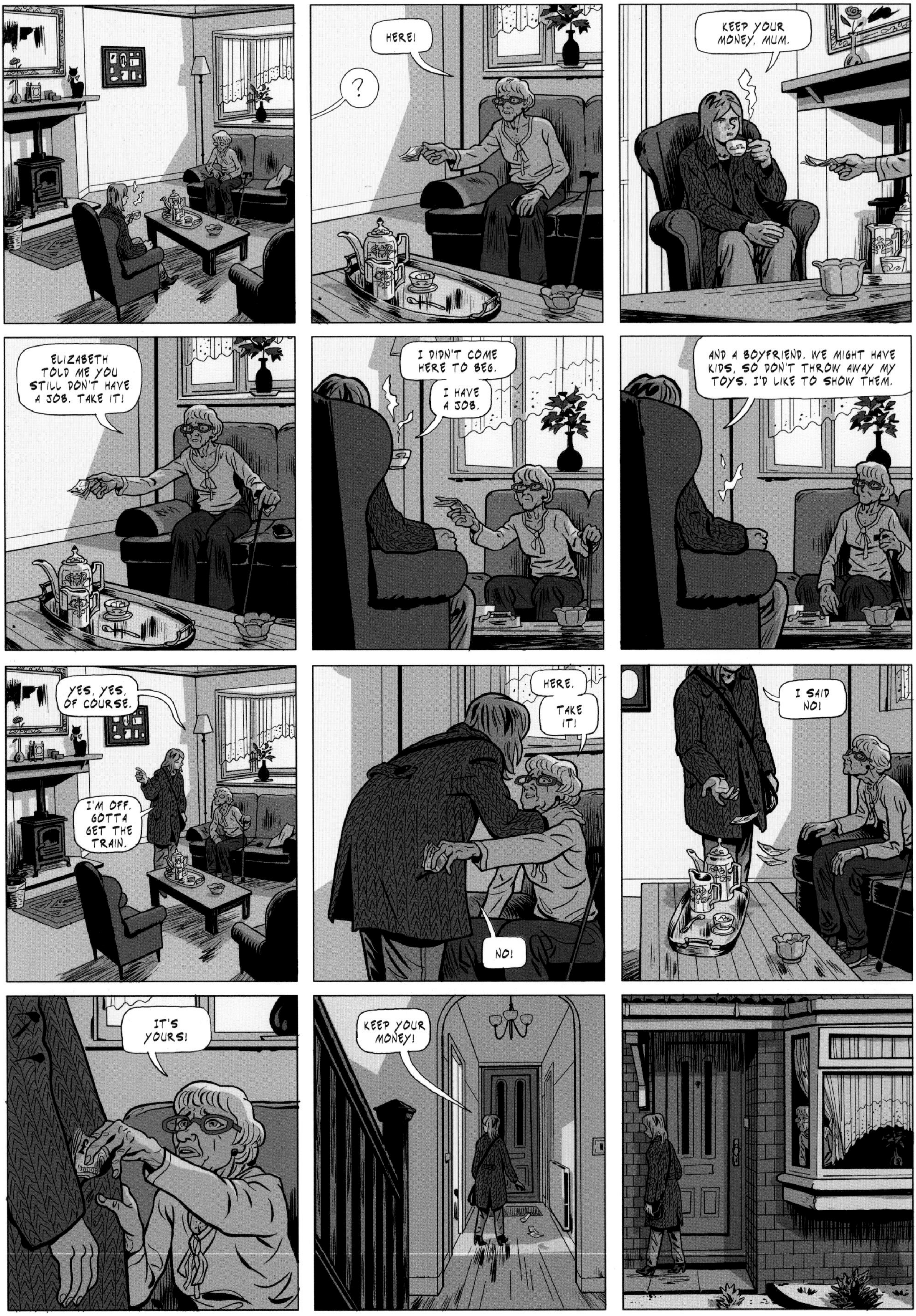
HERE!
?
KEEP YOUR MONEY, MUM.
ELIZABETH TOLD ME YOU STILL DON'T HAVE A JOB. TAKE IT!
I DIDN'T COME HERE TO BEG.
I HAVE A JOB.
AND A BOYFRIEND. WE MIGHT HAVE KIDS, SO DON'T THROW AWAY MY TOYS. I'D LIKE TO SHOW THEM.
YES, YES, OF COURSE.
I'M OFF. GOTTA GET THE TRAIN.
HERE.
TAKE IT!
NO!
I SAID NO!
IT'S YOURS!
KEEP YOUR MONEY!

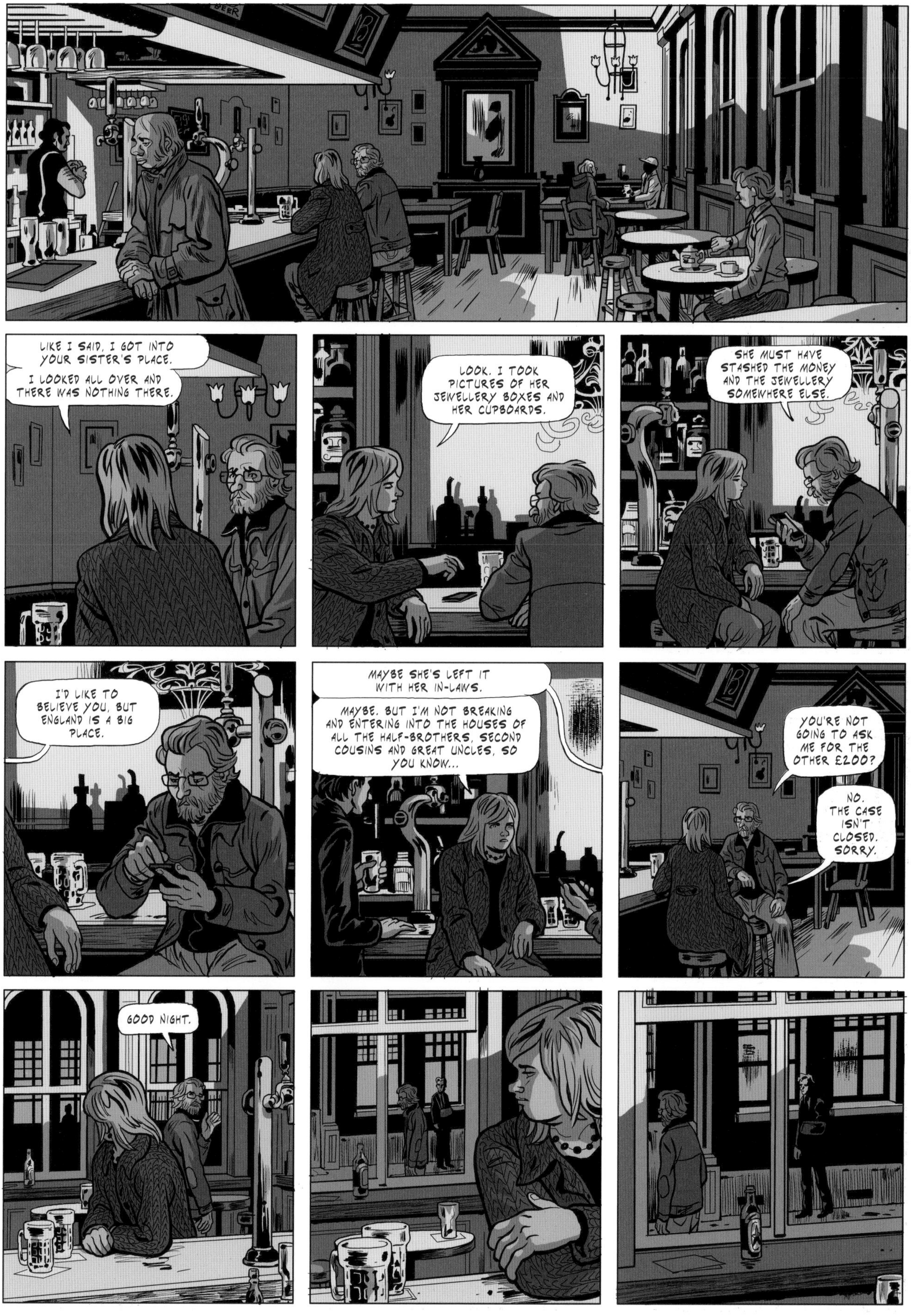
BEER
LIKE I SAID, I GOT INTO YOUR SISTER'S PLACE.
I LOOKED ALL OVER AND THERE WAS NOTHING THERE.
LOOK. I TOOK PICTURES OF HER JEWELLERY BOXES AND HER CUPBOARDS.
SHE MUST HAVE STASHED THE MONEY AND THE JEWELLERY SOMEWHERE ELSE.
I'D LIKE TO BELIEVE YOU, BUT ENGLAND IS A BIG PLACE.
MAYBE SHE'S LEFT IT WITH HER IN-LAWS.
MAYBE. BUT I'M NOT BREAKING AND ENTERING INTO THE HOUSES OF ALL THE HALF-BROTHERS, SECOND COUSINS AND GREAT UNCLES, SO YOU KNOW...
YOU'RE NOT GOING TO ASK ME FOR THE OTHER £200?
NO. THE CASE ISN'T CLOSED. SORRY.
GOOD NIGHT.

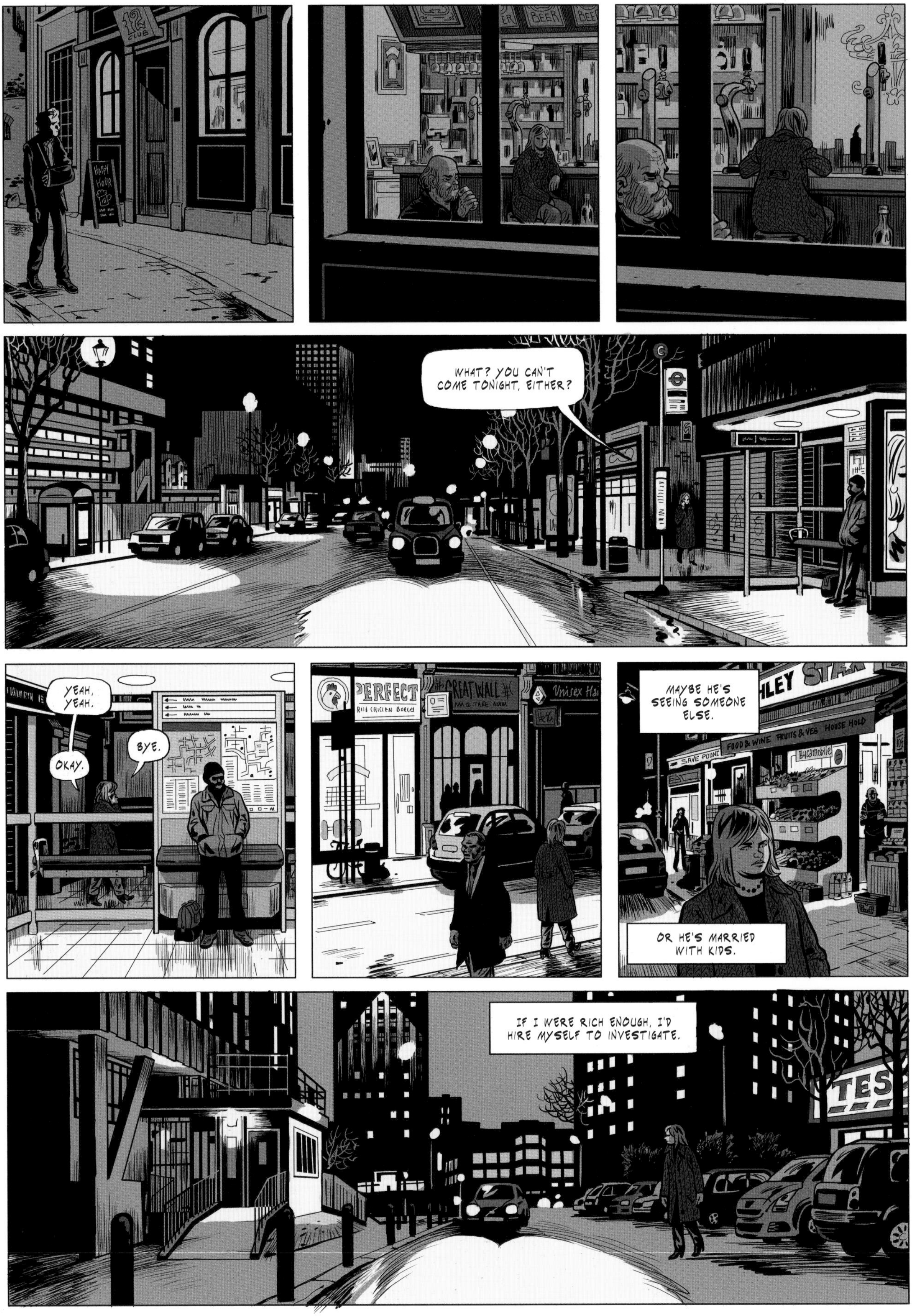

HAPPY HOUR
BEER
WHAT? YOU CAN'T COME TONIGHT, EITHER?
YEAH, YEAH.
OKAY.
BYE.
PERFECT
GREAT WALL
MAYBE HE'S SEEING SOMEONE ELSE.
FOOD & WINE FRUITS & VEG HOUSE HOLD
OR HE'S MARRIED WITH KIDS.
IF I WERE RICH ENOUGH, I'D HIRE MYSELF TO INVESTIGATE.

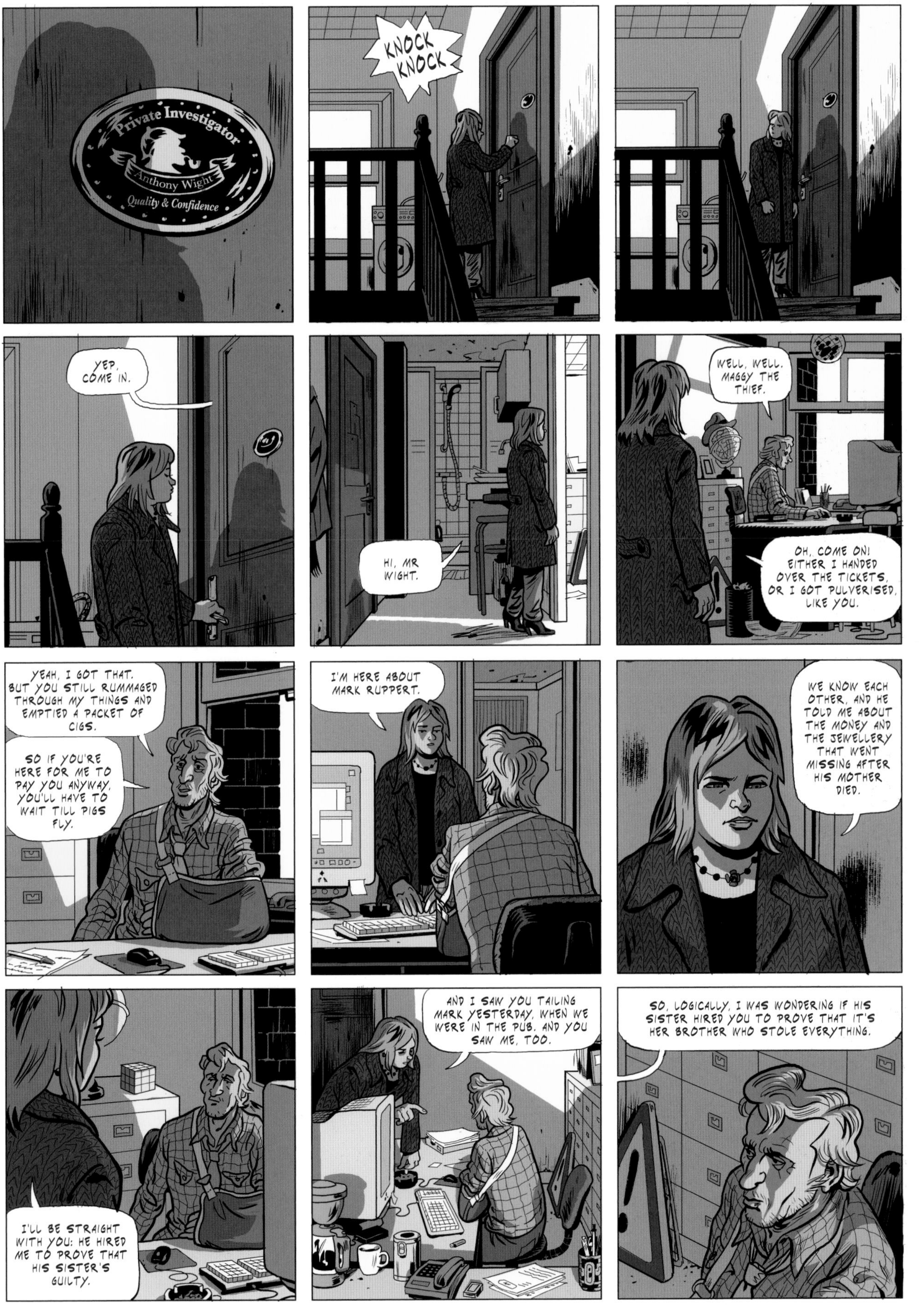
Private Investigator
Anthony Wight
Quality & Confidence
KNOCK KNOCK
YEP. COME IN.
HI, MR WIGHT.
WELL, WELL. MAGGY THE THIEF.
OH, COME ON! EITHER I HANDED OVER THE TICKETS, OR I GOT PULVERISED, LIKE YOU.
YEAH, I GOT THAT. BUT YOU STILL RUMMAGED THROUGH MY THINGS AND EMPTIED A PACKET OF CIGS.
SO IF YOU'RE HERE FOR ME TO PAY YOU ANYWAY, YOU'LL HAVE TO WAIT TILL PIGS FLY.
I'M HERE ABOUT MARK RUPPERT.
WE KNOW EACH OTHER, AND HE TOLD ME ABOUT THE MONEY AND THE JEWELLERY THAT WENT MISSING AFTER HIS MOTHER DIED.
I'LL BE STRAIGHT WITH YOU: HE HIRED ME TO PROVE THAT HIS SISTER'S GUILTY.
AND I SAW YOU TAILING MARK YESTERDAY, WHEN WE WERE IN THE PUB. AND YOU SAW ME, TOO.
SO, LOGICALLY, I WAS WONDERING IF HIS SISTER HIRED YOU TO PROVE THAT IT'S HER BROTHER WHO STOLE EVERYTHING.

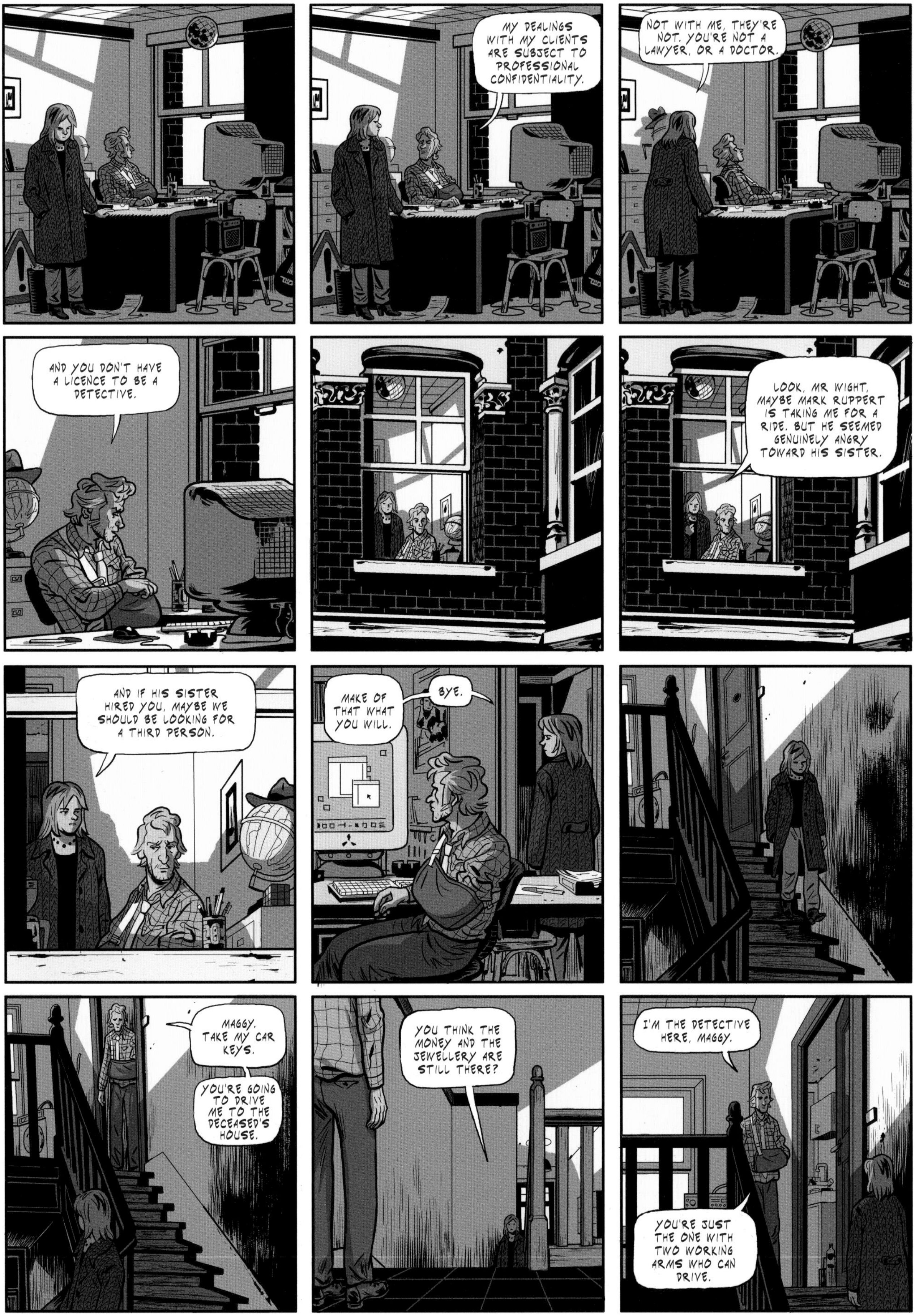

MY DEALINGS WITH MY CLIENTS ARE SUBJECT TO PROFESSIONAL CONFIDENTIALITY.
NOT WITH ME, THEY'RE NOT. YOU'RE NOT A LAWYER, OR A DOCTOR.
AND YOU DON'T HAVE A LICENCE TO BE A DETECTIVE.
LOOK, MR WIGHT, MAYBE MARK RUPPERT IS TAKING ME FOR A RIDE. BUT HE SEEMED GENUINELY ANGRY TOWARD HIS SISTER.
AND IF HIS SISTER HIRED YOU, MAYBE WE SHOULD BE LOOKING FOR A THIRD PERSON.
MAKE OF THAT WHAT YOU WILL.
BYE.
MAGGY. TAKE MY CAR KEYS.
YOU'RE GOING TO DRIVE ME TO THE DECEASED'S HOUSE.
YOU THINK THE MONEY AND THE JEWELLERY ARE STILL THERE?
I'M THE DETECTIVE HERE, MAGGY.
YOU'RE JUST THE ONE WITH TWO WORKING ARMS WHO CAN DRIVE.

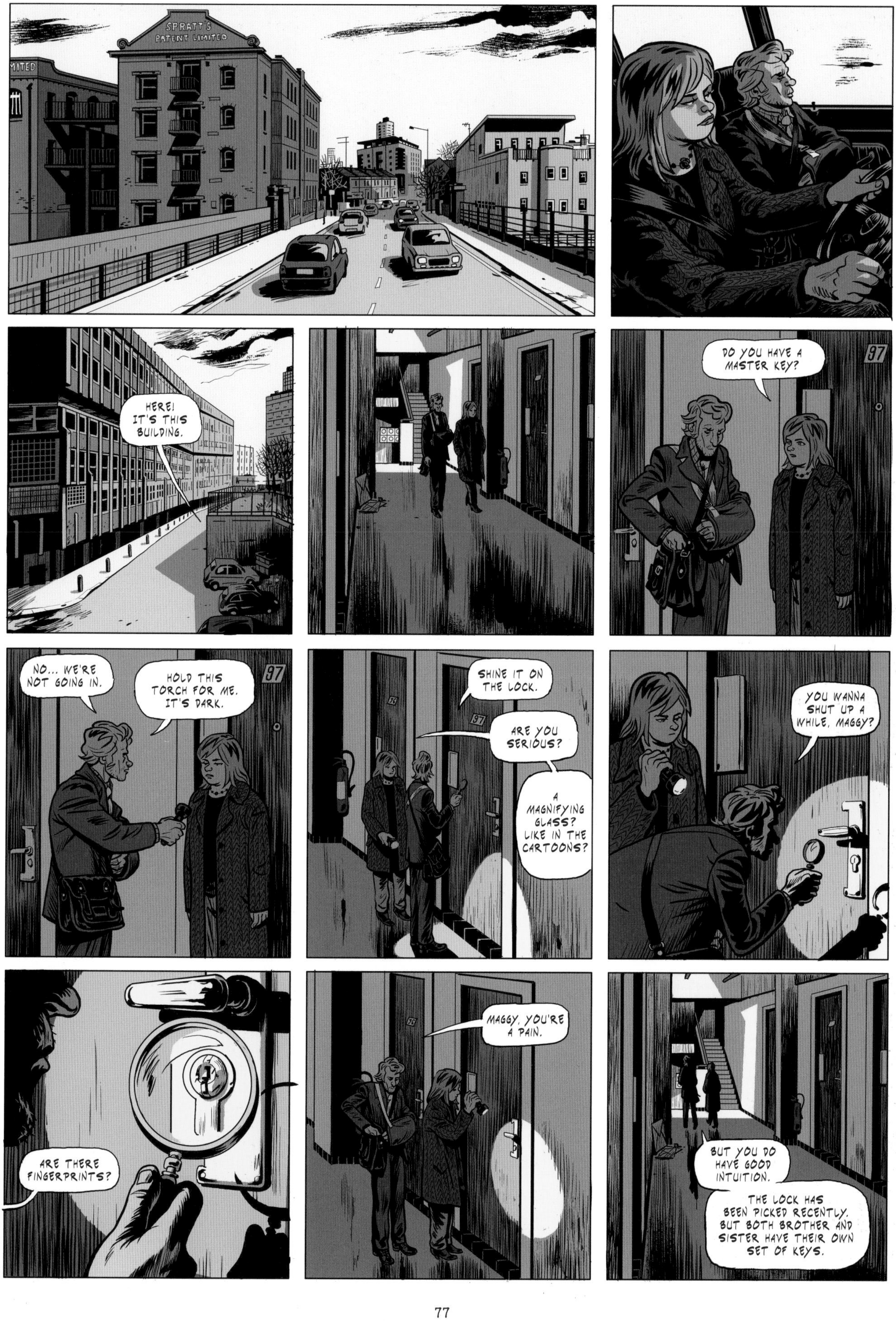
SPRATT'S PATENT LIMITED
MITED
HERE! IT'S THIS BUILDING.
DO YOU HAVE A MASTER KEY?
97
NO... WE'RE NOT GOING IN.
HOLD THIS TORCH FOR ME. IT'S DARK.
SHINE IT ON THE LOCK.
ARE YOU SERIOUS?
A MAGNIFYING GLASS? LIKE IN THE CARTOONS?
YOU WANNA SHUT UP A WHILE, MAGGY?
ARE THERE FINGERPRINTS?
MAGGY, YOU'RE A PAIN.
BUT YOU DO HAVE GOOD INTUITION.
THE LOCK HAS BEEN PICKED RECENTLY. BUT BOTH BROTHER AND SISTER HAVE THEIR OWN SET OF KEYS.

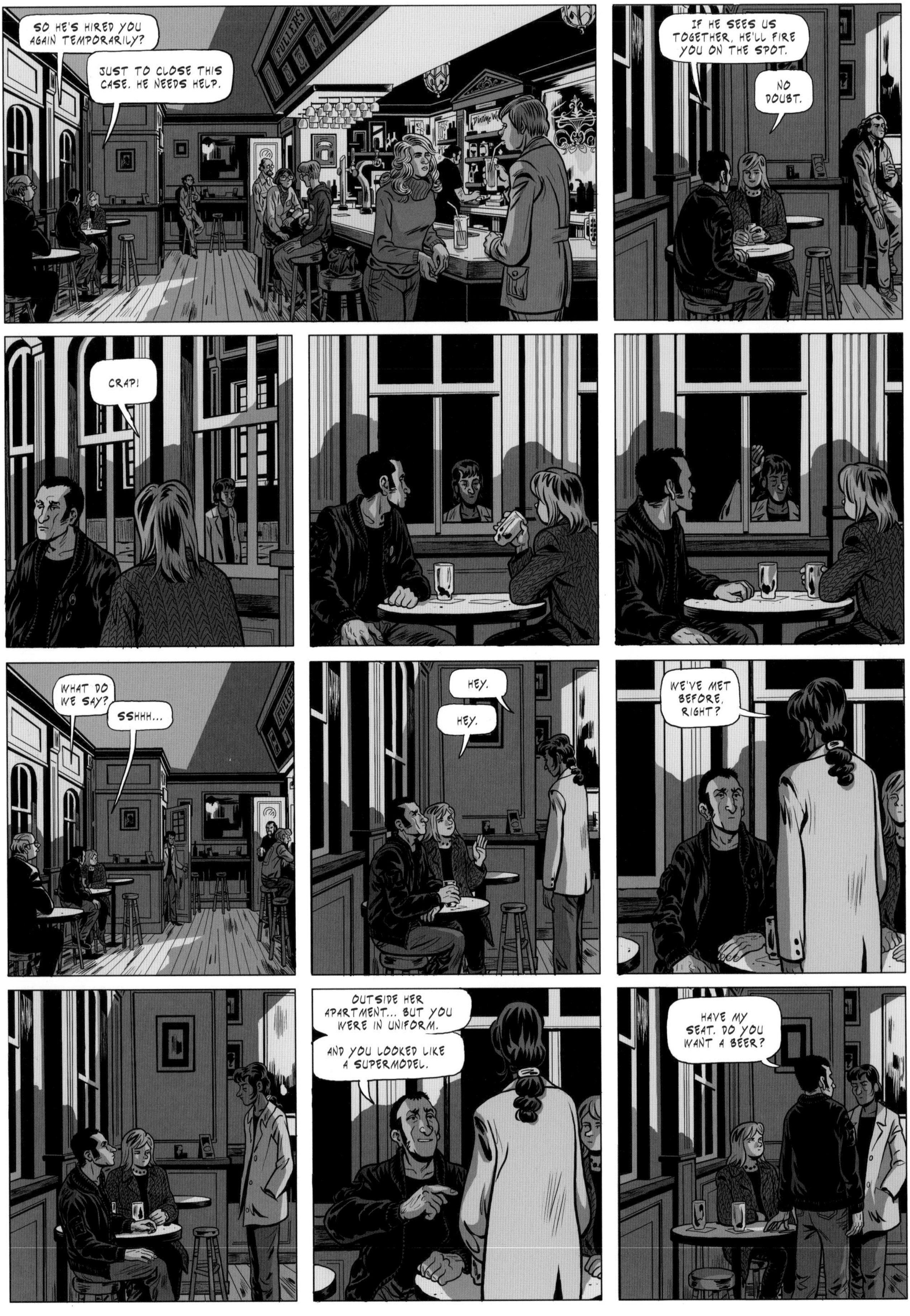
SO HE'S HIRED YOU AGAIN TEMPORARILY?
JUST TO CLOSE THIS CASE. HE NEEDS HELP.
IF HE SEES US TOGETHER, HE'LL FIRE YOU ON THE SPOT.
NO DOUBT.
CRAP!
WHAT DO WE SAY?
SSHHH...
HEY.
HEY.
WE'VE MET BEFORE, RIGHT?
OUTSIDE HER APARTMENT... BUT YOU WERE IN UNIFORM.
AND YOU LOOKED LIKE A SUPERMODEL.
HAVE MY SEAT. DO YOU WANT A BEER?

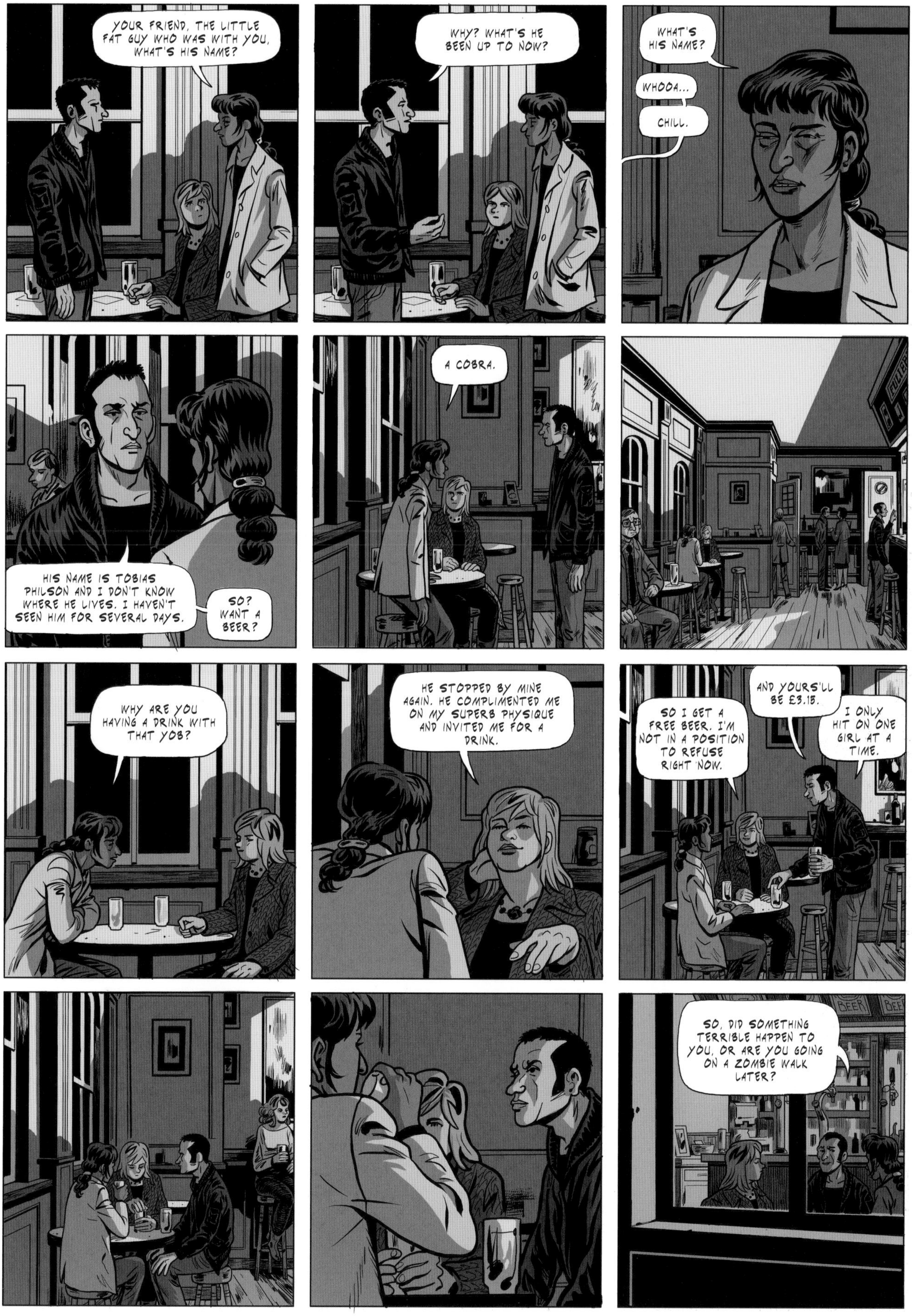
YOUR FRIEND, THE LITTLE FAT GUY WHO WAS WITH YOU, WHAT'S HIS NAME?
WHY? WHAT'S HE BEEN UP TO NOW?
WHAT'S HIS NAME?
WHOOA...
CHILL.
HIS NAME IS TOBIAS PHILSON AND I DON'T KNOW WHERE HE LIVES. I HAVEN'T SEEN HIM FOR SEVERAL DAYS.
SO? WANT A BEER?
A COBRA.
WHY ARE YOU HAVING A DRINK WITH THAT YOB?
HE STOPPED BY MINE AGAIN. HE COMPLIMENTED ME ON MY SUPERB PHYSIQUE AND INVITED ME FOR A DRINK.
SO I GET A FREE BEER. I'M NOT IN A POSITION TO REFUSE RIGHT NOW.
AND YOURS'LL BE £3.15.
I ONLY HIT ON ONE GIRL AT A TIME.
SO, DID SOMETHING TERRIBLE HAPPEN TO YOU, OR ARE YOU GOING ON A ZOMBIE WALK LATER?
BEER
BEER

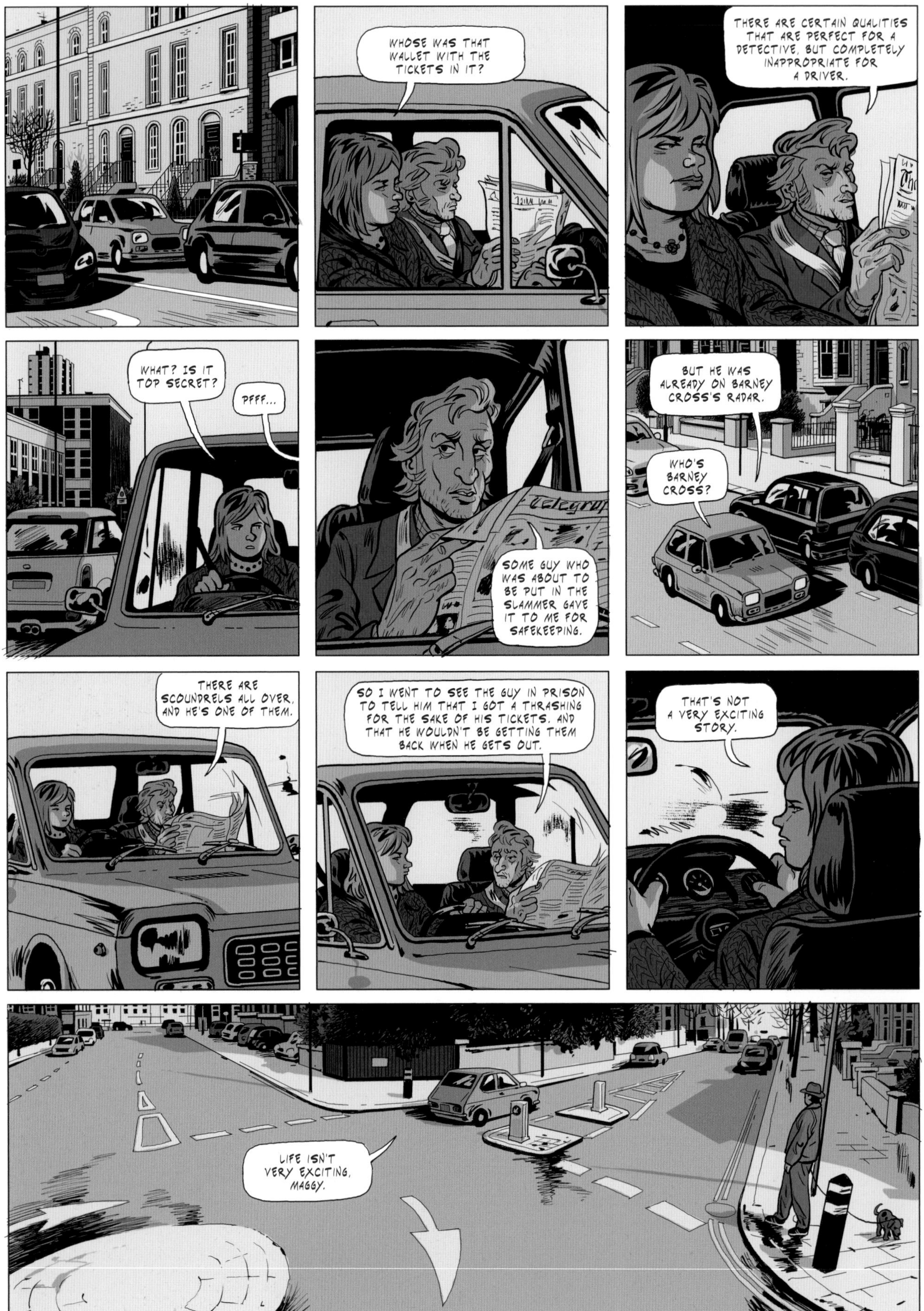
WHOSE WAS THAT WALLET WITH THE TICKETS IN IT?
THERE ARE CERTAIN QUALITIES THAT ARE PERFECT FOR A DETECTIVE, BUT COMPLETELY INAPPROPRIATE FOR A DRIVER.
WHAT? IS IT TOP SECRET?
PFFF...
SOME GUY WHO WAS ABOUT TO BE PUT IN THE SLAMMER GAVE IT TO ME FOR SAFEKEEPING.
BUT HE WAS ALREADY ON BARNEY CROSS'S RADAR.
WHO'S BARNEY CROSS?
THERE ARE SCOUNDRELS ALL OVER, AND HE'S ONE OF THEM.
SO I WENT TO SEE THE GUY IN PRISON TO TELL HIM THAT I GOT A THRASHING FOR THE SAKE OF HIS TICKETS. AND THAT HE WOULDN'T BE GETTING THEM BACK WHEN HE GETS OUT.
THAT'S NOT A VERY EXCITING STORY.
LIFE ISN'T VERY EXCITING, MAGGY.

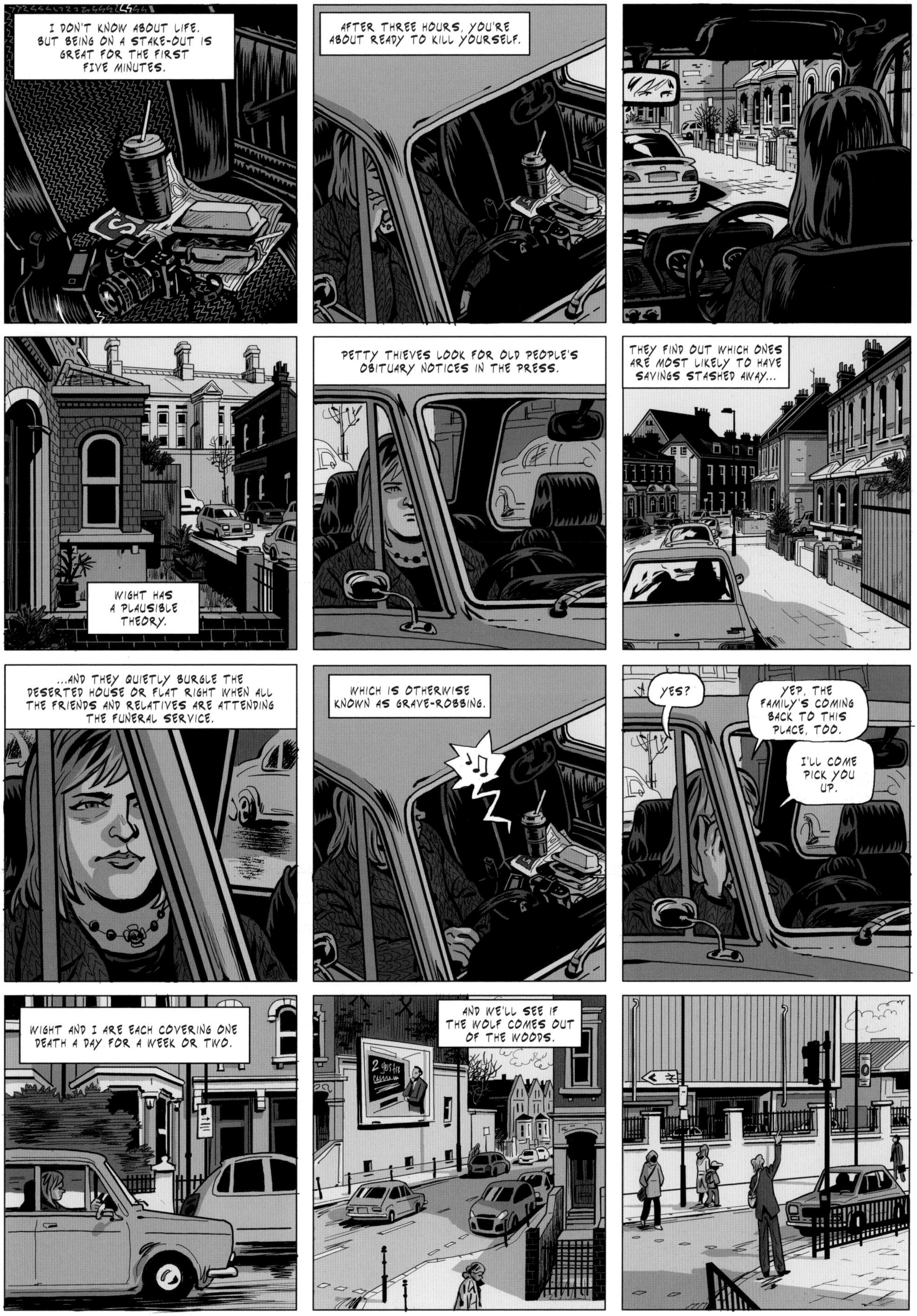
I DON'T KNOW ABOUT LIFE. BUT BEING ON A STAKE-OUT IS GREAT FOR THE FIRST FIVE MINUTES.
AFTER THREE HOURS, YOU'RE ABOUT READY TO KILL YOURSELF.
WIGHT HAS A PLAUSIBLE THEORY.
PETTY THIEVES LOOK FOR OLD PEOPLE'S OBITUARY NOTICES IN THE PRESS.
THEY FIND OUT WHICH ONES ARE MOST LIKELY TO HAVE SAVINGS STASHED AWAY...
...AND THEY QUIETLY BURGLE THE DESERTED HOUSE OR FLAT RIGHT WHEN ALL THE FRIENDS AND RELATIVES ARE ATTENDING THE FUNERAL SERVICE.
WHICH IS OTHERWISE KNOWN AS GRAVE-ROBBING.
YES?
YEP, THE FAMILY'S COMING BACK TO THIS PLACE, TOO.
I'LL COME PICK YOU UP.
WIGHT AND I ARE EACH COVERING ONE DEATH A DAY FOR A WEEK OR TWO.
AND WE'LL SEE IF THE WOLF COMES OUT OF THE WOODS.

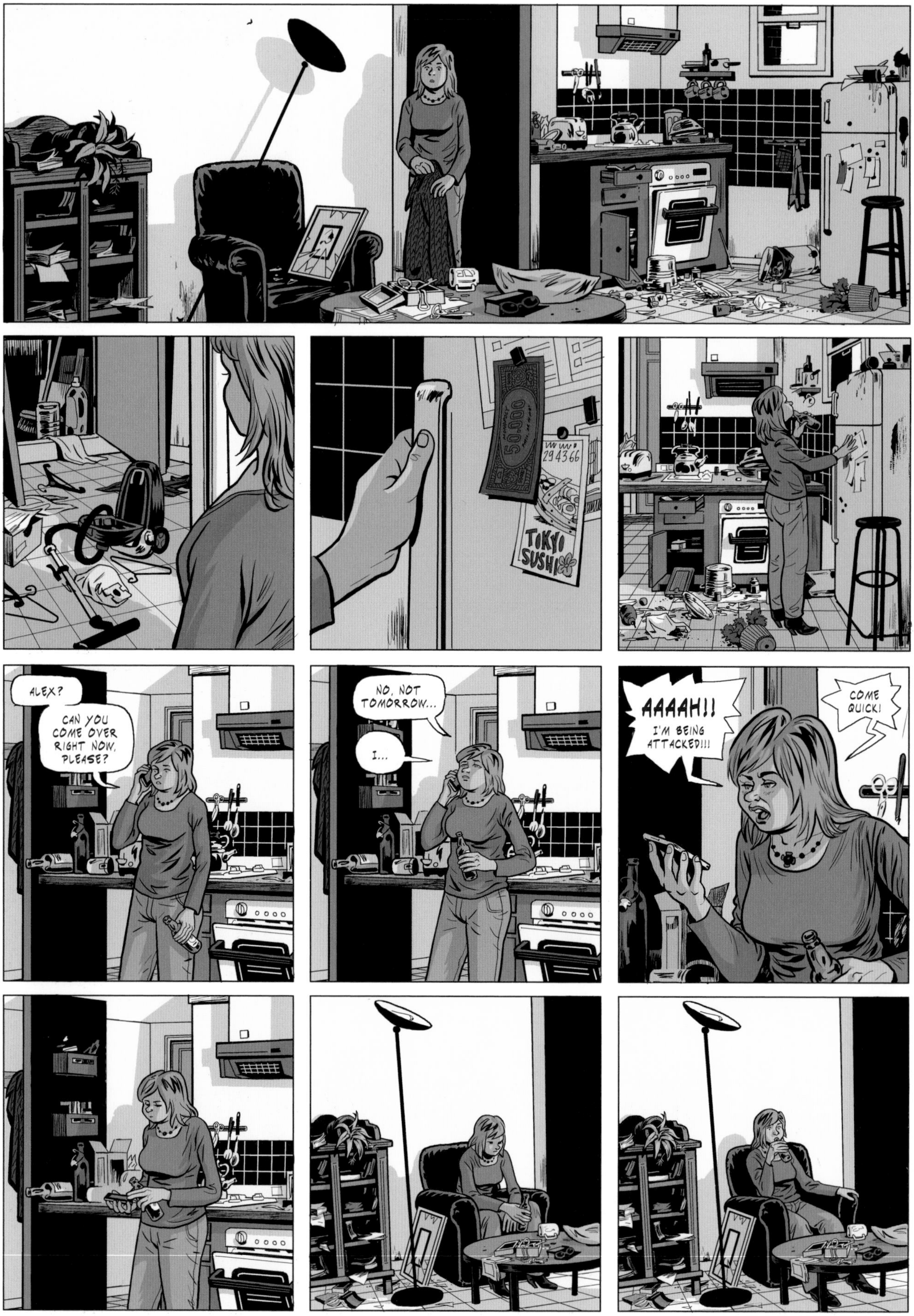
50.000
294366
TOKYO SUSHI
ALEX?
CAN YOU COME OVER RIGHT NOW, PLEASE?
NO, NOT TOMORROW...
I...
AAAAH!!
I'M BEING ATTACKED!!!
COME QUICK!

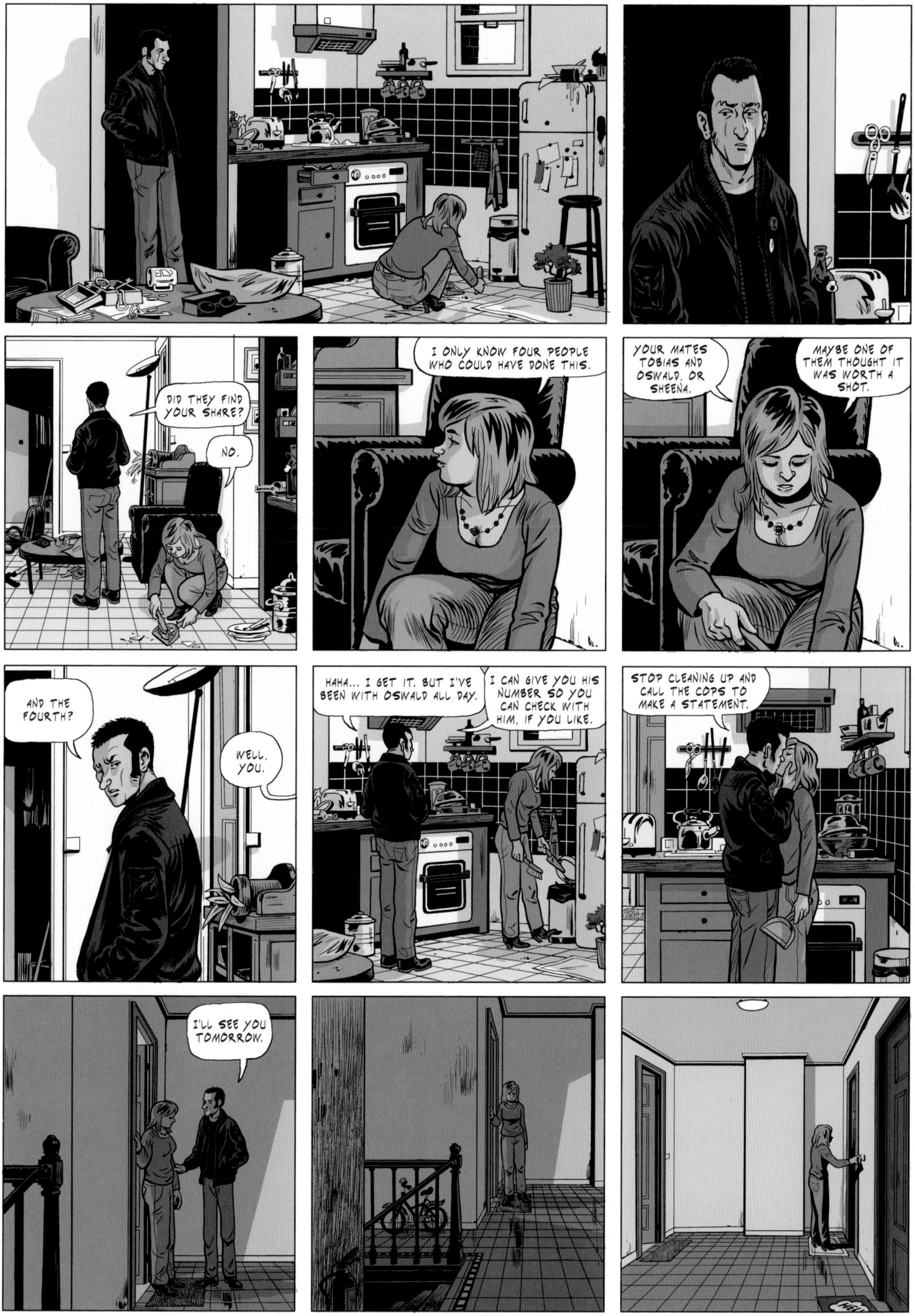
DID THEY FIND YOUR SHARE?
NO.
I ONLY KNOW FOUR PEOPLE WHO COULD HAVE DONE THIS.
YOUR MATES TOBIAS AND OSWALD, OR SHEENA.
MAYBE ONE OF THEM THOUGHT IT WAS WORTH A SHOT.
AND THE FOURTH?
WELL, YOU.
HAHA... I GET IT. BUT I'VE BEEN WITH OSWALD ALL DAY.
I CAN GIVE YOU HIS NUMBER SO YOU CAN CHECK WITH HIM, IF YOU LIKE.
STOP CLEANING UP AND CALL THE COPS TO MAKE A STATEMENT.
I'LL SEE YOU TOMORROW.

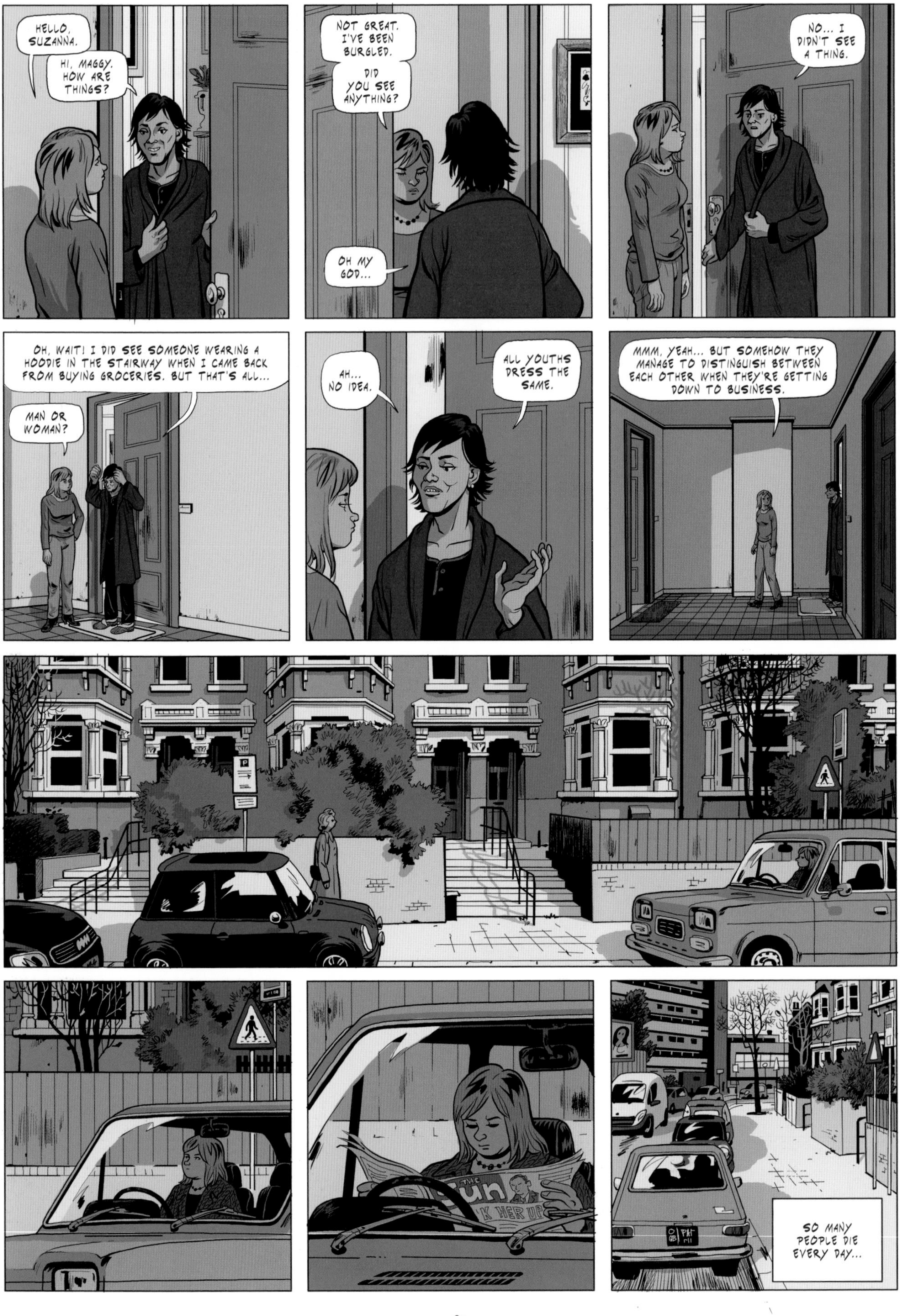
HELLO, SUZANNA.
HI, MAGGY. HOW ARE THINGS?
NOT GREAT. I'VE BEEN BURGLED.
DID YOU SEE ANYTHING?
OH MY GOD...
NO... I DIDN'T SEE A THING.
OH, WAIT! I DID SEE SOMEONE WEARING A HOODIE IN THE STAIRWAY WHEN I CAME BACK FROM BUYING GROCERIES. BUT THAT'S ALL...
MAN OR WOMAN?
AH... NO IDEA.
ALL YOUTHS DRESS THE SAME.
MMM, YEAH... BUT SOMEHOW THEY MANAGE TO DISTINGUISH BETWEEN EACH OTHER WHEN THEY'RE GETTING DOWN TO BUSINESS.
SO MANY PEOPLE DIE EVERY DAY...

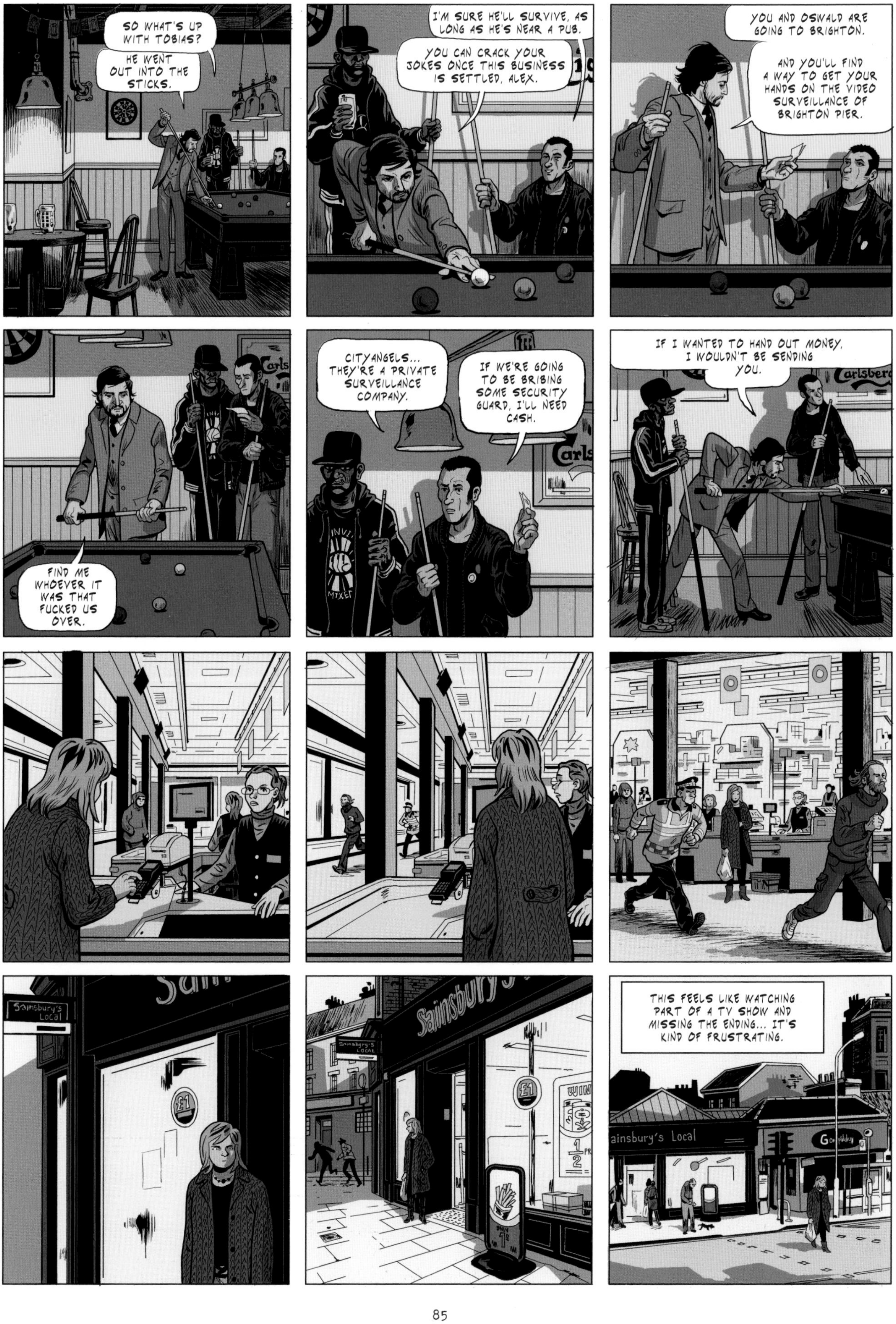
SO WHAT'S UP WITH TOBIAS?
HE WENT OUT INTO THE STICKS.
I'M SURE HE'LL SURVIVE, AS LONG AS HE'S NEAR A PUB.
YOU CAN CRACK YOUR JOKES ONCE THIS BUSINESS IS SETTLED, ALEX.
YOU AND OSWALD ARE GOING TO BRIGHTON.
AND YOU'LL FIND A WAY TO GET YOUR HANDS ON THE VIDEO SURVEILLANCE OF BRIGHTON PIER.
FIND ME WHOEVER IT WAS THAT FUCKED US OVER.
CITYANGELS... THEY'RE A PRIVATE SURVEILLANCE COMPANY.
IF WE'RE GOING TO BE BRIBING SOME SECURITY GUARD, I'LL NEED CASH.
IF I WANTED TO HAND OUT MONEY, I WOULDN'T BE SENDING YOU.
Sainsbury's Local
Sainsbury's
Sainsbury's Local
THIS FEELS LIKE WATCHING PART OF A TV SHOW AND MISSING THE ENDING... IT'S KIND OF FRUSTRATING.
Sainsbury's Local

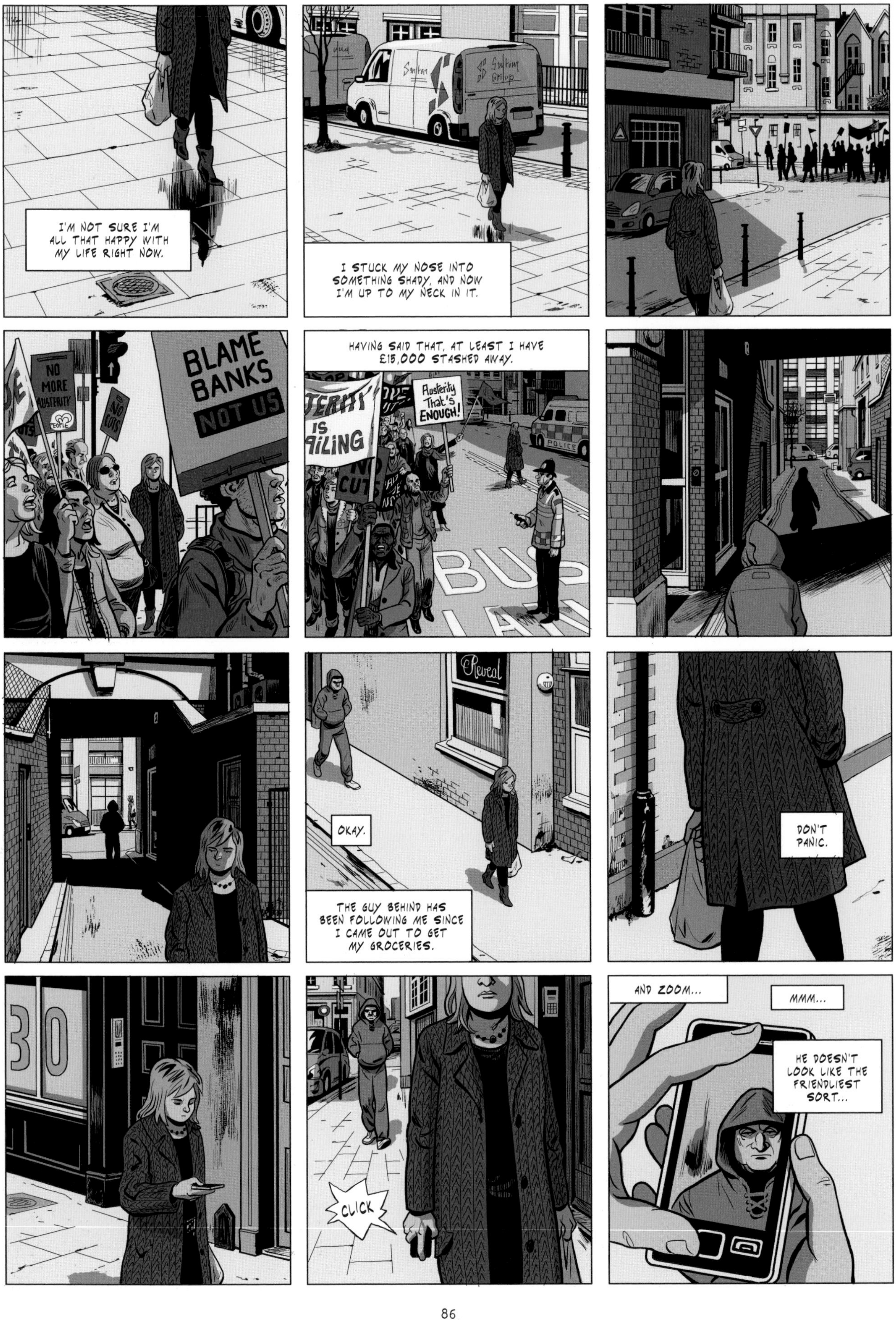
I'M NOT SURE I'M ALL THAT HAPPY WITH MY LIFE RIGHT NOW.
I STUCK MY NOSE INTO SOMETHING SHADY, AND NOW I'M UP TO MY NECK IN IT.
NO MORE AUSTERITY
NO CUTS
BLAME BANKS NOT US
HAVING SAID THAT, AT LEAST I HAVE £15,000 STASHED AWAY.
Austerity That's ENOUGH!
NO CUTS
POLICE
Reveal
OKAY.
THE GUY BEHIND HAS BEEN FOLLOWING ME SINCE I CAME OUT TO GET MY GROCERIES.
DON'T PANIC.
CLICK
AND ZOOM...
MMM...
HE DOESN'T LOOK LIKE THE FRIENDLIEST SORT...

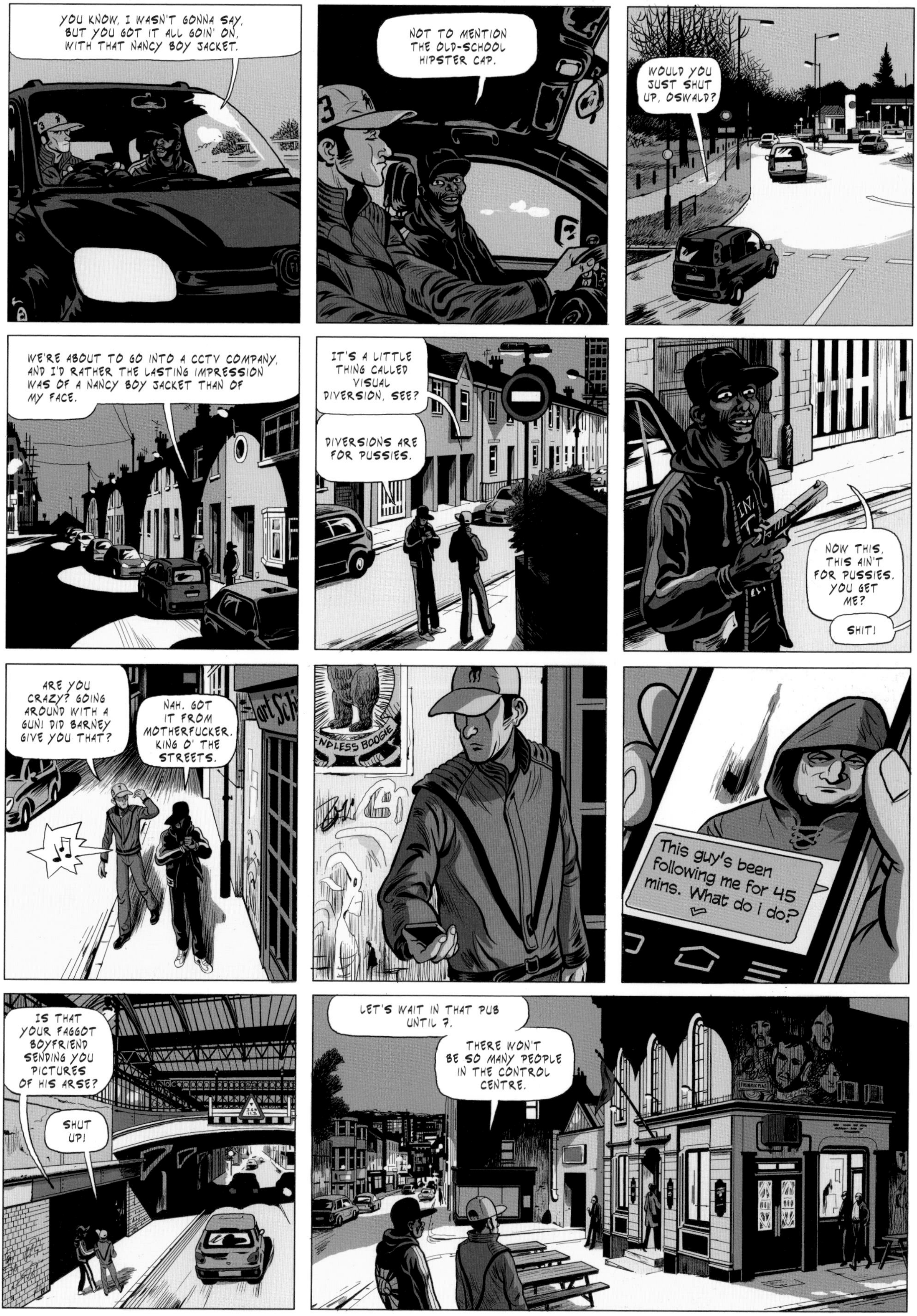
YOU KNOW, I WASN'T GONNA SAY, BUT YOU GOT IT ALL GOIN' ON, WITH THAT NANCY BOY JACKET.
NOT TO MENTION THE OLD-SCHOOL HIPSTER CAP.
WOULD YOU JUST SHUT UP, OSWALD?
WE'RE ABOUT TO GO INTO A CCTV COMPANY, AND I'D RATHER THE LASTING IMPRESSION WAS OF A NANCY BOY JACKET THAN OF MY FACE.
IT'S A LITTLE THING CALLED VISUAL DIVERSION, SEE?
DIVERSIONS ARE FOR PUSSIES.
NOW THIS, THIS AIN'T FOR PUSSIES. YOU GET ME?
SHIT!
ARE YOU CRAZY? GOING AROUND WITH A GUN! DID BARNEY GIVE YOU THAT?
NAH. GOT IT FROM MOTHERFUCKER. KING O' THE STREETS.
ENDLESS BOOGIE
This guy's been following me for 45 mins. What do i do?
IS THAT YOUR FAGGOT BOYFRIEND SENDING YOU PICTURES OF HIS ARSE?
SHUT UP!
LET'S WAIT IN THAT PUB UNTIL 7.
THERE WON'T BE SO MANY PEOPLE IN THE CONTROL CENTRE.

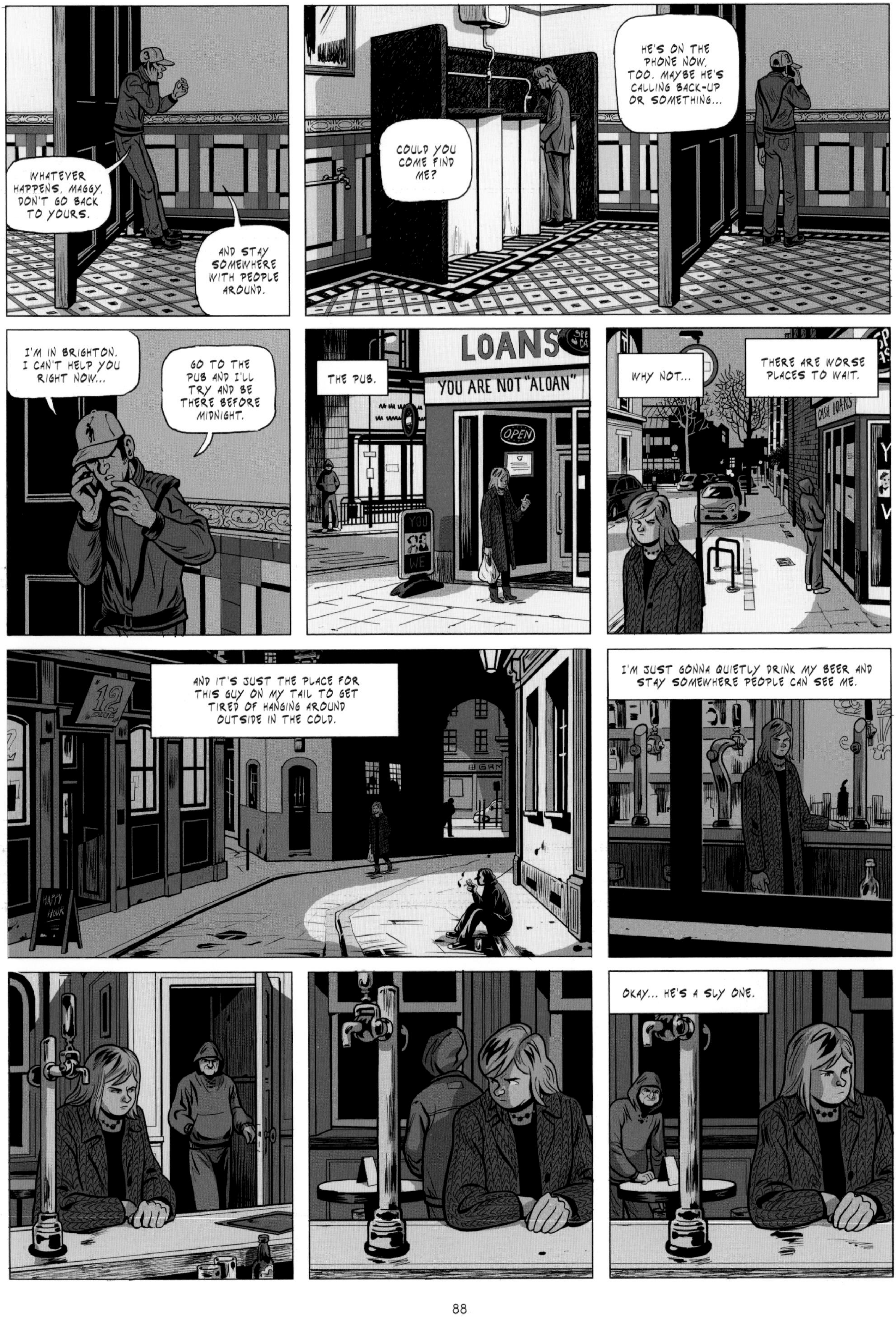

WHATEVER HAPPENS, MAGGY, DON'T GO BACK TO YOURS.
AND STAY SOMEWHERE WITH PEOPLE AROUND.
COULD YOU COME FIND ME?
HE'S ON THE PHONE NOW, TOO. MAYBE HE'S CALLING BACK-UP OR SOMETHING...
I'M IN BRIGHTON. I CAN'T HELP YOU RIGHT NOW...
GO TO THE PUB AND I'LL TRY AND BE THERE BEFORE MIDNIGHT.
THE PUB.
LOANS
YOU ARE NOT "ALOAN"
OPEN
YOU
WE
WHY NOT...
THERE ARE WORSE PLACES TO WAIT.
CASH LOANS
AND IT'S JUST THE PLACE FOR THIS GUY ON MY TAIL TO GET TIRED OF HANGING AROUND OUTSIDE IN THE COLD.
HAPPY HOUR
I'M JUST GONNA QUIETLY DRINK MY BEER AND STAY SOMEWHERE PEOPLE CAN SEE ME.
OKAY... HE'S A SLY ONE.

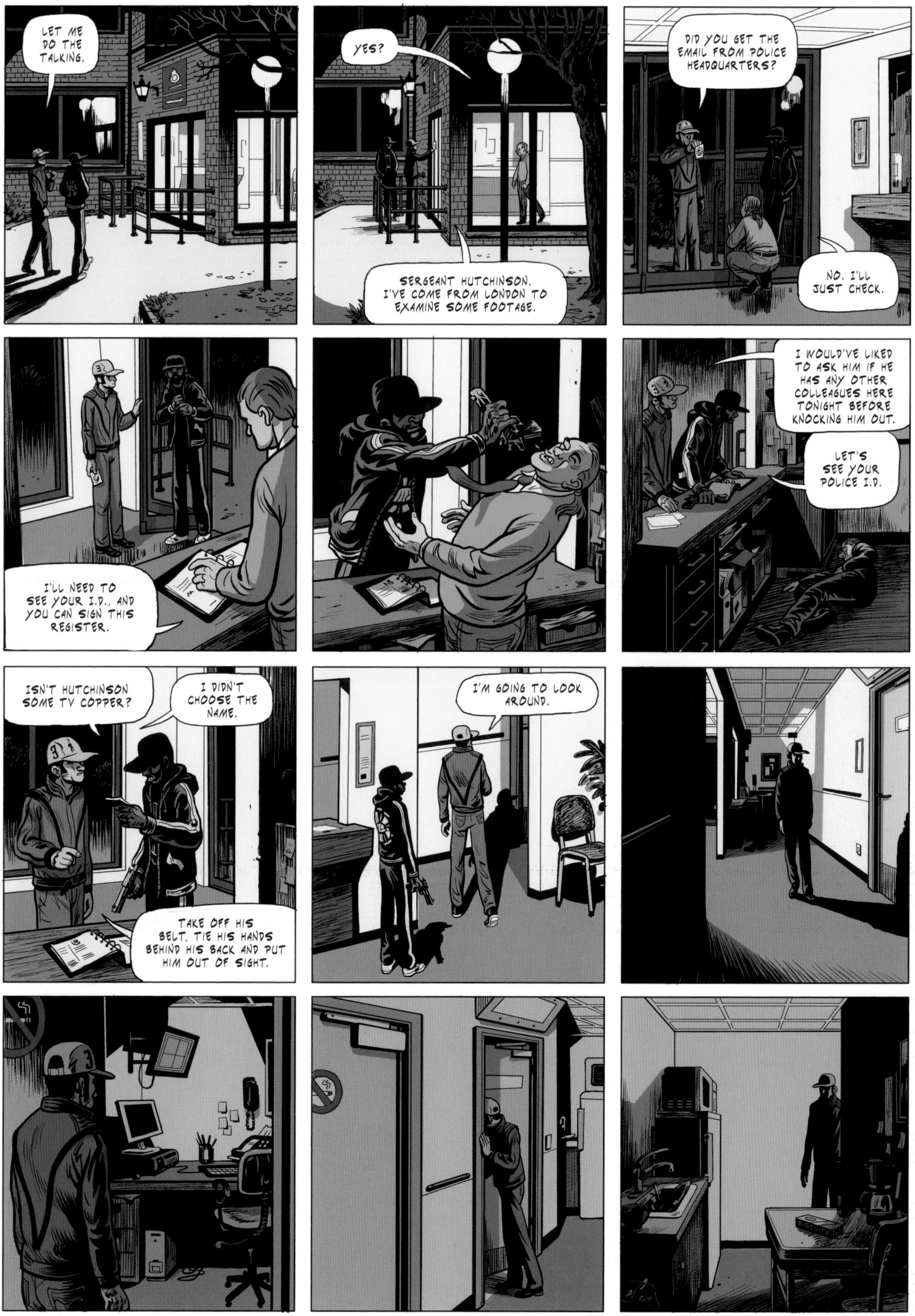
LET ME DO THE TALKING.
YES?
SERGEANT HUTCHINSON. I'VE COME FROM LONDON TO EXAMINE SOME FOOTAGE.
DID YOU GET THE EMAIL FROM POLICE HEADQUARTERS?
NO. I'LL JUST CHECK.
I'LL NEED TO SEE YOUR I.D., AND YOU CAN SIGN THIS REGISTER.
I WOULD'VE LIKED TO ASK HIM IF HE HAS ANY OTHER COLLEAGUES HERE TONIGHT BEFORE KNOCKING HIM OUT.
LET'S SEE YOUR POLICE I.D.
ISN'T HUTCHINSON SOME TV COPPER?
I DIDN'T CHOOSE THE NAME.
TAKE OFF HIS BELT, TIE HIS HANDS BEHIND HIS BACK AND PUT HIM OUT OF SIGHT.
I'M GOING TO LOOK AROUND.

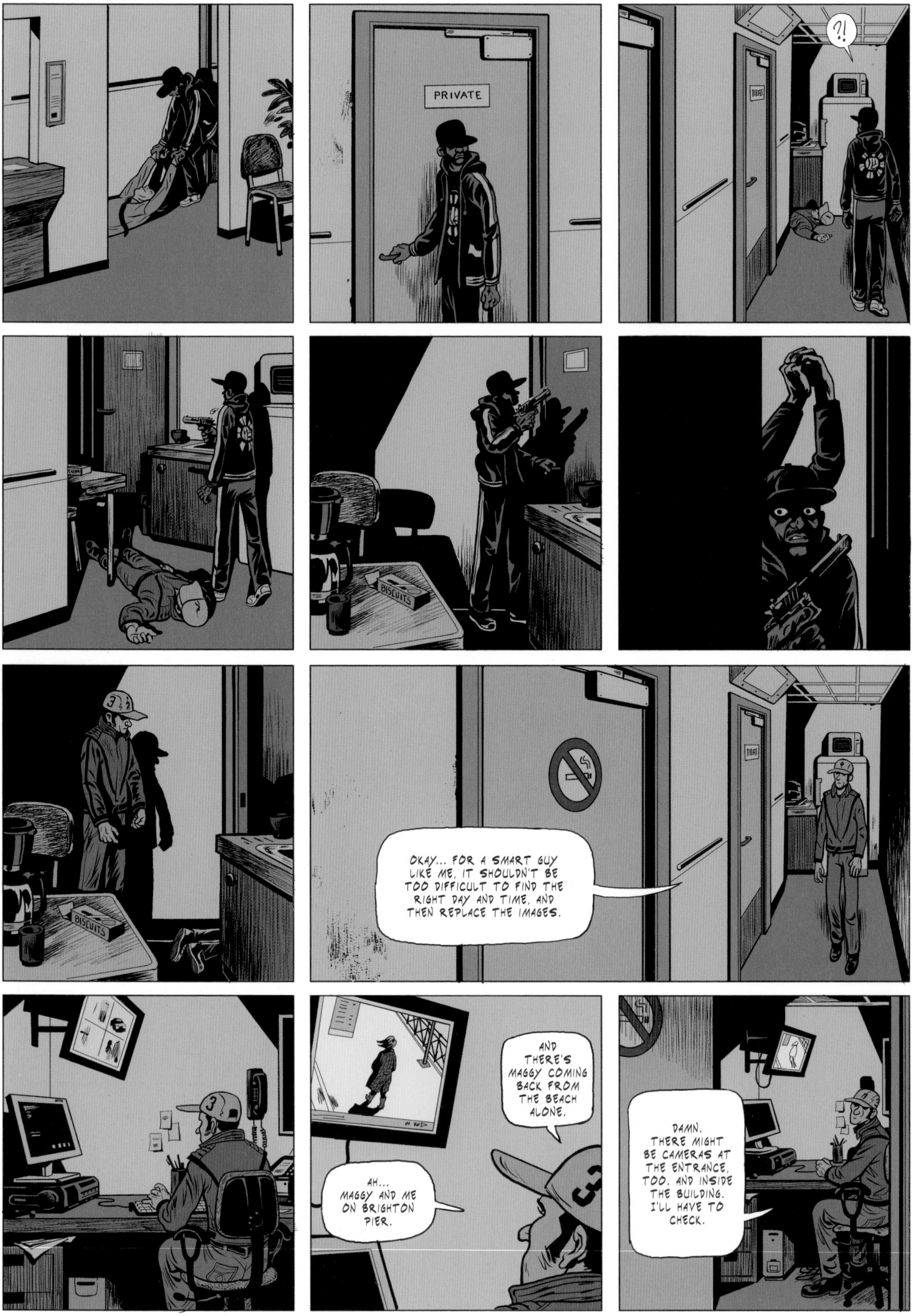
PRIVATE
?!
BISCUITS
BISCUITS
OKAY... FOR A SMART GUY LIKE ME, IT SHOULDN'T BE TOO DIFFICULT TO FIND THE RIGHT DAY AND TIME, AND THEN REPLACE THE IMAGES.
AND THERE'S MAGGY COMING BACK FROM THE BEACH ALONE.
AH... MAGGY AND ME ON BRIGHTON PIER.
DAMN. THERE MIGHT BE CAMERAS AT THE ENTRANCE, TOO. AND INSIDE THE BUILDING. I'LL HAVE TO CHECK.

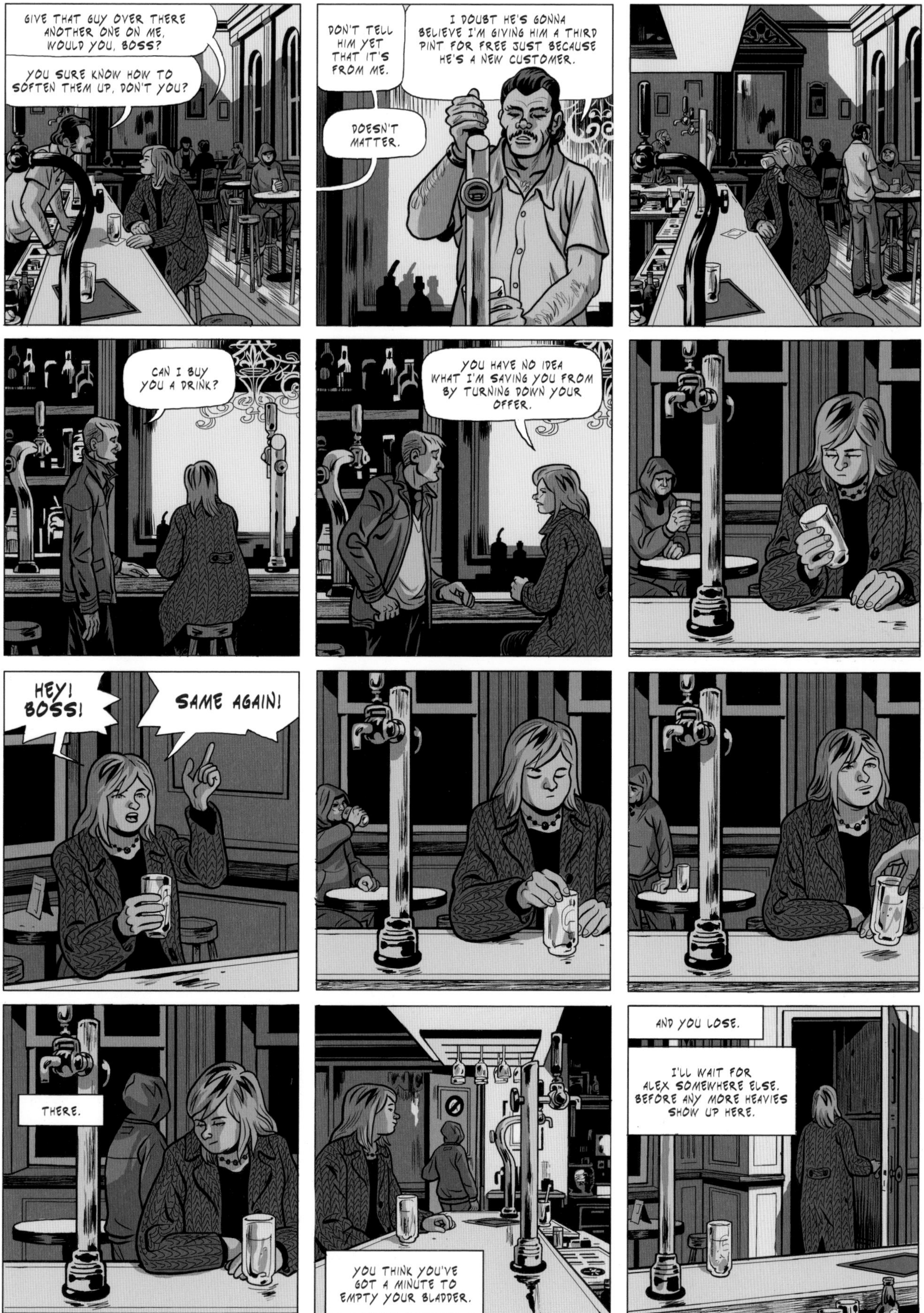

GIVE THAT GUY OVER THERE ANOTHER ONE ON ME, WOULD YOU, BOSS?
YOU SURE KNOW HOW TO SOFTEN THEM UP, DON'T YOU?
DON'T TELL HIM YET THAT IT'S FROM ME.
I DOUBT HE'S GONNA BELIEVE I'M GIVING HIM A THIRD PINT FOR FREE JUST BECAUSE HE'S A NEW CUSTOMER.
DOESN'T MATTER.
CAN I BUY YOU A DRINK?
YOU HAVE NO IDEA WHAT I'M SAVING YOU FROM BY TURNING DOWN YOUR OFFER.
HEY! BOSS!
SAME AGAIN!
THERE.
YOU THINK YOU'VE GOT A MINUTE TO EMPTY YOUR BLADDER.
AND YOU LOSE.
I'LL WAIT FOR ALEX SOMEWHERE ELSE. BEFORE ANY MORE HEAVIES SHOW UP HERE.

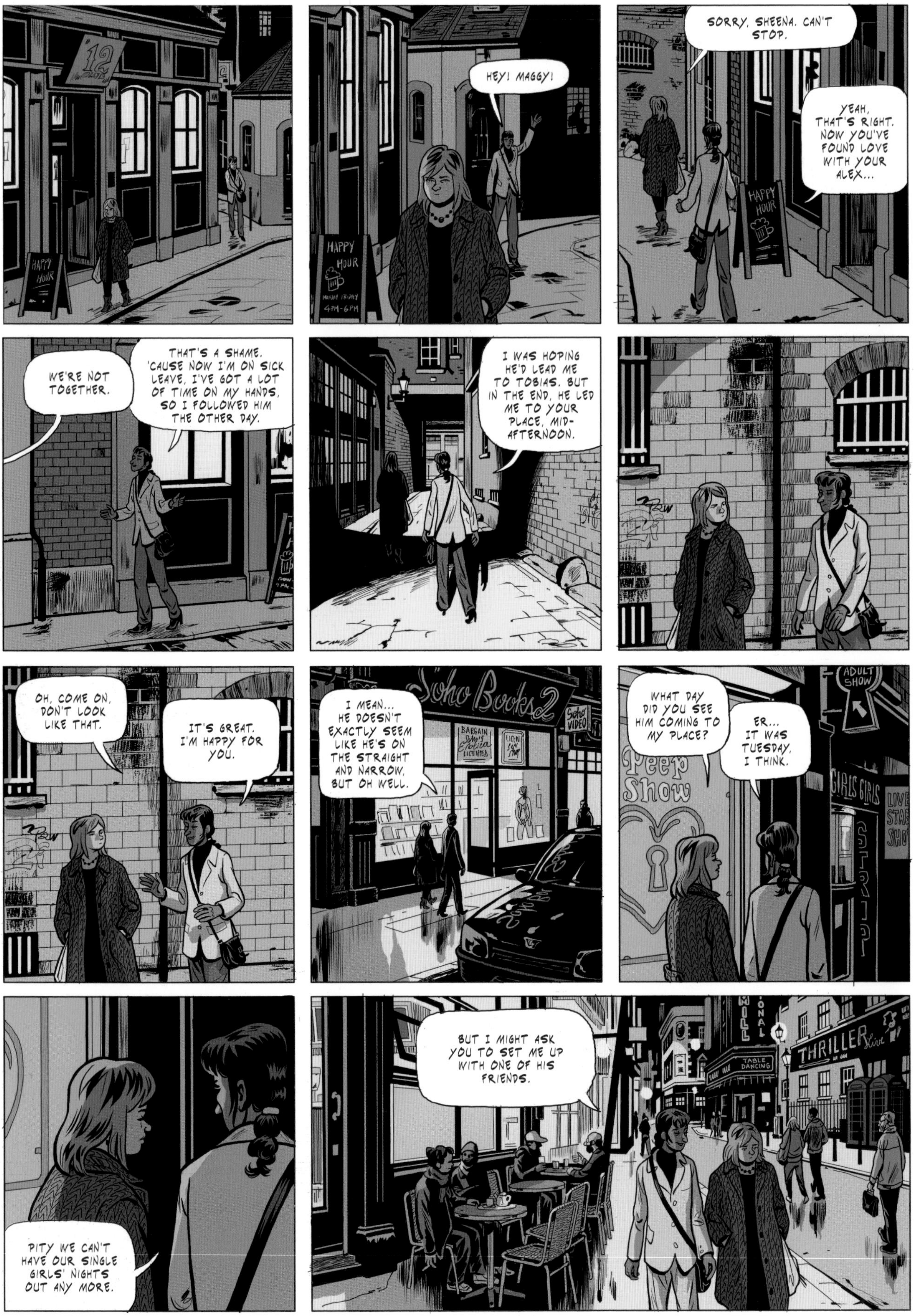

HEY! MAGGY!
SORRY, SHEENA. CAN'T STOP.
YEAH, THAT'S RIGHT. NOW YOU'VE FOUND LOVE WITH YOUR ALEX...
WE'RE NOT TOGETHER.
THAT'S A SHAME. 'CAUSE NOW I'M ON SICK LEAVE, I'VE GOT A LOT OF TIME ON MY HANDS, SO I FOLLOWED HIM THE OTHER DAY.
I WAS HOPING HE'D LEAD ME TO TOBIAS. BUT IN THE END, HE LED ME TO YOUR PLACE, MID-AFTERNOON.
OH, COME ON, DON'T LOOK LIKE THAT.
IT'S GREAT. I'M HAPPY FOR YOU.
I MEAN... HE DOESN'T EXACTLY SEEM LIKE HE'S ON THE STRAIGHT AND NARROW, BUT OH WELL.
WHAT DAY DID YOU SEE HIM COMING TO MY PLACE?
ER... IT WAS TUESDAY, I THINK.
PITY WE CAN'T HAVE OUR SINGLE GIRLS' NIGHTS OUT ANY MORE.
BUT I MIGHT ASK YOU TO SET ME UP WITH ONE OF HIS FRIENDS.

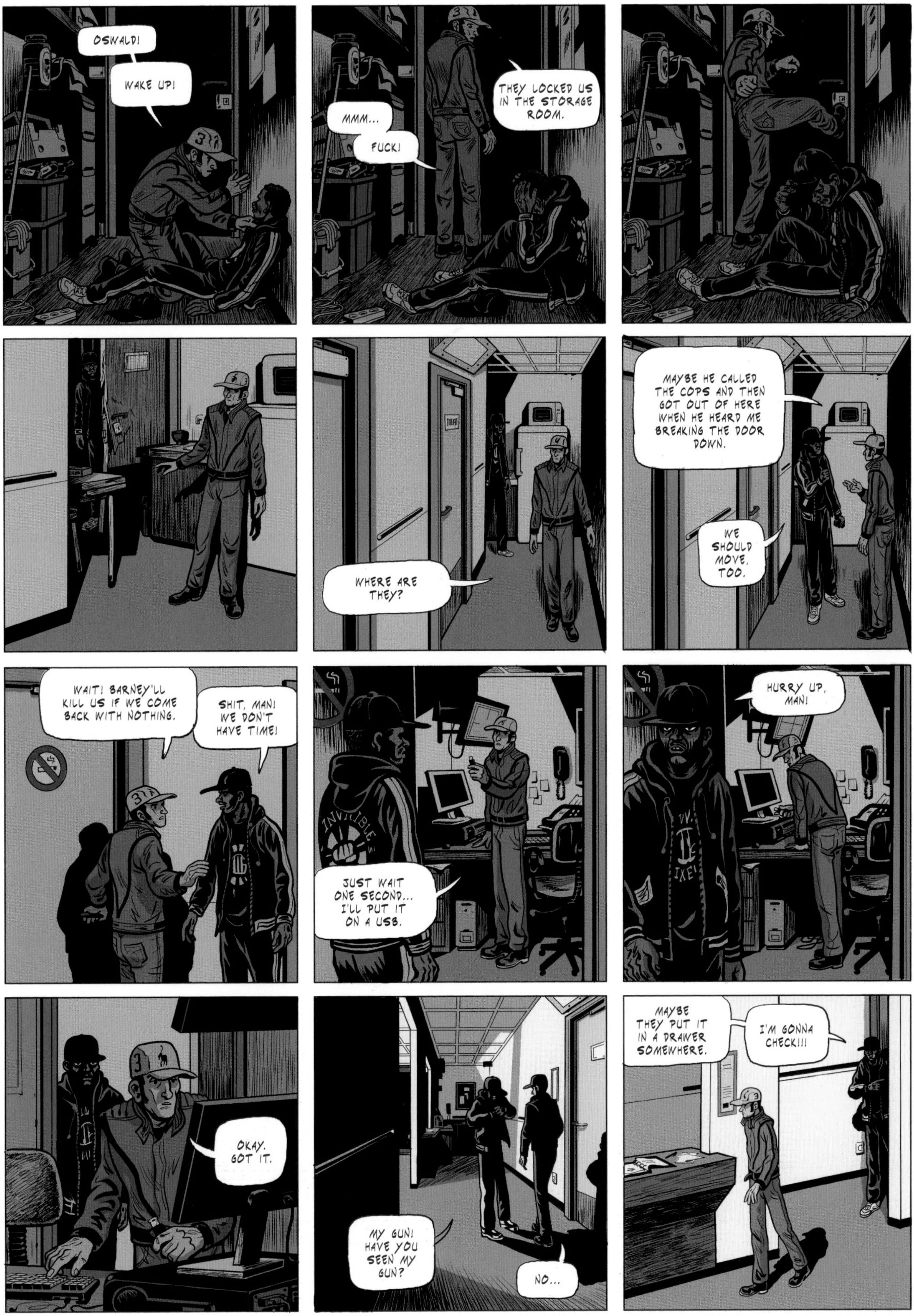
OSWALD!
WAKE UP!
MMM...
FUCK!
THEY LOCKED US IN THE STORAGE ROOM.
WHERE ARE THEY?
MAYBE HE CALLED THE COPS AND THEN GOT OUT OF HERE WHEN HE HEARD ME BREAKING THE DOOR DOWN.
WE SHOULD MOVE, TOO.
WAIT! BARNEY'LL KILL US IF WE COME BACK WITH NOTHING.
SHIT, MAN! WE DON'T HAVE TIME!
JUST WAIT ONE SECOND... I'LL PUT IT ON A USB.
HURRY UP, MAN!
OKAY. GOT IT.
MY GUN! HAVE YOU SEEN MY GUN?
NO...
MAYBE THEY PUT IT IN A DRAWER SOMEWHERE.
I'M GONNA CHECK!!!

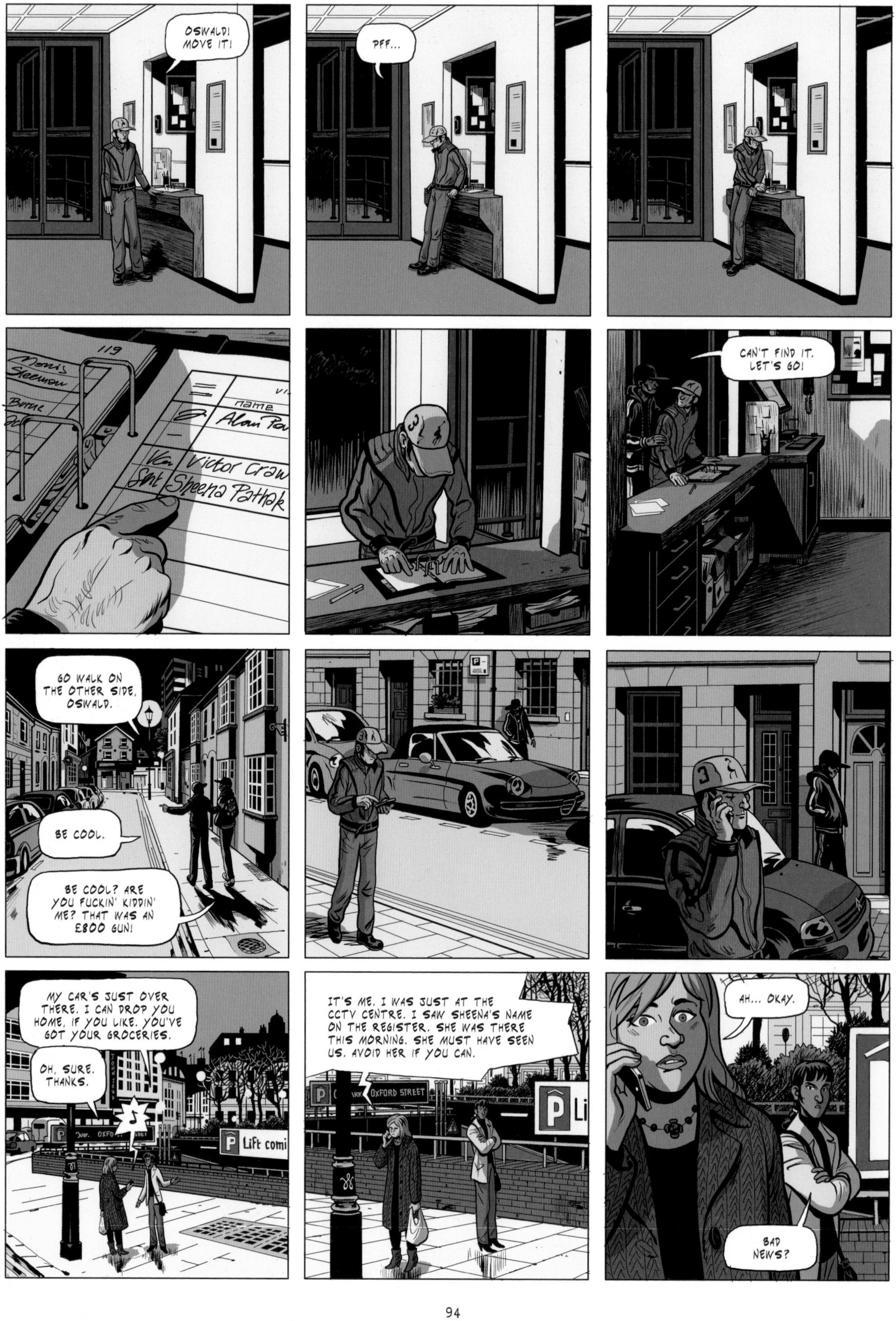
OSWALD! MOVE IT!
PFF...
119
Morris
Sleemow
Burne
name
Alan Pa
Victor Craw
Sheena Pathak
CAN'T FIND IT. LET'S GO!
GO WALK ON THE OTHER SIDE, OSWALD.
BE COOL.
BE COOL? ARE YOU FUCKIN' KIDDIN' ME? THAT WAS AN £800 GUN!
MY CAR'S JUST OVER THERE. I CAN DROP YOU HOME, IF YOU LIKE. YOU'VE GOT YOUR GROCERIES.
OH, SURE. THANKS.
Lift comi
IT'S ME. I WAS JUST AT THE CCTV CENTRE. I SAW SHEENA'S NAME ON THE REGISTER. SHE WAS THERE THIS MORNING. SHE MUST HAVE SEEN US. AVOID HER IF YOU CAN.
OXFORD STREET
AH... OKAY.
BAD NEWS?

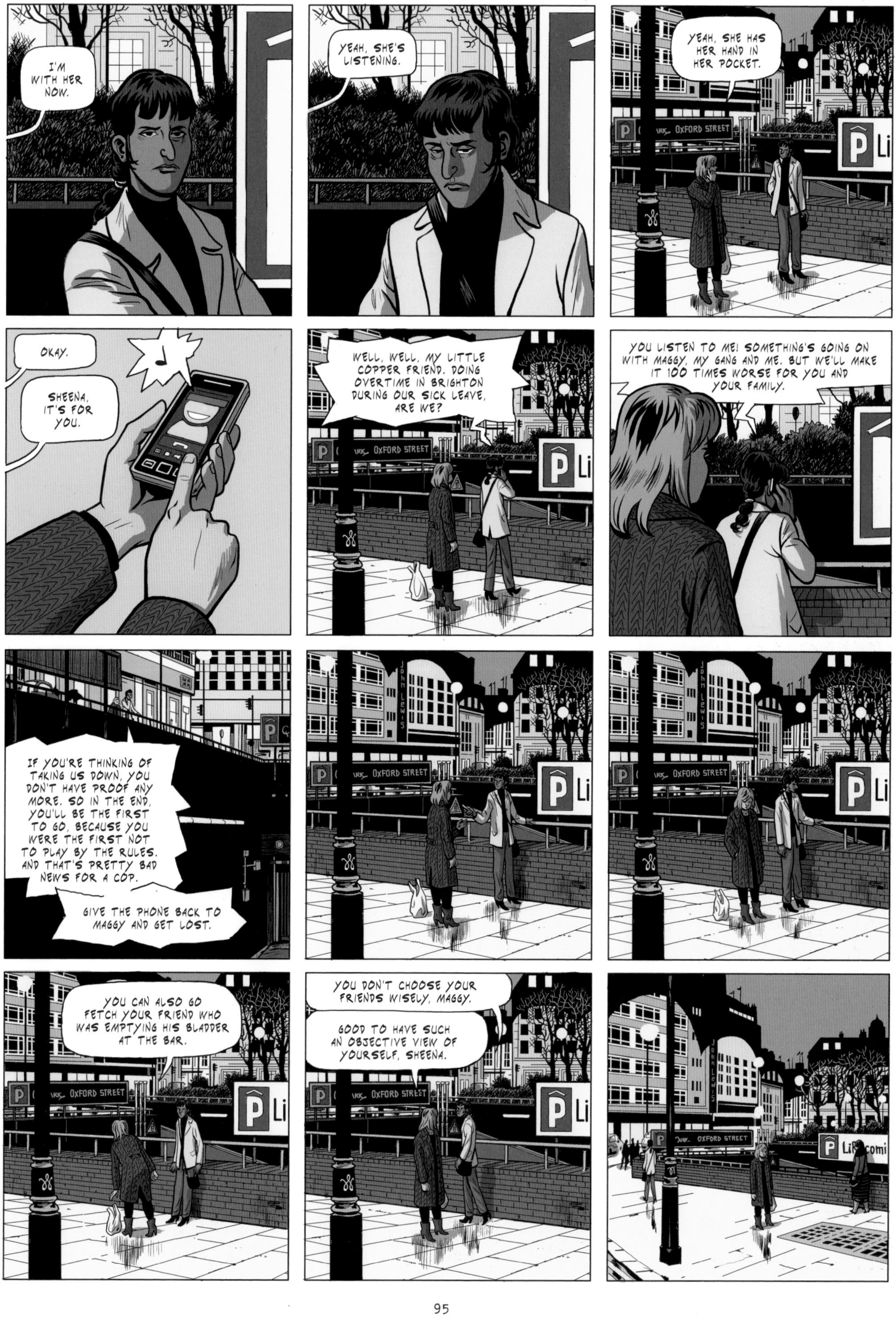

I'M WITH HER NOW.
YEAH, SHE'S LISTENING.
YEAH, SHE HAS HER HAND IN HER POCKET.
OXFORD STREET
OKAY.
SHEENA, IT'S FOR YOU.
WELL, WELL, MY LITTLE COPPER FRIEND. DOING OVERTIME IN BRIGHTON DURING OUR SICK LEAVE, ARE WE?
YOU LISTEN TO ME! SOMETHING'S GOING ON WITH MAGGY, MY GANG AND ME. BUT WE'LL MAKE IT 100 TIMES WORSE FOR YOU AND YOUR FAMILY.
IF YOU'RE THINKING OF TAKING US DOWN, YOU DON'T HAVE PROOF ANY MORE. SO IN THE END, YOU'LL BE THE FIRST TO GO, BECAUSE YOU WERE THE FIRST NOT TO PLAY BY THE RULES. AND THAT'S PRETTY BAD NEWS FOR A COP.
GIVE THE PHONE BACK TO MAGGY AND GET LOST.
JOHN LEWIS
YOU CAN ALSO GO FETCH YOUR FRIEND WHO WAS EMPTYING HIS BLADDER AT THE BAR.
YOU DON'T CHOOSE YOUR FRIENDS WISELY, MAGGY.
GOOD TO HAVE SUCH AN OBJECTIVE VIEW OF YOURSELF, SHEENA.

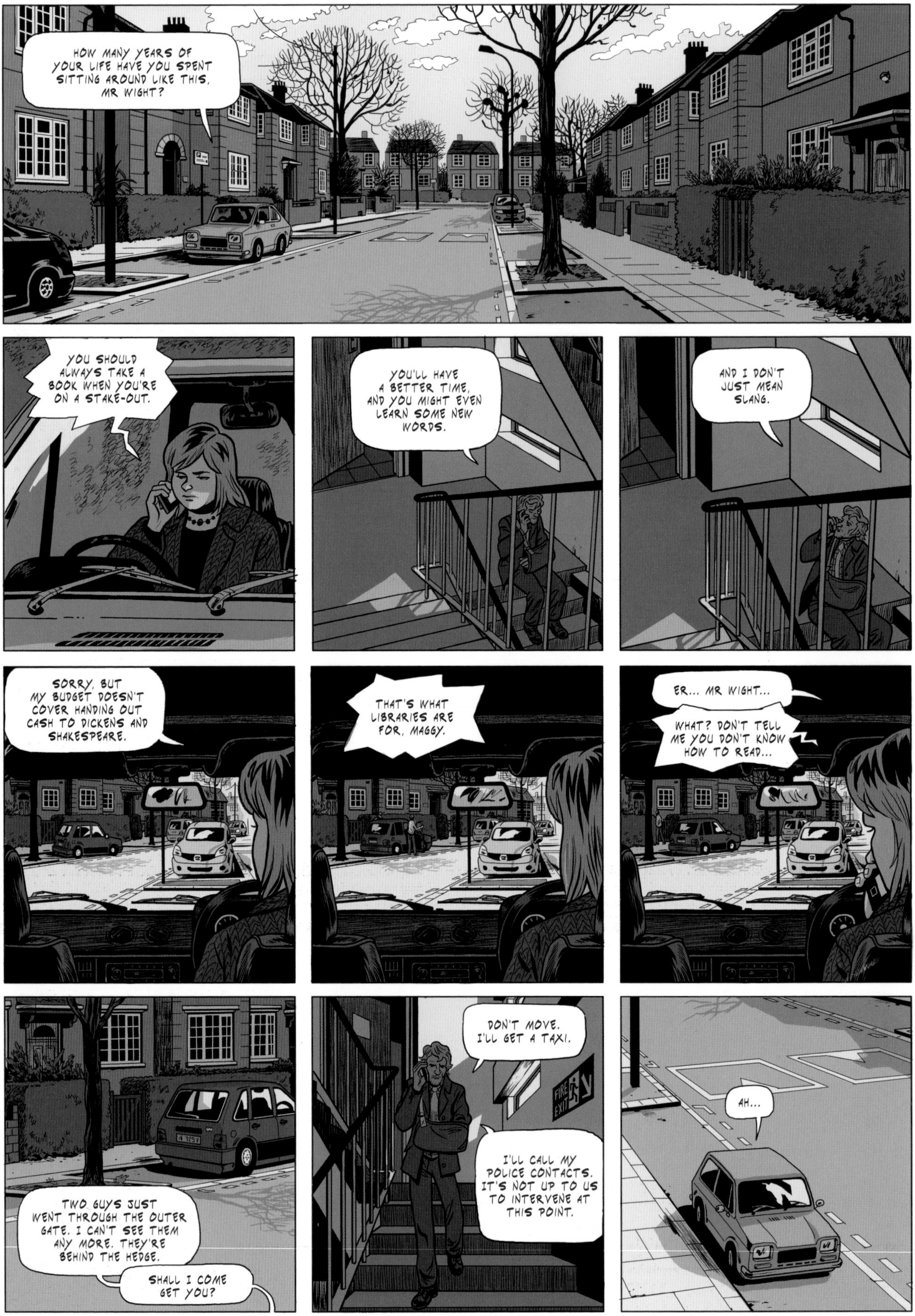
HOW MANY YEARS OF YOUR LIFE HAVE YOU SPENT SITTING AROUND LIKE THIS, MR WIGHT?
YOU SHOULD ALWAYS TAKE A BOOK WHEN YOU'RE ON A STAKE-OUT.
YOU'LL HAVE A BETTER TIME, AND YOU MIGHT EVEN LEARN SOME NEW WORDS.
AND I DON'T JUST MEAN SLANG.
SORRY, BUT MY BUDGET DOESN'T COVER HANDING OUT CASH TO DICKENS AND SHAKESPEARE.
THAT'S WHAT LIBRARIES ARE FOR, MAGGY.
ER... MR WIGHT...
WHAT? DON'T TELL ME YOU DON'T KNOW HOW TO READ...
TWO GUYS JUST WENT THROUGH THE OUTER GATE. I CAN'T SEE THEM ANY MORE. THEY'RE BEHIND THE HEDGE.
SHALL I COME GET YOU?
DON'T MOVE. I'LL GET A TAXI.
FIRE EXIT
I'LL CALL MY POLICE CONTACTS. IT'S NOT UP TO US TO INTERVENE AT THIS POINT.
AH...

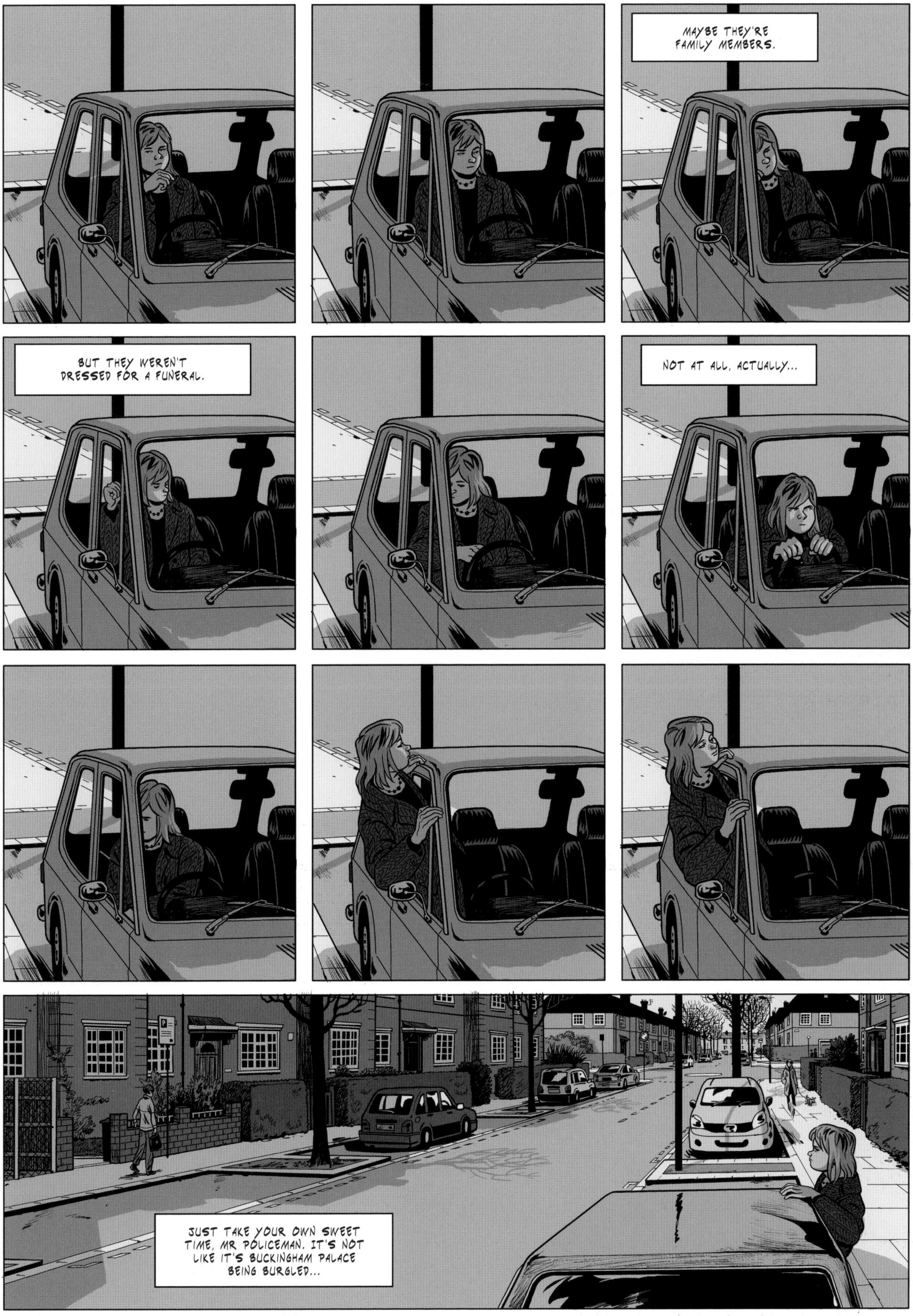
MAYBE THEY'RE FAMILY MEMBERS.
BUT THEY WEREN'T DRESSED FOR A FUNERAL.
NOT AT ALL, ACTUALLY...
JUST TAKE YOUR OWN SWEET TIME, MR POLICEMAN. IT'S NOT LIKE IT'S BUCKINGHAM PALACE BEING BURGLED...

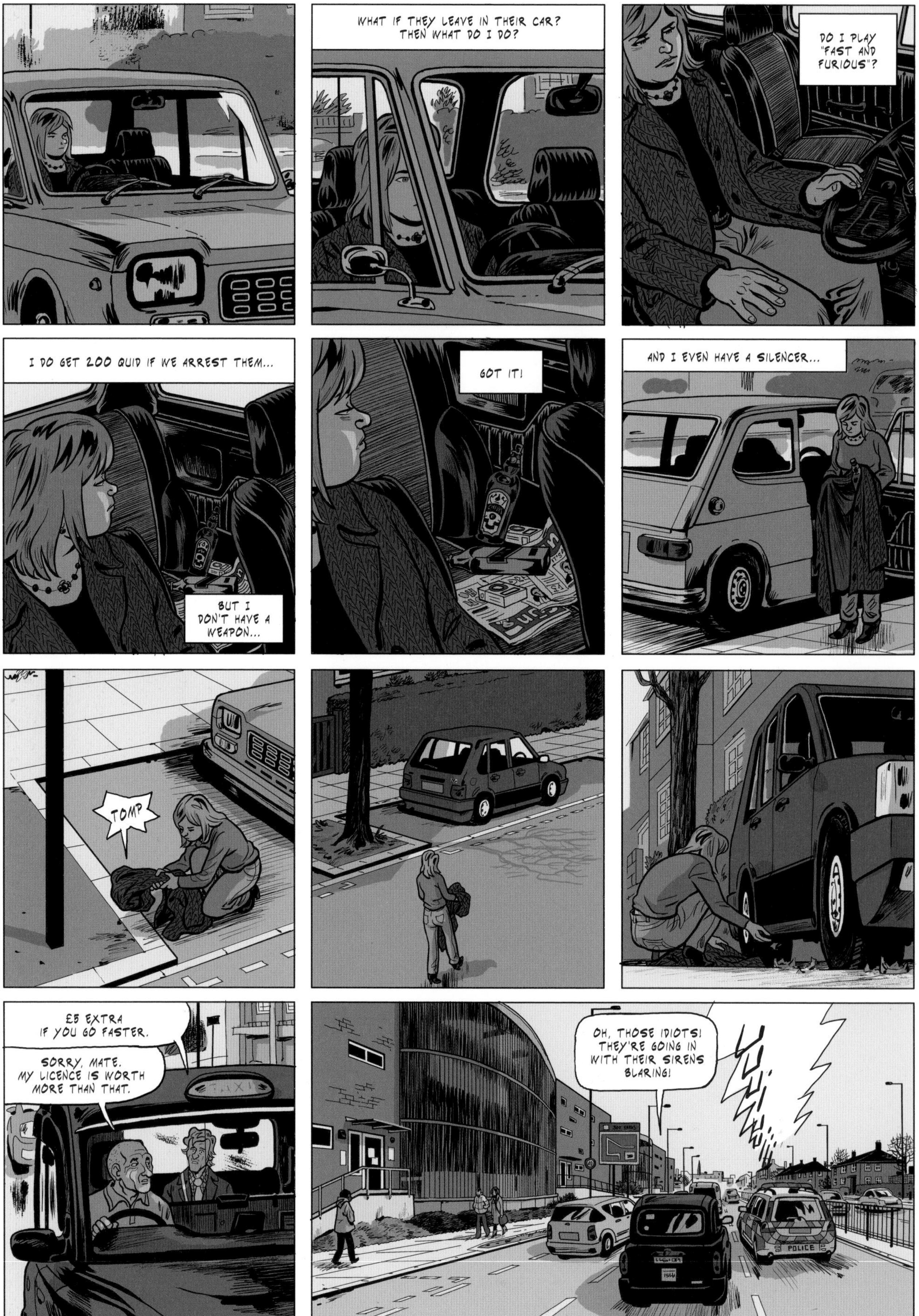
WHAT IF THEY LEAVE IN THEIR CAR? THEN WHAT DO I DO?
DO I PLAY "FAST AND FURIOUS"?
I DO GET 200 QUID IF WE ARREST THEM...
BUT I DON'T HAVE A WEAPON...
GOT IT!
AND I EVEN HAVE A SILENCER...
TOMP
£5 EXTRA IF YOU GO FASTER.
SORRY, MATE. MY LICENCE IS WORTH MORE THAN THAT.
OH, THOSE IDIOTS! THEY'RE GOING IN WITH THEIR SIRENS BLARING!
POLICE

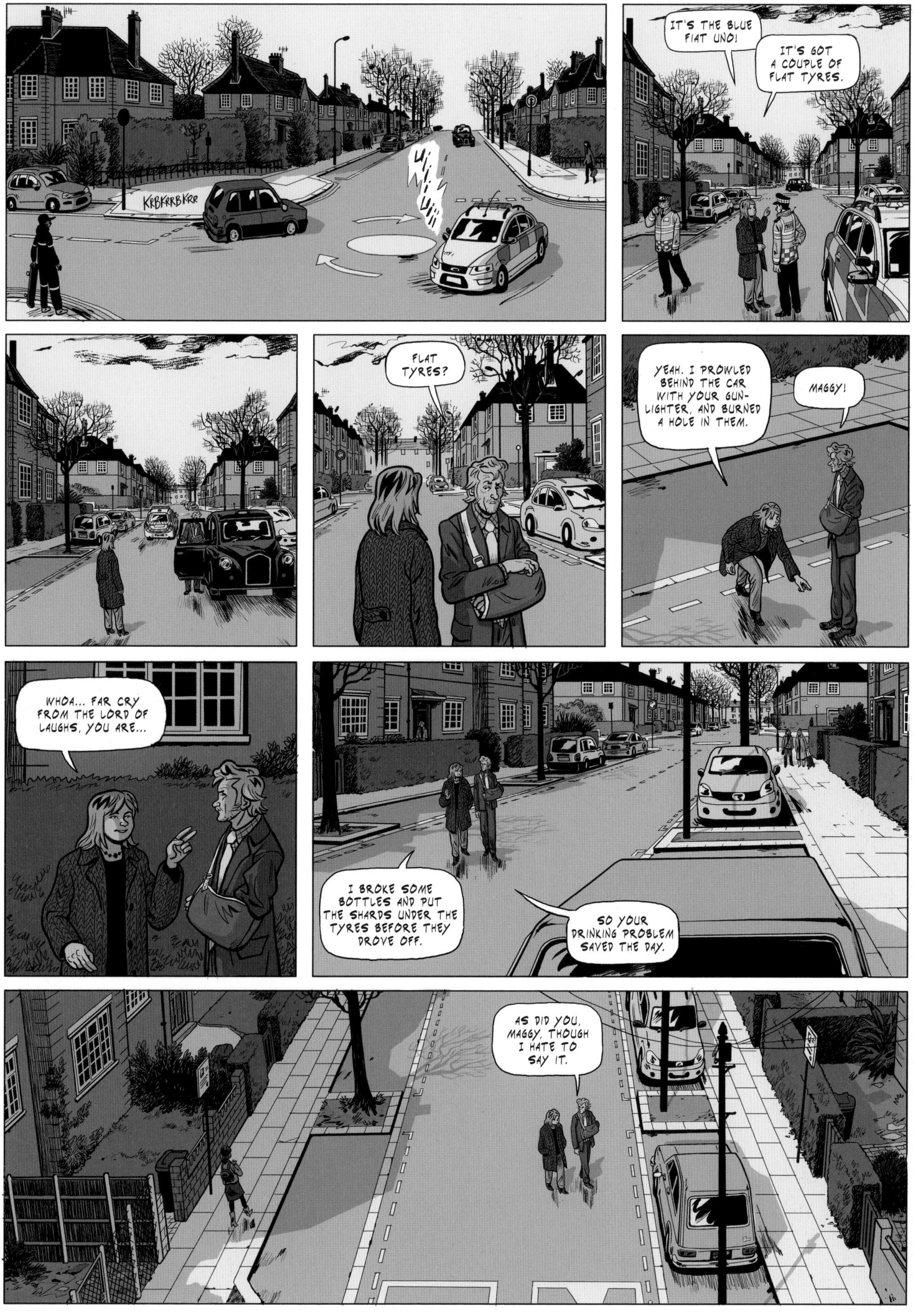
KRBKRRBKRR
IT'S THE BLUE FIAT UNO!
IT'S GOT A COUPLE OF FLAT TYRES.
FLAT TYRES?
YEAH. I PROWLED BEHIND THE CAR WITH YOUR GUN-LIGHTER, AND BURNED A HOLE IN THEM.
MAGGY!
WHOA... FAR CRY FROM THE LORD OF LAUGHS, YOU ARE...
I BROKE SOME BOTTLES AND PUT THE SHARDS UNDER THE TYRES BEFORE THEY DROVE OFF.
SO YOUR DRINKING PROBLEM SAVED THE DAY.
AS DID YOU, MAGGY, THOUGH I HATE TO SAY IT.

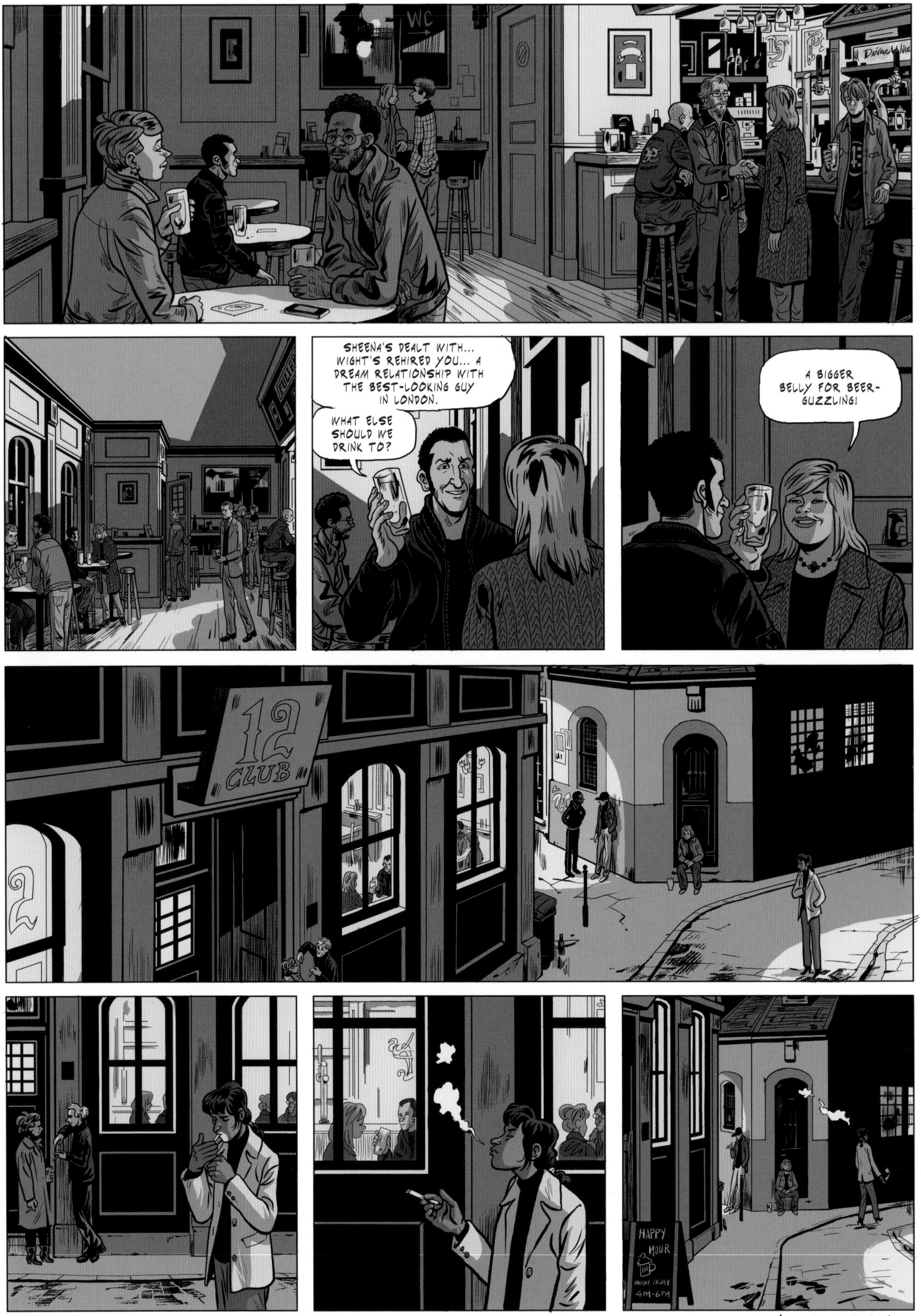

WC
SHEENA'S DEALT WITH... WIGHT'S REHIRED YOU... A DREAM RELATIONSHIP WITH THE BEST-LOOKING GUY IN LONDON.
WHAT ELSE SHOULD WE DRINK TO?
A BIGGER BELLY FOR BEER-GUZZLING!
12 CLUB
HAPPY HOUR
MONDAY FRIDAY
4PM-6PM

3. SHAME IT HAD TO END THIS WAY

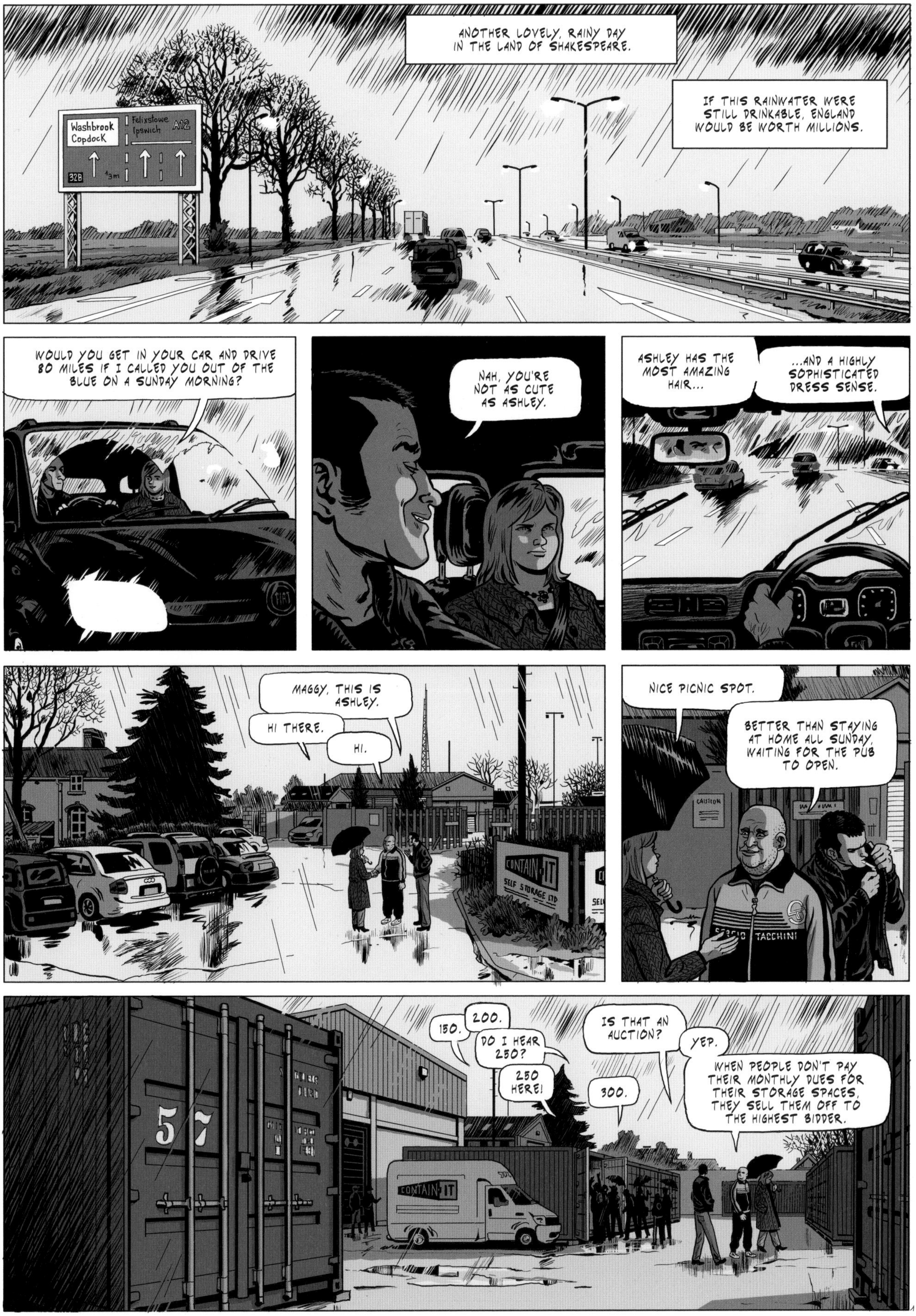
ANOTHER LOVELY, RAINY DAY IN THE LAND OF SHAKESPEARE.
IF THIS RAINWATER WERE STILL DRINKABLE, ENGLAND WOULD BE WORTH MILLIONS.
Washbrook Copdock
Felixstowe Ipswich A12
32B
WOULD YOU GET IN YOUR CAR AND DRIVE 80 MILES IF I CALLED YOU OUT OF THE BLUE ON A SUNDAY MORNING?
NAH, YOU'RE NOT AS CUTE AS ASHLEY.
ASHLEY HAS THE MOST AMAZING HAIR...
...AND A HIGHLY SOPHISTICATED DRESS SENSE.
MAGGY, THIS IS ASHLEY.
HI THERE.
HI.
CONTAIN IT SELF STORAGE LTD
NICE PICNIC SPOT.
BETTER THAN STAYING AT HOME ALL SUNDAY, WAITING FOR THE PUB TO OPEN.
TACCHINI
150.
200.
DO I HEAR 250?
250 HERE!
300.
IS THAT AN AUCTION?
YEP.
WHEN PEOPLE DON'T PAY THEIR MONTHLY DUES FOR THEIR STORAGE SPACES, THEY SELL THEM OFF TO THE HIGHEST BIDDER.
57
CONTAIN IT

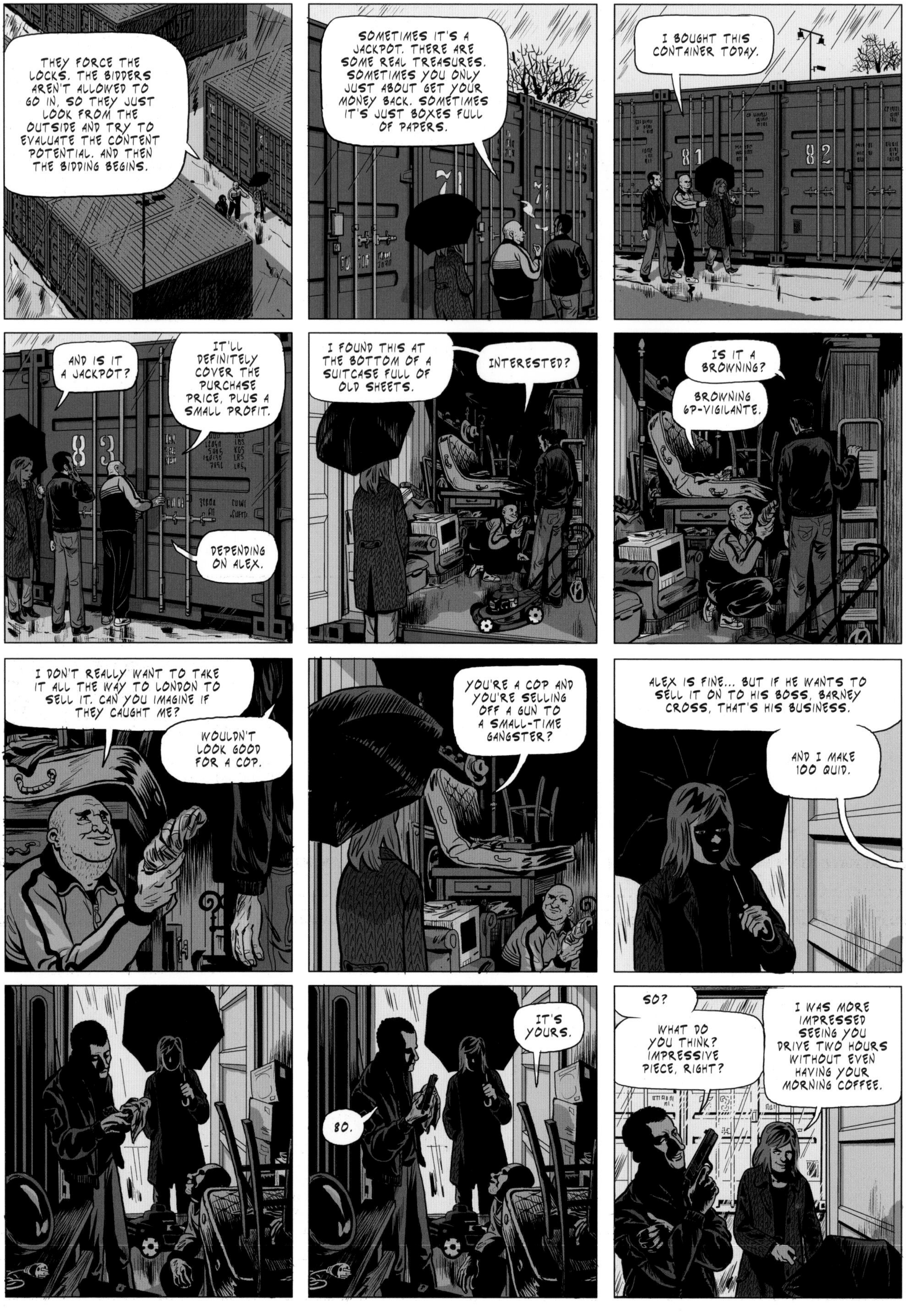
THEY FORCE THE LOCKS. THE BIDDERS AREN'T ALLOWED TO GO IN, SO THEY JUST LOOK FROM THE OUTSIDE AND TRY TO EVALUATE THE CONTENT POTENTIAL. AND THEN THE BIDDING BEGINS.
SOMETIMES IT'S A JACKPOT. THERE ARE SOME REAL TREASURES. SOMETIMES YOU ONLY JUST ABOUT GET YOUR MONEY BACK. SOMETIMES IT'S JUST BOXES FULL OF PAPERS.
I BOUGHT THIS CONTAINER TODAY.
AND IS IT A JACKPOT?
IT'LL DEFINITELY COVER THE PURCHASE PRICE, PLUS A SMALL PROFIT.
DEPENDING ON ALEX.
I FOUND THIS AT THE BOTTOM OF A SUITCASE FULL OF OLD SHEETS.
INTERESTED?
IS IT A BROWNING?
BROWNING GP-VIGILANTE.
I DON'T REALLY WANT TO TAKE IT ALL THE WAY TO LONDON TO SELL IT. CAN YOU IMAGINE IF THEY CAUGHT ME?
WOULDN'T LOOK GOOD FOR A COP.
YOU'RE A COP AND YOU'RE SELLING OFF A GUN TO A SMALL-TIME GANGSTER?
ALEX IS FINE... BUT IF HE WANTS TO SELL IT ON TO HIS BOSS, BARNEY CROSS, THAT'S HIS BUSINESS.
AND I MAKE 100 QUID.
IT'S YOURS.
80.
SO?
WHAT DO YOU THINK? IMPRESSIVE PIECE, RIGHT?
I WAS MORE IMPRESSED SEEING YOU DRIVE TWO HOURS WITHOUT EVEN HAVING YOUR MORNING COFFEE.

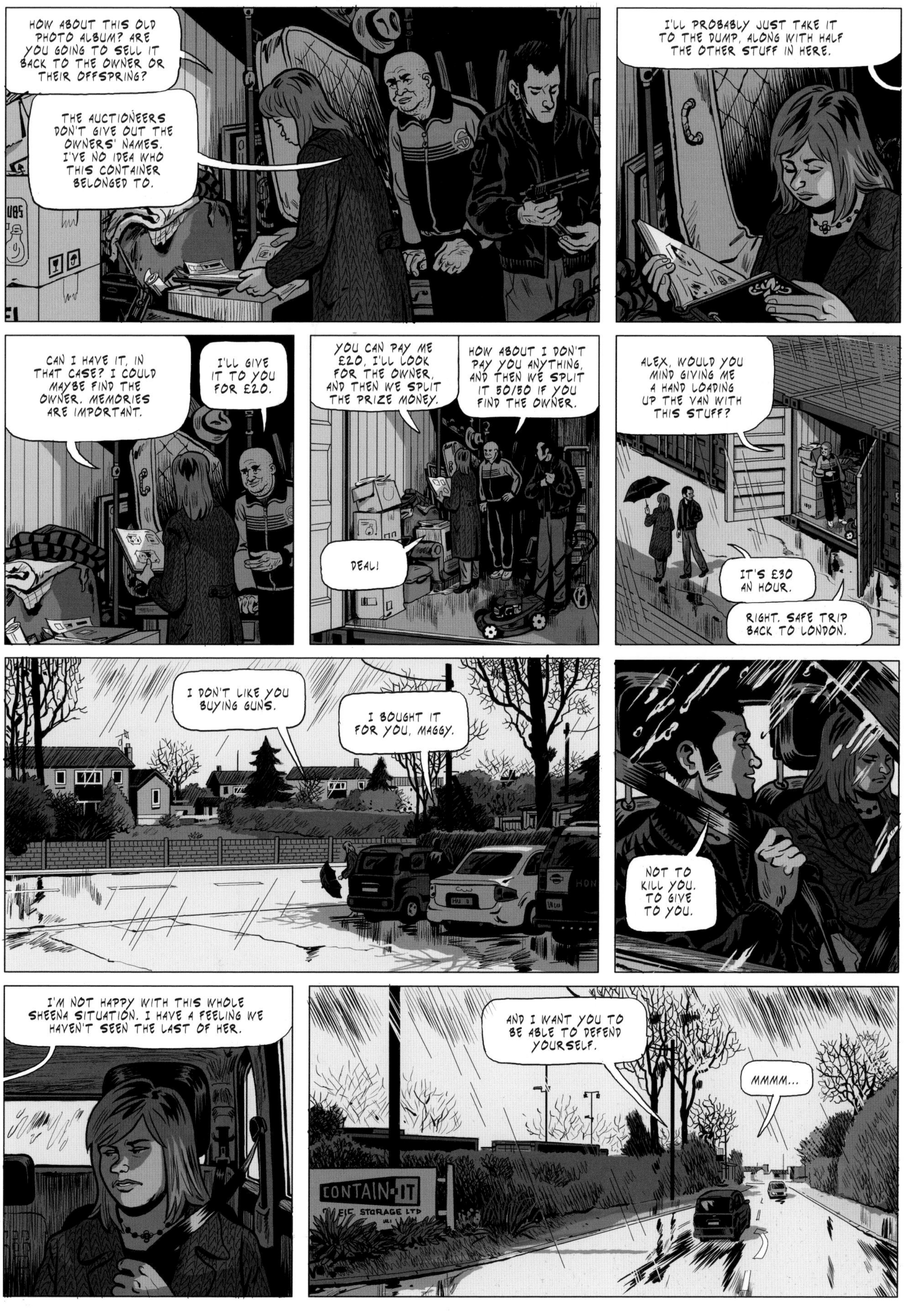
HOW ABOUT THIS OLD PHOTO ALBUM? ARE YOU GOING TO SELL IT BACK TO THE OWNER OR THEIR OFFSPRING?
THE AUCTIONEERS DON'T GIVE OUT THE OWNERS' NAMES. I'VE NO IDEA WHO THIS CONTAINER BELONGED TO.
I'LL PROBABLY JUST TAKE IT TO THE DUMP, ALONG WITH HALF THE OTHER STUFF IN HERE.
CAN I HAVE IT, IN THAT CASE? I COULD MAYBE FIND THE OWNER. MEMORIES ARE IMPORTANT.
I'LL GIVE IT TO YOU FOR £20.
YOU CAN PAY ME £20, I'LL LOOK FOR THE OWNER, AND THEN WE SPLIT THE PRIZE MONEY.
HOW ABOUT I DON'T PAY YOU ANYTHING, AND THEN WE SPLIT IT 50/50 IF YOU FIND THE OWNER.
DEAL!
ALEX, WOULD YOU MIND GIVING ME A HAND LOADING UP THE VAN WITH THIS STUFF?
IT'S £30 AN HOUR.
RIGHT. SAFE TRIP BACK TO LONDON.
I DON'T LIKE YOU BUYING GUNS.
I BOUGHT IT FOR YOU, MAGGY.
NOT TO KILL YOU. TO GIVE TO YOU.
I'M NOT HAPPY WITH THIS WHOLE SHEENA SITUATION. I HAVE A FEELING WE HAVEN'T SEEN THE LAST OF HER.
AND I WANT YOU TO BE ABLE TO DEFEND YOURSELF.
MMMM...
CONTAIN-IT
STORAGE LTD

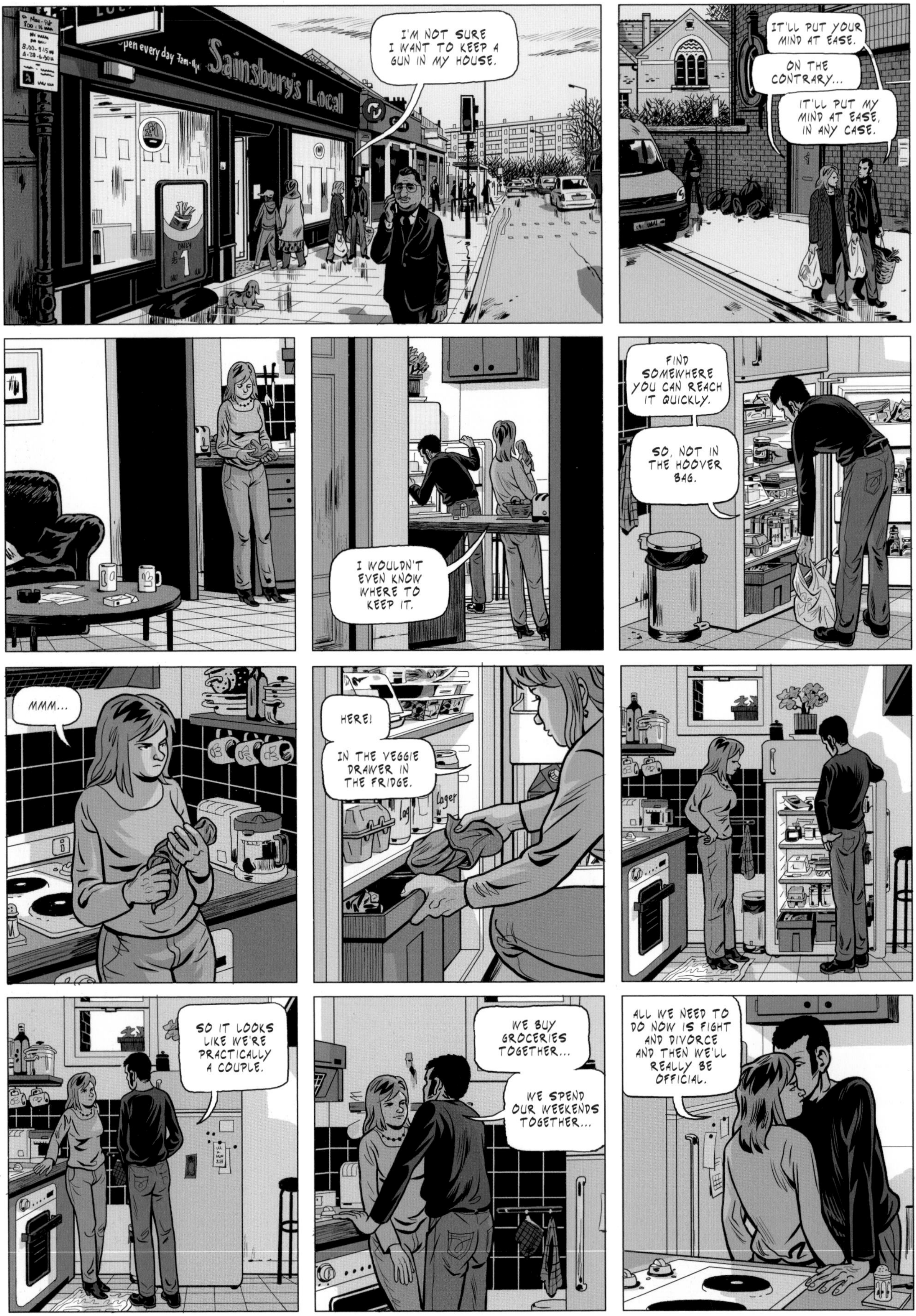
Sainsbury's Local
I'M NOT SURE I WANT TO KEEP A GUN IN MY HOUSE.
IT'LL PUT YOUR MIND AT EASE.
ON THE CONTRARY...
IT'LL PUT MY MIND AT EASE, IN ANY CASE.
I WOULDN'T EVEN KNOW WHERE TO KEEP IT.
FIND SOMEWHERE YOU CAN REACH IT QUICKLY.
SO, NOT IN THE HOOVER BAG.
MMM...
HERE!
IN THE VEGGIE DRAWER IN THE FRIDGE.
SO IT LOOKS LIKE WE'RE PRACTICALLY A COUPLE.
WE BUY GROCERIES TOGETHER...
WE SPEND OUR WEEKENDS TOGETHER...
ALL WE NEED TO DO NOW IS FIGHT AND DIVORCE AND THEN WE'LL REALLY BE OFFICIAL.

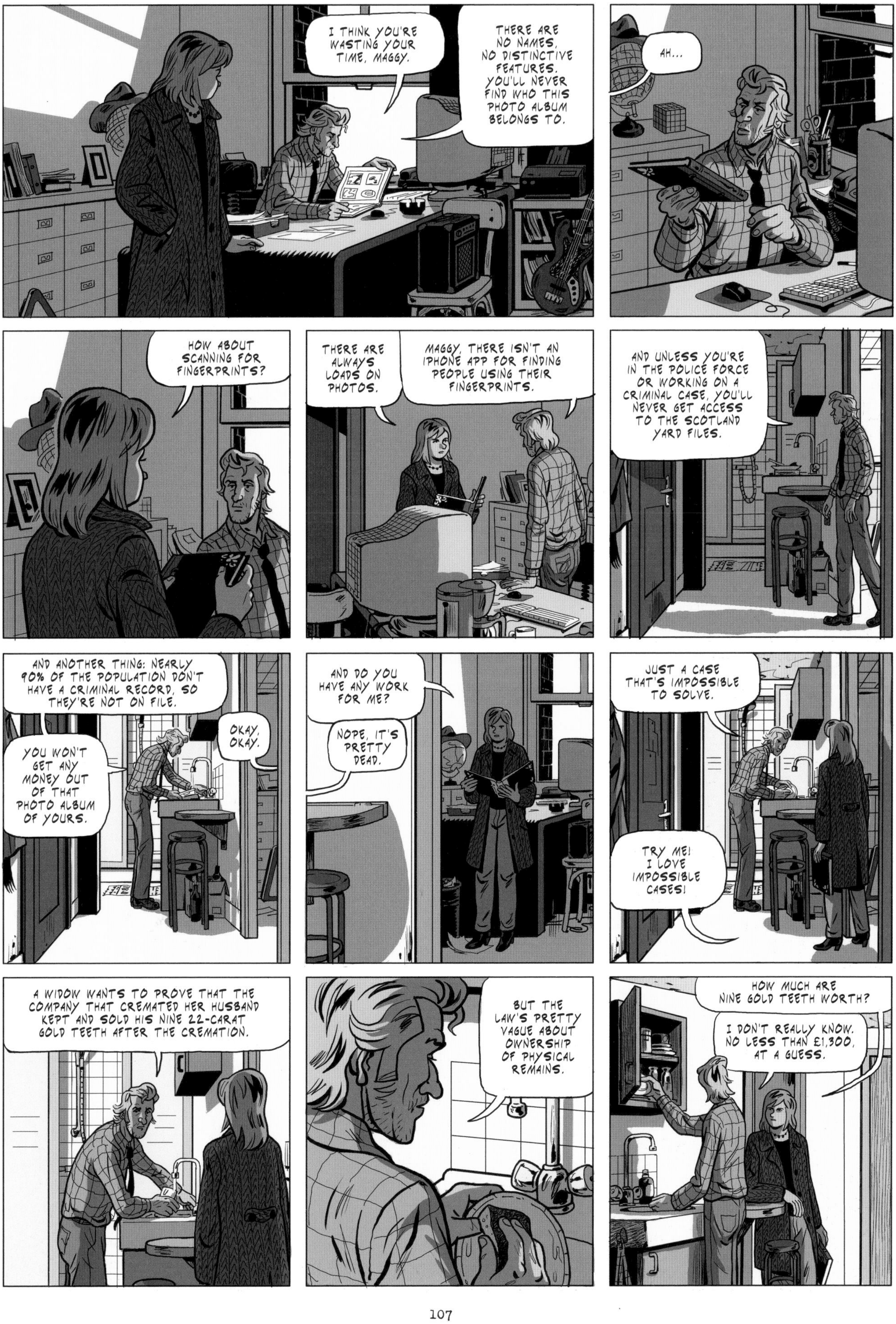
I THINK YOU'RE WASTING YOUR TIME, MAGGY.
THERE ARE NO NAMES, NO DISTINCTIVE FEATURES. YOU'LL NEVER FIND WHO THIS PHOTO ALBUM BELONGS TO.
AH...
HOW ABOUT SCANNING FOR FINGERPRINTS?
THERE ARE ALWAYS LOADS ON PHOTOS.
MAGGY, THERE ISN'T AN IPHONE APP FOR FINDING PEOPLE USING THEIR FINGERPRINTS.
AND UNLESS YOU'RE IN THE POLICE FORCE OR WORKING ON A CRIMINAL CASE, YOU'LL NEVER GET ACCESS TO THE SCOTLAND YARD FILES.
AND ANOTHER THING: NEARLY 90% OF THE POPULATION DON'T HAVE A CRIMINAL RECORD, SO THEY'RE NOT ON FILE.
YOU WON'T GET ANY MONEY OUT OF THAT PHOTO ALBUM OF YOURS.
OKAY, OKAY.
AND DO YOU HAVE ANY WORK FOR ME?
NOPE, IT'S PRETTY DEAD.
JUST A CASE THAT'S IMPOSSIBLE TO SOLVE.
TRY ME! I LOVE IMPOSSIBLE CASES!
A WIDOW WANTS TO PROVE THAT THE COMPANY THAT CREMATED HER HUSBAND KEPT AND SOLD HIS NINE 22-CARAT GOLD TEETH AFTER THE CREMATION.
BUT THE LAW'S PRETTY VAGUE ABOUT OWNERSHIP OF PHYSICAL REMAINS.
HOW MUCH ARE NINE GOLD TEETH WORTH?
I DON'T REALLY KNOW. NO LESS THAN £1,300, AT A GUESS.

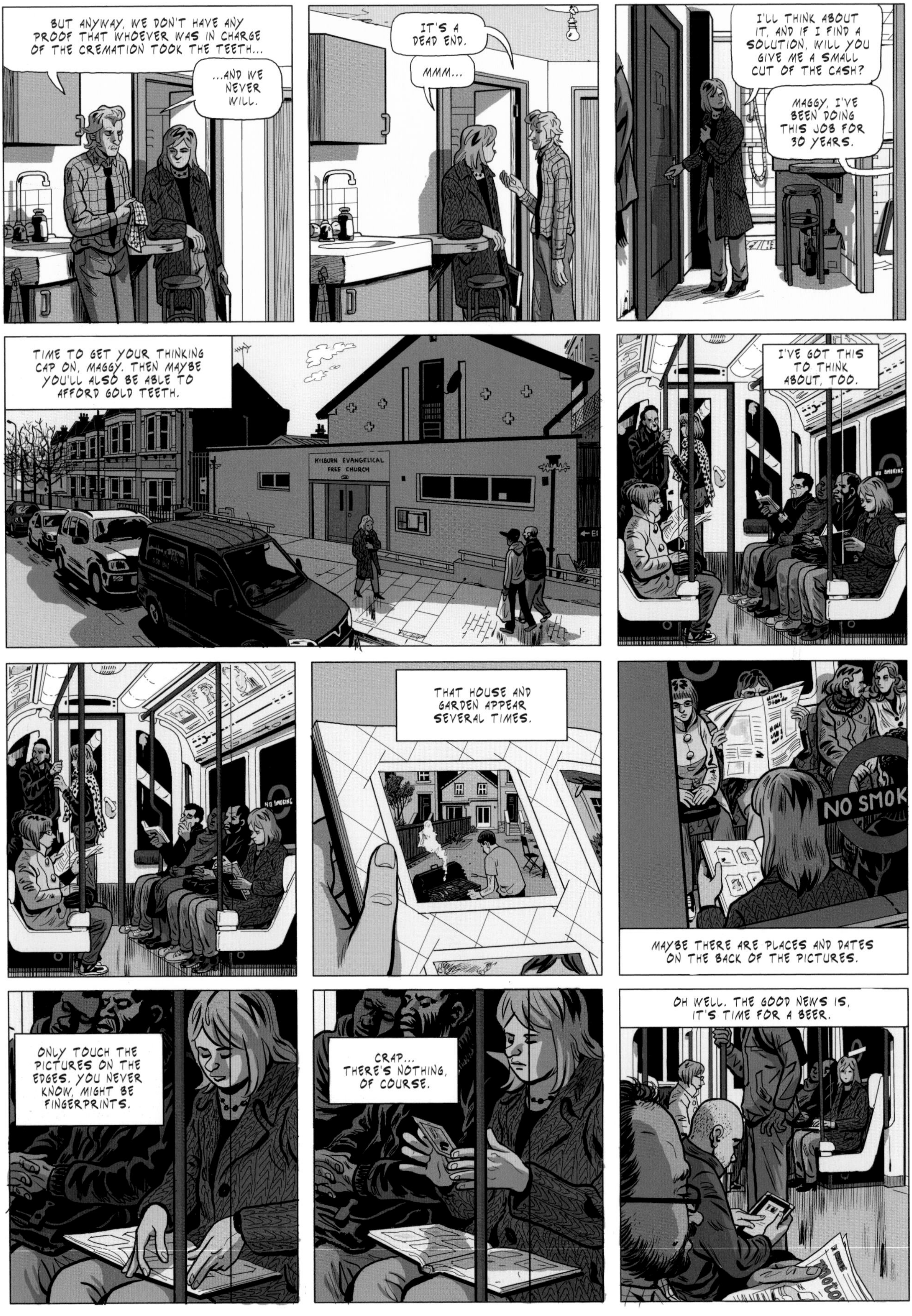
BUT ANYWAY, WE DON'T HAVE ANY PROOF THAT WHOEVER WAS IN CHARGE OF THE CREMATION TOOK THE TEETH...
...AND WE NEVER WILL.
IT'S A DEAD END.
MMM...
I'LL THINK ABOUT IT, AND IF I FIND A SOLUTION, WILL YOU GIVE ME A SMALL CUT OF THE CASH?
MAGGY, I'VE BEEN DOING THIS JOB FOR 30 YEARS.
TIME TO GET YOUR THINKING CAP ON, MAGGY. THEN MAYBE YOU'LL ALSO BE ABLE TO AFFORD GOLD TEETH.
KILBURN EVANGELICAL FREE CHURCH
I'VE GOT THIS TO THINK ABOUT, TOO.
NO SMOKING
THAT HOUSE AND GARDEN APPEAR SEVERAL TIMES.
NO SMOK
MAYBE THERE ARE PLACES AND DATES ON THE BACK OF THE PICTURES.
ONLY TOUCH THE PICTURES ON THE EDGES. YOU NEVER KNOW, MIGHT BE FINGERPRINTS.
CRAP... THERE'S NOTHING, OF COURSE.
OH WELL. THE GOOD NEWS IS, IT'S TIME FOR A BEER.

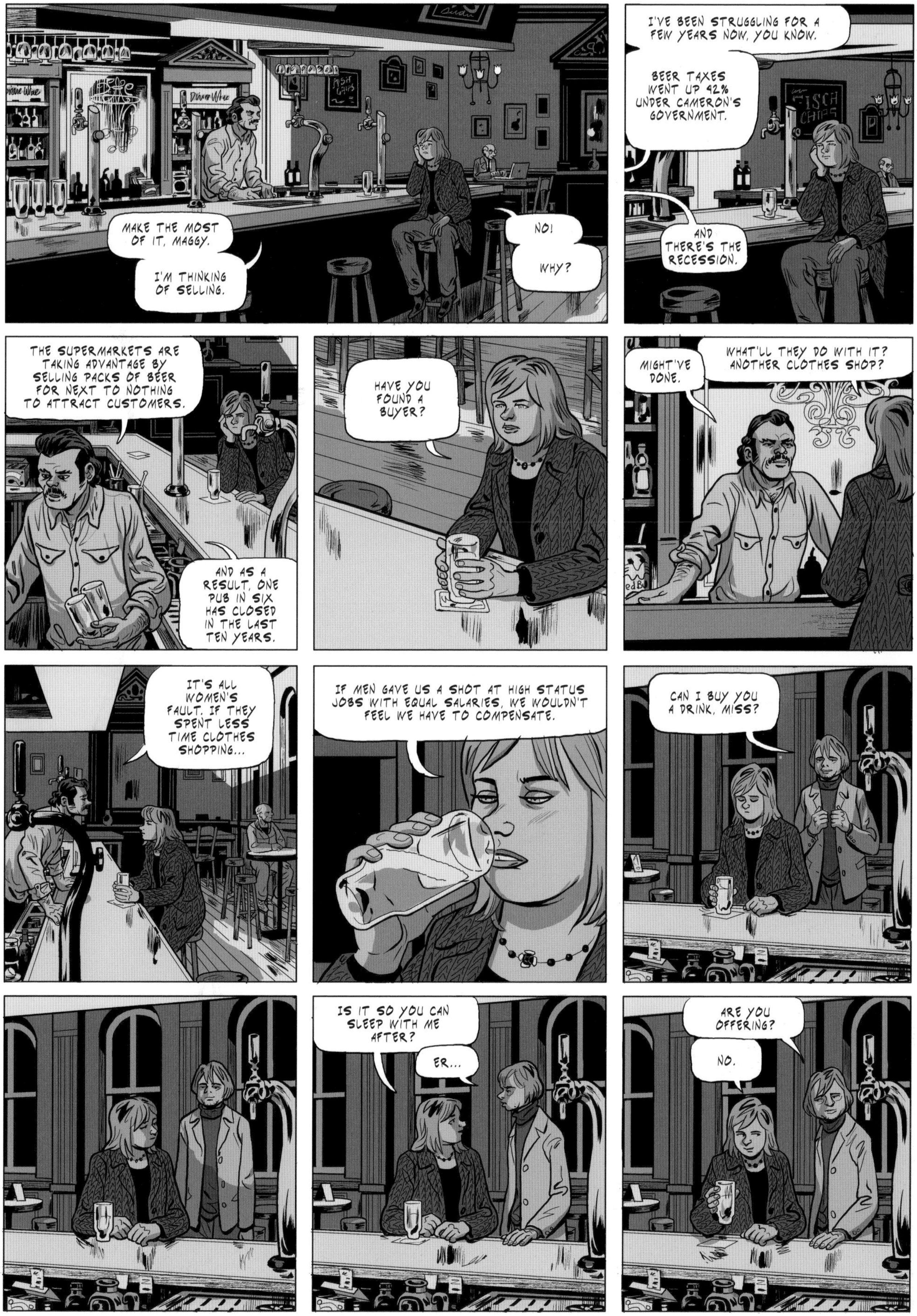
MAKE THE MOST OF IT, MAGGY.
I'M THINKING OF SELLING.
NO!
WHY?
I'VE BEEN STRUGGLING FOR A FEW YEARS NOW, YOU KNOW.
BEER TAXES WENT UP 42% UNDER CAMERON'S GOVERNMENT.
AND THERE'S THE RECESSION.
THE SUPERMARKETS ARE TAKING ADVANTAGE BY SELLING PACKS OF BEER FOR NEXT TO NOTHING TO ATTRACT CUSTOMERS.
AND AS A RESULT, ONE PUB IN SIX HAS CLOSED IN THE LAST TEN YEARS.
HAVE YOU FOUND A BUYER?
MIGHT'VE DONE.
WHAT'LL THEY DO WITH IT? ANOTHER CLOTHES SHOP?
IT'S ALL WOMEN'S FAULT. IF THEY SPENT LESS TIME CLOTHES SHOPPING...
IF MEN GAVE US A SHOT AT HIGH STATUS JOBS WITH EQUAL SALARIES, WE WOULDN'T FEEL WE HAVE TO COMPENSATE.
CAN I BUY YOU A DRINK, MISS?
IS IT SO YOU CAN SLEEP WITH ME AFTER?
ER...
ARE YOU OFFERING?
NO.

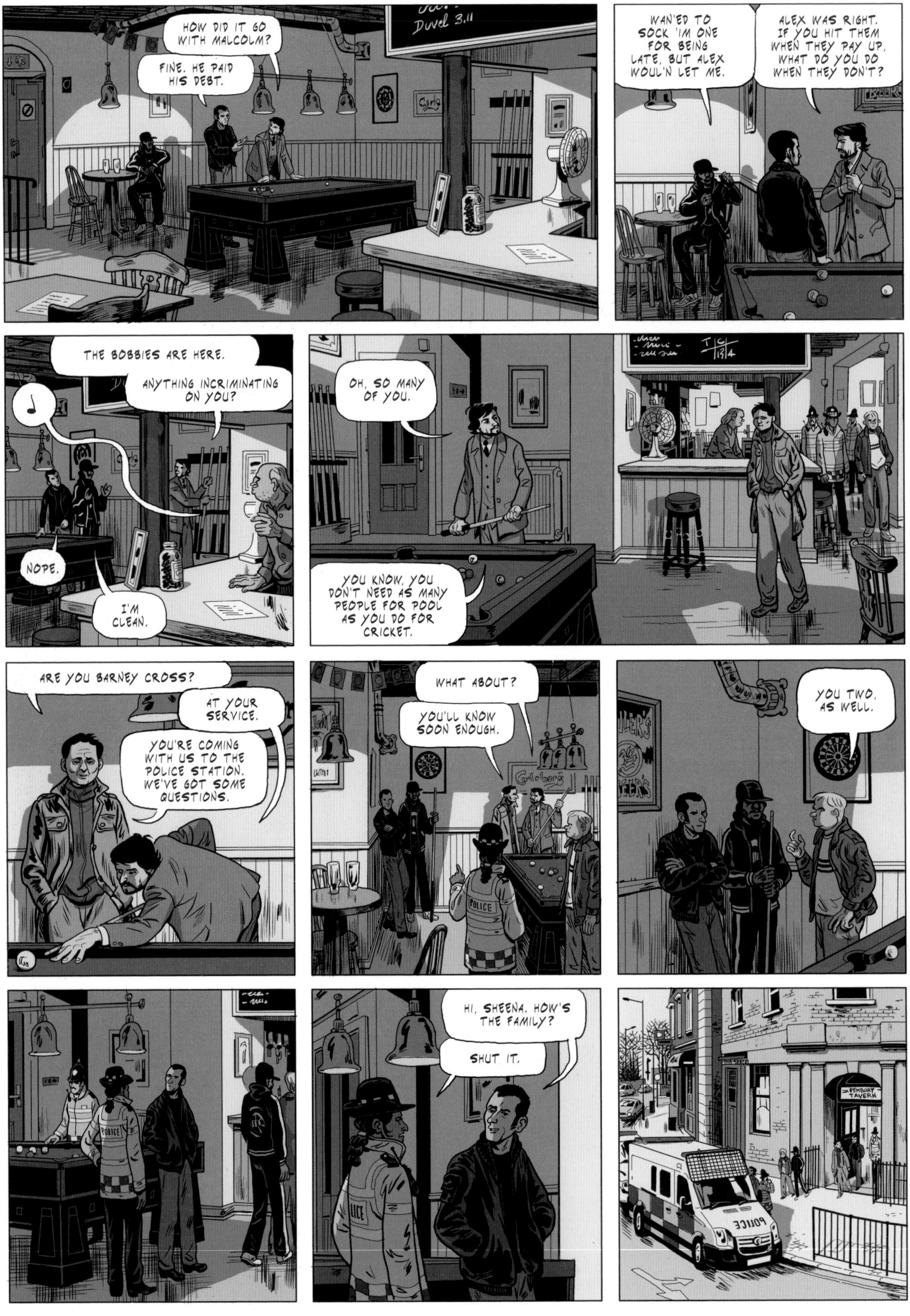

Duvel 3.11
HOW DID IT GO WITH MALCOLM?
FINE. HE PAID HIS DEBT.
WAN'ED TO SOCK 'IM ONE FOR BEING LATE, BUT ALEX WOUL'N LET ME.
ALEX WAS RIGHT. IF YOU HIT THEM WHEN THEY PAY UP, WHAT DO YOU DO WHEN THEY DON'T?
THE BOBBIES ARE HERE.
ANYTHING INCRIMINATING ON YOU?
NOPE.
I'M CLEAN.
OH, SO MANY OF YOU.
YOU KNOW, YOU DON'T NEED AS MANY PEOPLE FOR POOL AS YOU DO FOR CRICKET.
ARE YOU BARNEY CROSS?
AT YOUR SERVICE.
YOU'RE COMING WITH US TO THE POLICE STATION. WE'VE GOT SOME QUESTIONS.
WHAT ABOUT?
YOU'LL KNOW SOON ENOUGH.
POLICE
YOU TWO, AS WELL.
POLICE
HI, SHEENA. HOW'S THE FAMILY?
SHUT IT.
TAVERN
POLICE

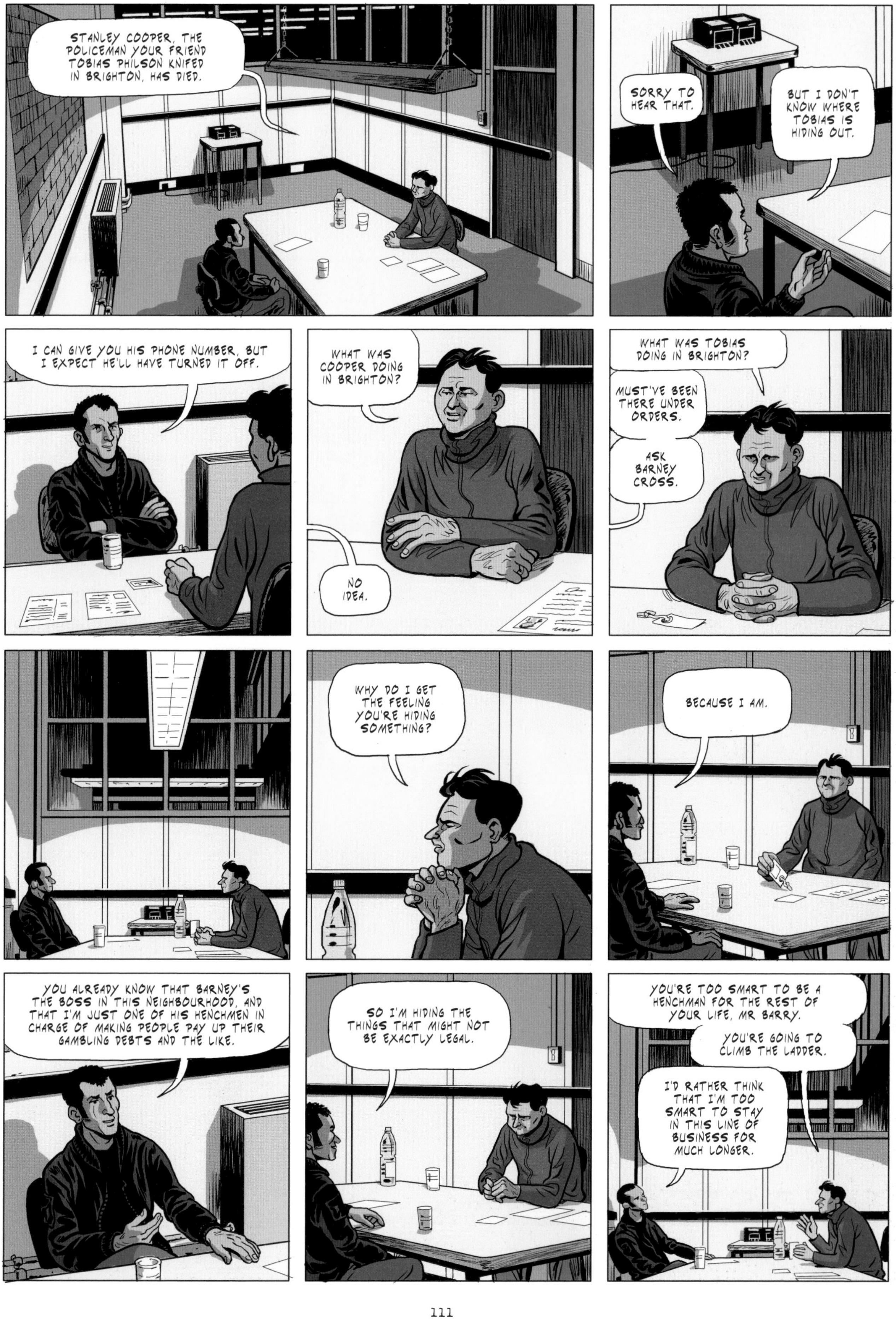
STANLEY COOPER, THE POLICEMAN YOUR FRIEND TOBIAS PHILSON KNIFED IN BRIGHTON, HAS DIED.
SORRY TO HEAR THAT.
BUT I DON'T KNOW WHERE TOBIAS IS HIDING OUT.
I CAN GIVE YOU HIS PHONE NUMBER, BUT I EXPECT HE'LL HAVE TURNED IT OFF.
WHAT WAS COOPER DOING IN BRIGHTON?
NO IDEA.
WHAT WAS TOBIAS DOING IN BRIGHTON?
MUST'VE BEEN THERE UNDER ORDERS.
ASK BARNEY CROSS.
WHY DO I GET THE FEELING YOU'RE HIDING SOMETHING?
BECAUSE I AM.
YOU ALREADY KNOW THAT BARNEY'S THE BOSS IN THIS NEIGHBOURHOOD, AND THAT I'M JUST ONE OF HIS HENCHMEN IN CHARGE OF MAKING PEOPLE PAY UP THEIR GAMBLING DEBTS AND THE LIKE.
SO I'M HIDING THE THINGS THAT MIGHT NOT BE EXACTLY LEGAL.
YOU'RE TOO SMART TO BE A HENCHMAN FOR THE REST OF YOUR LIFE, MR BARRY.
YOU'RE GOING TO CLIMB THE LADDER.
I'D RATHER THINK THAT I'M TOO SMART TO STAY IN THIS LINE OF BUSINESS FOR MUCH LONGER.

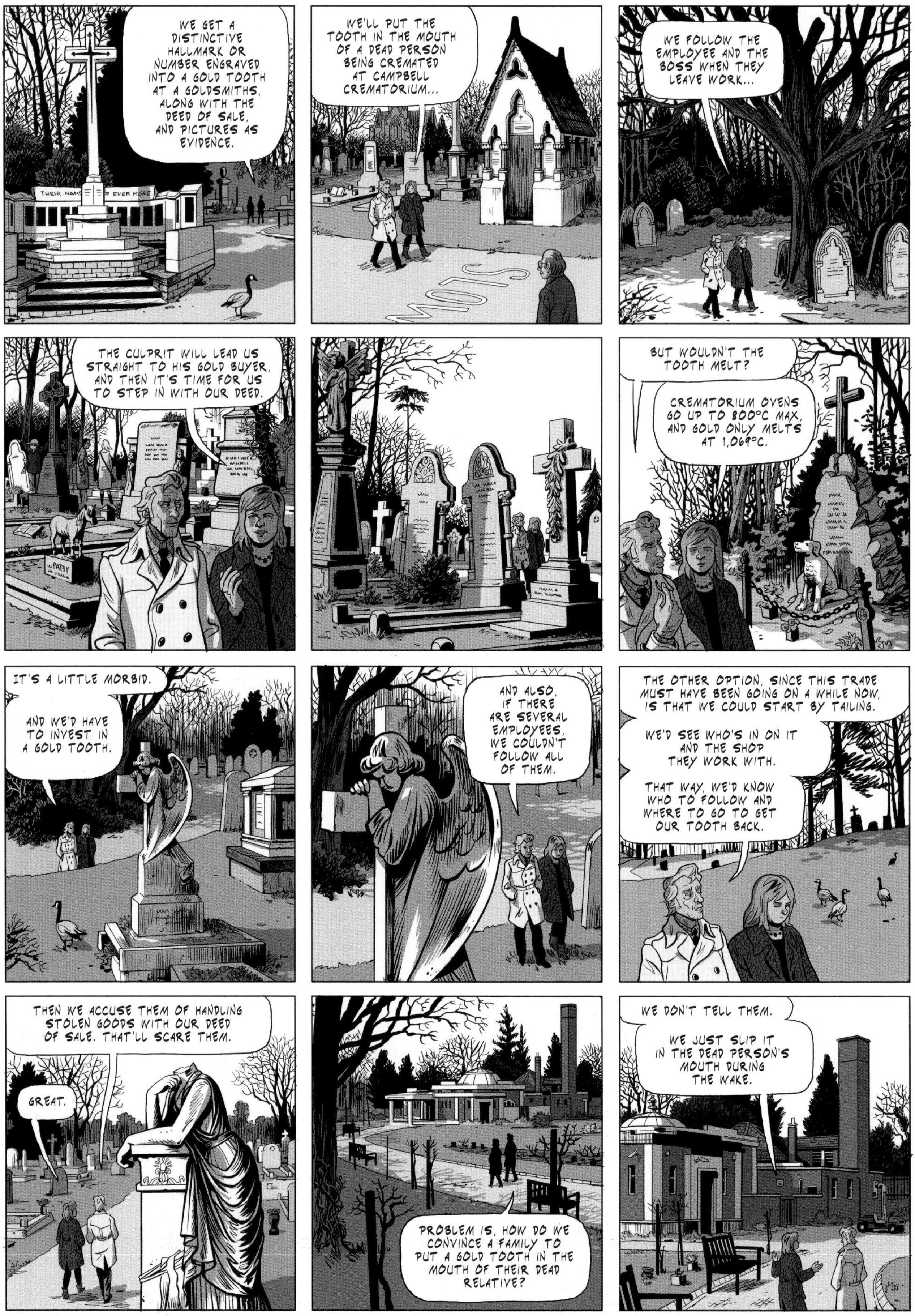
WE GET A DISTINCTIVE HALLMARK OR NUMBER ENGRAVED INTO A GOLD TOOTH AT A GOLDSMITHS, ALONG WITH THE DEED OF SALE, AND PICTURES AS EVIDENCE.
WE'LL PUT THE TOOTH IN THE MOUTH OF A DEAD PERSON BEING CREMATED AT CAMPBELL CREMATORIUM...
SLOW
WE FOLLOW THE EMPLOYEE AND THE BOSS WHEN THEY LEAVE WORK...
THE CULPRIT WILL LEAD US STRAIGHT TO HIS GOLD BUYER, AND THEN IT'S TIME FOR US TO STEP IN WITH OUR DEED.
PATSY
BUT WOULDN'T THE TOOTH MELT?
CREMATORIUM OVENS GO UP TO 800°C MAX, AND GOLD ONLY MELTS AT 1,069°C.
IT'S A LITTLE MORBID.
AND WE'D HAVE TO INVEST IN A GOLD TOOTH.
AND ALSO, IF THERE ARE SEVERAL EMPLOYEES, WE COULDN'T FOLLOW ALL OF THEM.
THE OTHER OPTION, SINCE THIS TRADE MUST HAVE BEEN GOING ON A WHILE NOW, IS THAT WE COULD START BY TAILING.
WE'D SEE WHO'S IN ON IT AND THE SHOP THEY WORK WITH.
THAT WAY, WE'D KNOW WHO TO FOLLOW AND WHERE TO GO TO GET OUR TOOTH BACK.
THEN WE ACCUSE THEM OF HANDLING STOLEN GOODS WITH OUR DEED OF SALE. THAT'LL SCARE THEM.
GREAT.
PROBLEM IS, HOW DO WE CONVINCE A FAMILY TO PUT A GOLD TOOTH IN THE MOUTH OF THEIR DEAD RELATIVE?
WE DON'T TELL THEM.
WE JUST SLIP IT IN THE DEAD PERSON'S MOUTH DURING THE WAKE.

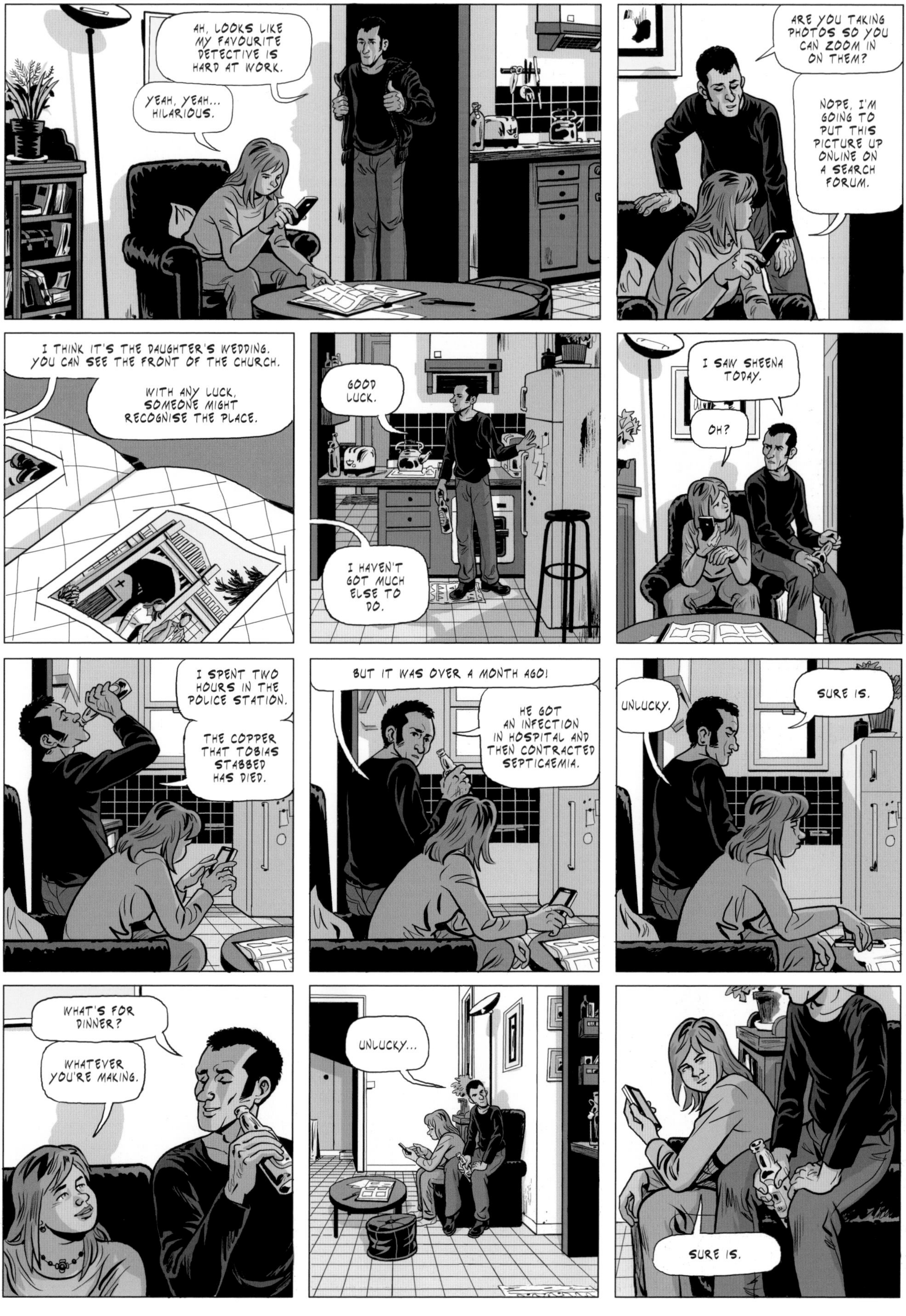
AH, LOOKS LIKE MY FAVOURITE DETECTIVE IS HARD AT WORK.
YEAH, YEAH... HILARIOUS.
ARE YOU TAKING PHOTOS SO YOU CAN ZOOM IN ON THEM?
NOPE, I'M GOING TO PUT THIS PICTURE UP ONLINE ON A SEARCH FORUM.
I THINK IT'S THE DAUGHTER'S WEDDING. YOU CAN SEE THE FRONT OF THE CHURCH.
WITH ANY LUCK, SOMEONE MIGHT RECOGNISE THE PLACE.
GOOD LUCK.
I HAVEN'T GOT MUCH ELSE TO DO.
I SAW SHEENA TODAY.
OH?
I SPENT TWO HOURS IN THE POLICE STATION.
THE COPPER THAT TOBIAS STABBED HAS DIED.
BUT IT WAS OVER A MONTH AGO!
HE GOT AN INFECTION IN HOSPITAL AND THEN CONTRACTED SEPTICAEMIA.
UNLUCKY.
SURE IS.
WHAT'S FOR DINNER?
WHATEVER YOU'RE MAKING.
UNLUCKY...
SURE IS.

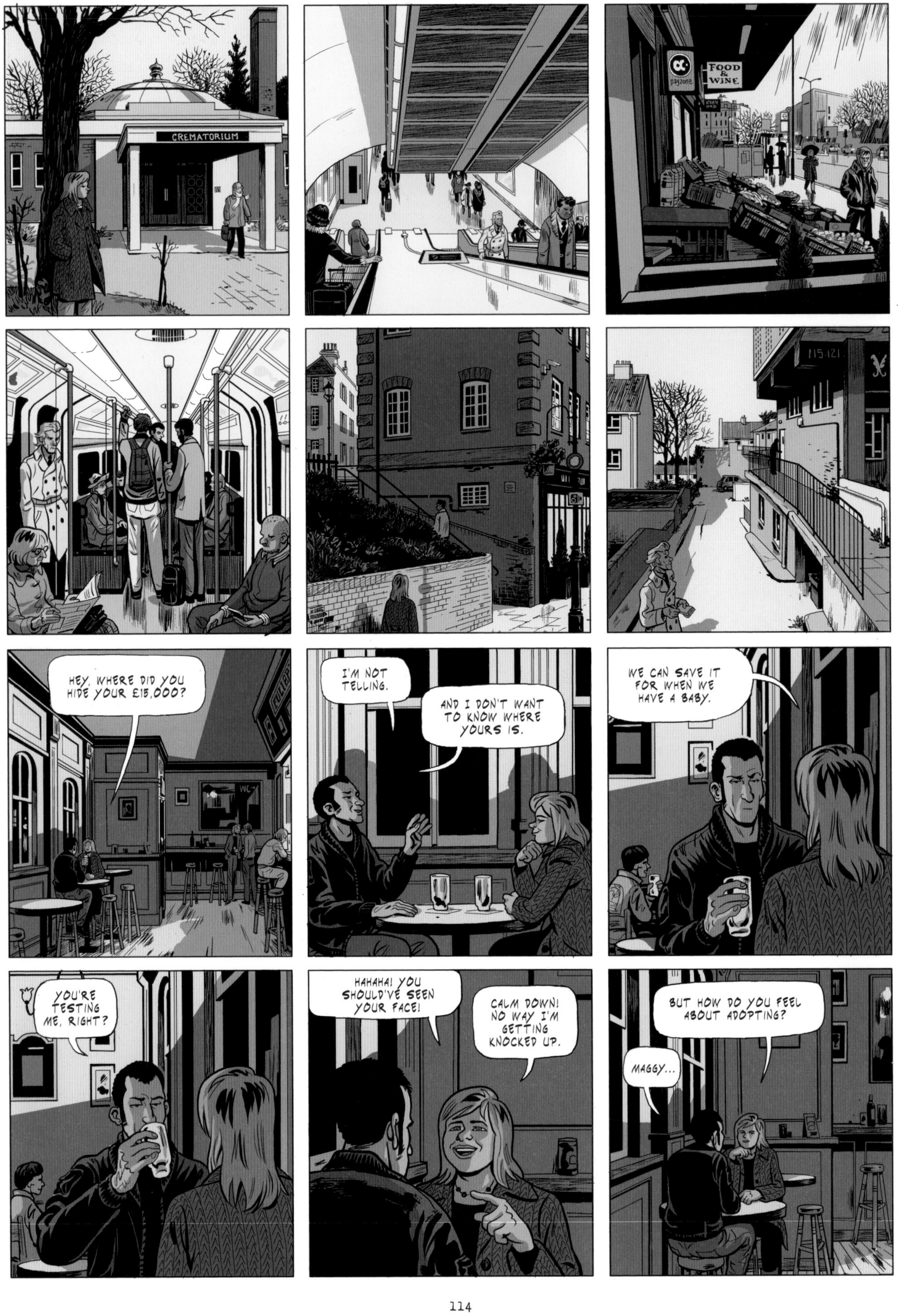
CREMATORIUM
payzone
FOOD & WINE
HEY, WHERE DID YOU HIDE YOUR £15,000?
I'M NOT TELLING.
AND I DON'T WANT TO KNOW WHERE YOURS IS.
WE CAN SAVE IT FOR WHEN WE HAVE A BABY.
YOU'RE TESTING ME, RIGHT?
HAHAHA! YOU SHOULD'VE SEEN YOUR FACE!
CALM DOWN! NO WAY I'M GETTING KNOCKED UP.
BUT HOW DO YOU FEEL ABOUT ADOPTING?
MAGGY...

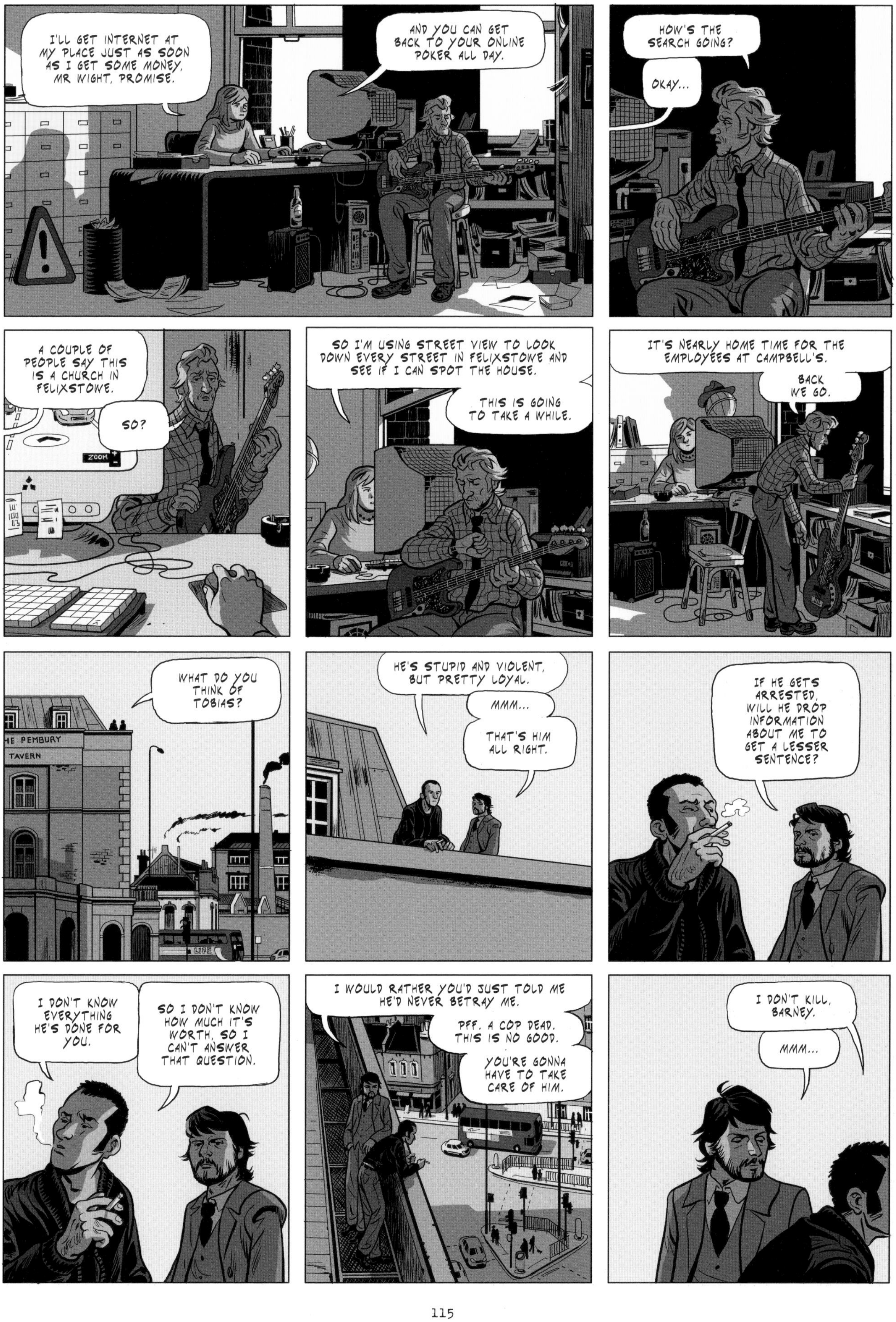
I'LL GET INTERNET AT MY PLACE JUST AS SOON AS I GET SOME MONEY, MR WIGHT, PROMISE.
AND YOU CAN GET BACK TO YOUR ONLINE POKER ALL DAY.
HOW'S THE SEARCH GOING?
OKAY...
A COUPLE OF PEOPLE SAY THIS IS A CHURCH IN FELIXSTOWE.
SO?
ZOOM
SO I'M USING STREET VIEW TO LOOK DOWN EVERY STREET IN FELIXSTOWE AND SEE IF I CAN SPOT THE HOUSE.
THIS IS GOING TO TAKE A WHILE.
IT'S NEARLY HOME TIME FOR THE EMPLOYEES AT CAMPBELL'S.
BACK WE GO.
WHAT DO YOU THINK OF TOBIAS?
HE PEMBURY
TAVERN
HE'S STUPID AND VIOLENT, BUT PRETTY LOYAL.
MMM...
THAT'S HIM ALL RIGHT.
IF HE GETS ARRESTED, WILL HE DROP INFORMATION ABOUT ME TO GET A LESSER SENTENCE?
I DON'T KNOW EVERYTHING HE'S DONE FOR YOU.
SO I DON'T KNOW HOW MUCH IT'S WORTH, SO I CAN'T ANSWER THAT QUESTION.
I WOULD RATHER YOU'D JUST TOLD ME HE'D NEVER BETRAY ME.
PFF. A COP DEAD. THIS IS NO GOOD.
YOU'RE GONNA HAVE TO TAKE CARE OF HIM.
I DON'T KILL, BARNEY.
MMM...

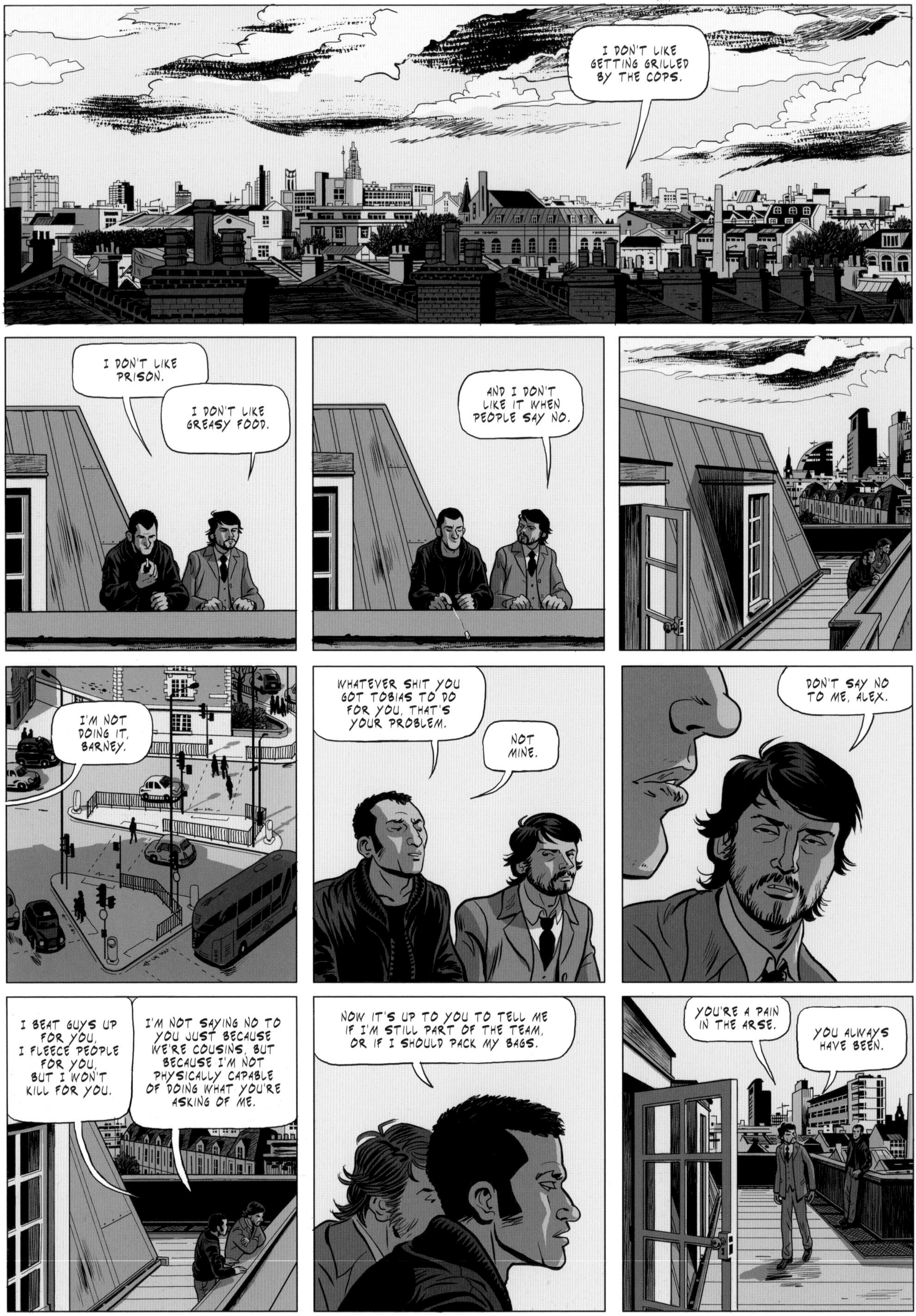
I DON'T LIKE GETTING GRILLED BY THE COPS.
I DON'T LIKE PRISON.
I DON'T LIKE GREASY FOOD.
AND I DON'T LIKE IT WHEN PEOPLE SAY NO.
I'M NOT DOING IT, BARNEY.
WHATEVER SHIT YOU GOT TOBIAS TO DO FOR YOU, THAT'S YOUR PROBLEM.
NOT MINE.
DON'T SAY NO TO ME, ALEX.
I BEAT GUYS UP FOR YOU, I FLEECE PEOPLE FOR YOU, BUT I WON'T KILL FOR YOU.
I'M NOT SAYING NO TO YOU JUST BECAUSE WE'RE COUSINS, BUT BECAUSE I'M NOT PHYSICALLY CAPABLE OF DOING WHAT YOU'RE ASKING OF ME.
NOW IT'S UP TO YOU TO TELL ME IF I'M STILL PART OF THE TEAM, OR IF I SHOULD PACK MY BAGS.
YOU'RE A PAIN IN THE ARSE.
YOU ALWAYS HAVE BEEN.

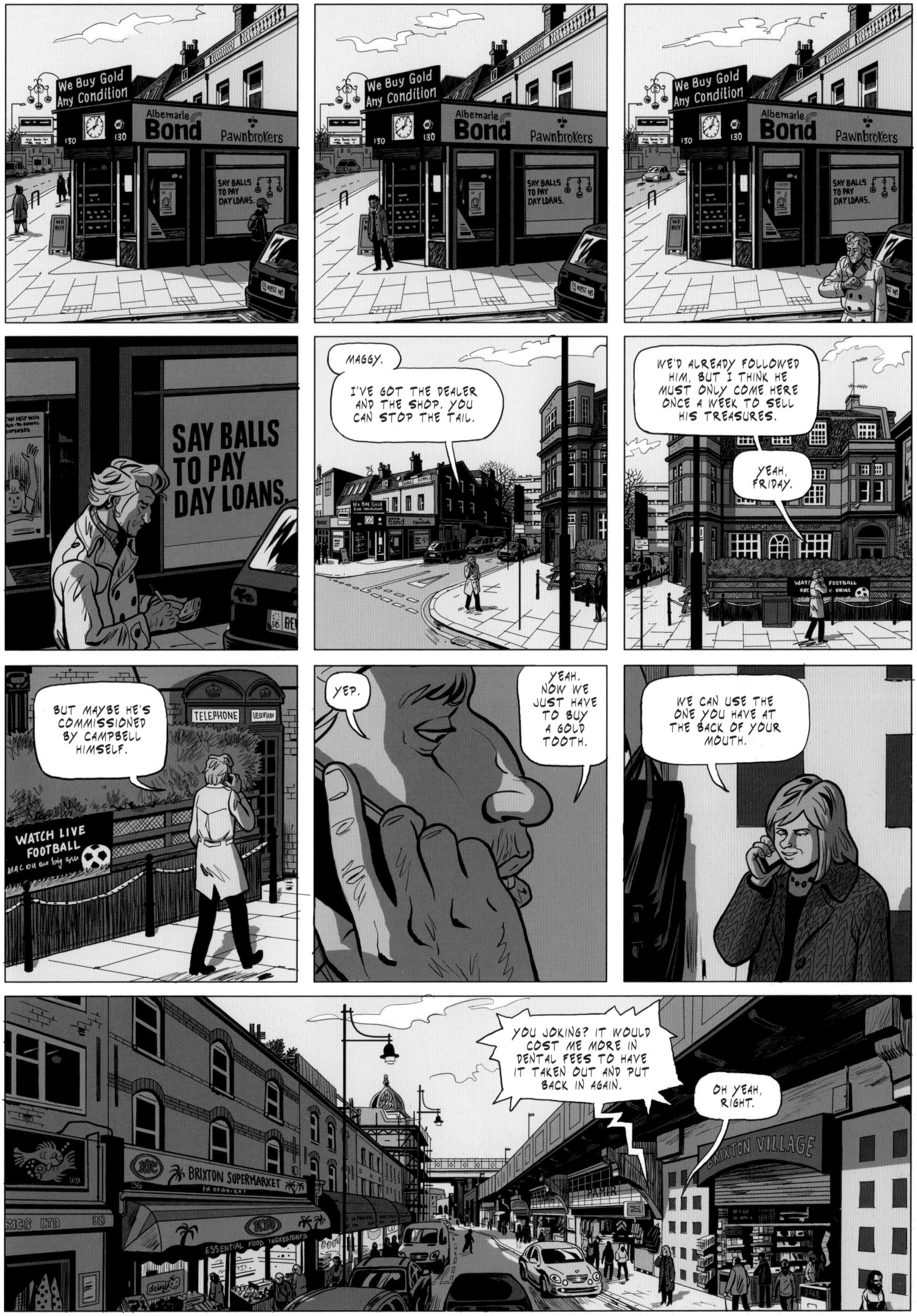
We Buy Gold
Any Condition
Albemarle Bond
Pawnbrokers
130
SAY BALLS TO PAY DAY LOANS.
We Buy Gold
Any Condition
Albemarle Bond
Pawnbrokers
130
SAY BALLS TO PAY DAY LOANS.
We Buy Gold
Any Condition
Albemarle Bond
Pawnbrokers
130
SAY BALLS TO PAY DAY LOANS.
SAY BALLS TO PAY DAY LOANS.
MAGGY.
I'VE GOT THE DEALER AND THE SHOP. YOU CAN STOP THE TAIL.
WE'D ALREADY FOLLOWED HIM, BUT I THINK HE MUST ONLY COME HERE ONCE A WEEK TO SELL HIS TREASURES.
YEAH, FRIDAY.
BUT MAYBE HE'S COMMISSIONED BY CAMPBELL HIMSELF.
TELEPHONE
WATCH LIVE FOOTBALL
YEP.
YEAH. NOW WE JUST HAVE TO BUY A GOLD TOOTH.
WE CAN USE THE ONE YOU HAVE AT THE BACK OF YOUR MOUTH.
YOU JOKING? IT WOULD COST ME MORE IN DENTAL FEES TO HAVE IT TAKEN OUT AND PUT BACK IN AGAIN.
OH YEAH, RIGHT.
BRIXTON SUPERMARKET
ESSENTIAL FOOD INGREDIENTS
BRIXTON VILLAGE

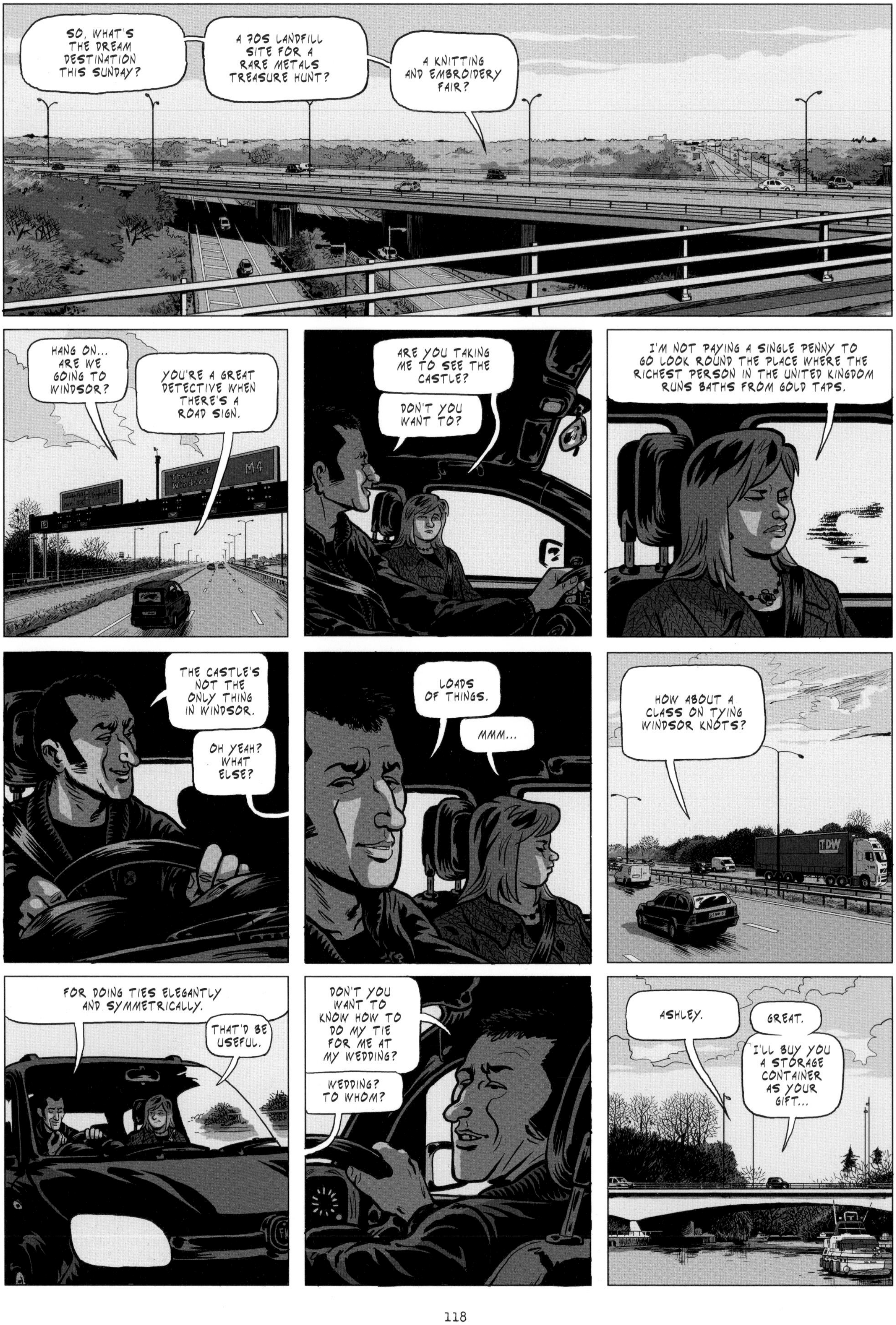
SO, WHAT'S THE DREAM DESTINATION THIS SUNDAY?
A 70S LANDFILL SITE FOR A RARE METALS TREASURE HUNT?
A KNITTING AND EMBROIDERY FAIR?
HANG ON... ARE WE GOING TO WINDSOR?
YOU'RE A GREAT DETECTIVE WHEN THERE'S A ROAD SIGN.
M4
ARE YOU TAKING ME TO SEE THE CASTLE?
DON'T YOU WANT TO?
I'M NOT PAYING A SINGLE PENNY TO GO LOOK ROUND THE PLACE WHERE THE RICHEST PERSON IN THE UNITED KINGDOM RUNS BATHS FROM GOLD TAPS.
THE CASTLE'S NOT THE ONLY THING IN WINDSOR.
OH YEAH? WHAT ELSE?
LOADS OF THINGS.
MMM...
HOW ABOUT A CLASS ON TYING WINDSOR KNOTS?
TDW
FOR DOING TIES ELEGANTLY AND SYMMETRICALLY.
THAT'D BE USEFUL.
DON'T YOU WANT TO KNOW HOW TO DO MY TIE FOR ME AT MY WEDDING?
WEDDING? TO WHOM?
ASHLEY.
GREAT.
I'LL BUY YOU A STORAGE CONTAINER AS YOUR GIFT...

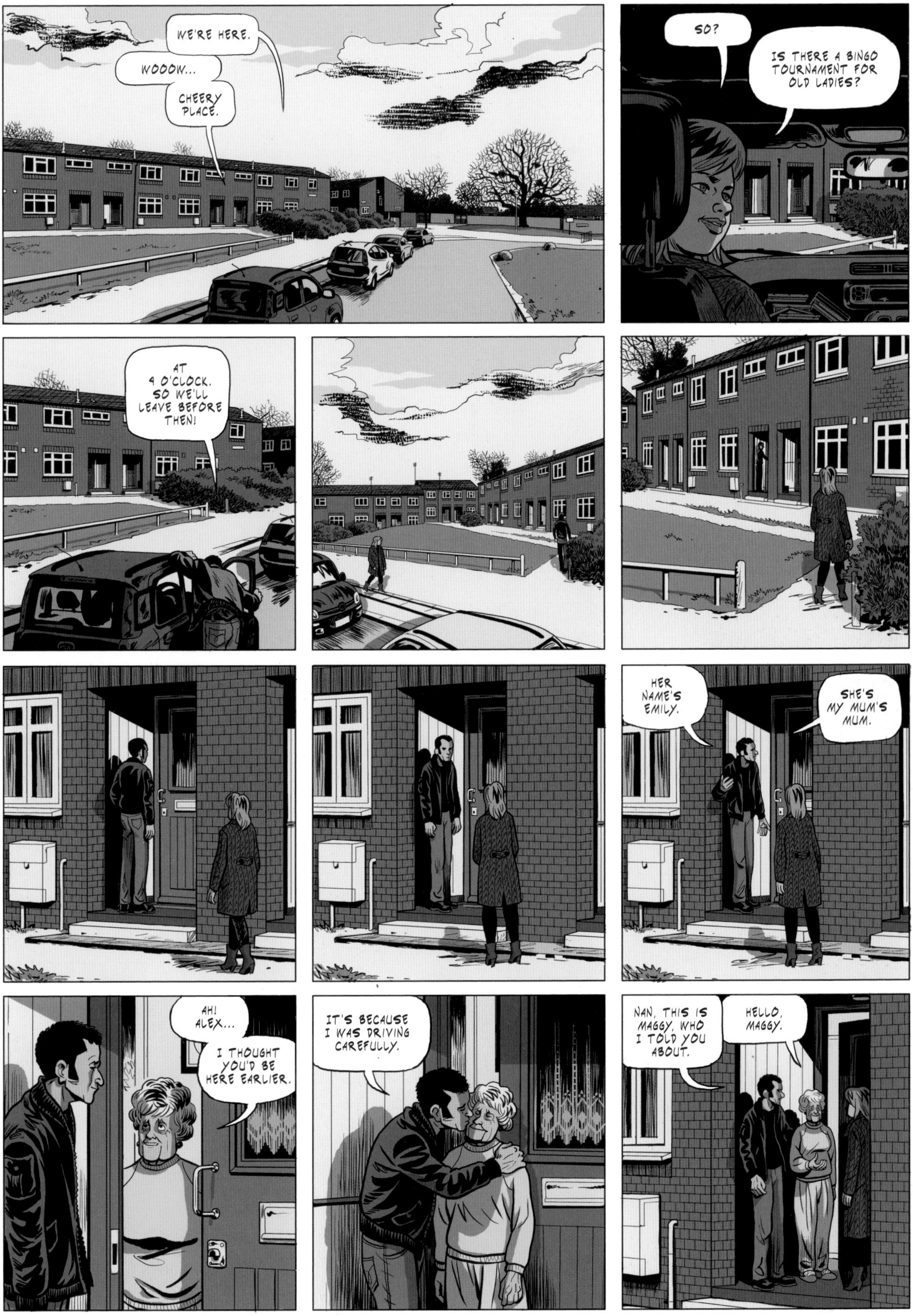
WE'RE HERE.
WOOOW...
CHEERY PLACE.
SO?
IS THERE A BINGO TOURNAMENT FOR OLD LADIES?
AT 4 O'CLOCK. SO WE'LL LEAVE BEFORE THEN!
HER NAME'S EMILY.
SHE'S MY MUM'S MUM.
AH! ALEX...
I THOUGHT YOU'D BE HERE EARLIER.
IT'S BECAUSE I WAS DRIVING CAREFULLY.
NAN, THIS IS MAGGY, WHO I TOLD YOU ABOUT.
HELLO, MAGGY.

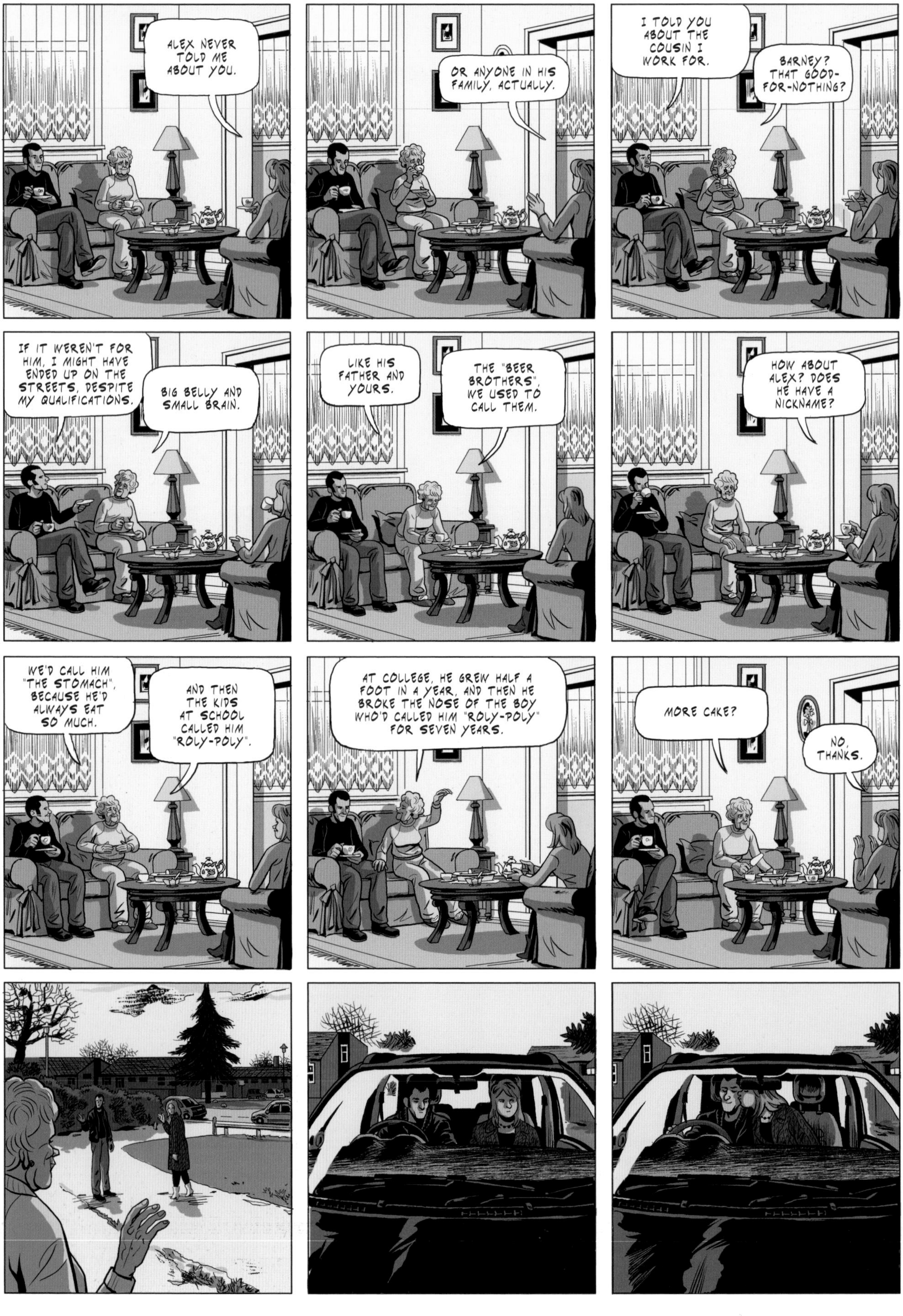
ALEX NEVER TOLD ME ABOUT YOU.
OR ANYONE IN HIS FAMILY, ACTUALLY.
I TOLD YOU ABOUT THE COUSIN I WORK FOR.
BARNEY? THAT GOOD-FOR-NOTHING?
IF IT WEREN'T FOR HIM, I MIGHT HAVE ENDED UP ON THE STREETS, DESPITE MY QUALIFICATIONS.
BIG BELLY AND SMALL BRAIN.
LIKE HIS FATHER AND YOURS.
THE "BEER BROTHERS", WE USED TO CALL THEM.
HOW ABOUT ALEX? DOES HE HAVE A NICKNAME?
WE'D CALL HIM "THE STOMACH", BECAUSE HE'D ALWAYS EAT SO MUCH.
AND THEN THE KIDS AT SCHOOL CALLED HIM "ROLY-POLY".
AT COLLEGE, HE GREW HALF A FOOT IN A YEAR, AND THEN HE BROKE THE NOSE OF THE BOY WHO'D CALLED HIM "ROLY-POLY" FOR SEVEN YEARS.
MORE CAKE?
NO, THANKS.

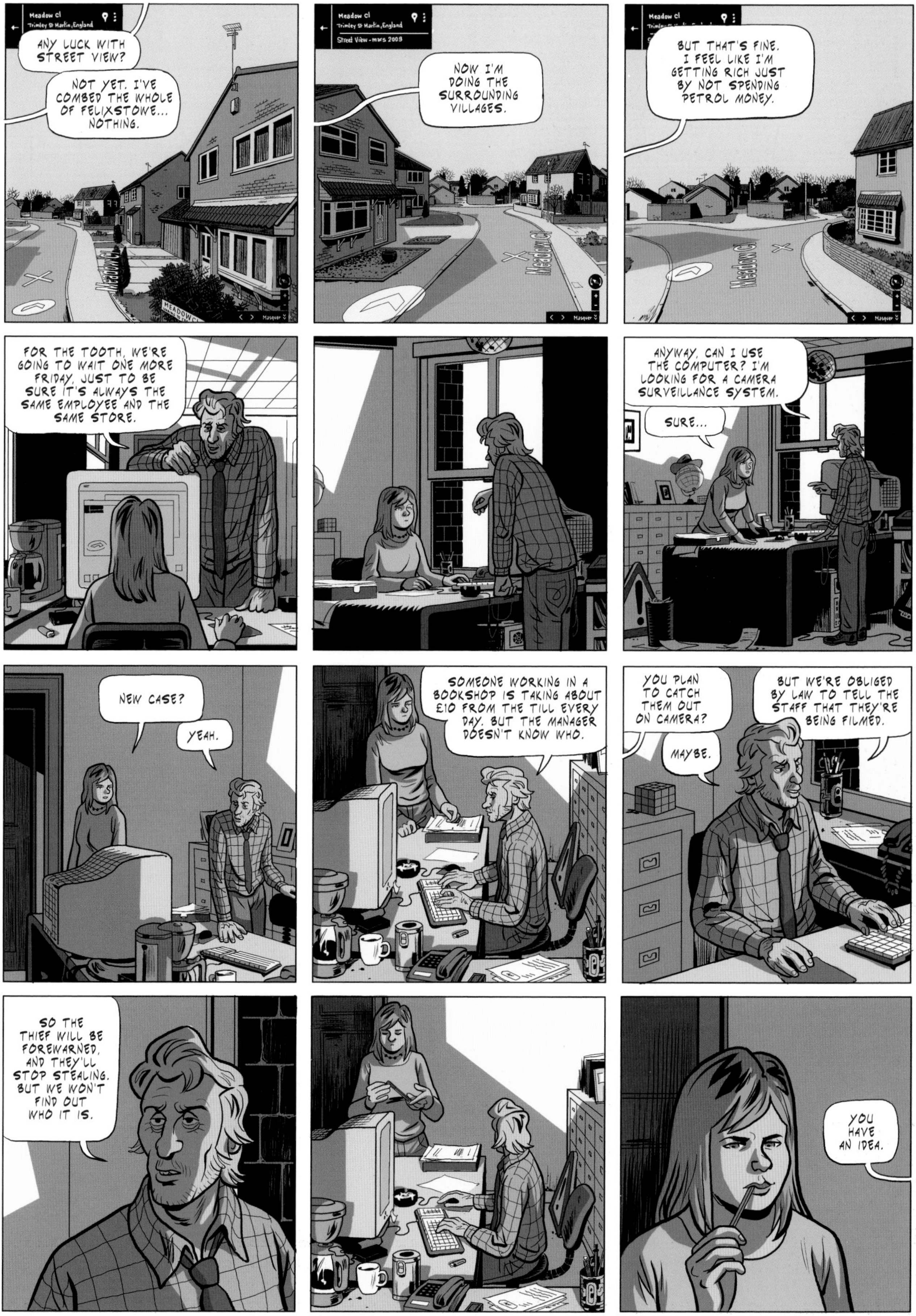
Meadow Cl
Trimley St Martin, England
ANY LUCK WITH STREET VIEW?
NOT YET. I'VE COMBED THE WHOLE OF FELIXSTOWE... NOTHING.
Meadow Cl
Masquer
Meadow Cl
Trimley St Martin, England
Street View - mars 2009
NOW I'M DOING THE SURROUNDING VILLAGES.
Meadow Cl
Masquer
Meadow Cl
BUT THAT'S FINE. I FEEL LIKE I'M GETTING RICH JUST BY NOT SPENDING PETROL MONEY.
Meadow Cl
Masquer
FOR THE TOOTH, WE'RE GOING TO WAIT ONE MORE FRIDAY, JUST TO BE SURE IT'S ALWAYS THE SAME EMPLOYEE AND THE SAME STORE.
ANYWAY, CAN I USE THE COMPUTER? I'M LOOKING FOR A CAMERA SURVEILLANCE SYSTEM.
SURE...
NEW CASE?
YEAH.
SOMEONE WORKING IN A BOOKSHOP IS TAKING ABOUT £10 FROM THE TILL EVERY DAY. BUT THE MANAGER DOESN'T KNOW WHO.
YOU PLAN TO CATCH THEM OUT ON CAMERA?
MAYBE.
BUT WE'RE OBLIGED BY LAW TO TELL THE STAFF THAT THEY'RE BEING FILMED.
SO THE THIEF WILL BE FOREWARNED, AND THEY'LL STOP STEALING. BUT WE WON'T FIND OUT WHO IT IS.
YOU HAVE AN IDEA.

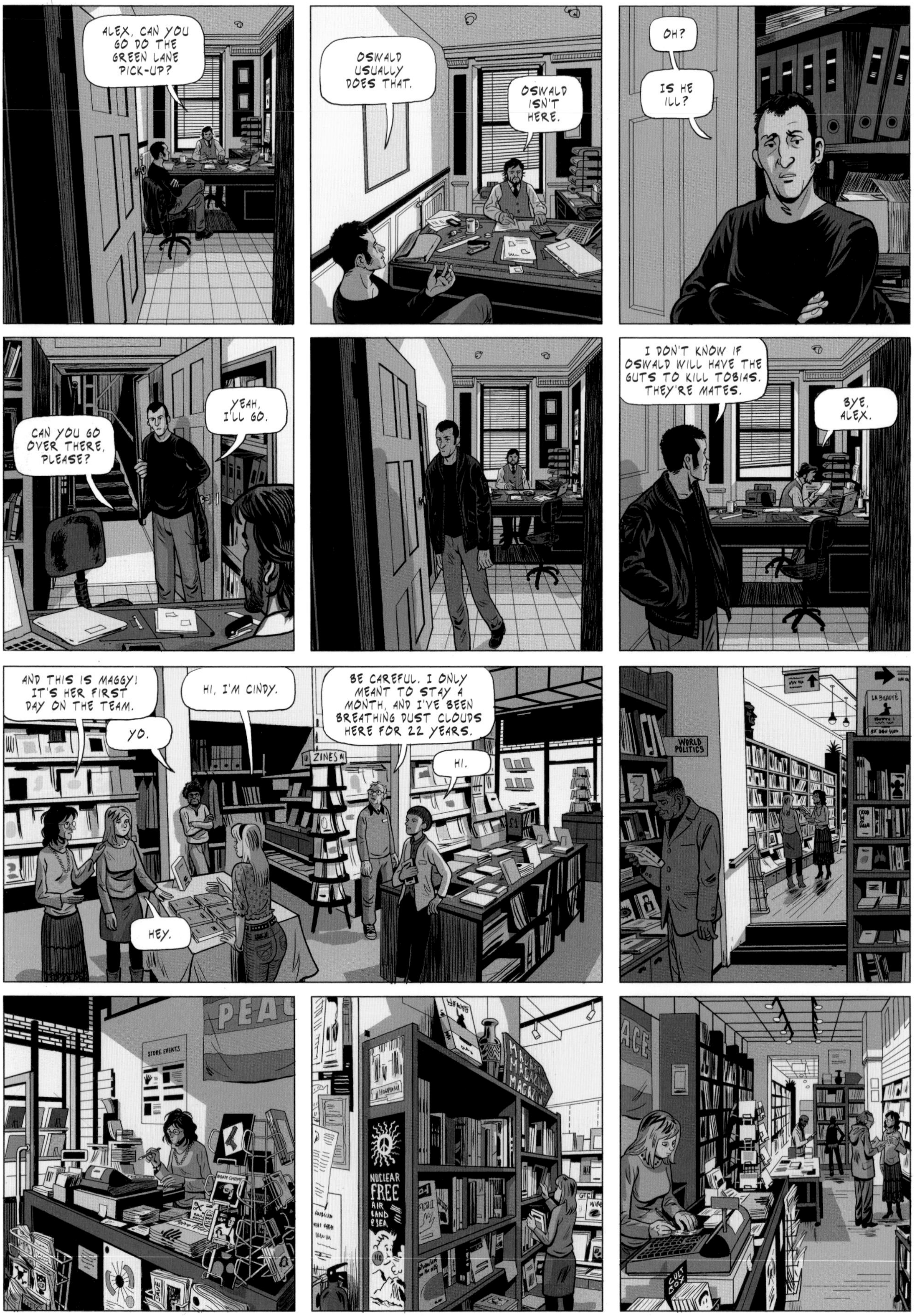
ALEX, CAN YOU GO DO THE GREEN LANE PICK-UP?
OSWALD USUALLY DOES THAT.
OSWALD ISN'T HERE.
OH?
IS HE ILL?
CAN YOU GO OVER THERE, PLEASE?
YEAH, I'LL GO.
I DON'T KNOW IF OSWALD WILL HAVE THE GUTS TO KILL TOBIAS. THEY'RE MATES.
BYE, ALEX.
AND THIS IS MAGGY! IT'S HER FIRST DAY ON THE TEAM.
YO.
HI, I'M CINDY.
HEY.
BE CAREFUL. I ONLY MEANT TO STAY A MONTH, AND I'VE BEEN BREATHING DUST CLOUDS HERE FOR 22 YEARS.
HI.
ZINES
WORLD POLITICS
STORE EVENTS
NUCLEAR FREE AIR LAND & SEA

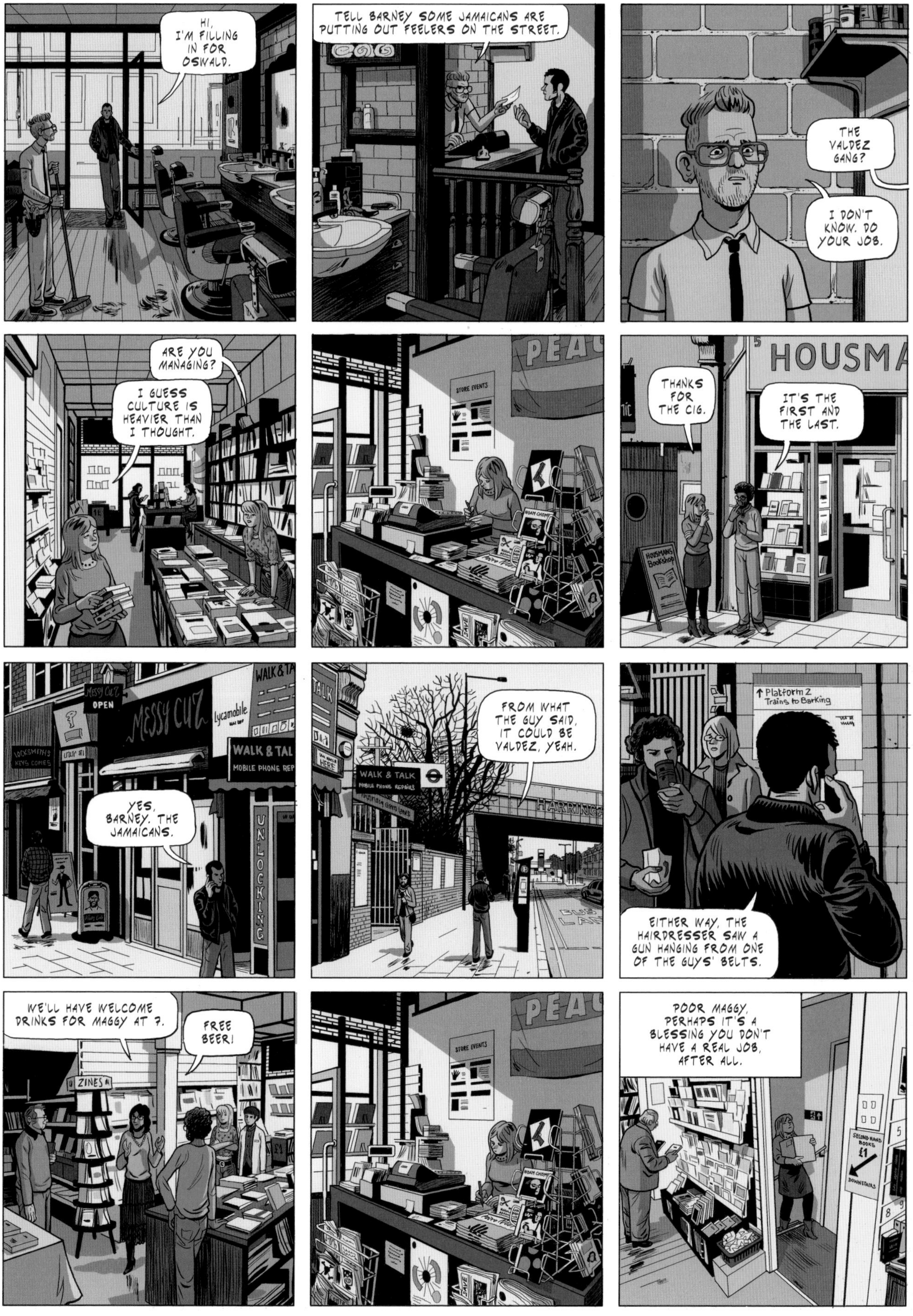
HI, I'M FILLING IN FOR OSWALD.
TELL BARNEY SOME JAMAICANS ARE PUTTING OUT FEELERS ON THE STREET.
THE VALDEZ GANG?
I DON'T KNOW. DO YOUR JOB.
ARE YOU MANAGING?
I GUESS CULTURE IS HEAVIER THAN I THOUGHT.
STORE EVENTS
HOUSMA
THANKS FOR THE CIG.
IT'S THE FIRST AND THE LAST.
HOUSMANS Bookshop
MESSY CUZ
OPEN
WALK & TAL
MOBILE PHONE REP
UNLOCKING
YES, BARNEY. THE JAMAICANS.
WALK & TALK
MOBILE PHONE REPAIRS
FROM WHAT THE GUY SAID, IT COULD BE VALDEZ, YEAH.
Platform 2
Trains to Barking
EITHER WAY, THE HAIRDRESSER SAW A GUN HANGING FROM ONE OF THE GUYS' BELTS.
WE'LL HAVE WELCOME DRINKS FOR MAGGY AT 7.
FREE BEER!
ZINES
STORE EVENTS
POOR MAGGY, PERHAPS IT'S A BLESSING YOU DON'T HAVE A REAL JOB, AFTER ALL.
SECOND HAND BOOKS £1
DOWNSTAIRS

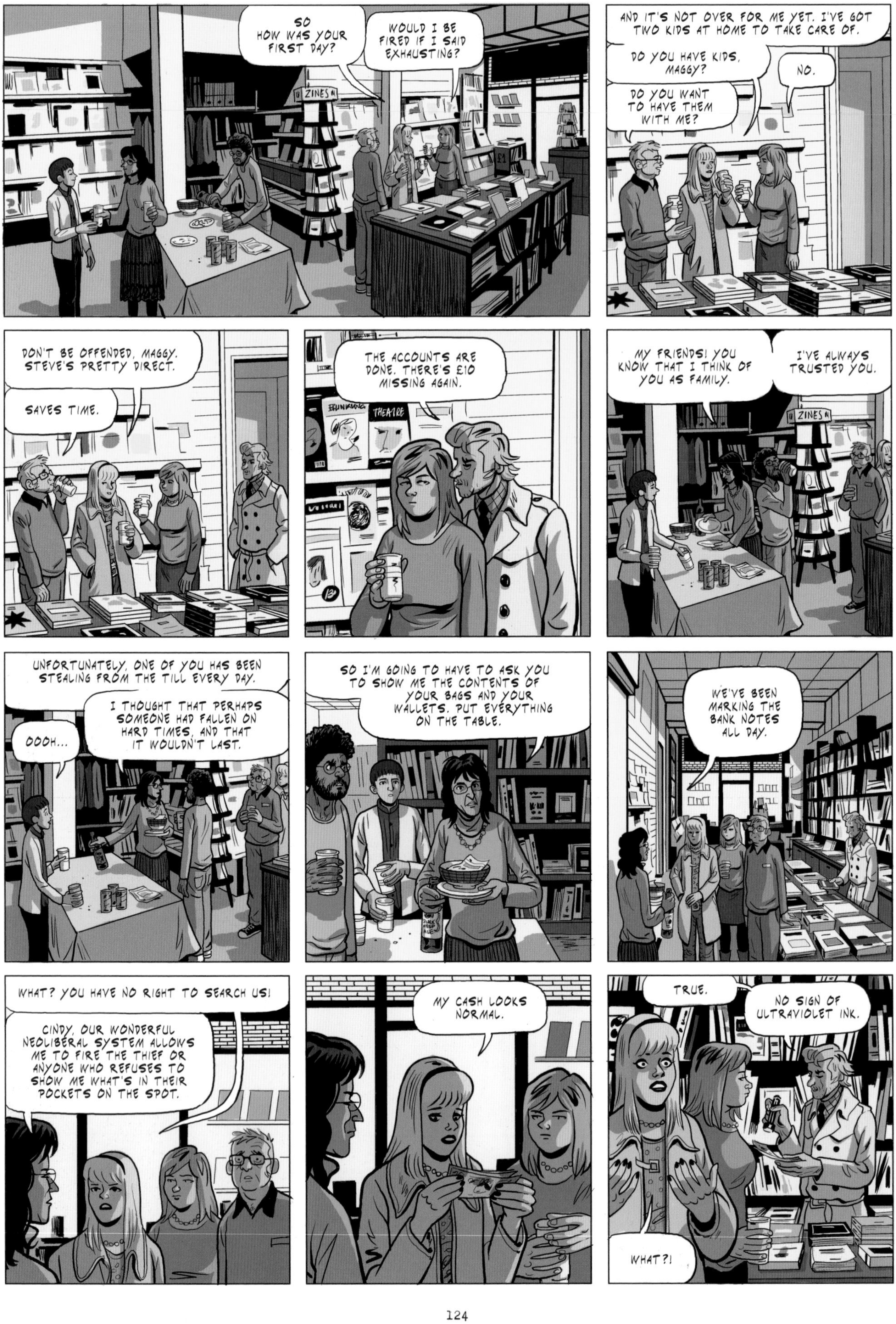
SO HOW WAS YOUR FIRST DAY?
WOULD I BE FIRED IF I SAID EXHAUSTING?
ZINES
AND IT'S NOT OVER FOR ME YET. I'VE GOT TWO KIDS AT HOME TO TAKE CARE OF.
DO YOU HAVE KIDS, MAGGY?
NO.
DO YOU WANT TO HAVE THEM WITH ME?
DON'T BE OFFENDED, MAGGY. STEVE'S PRETTY DIRECT.
SAVES TIME.
THE ACCOUNTS ARE DONE. THERE'S £10 MISSING AGAIN.
THEATRE
MY FRIENDS! YOU KNOW THAT I THINK OF YOU AS FAMILY.
I'VE ALWAYS TRUSTED YOU.
ZINES
UNFORTUNATELY, ONE OF YOU HAS BEEN STEALING FROM THE TILL EVERY DAY.
OOOH...
I THOUGHT THAT PERHAPS SOMEONE HAD FALLEN ON HARD TIMES, AND THAT IT WOULDN'T LAST.
SO I'M GOING TO HAVE TO ASK YOU TO SHOW ME THE CONTENTS OF YOUR BAGS AND YOUR WALLETS. PUT EVERYTHING ON THE TABLE.
WE'VE BEEN MARKING THE BANK NOTES ALL DAY.
WHAT? YOU HAVE NO RIGHT TO SEARCH US!
CINDY, OUR WONDERFUL NEOLIBERAL SYSTEM ALLOWS ME TO FIRE THE THIEF OR ANYONE WHO REFUSES TO SHOW ME WHAT'S IN THEIR POCKETS ON THE SPOT.
MY CASH LOOKS NORMAL.
TRUE.
NO SIGN OF ULTRAVIOLET INK.
WHAT?!

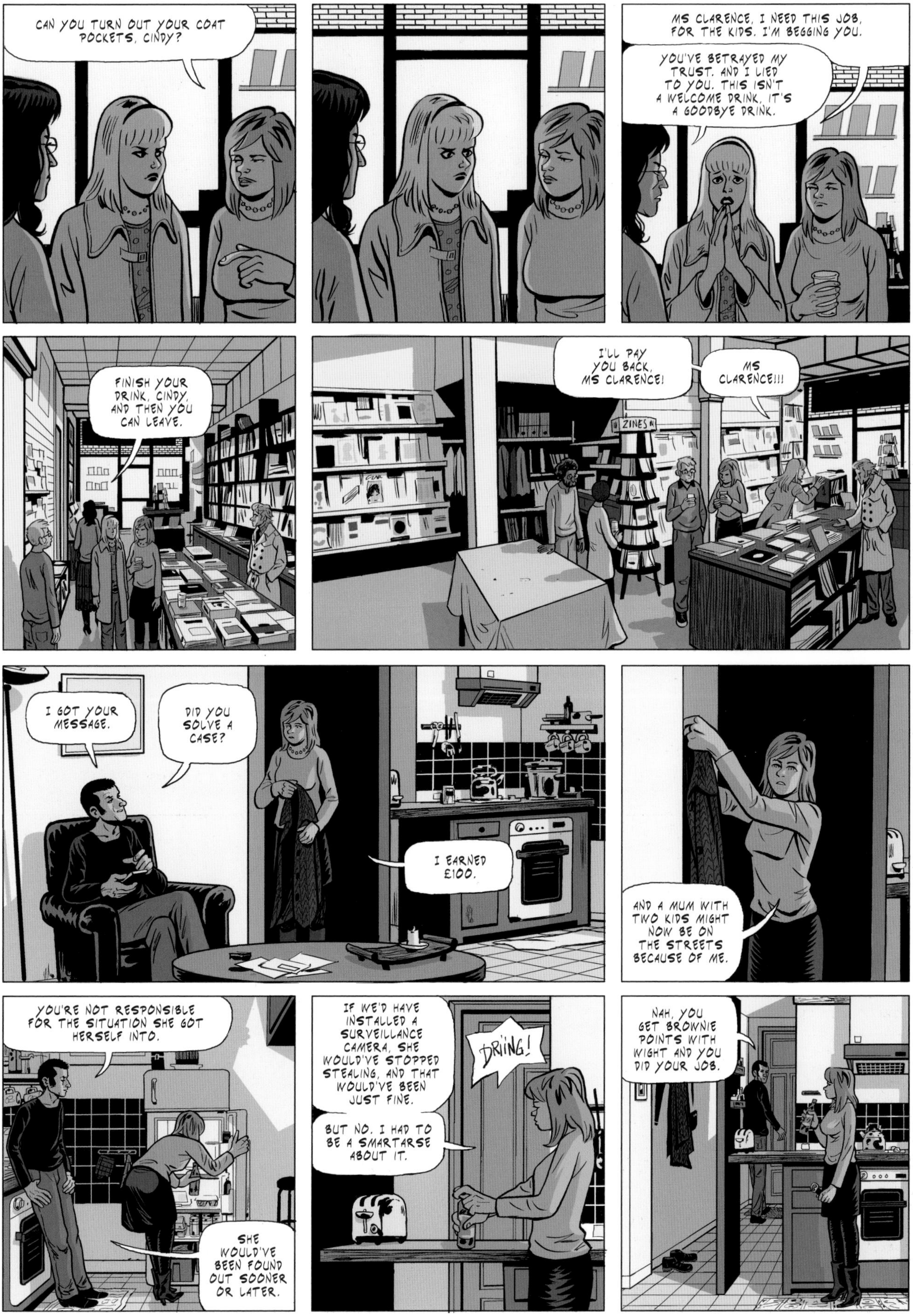
CAN YOU TURN OUT YOUR COAT POCKETS, CINDY?
MS CLARENCE, I NEED THIS JOB, FOR THE KIDS. I'M BEGGING YOU.
YOU'VE BETRAYED MY TRUST. AND I LIED TO YOU. THIS ISN'T A WELCOME DRINK, IT'S A GOODBYE DRINK.
FINISH YOUR DRINK, CINDY, AND THEN YOU CAN LEAVE.
I'LL PAY YOU BACK, MS CLARENCE!
MS CLARENCE!!!
ZINES
I GOT YOUR MESSAGE.
DID YOU SOLVE A CASE?
I EARNED £100.
AND A MUM WITH TWO KIDS MIGHT NOW BE ON THE STREETS BECAUSE OF ME.
YOU'RE NOT RESPONSIBLE FOR THE SITUATION SHE GOT HERSELF INTO.
SHE WOULD'VE BEEN FOUND OUT SOONER OR LATER.
IF WE'D HAVE INSTALLED A SURVEILLANCE CAMERA, SHE WOULD'VE STOPPED STEALING, AND THAT WOULD'VE BEEN JUST FINE.
DRIING!
BUT NO. I HAD TO BE A SMARTARSE ABOUT IT.
NAH, YOU GET BROWNIE POINTS WITH WIGHT AND YOU DID YOUR JOB.

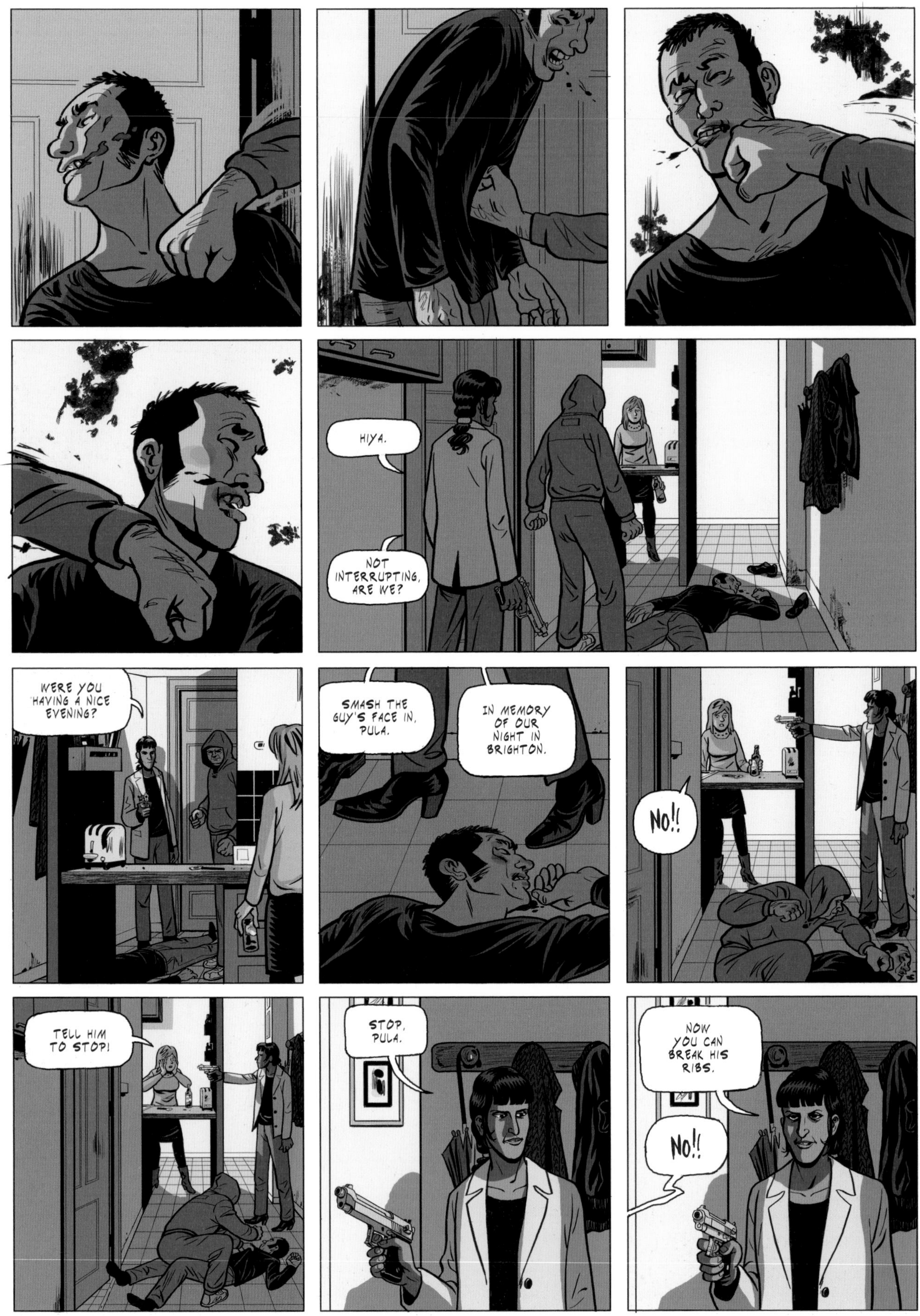
HIYA.
NOT INTERRUPTING, ARE WE?
WERE YOU HAVING A NICE EVENING?
SMASH THE GUY'S FACE IN, PULA.
IN MEMORY OF OUR NIGHT IN BRIGHTON.
NO!!
TELL HIM TO STOP!
STOP, PULA.
NOW YOU CAN BREAK HIS RIBS.
NO!!

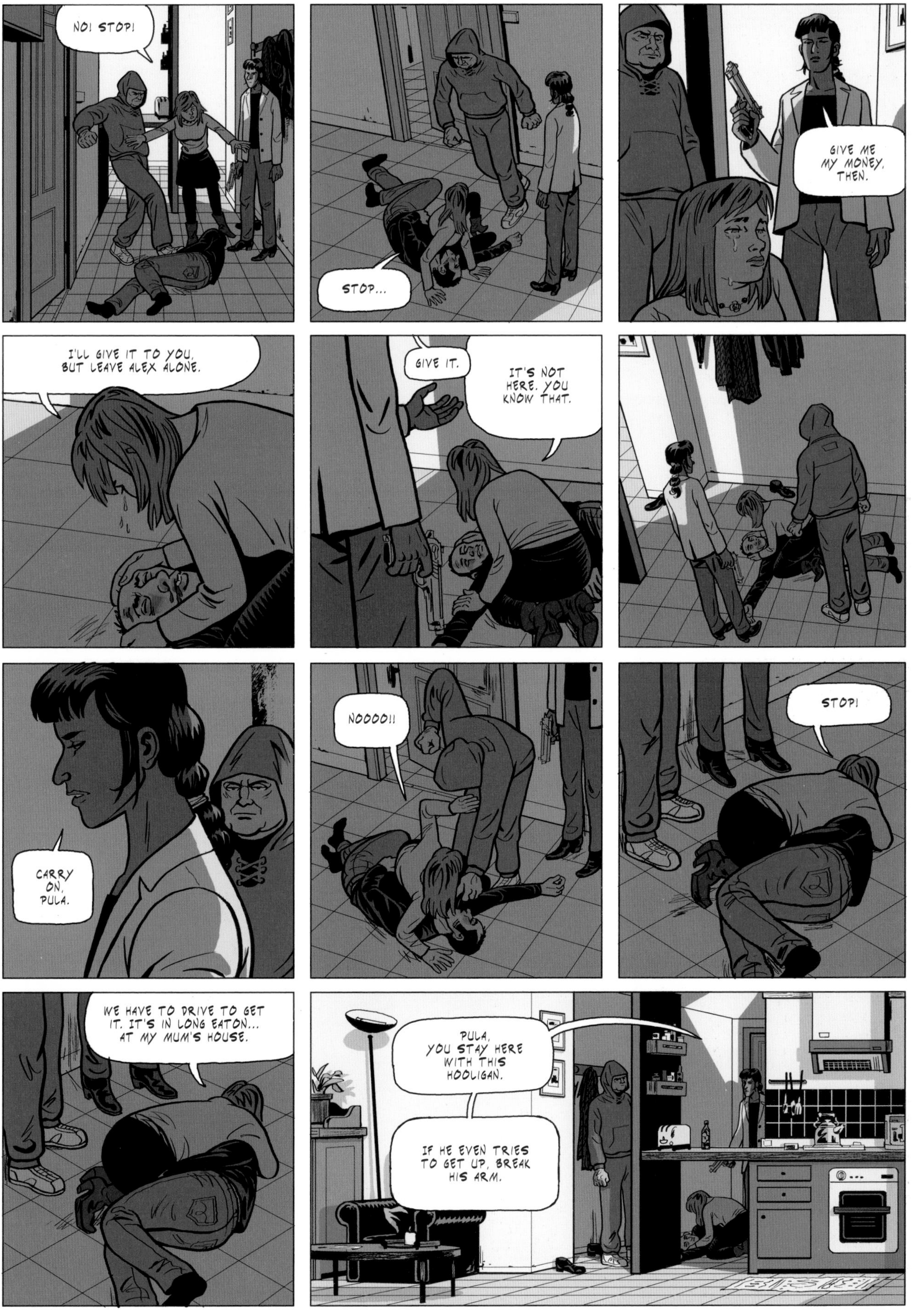
NO! STOP!
STOP...
GIVE ME MY MONEY, THEN.
I'LL GIVE IT TO YOU, BUT LEAVE ALEX ALONE.
GIVE IT.
IT'S NOT HERE. YOU KNOW THAT.
CARRY ON, PULA.
NOOOO!!
STOP!
WE HAVE TO DRIVE TO GET IT. IT'S IN LONG EATON... AT MY MUM'S HOUSE.
PULA, YOU STAY HERE WITH THIS HOOLIGAN.
IF HE EVEN TRIES TO GET UP, BREAK HIS ARM.

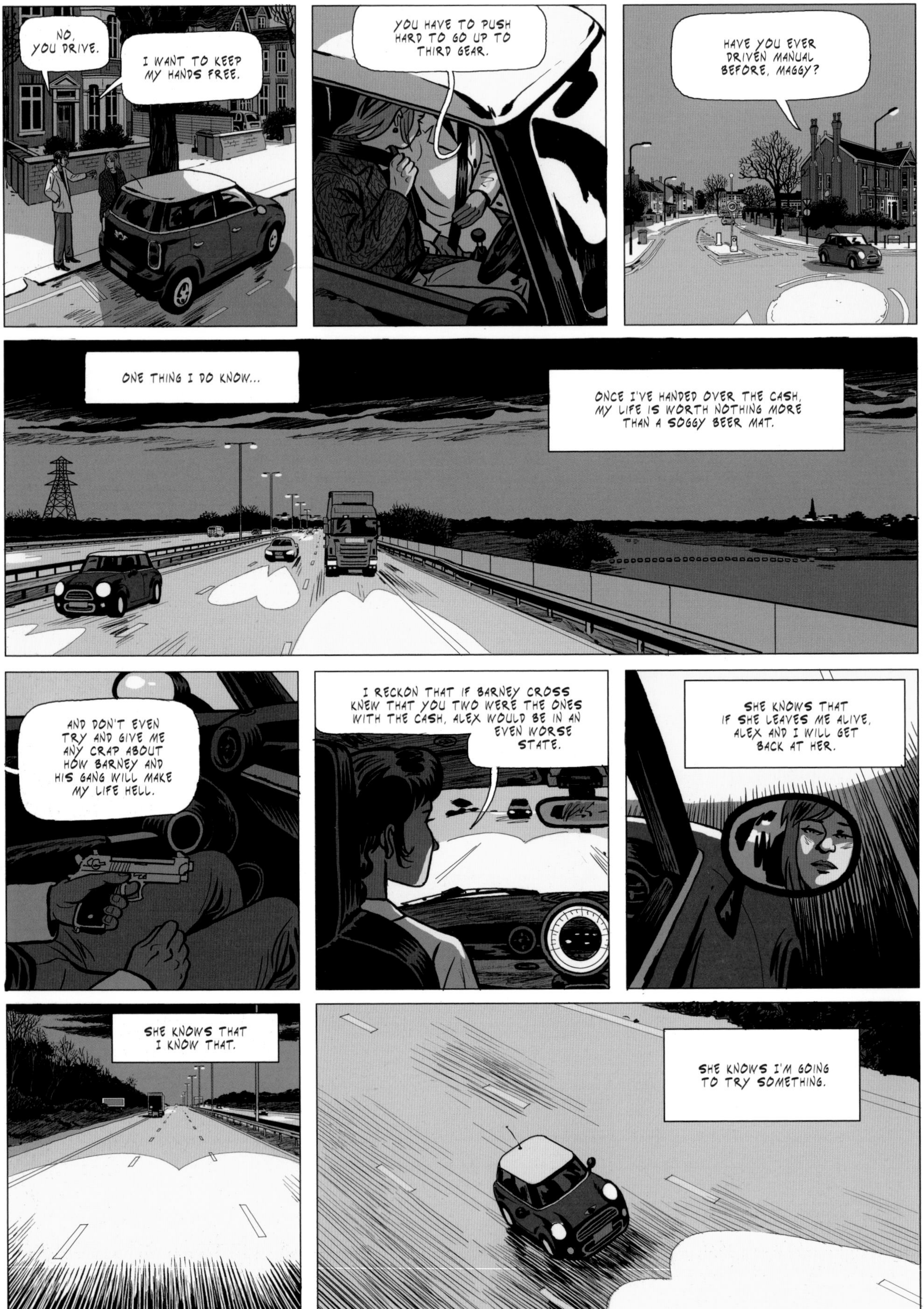
NO, YOU DRIVE.
I WANT TO KEEP MY HANDS FREE.
YOU HAVE TO PUSH HARD TO GO UP TO THIRD GEAR.
HAVE YOU EVER DRIVEN MANUAL BEFORE, MAGGY?
ONE THING I DO KNOW...
ONCE I'VE HANDED OVER THE CASH, MY LIFE IS WORTH NOTHING MORE THAN A SOGGY BEER MAT.
AND DON'T EVEN TRY AND GIVE ME ANY CRAP ABOUT HOW BARNEY AND HIS GANG WILL MAKE MY LIFE HELL.
I RECKON THAT IF BARNEY CROSS KNEW THAT YOU TWO WERE THE ONES WITH THE CASH, ALEX WOULD BE IN AN EVEN WORSE STATE.
SHE KNOWS THAT IF SHE LEAVES ME ALIVE, ALEX AND I WILL GET BACK AT HER.
SHE KNOWS THAT I KNOW THAT.
SHE KNOWS I'M GOING TO TRY SOMETHING.

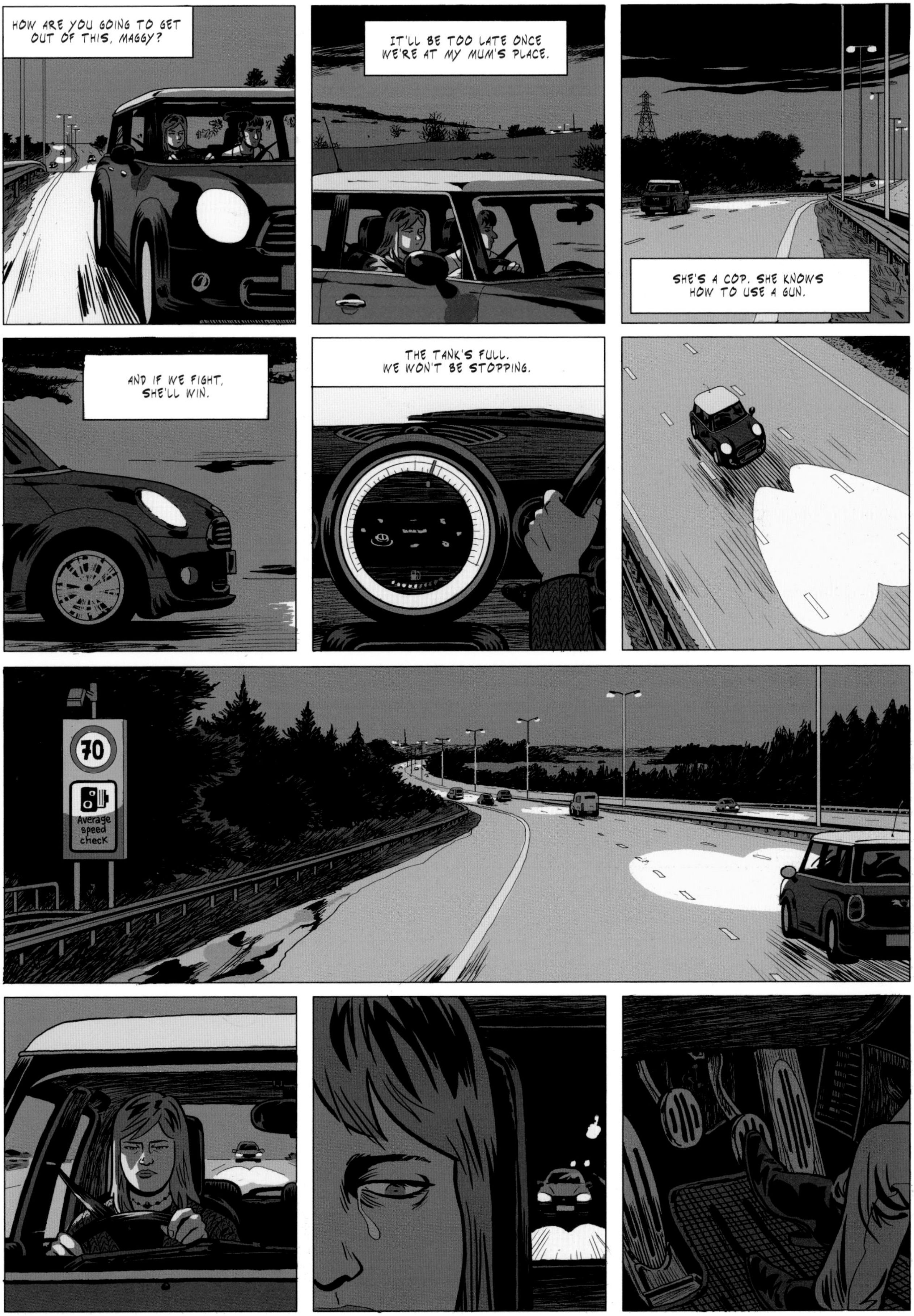
HOW ARE YOU GOING TO GET OUT OF THIS, MAGGY?
IT'LL BE TOO LATE ONCE WE'RE AT MY MUM'S PLACE.
SHE'S A COP. SHE KNOWS HOW TO USE A GUN.
AND IF WE FIGHT, SHE'LL WIN.
THE TANK'S FULL. WE WON'T BE STOPPING.
70
Average speed check

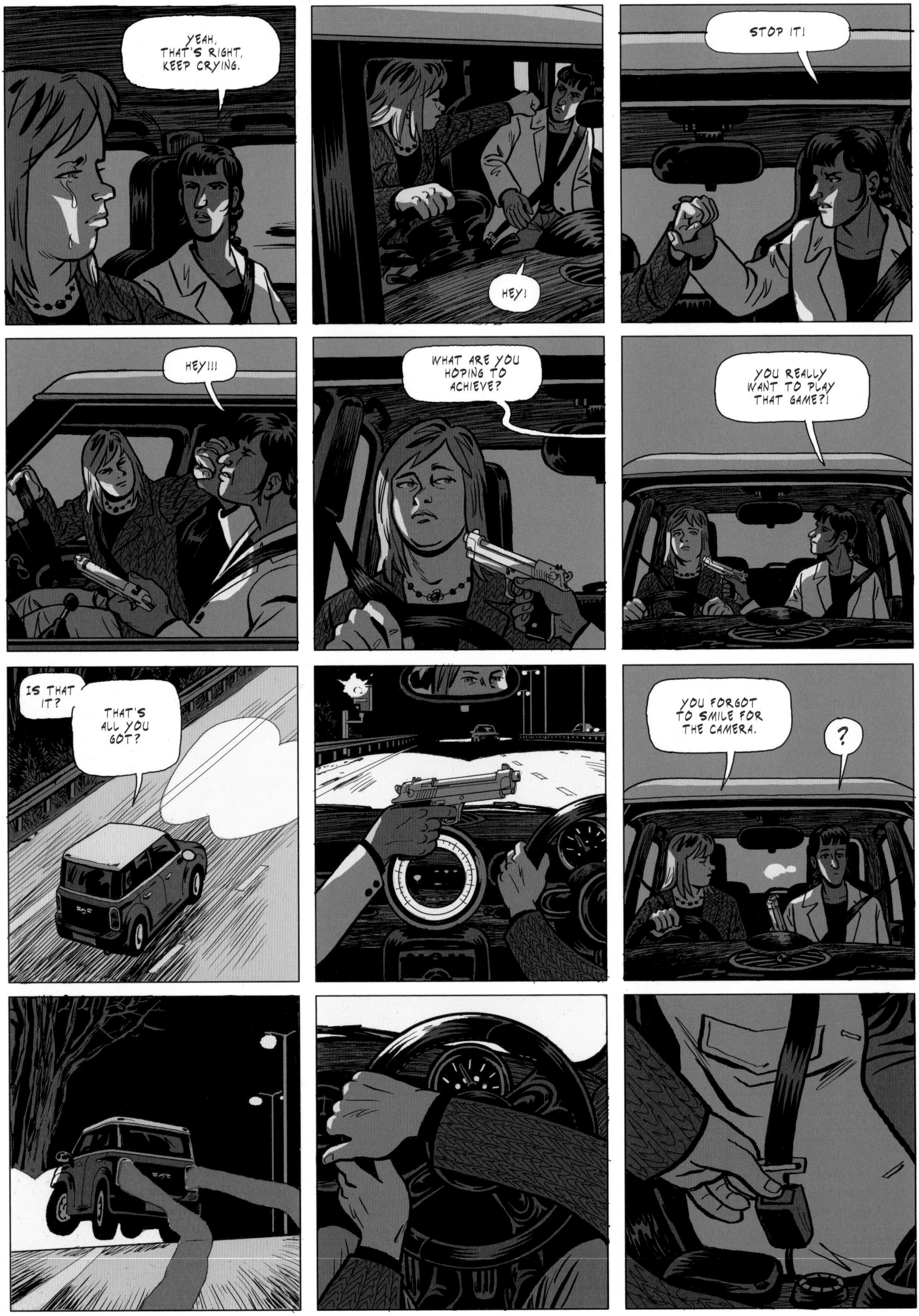
YEAH, THAT'S RIGHT, KEEP CRYING.
HEY!
STOP IT!
HEY!!!
WHAT ARE YOU HOPING TO ACHIEVE?
YOU REALLY WANT TO PLAY THAT GAME?!
IS THAT IT?
THAT'S ALL YOU GOT?
YOU FORGOT TO SMILE FOR THE CAMERA.
?

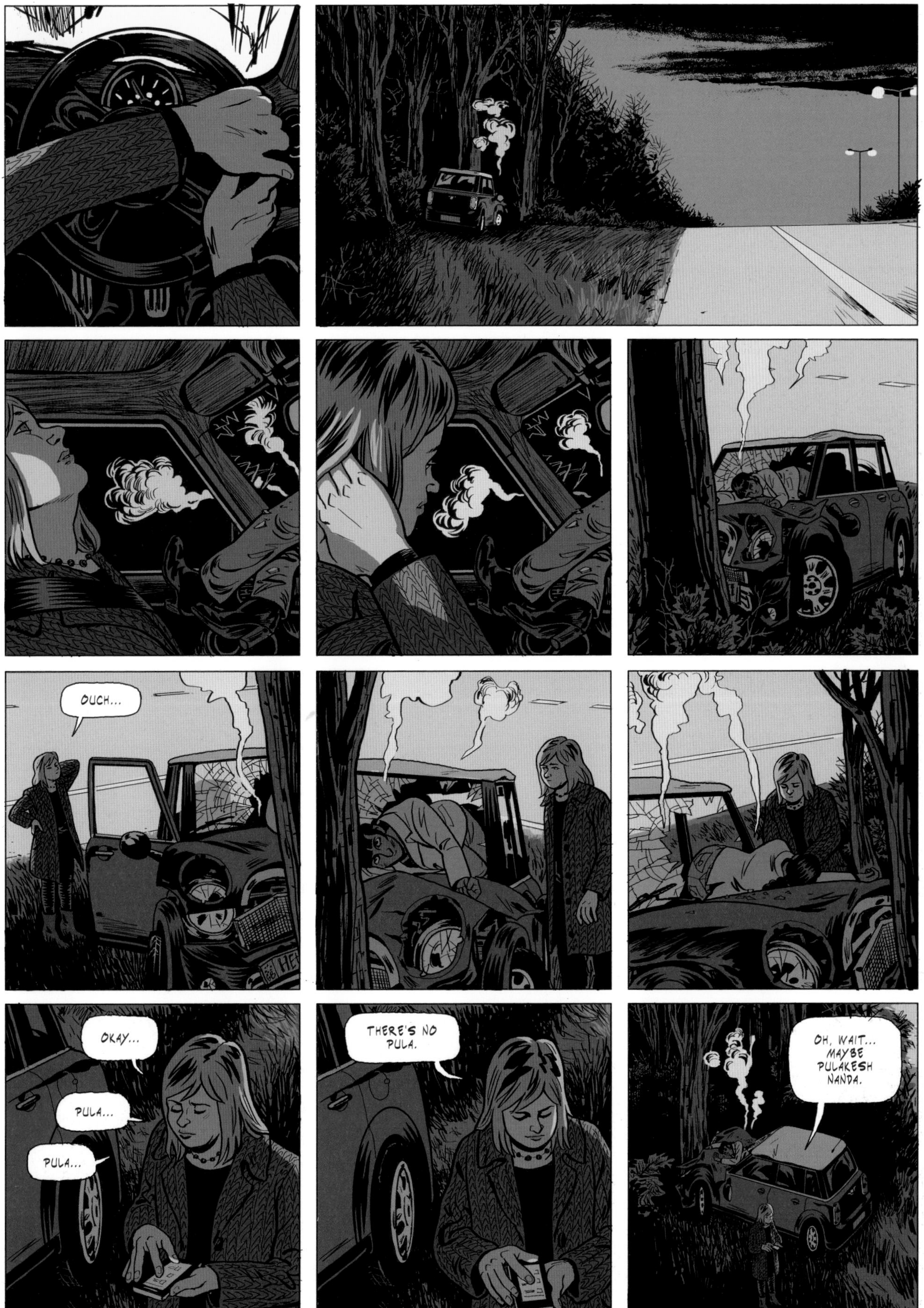
OUCH...
OKAY...
PULA...
PULA...
THERE'S NO PULA.
OH, WAIT... MAYBE PULAKESH NANDA.

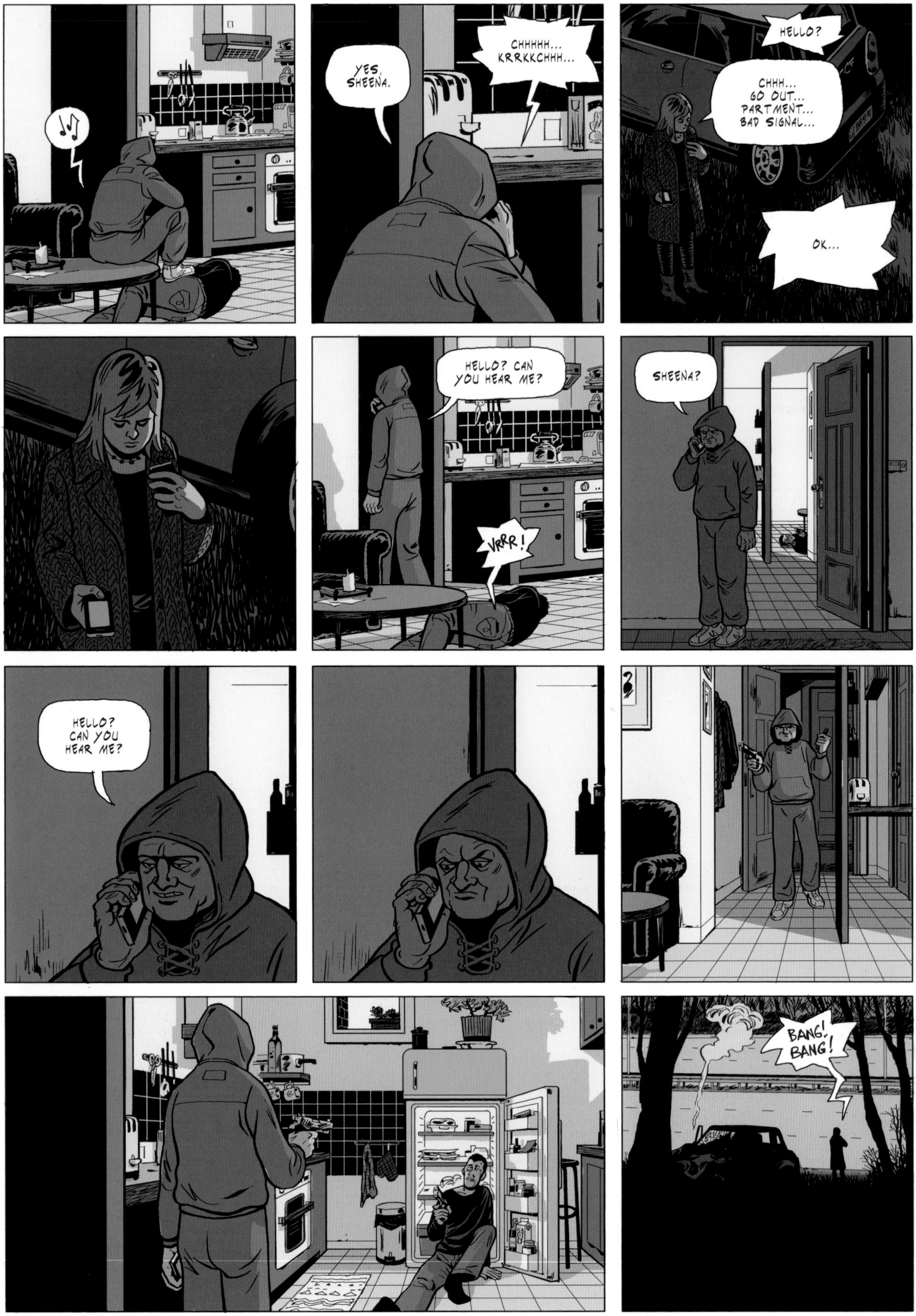
YES, SHEENA.
CHHHHH... KRRKKCHHH...
HELLO?
CHHH... GO OUT... PARTMENT... BAD SIGNAL...
OK...
HELLO? CAN YOU HEAR ME?
VRRR!
SHEENA?
HELLO? CAN YOU HEAR ME?
BANG! BANG!

ONE MORE QUESTION, MISS GARRISSON.

WHY DID ALEX SAY THAT TOBIAS PHILSON MIGHT BE IN LONG EATON?

HE NEVER MENTIONED LONG EATON DURING THE LAST INTERROGATION.

I DON'T KNOW... MAYBE JUST A RANDOM ADDRESS.

SO THEY'D STOP HITTING HIM...?

TO BUY TIME...?

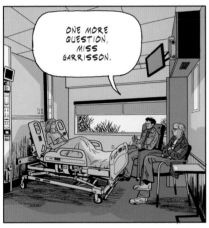

WHAT THE HELL WAS SHEENA THINKING?! TRYING TO PICK UP TOBIAS' TRAIL ON HER OWN LIKE THAT!

I GET THAT STANLEY COOPER WAS HER PARTNER AND ALL, BUT STILL...

I'D HAVE A HARD TIME BELIEVING IT, TOO, IF IT WEREN'T FOR THAT SPEED CAMERA IMAGE.

AND YOU DEFINITELY WOULDN'T HAVE BEEN GOING HOME TODAY.

THANK YOU FOR YOUR UNDERSTANDING. CAN I FILE A COMPLAINT AGAINST THAT BITCH, EVEN IF SHE'S DEAD?

NO, MISS GARRISSON.

YOU CAN'T TAKE DEAD PEOPLE TO COURT OR PUT THEM IN PRISON.

HOW'S ALEX? IS HE OKAY?

IF WE DON'T GET HIM FOR MURDER ON THE GROUNDS OF SELF-DEFENCE, WE'LL GET HIM FOR POSSESSION OF AN ILLEGAL WEAPON.

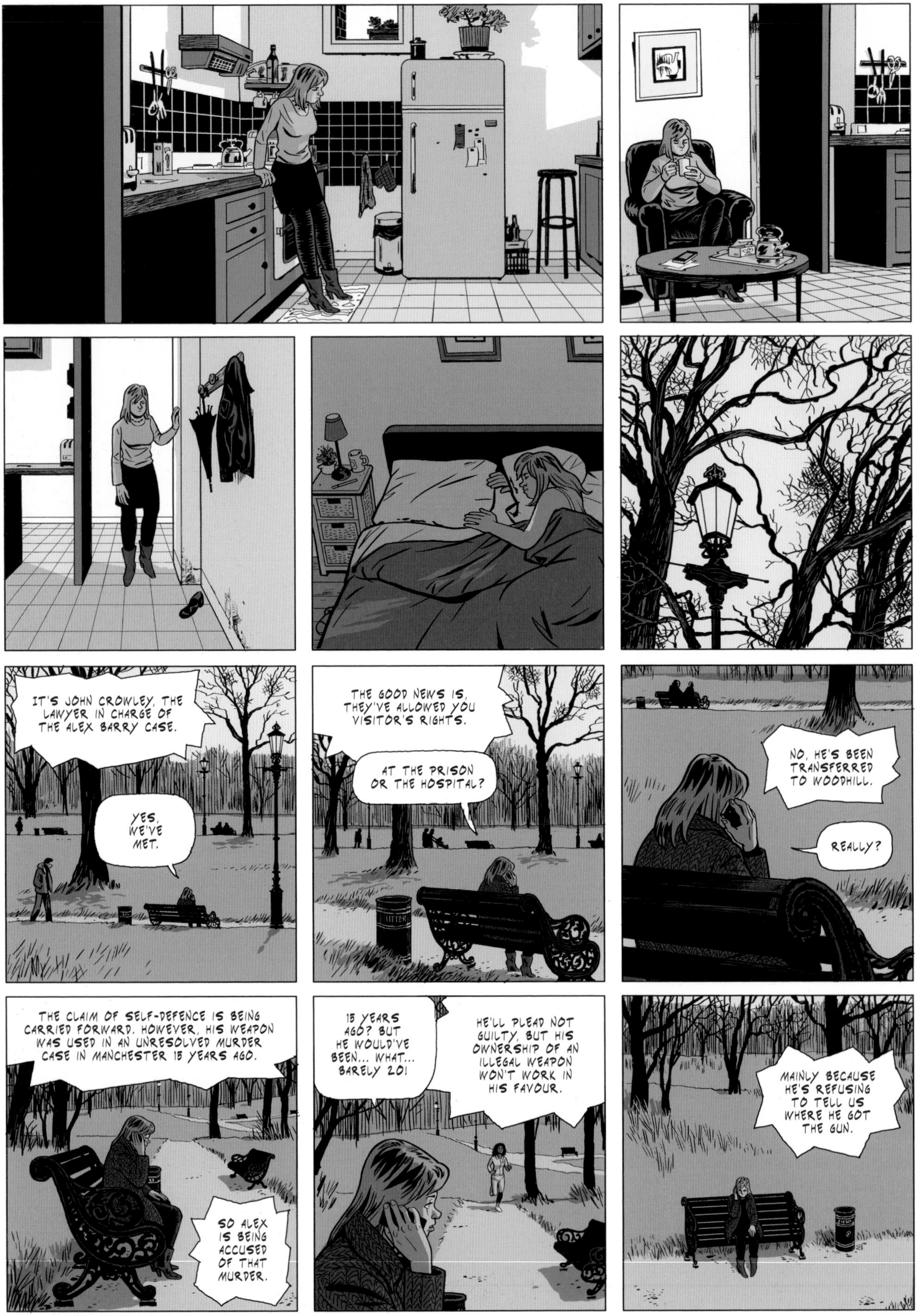
IT'S JOHN CROWLEY, THE LAWYER IN CHARGE OF THE ALEX BARRY CASE.
YES, WE'VE MET.
THE GOOD NEWS IS, THEY'VE ALLOWED YOU VISITOR'S RIGHTS.
AT THE PRISON OR THE HOSPITAL?
NO, HE'S BEEN TRANSFERRED TO WOODHILL.
REALLY?
THE CLAIM OF SELF-DEFENCE IS BEING CARRIED FORWARD. HOWEVER, HIS WEAPON WAS USED IN AN UNRESOLVED MURDER CASE IN MANCHESTER 15 YEARS AGO.
SO ALEX IS BEING ACCUSED OF THAT MURDER.
15 YEARS AGO? BUT HE WOULD'VE BEEN... WHAT... BARELY 20!
HE'LL PLEAD NOT GUILTY, BUT HIS OWNERSHIP OF AN ILLEGAL WEAPON WON'T WORK IN HIS FAVOUR.
MAINLY BECAUSE HE'S REFUSING TO TELL US WHERE HE GOT THE GUN.

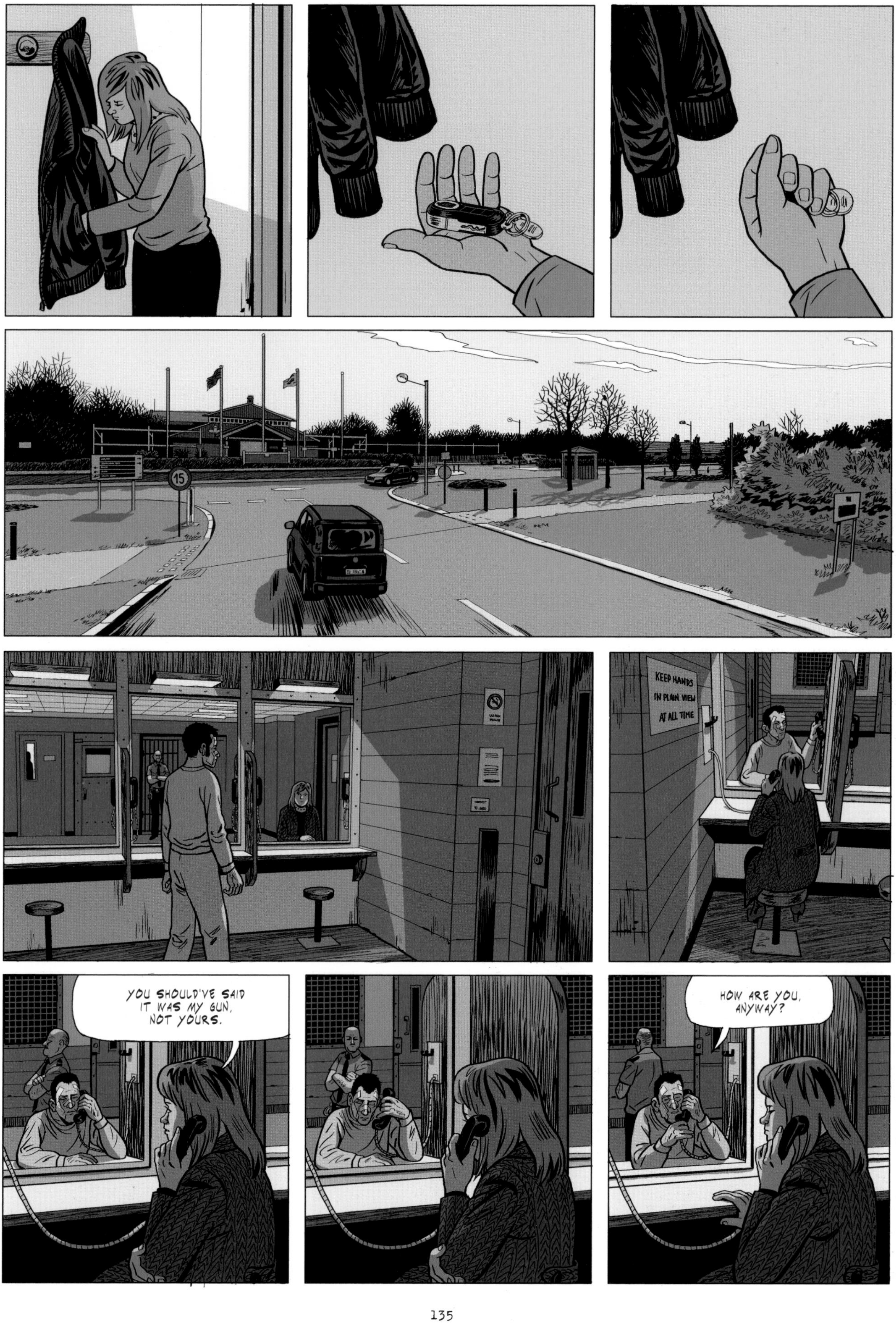
KEEP HANDS IN PLAIN VIEW AT ALL TIME
YOU SHOULD'VE SAID IT WAS MY GUN, NOT YOURS.
HOW ARE YOU, ANYWAY?

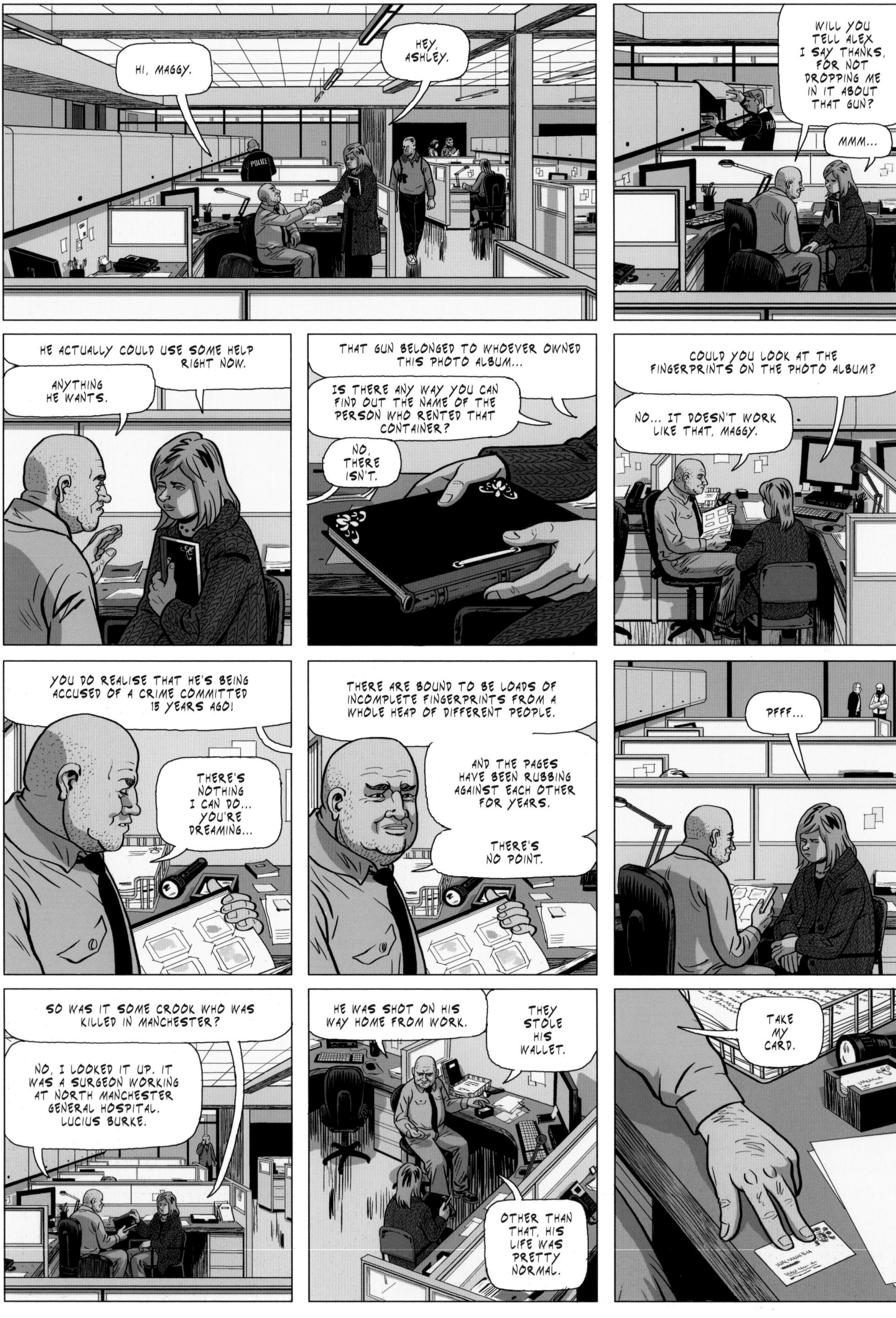
HI, MAGGY.
HEY, ASHLEY.
POLICE
WILL YOU TELL ALEX I SAY THANKS, FOR NOT DROPPING ME IN IT ABOUT THAT GUN?
MMM...
HE ACTUALLY COULD USE SOME HELP RIGHT NOW.
ANYTHING HE WANTS.
THAT GUN BELONGED TO WHOEVER OWNED THIS PHOTO ALBUM...
IS THERE ANY WAY YOU CAN FIND OUT THE NAME OF THE PERSON WHO RENTED THAT CONTAINER?
NO, THERE ISN'T.
COULD YOU LOOK AT THE FINGERPRINTS ON THE PHOTO ALBUM?
NO... IT DOESN'T WORK LIKE THAT, MAGGY.
YOU DO REALISE THAT HE'S BEING ACCUSED OF A CRIME COMMITTED 15 YEARS AGO!
THERE'S NOTHING I CAN DO... YOU'RE DREAMING...
THERE ARE BOUND TO BE LOADS OF INCOMPLETE FINGERPRINTS FROM A WHOLE HEAP OF DIFFERENT PEOPLE.
AND THE PAGES HAVE BEEN RUBBING AGAINST EACH OTHER FOR YEARS.
THERE'S NO POINT.
PFFF...
SO WAS IT SOME CROOK WHO WAS KILLED IN MANCHESTER?
NO, I LOOKED IT UP. IT WAS A SURGEON WORKING AT NORTH MANCHESTER GENERAL HOSPITAL. LUCIUS BURKE.
HE WAS SHOT ON HIS WAY HOME FROM WORK.
THEY STOLE HIS WALLET.
OTHER THAN THAT, HIS LIFE WAS PRETTY NORMAL.
TAKE MY CARD.

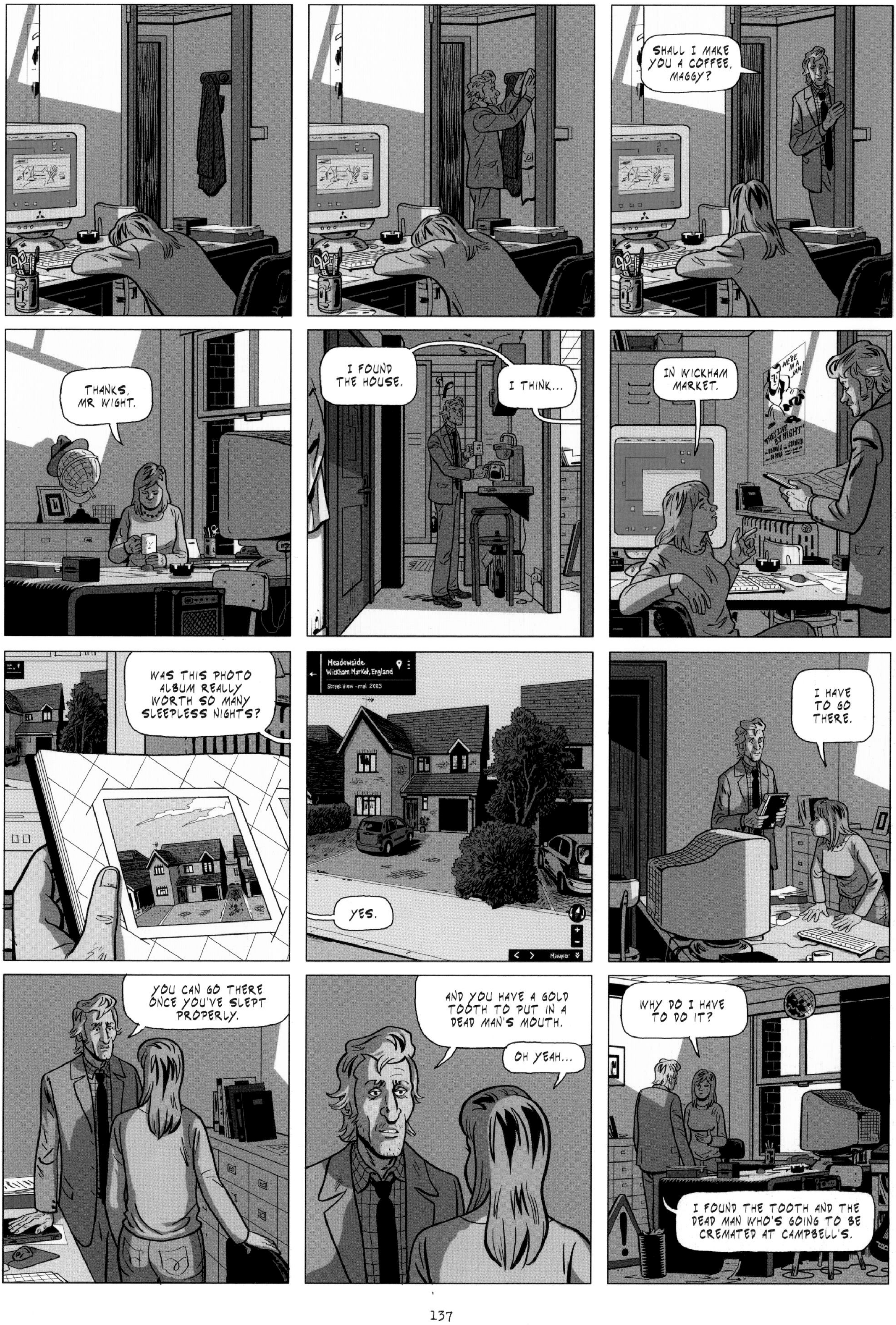
SHALL I MAKE YOU A COFFEE, MAGGY?
THANKS, MR WIGHT.
I FOUND THE HOUSE.
I THINK...
IN WICKHAM MARKET.
WAS THIS PHOTO ALBUM REALLY WORTH SO MANY SLEEPLESS NIGHTS?
Meadowside
Wickham Market, England
Street View - mai 2009
YES.
Masquer
I HAVE TO GO THERE.
YOU CAN GO THERE ONCE YOU'VE SLEPT PROPERLY.
AND YOU HAVE A GOLD TOOTH TO PUT IN A DEAD MAN'S MOUTH.
OH YEAH...
WHY DO I HAVE TO DO IT?
I FOUND THE TOOTH AND THE DEAD MAN WHO'S GOING TO BE CREMATED AT CAMPBELL'S.

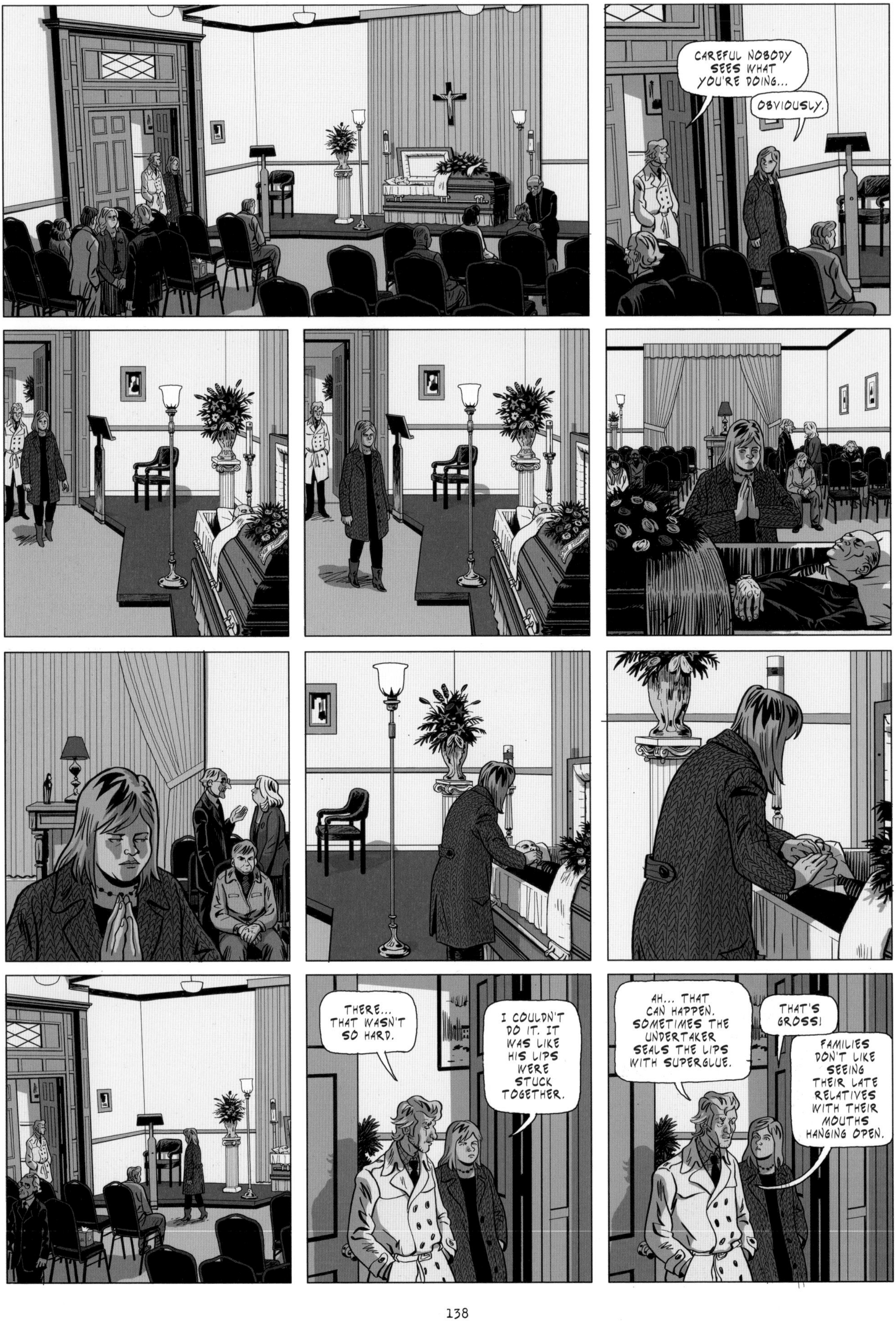
CAREFUL NOBODY SEES WHAT YOU'RE DOING...
OBVIOUSLY.
THERE... THAT WASN'T SO HARD.
I COULDN'T DO IT. IT WAS LIKE HIS LIPS WERE STUCK TOGETHER.
AH... THAT CAN HAPPEN. SOMETIMES THE UNDERTAKER SEALS THE LIPS WITH SUPERGLUE.
THAT'S GROSS!
FAMILIES DON'T LIKE SEEING THEIR LATE RELATIVES WITH THEIR MOUTHS HANGING OPEN.

OKAY, WE'LL TRY ANOTHER ONE.

NO!

GO BACK AND PUT IT IN HIS NOSE.

PUSH IT RIGHT UP THERE.

WHAT?

IT WON'T MAKE ANY DIFFERENCE ONCE HE'S CREMATED.

THERE'S SOMETHING I FORGOT TO SAY TO HIM.

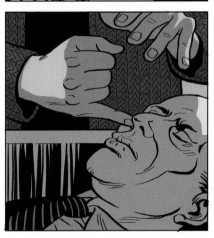

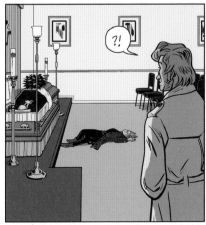

?!

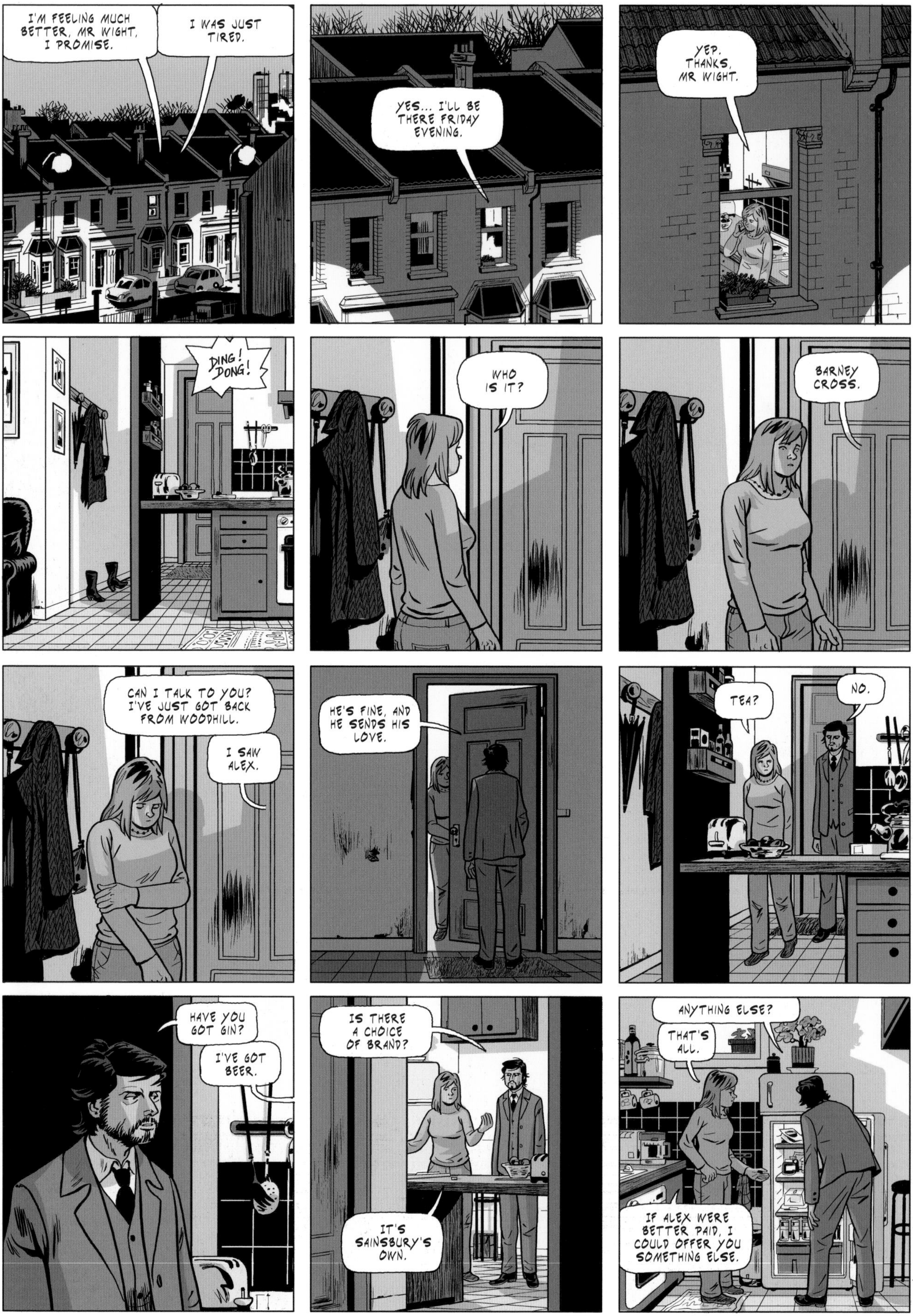
I'M FEELING MUCH BETTER, MR WIGHT, I PROMISE.
I WAS JUST TIRED.
YES... I'LL BE THERE FRIDAY EVENING.
YEP. THANKS, MR WIGHT.
DING! DONG!
WHO IS IT?
BARNEY CROSS.
CAN I TALK TO YOU? I'VE JUST GOT BACK FROM WOODHILL.
I SAW ALEX.
HE'S FINE, AND HE SENDS HIS LOVE.
TEA?
NO.
HAVE YOU GOT GIN?
I'VE GOT BEER.
IS THERE A CHOICE OF BRAND?
IT'S SAINSBURY'S OWN.
ANYTHING ELSE?
THAT'S ALL.
IF ALEX WERE BETTER PAID, I COULD OFFER YOU SOMETHING ELSE.

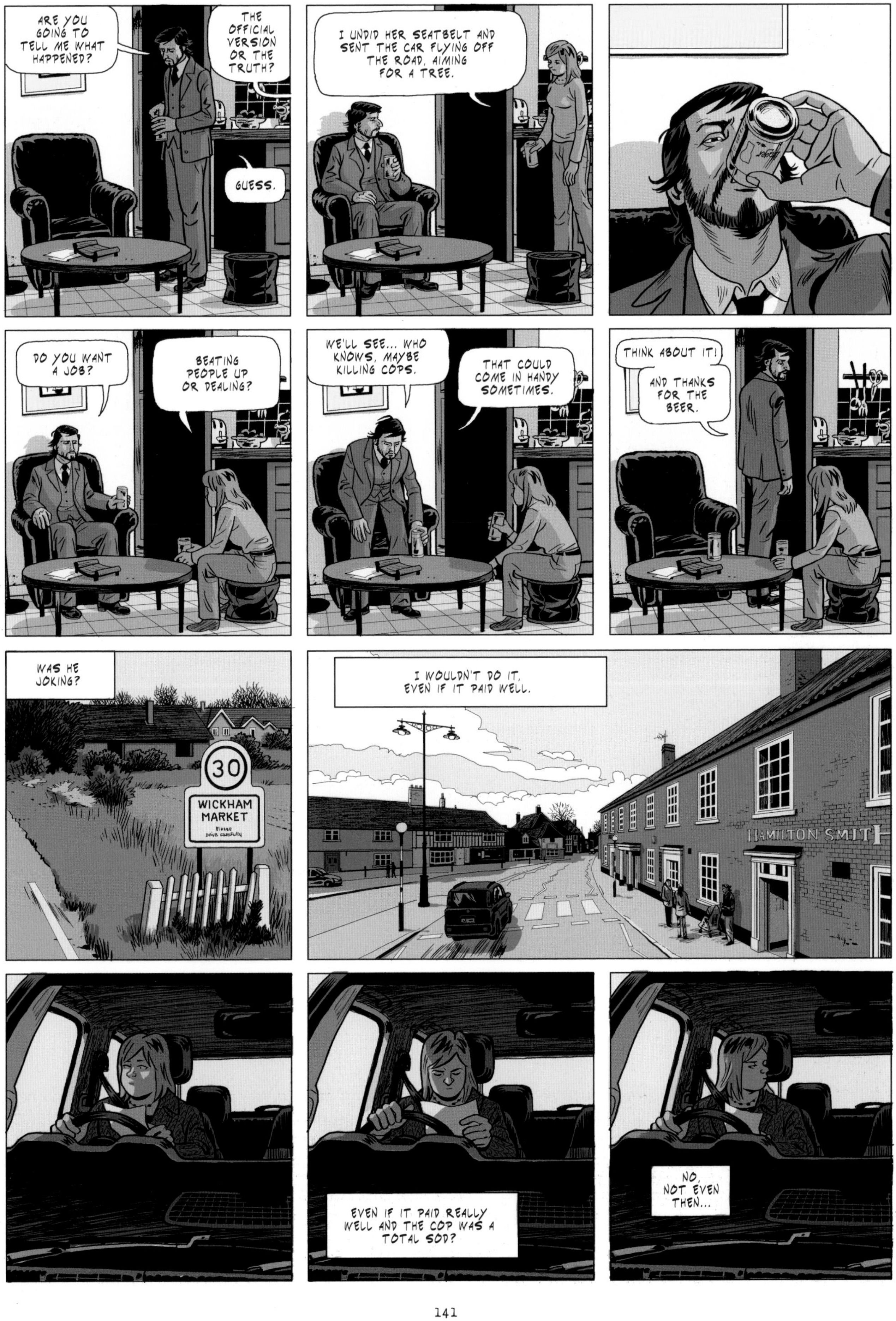

ARE YOU GOING TO TELL ME WHAT HAPPENED?
THE OFFICIAL VERSION OR THE TRUTH?
GUESS.
I UNDID HER SEATBELT AND SENT THE CAR FLYING OFF THE ROAD, AIMING FOR A TREE.
DO YOU WANT A JOB?
BEATING PEOPLE UP OR DEALING?
WE'LL SEE... WHO KNOWS, MAYBE KILLING COPS.
THAT COULD COME IN HANDY SOMETIMES.
THINK ABOUT IT!
AND THANKS FOR THE BEER.
WAS HE JOKING?
30
WICKHAM MARKET
Please drive carefully
I WOULDN'T DO IT, EVEN IF IT PAID WELL.
HAMILTON SMITH
EVEN IF IT PAID REALLY WELL AND THE COP WAS A TOTAL SOD?
NO, NOT EVEN THEN...

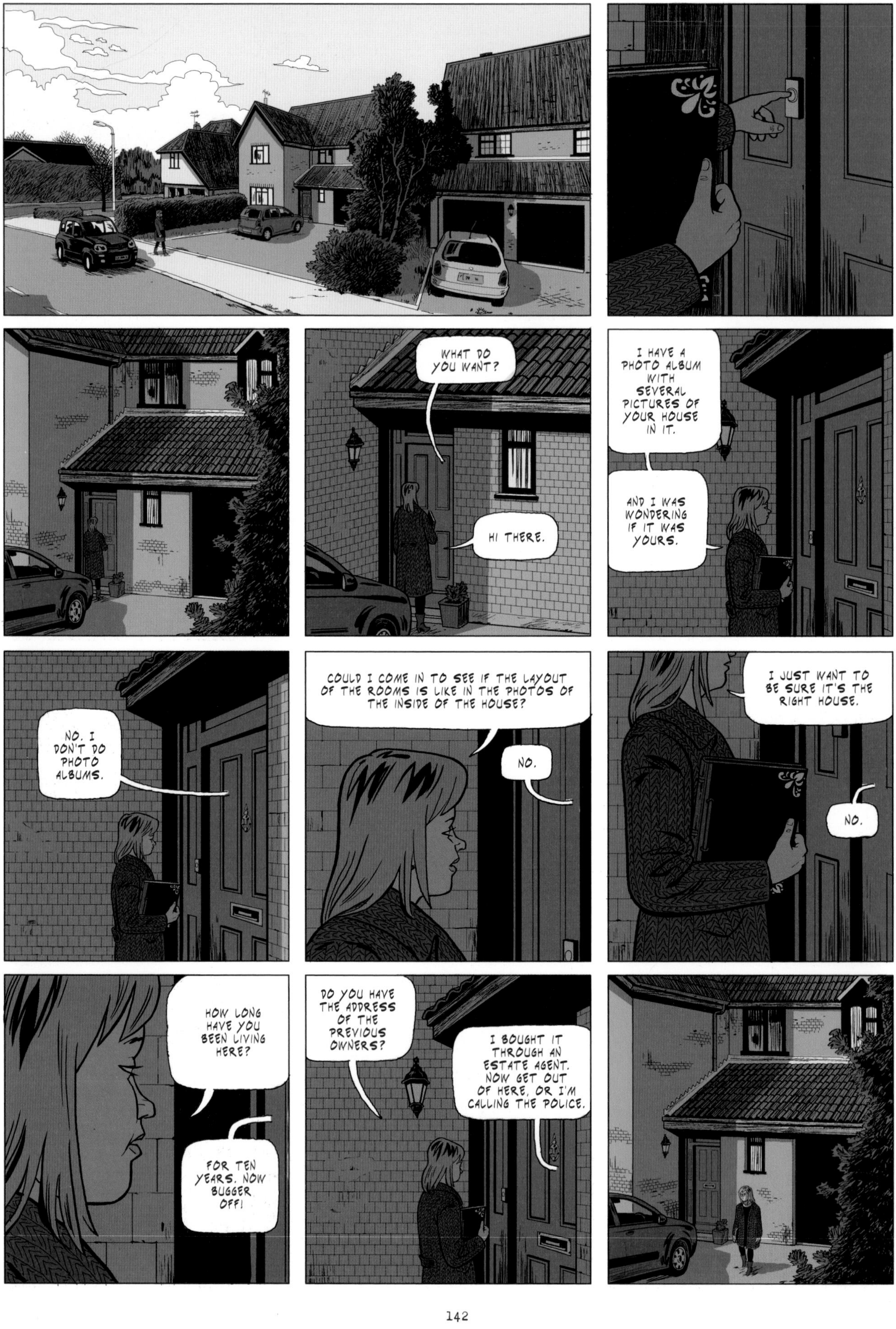

WHAT DO YOU WANT?
HI THERE.
I HAVE A PHOTO ALBUM WITH SEVERAL PICTURES OF YOUR HOUSE IN IT.
AND I WAS WONDERING IF IT WAS YOURS.
NO. I DON'T DO PHOTO ALBUMS.
COULD I COME IN TO SEE IF THE LAYOUT OF THE ROOMS IS LIKE IN THE PHOTOS OF THE INSIDE OF THE HOUSE?
NO.
I JUST WANT TO BE SURE IT'S THE RIGHT HOUSE.
NO.
HOW LONG HAVE YOU BEEN LIVING HERE?
FOR TEN YEARS. NOW BUGGER OFF!
DO YOU HAVE THE ADDRESS OF THE PREVIOUS OWNERS?
I BOUGHT IT THROUGH AN ESTATE AGENT. NOW GET OUT OF HERE, OR I'M CALLING THE POLICE.

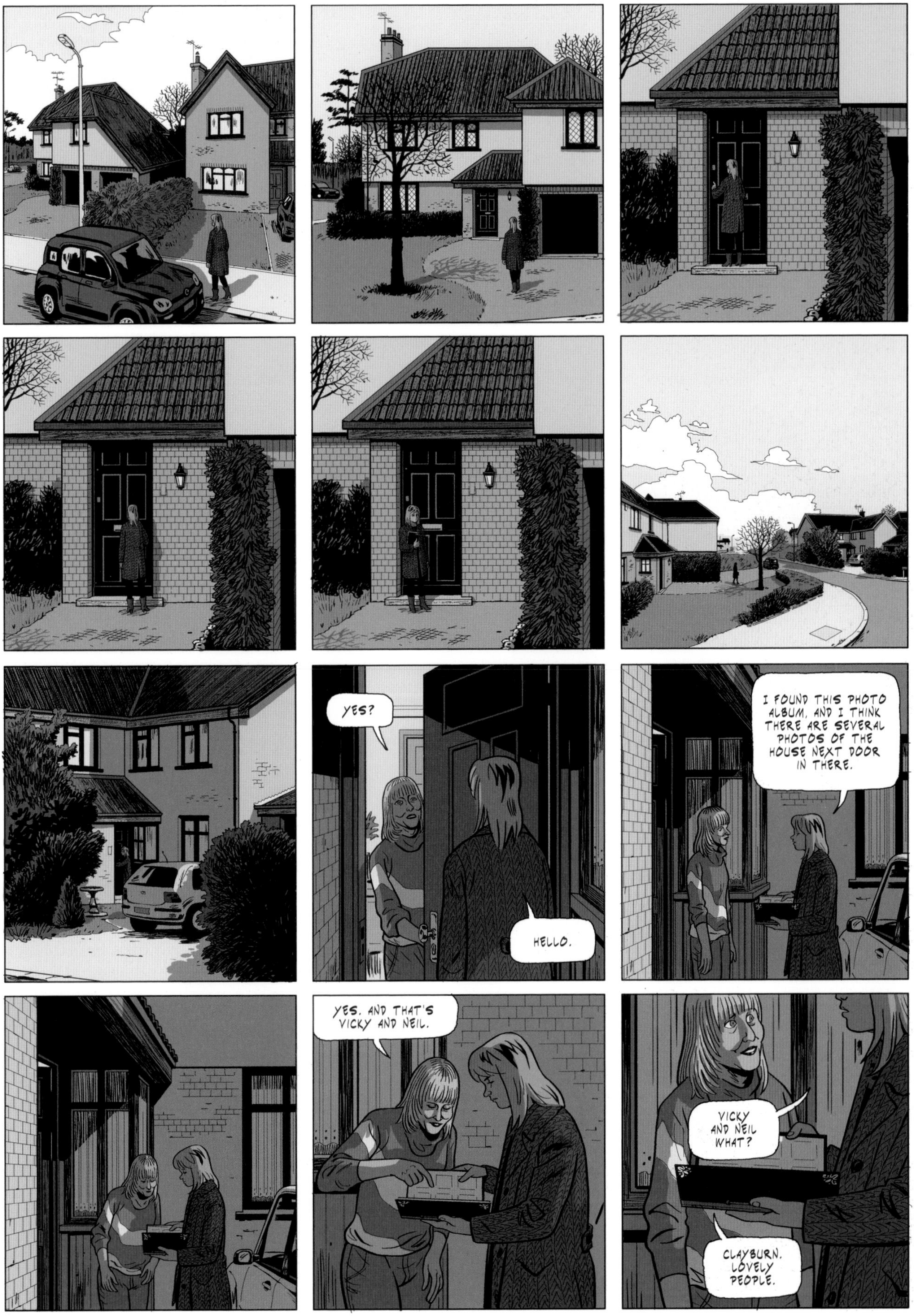
YES?
HELLO.
I FOUND THIS PHOTO ALBUM, AND I THINK THERE ARE SEVERAL PHOTOS OF THE HOUSE NEXT DOOR IN THERE.
YES. AND THAT'S VICKY AND NEIL.
VICKY AND NEIL WHAT?
CLAYBURN. LOVELY PEOPLE.

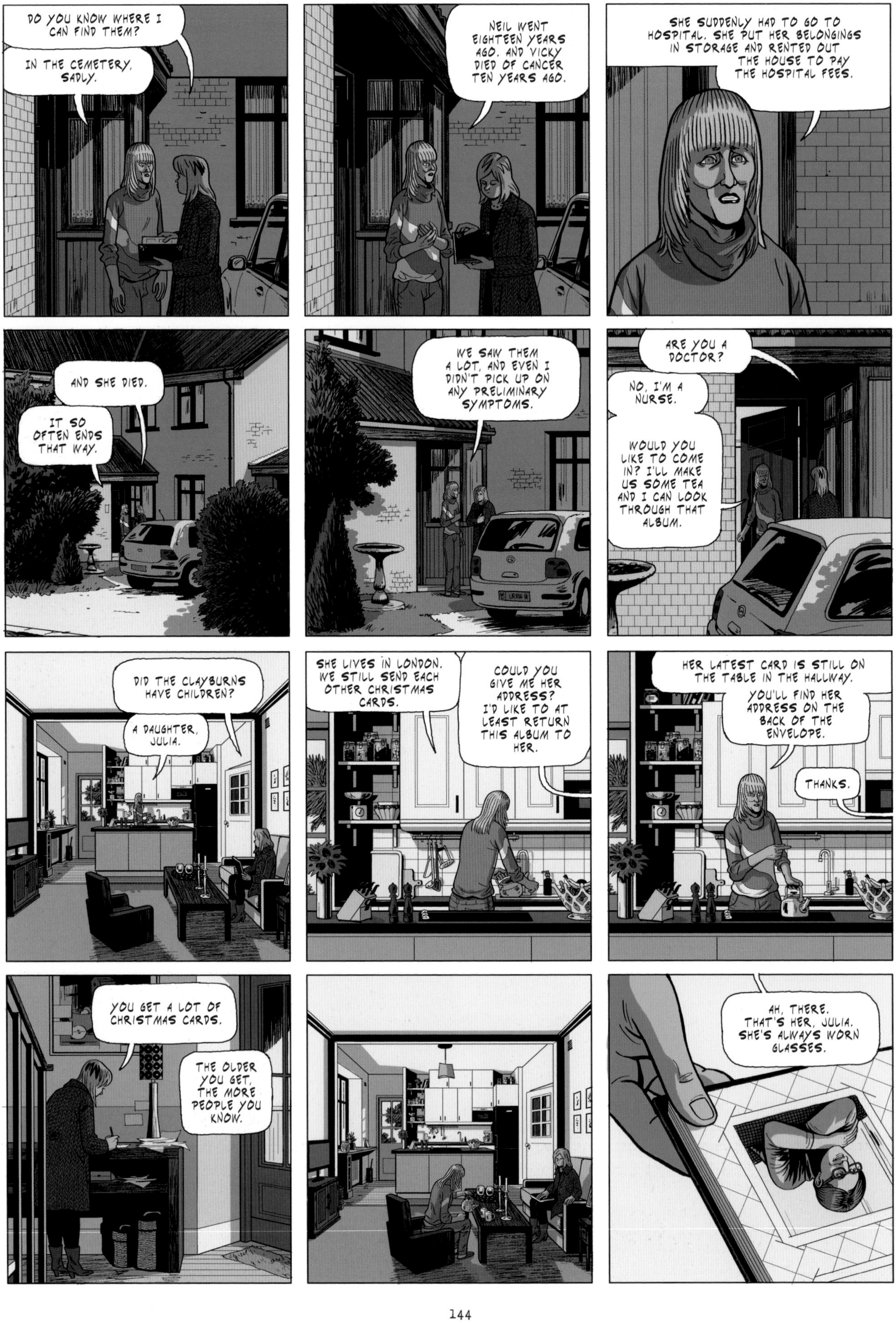
DO YOU KNOW WHERE I CAN FIND THEM?
IN THE CEMETERY, SADLY.
NEIL WENT EIGHTEEN YEARS AGO. AND VICKY DIED OF CANCER TEN YEARS AGO.
SHE SUDDENLY HAD TO GO TO HOSPITAL. SHE PUT HER BELONGINGS IN STORAGE AND RENTED OUT THE HOUSE TO PAY THE HOSPITAL FEES.
AND SHE DIED.
IT SO OFTEN ENDS THAT WAY.
WE SAW THEM A LOT, AND EVEN I DIDN'T PICK UP ON ANY PRELIMINARY SYMPTOMS.
ARE YOU A DOCTOR?
NO, I'M A NURSE.
WOULD YOU LIKE TO COME IN? I'LL MAKE US SOME TEA AND I CAN LOOK THROUGH THAT ALBUM.
DID THE CLAYBURNS HAVE CHILDREN?
A DAUGHTER, JULIA.
SHE LIVES IN LONDON. WE STILL SEND EACH OTHER CHRISTMAS CARDS.
COULD YOU GIVE ME HER ADDRESS? I'D LIKE TO AT LEAST RETURN THIS ALBUM TO HER.
HER LATEST CARD IS STILL ON THE TABLE IN THE HALLWAY.
YOU'LL FIND HER ADDRESS ON THE BACK OF THE ENVELOPE.
THANKS.
YOU GET A LOT OF CHRISTMAS CARDS.
THE OLDER YOU GET, THE MORE PEOPLE YOU KNOW.
AH, THERE. THAT'S HER, JULIA. SHE'S ALWAYS WORN GLASSES.

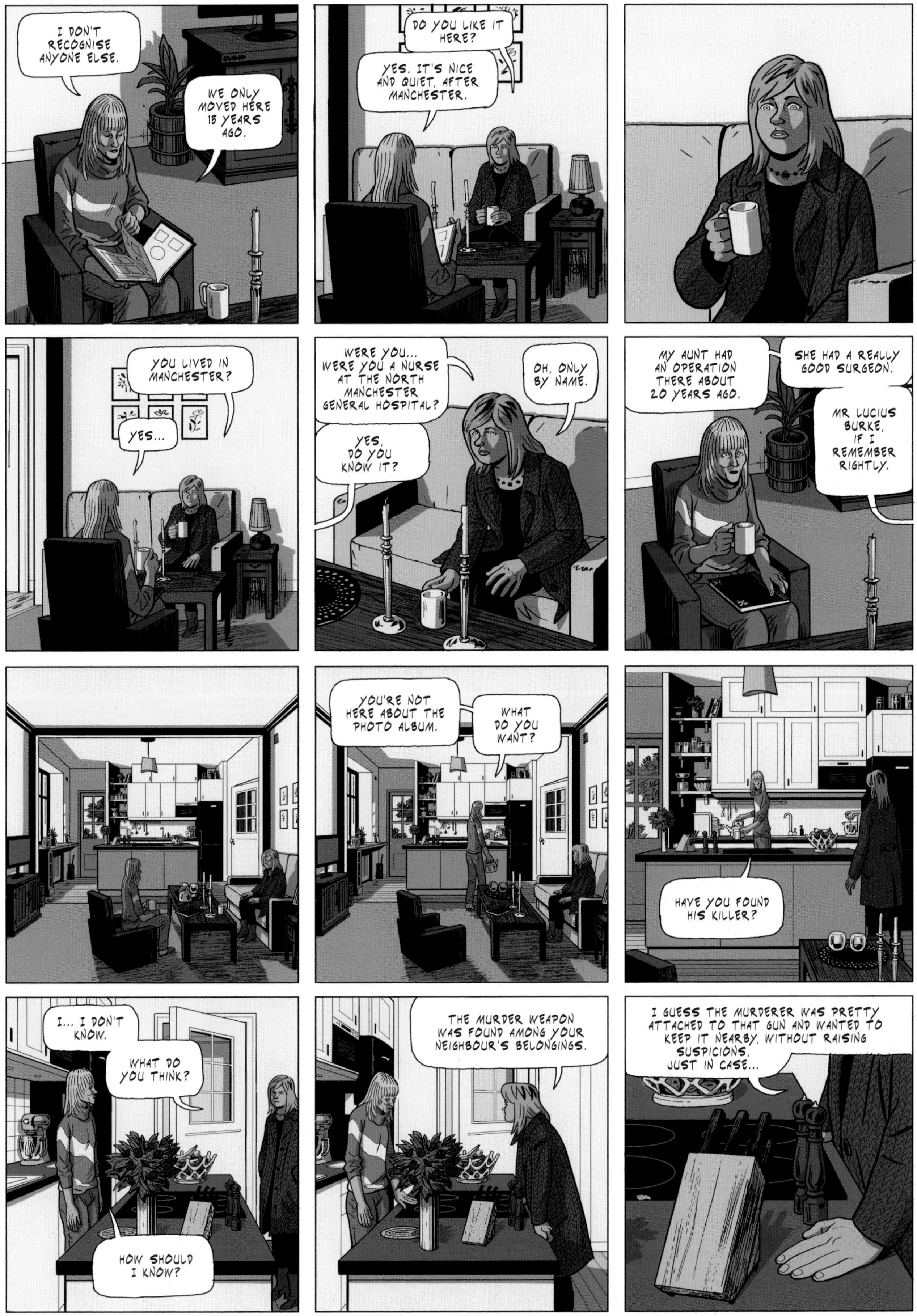
I DON'T RECOGNISE ANYONE ELSE.
WE ONLY MOVED HERE 15 YEARS AGO.
DO YOU LIKE IT HERE?
YES. IT'S NICE AND QUIET, AFTER MANCHESTER.
YOU LIVED IN MANCHESTER?
YES...
WERE YOU... WERE YOU A NURSE AT THE NORTH MANCHESTER GENERAL HOSPITAL?
YES, DO YOU KNOW IT?
OH, ONLY BY NAME.
MY AUNT HAD AN OPERATION THERE ABOUT 20 YEARS AGO.
SHE HAD A REALLY GOOD SURGEON.
MR LUCIUS BURKE, IF I REMEMBER RIGHTLY.
YOU'RE NOT HERE ABOUT THE PHOTO ALBUM.
WHAT DO YOU WANT?
HAVE YOU FOUND HIS KILLER?
I... I DON'T KNOW.
WHAT DO YOU THINK?
HOW SHOULD I KNOW?
THE MURDER WEAPON WAS FOUND AMONG YOUR NEIGHBOUR'S BELONGINGS.
I GUESS THE MURDERER WAS PRETTY ATTACHED TO THAT GUN AND WANTED TO KEEP IT NEARBY, WITHOUT RAISING SUSPICIONS, JUST IN CASE...

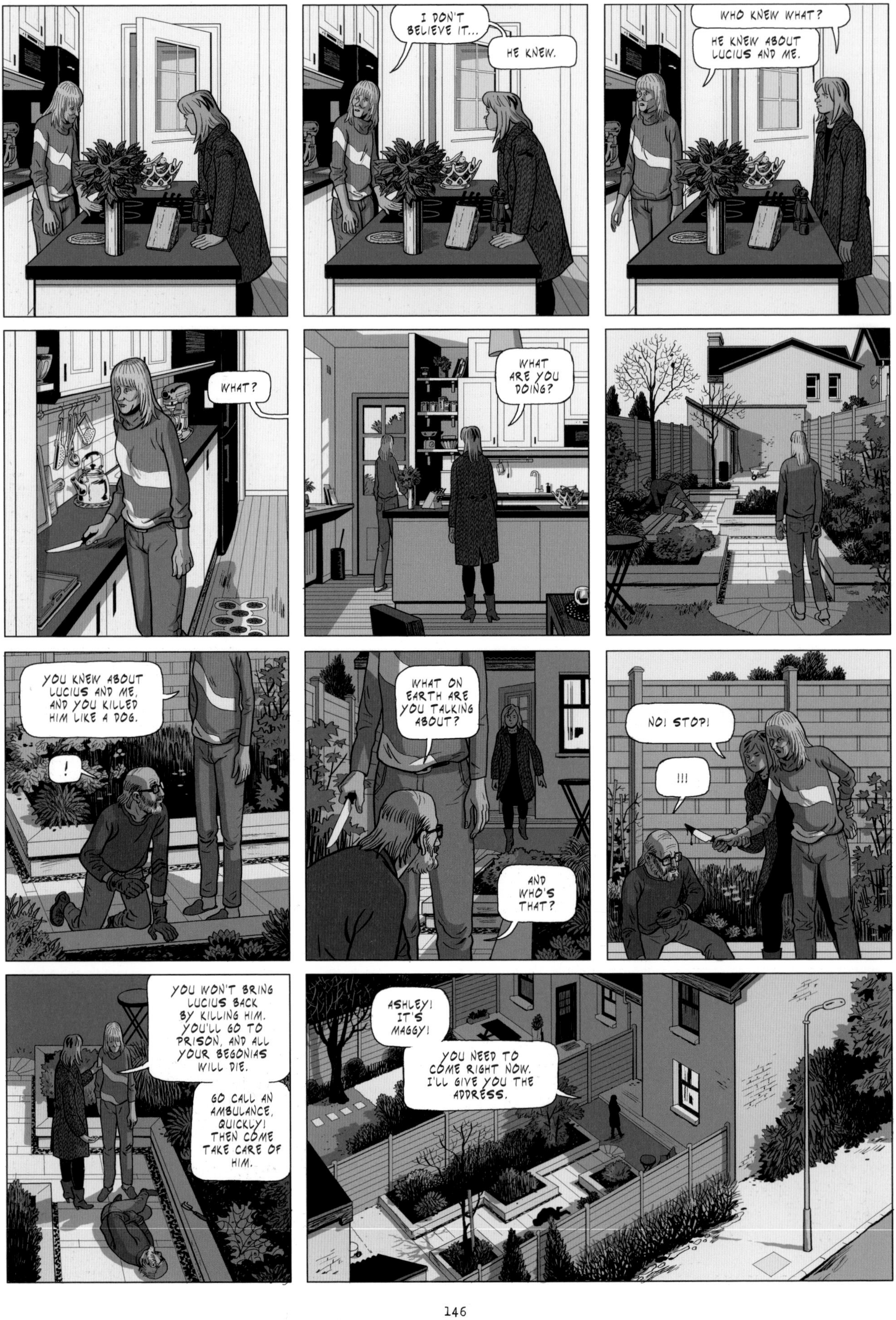
I DON'T BELIEVE IT...
HE KNEW.
WHO KNEW WHAT?
HE KNEW ABOUT LUCIUS AND ME.
WHAT?
WHAT ARE YOU DOING?
YOU KNEW ABOUT LUCIUS AND ME, AND YOU KILLED HIM LIKE A DOG.
!
WHAT ON EARTH ARE YOU TALKING ABOUT?
AND WHO'S THAT?
NO! STOP!
!!!
YOU WON'T BRING LUCIUS BACK BY KILLING HIM. YOU'LL GO TO PRISON, AND ALL YOUR BEGONIAS WILL DIE.
GO CALL AN AMBULANCE, QUICKLY! THEN COME TAKE CARE OF HIM.
ASHLEY! IT'S MAGGY!
YOU NEED TO COME RIGHT NOW. I'LL GIVE YOU THE ADDRESS.

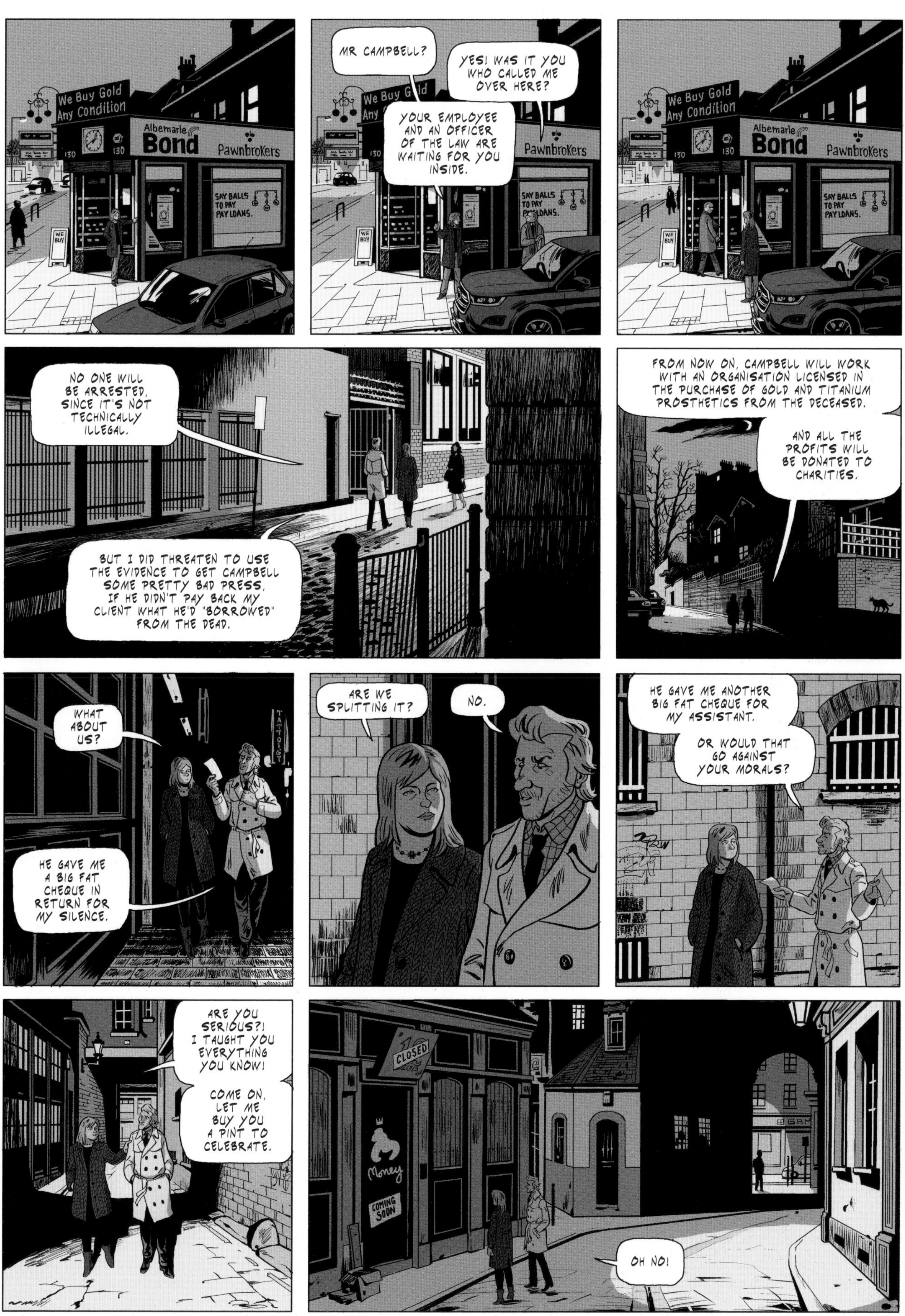
We Buy Gold Any Condition
Albemarle Bond
Pawnbrokers
SAY BALLS TO PAY PAY LOANS.
WE BUY
MR CAMPBELL?
YES! WAS IT YOU WHO CALLED ME OVER HERE?
YOUR EMPLOYEE AND AN OFFICER OF THE LAW ARE WAITING FOR YOU INSIDE.
NO ONE WILL BE ARRESTED, SINCE IT'S NOT TECHNICALLY ILLEGAL.
BUT I DID THREATEN TO USE THE EVIDENCE TO GET CAMPBELL SOME PRETTY BAD PRESS, IF HE DIDN'T PAY BACK MY CLIENT WHAT HE'D "BORROWED" FROM THE DEAD.
FROM NOW ON, CAMPBELL WILL WORK WITH AN ORGANISATION LICENSED IN THE PURCHASE OF GOLD AND TITANIUM PROSTHETICS FROM THE DECEASED.
AND ALL THE PROFITS WILL BE DONATED TO CHARITIES.
WHAT ABOUT US?
TATTOIST
HE GAVE ME A BIG FAT CHEQUE IN RETURN FOR MY SILENCE.
ARE WE SPLITTING IT?
NO.
HE GAVE ME ANOTHER BIG FAT CHEQUE FOR MY ASSISTANT.
OR WOULD THAT GO AGAINST YOUR MORALS?
ARE YOU SERIOUS?! I TAUGHT YOU EVERYTHING YOU KNOW!
COME ON, LET ME BUY YOU A PINT TO CELEBRATE.
CLOSED
Money
COMING SOON
OH NO!

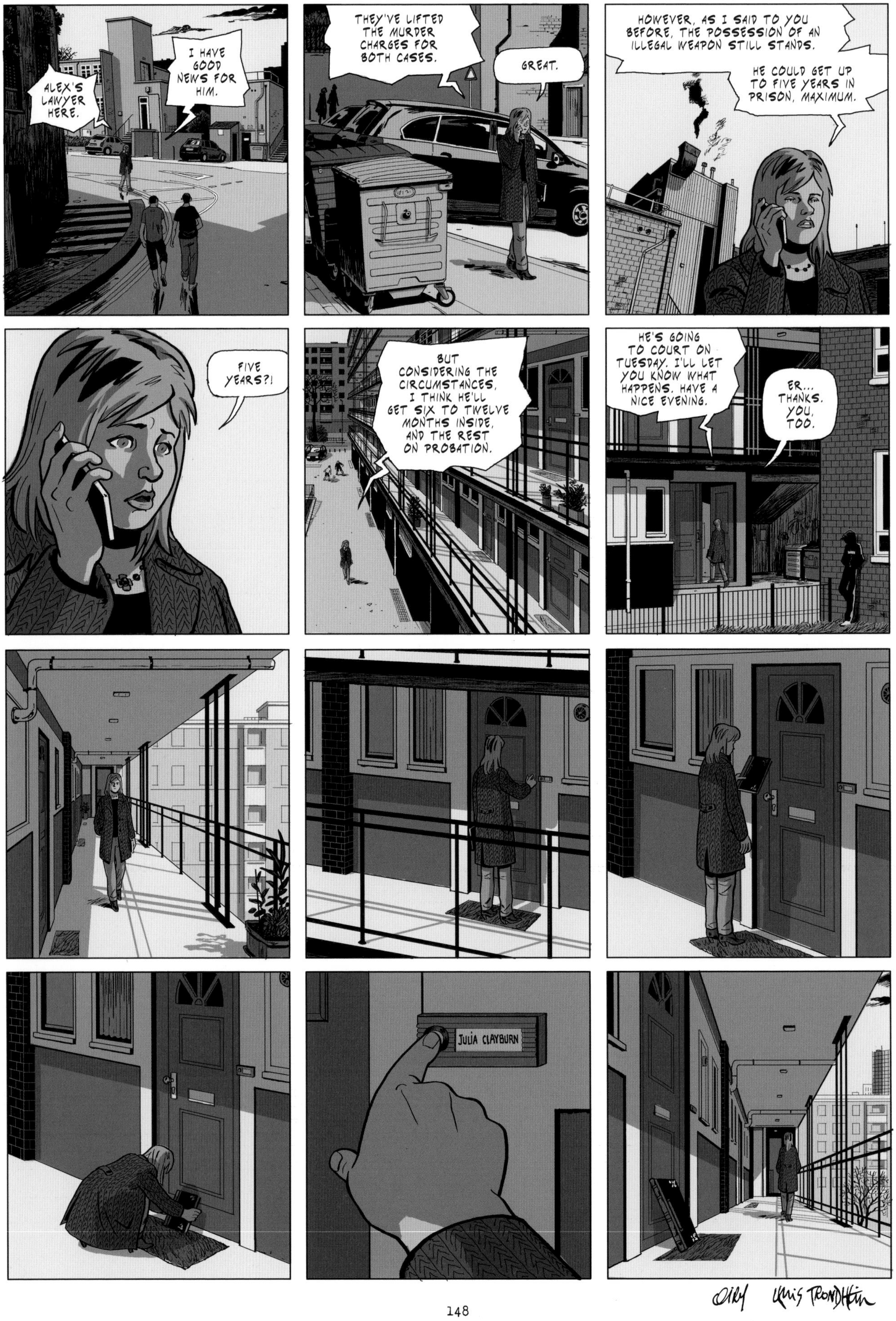

ALEX'S LAWYER HERE.
I HAVE GOOD NEWS FOR HIM.
THEY'VE LIFTED THE MURDER CHARGES FOR BOTH CASES.
GREAT.
HOWEVER, AS I SAID TO YOU BEFORE, THE POSSESSION OF AN ILLEGAL WEAPON STILL STANDS.
HE COULD GET UP TO FIVE YEARS IN PRISON, MAXIMUM.
FIVE YEARS?!
BUT CONSIDERING THE CIRCUMSTANCES, I THINK HE'LL GET SIX TO TWELVE MONTHS INSIDE, AND THE REST ON PROBATION.
HE'S GOING TO COURT ON TUESDAY. I'LL LET YOU KNOW WHAT HAPPENS. HAVE A NICE EVENING.
ER... THANKS. YOU, TOO.
JULIA CLAYBURN

Pocket Atlas of London

STREET PL

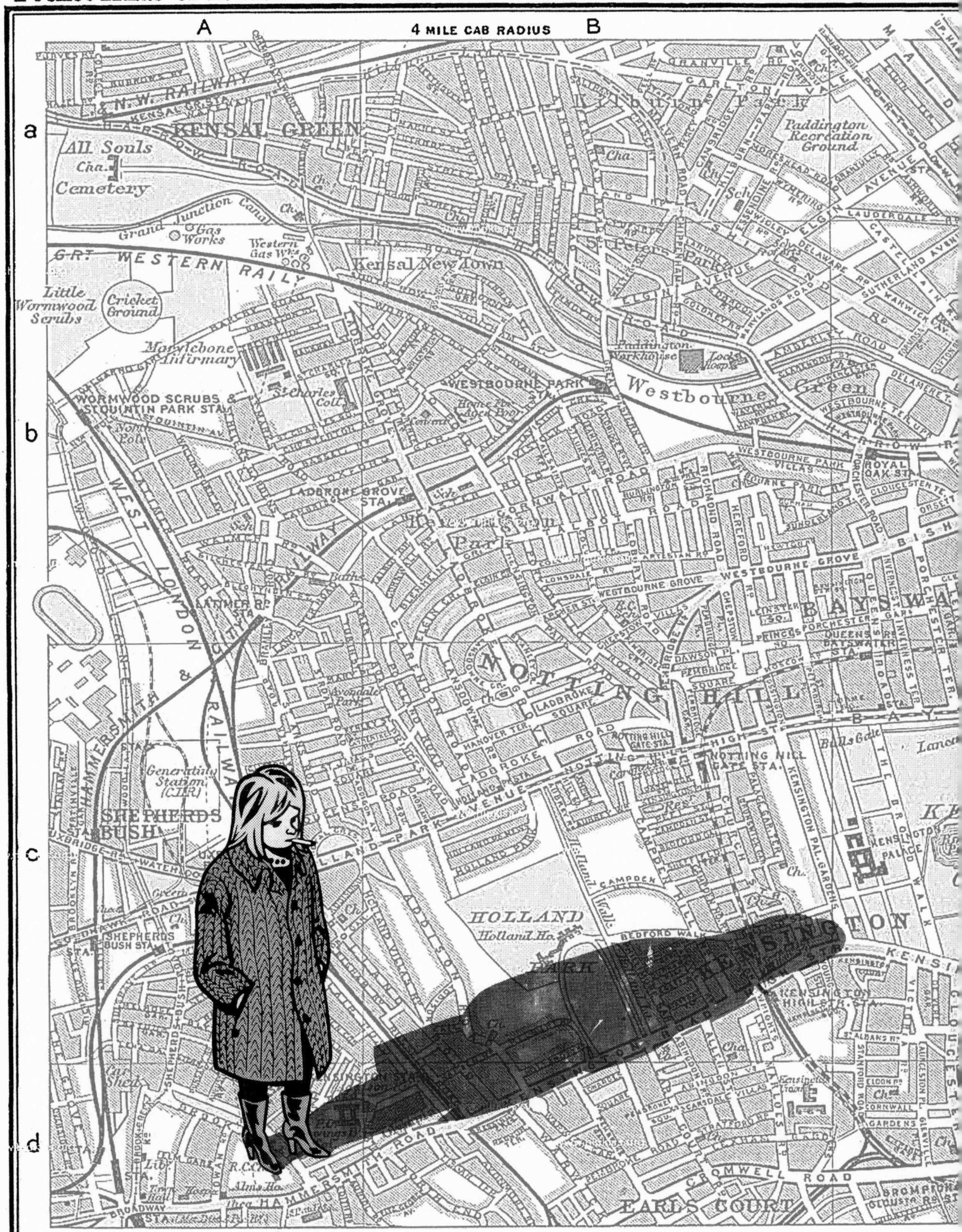
A
4 MILE CAB RADIUS
B
a
b
c
d
KENSAL GREEN
All Souls Cemetery
Grand Junction Canal
GR.T WESTERN RAILY
Little Wormwood Scrubs
Cricket Ground
Kensal New Town
Marylebone Infirmary
WORMWOOD SCRUBS & ST. QUINTIN PARK STA.
WESTBOURNE PARK STA.
Paddington Recreation Ground
Westbourne Green
LADBROKE GROVE STA.
WEST LONDON RAILWAY
NOTTING HILL
BAYSWATER
SHEPHERDS BUSH
HOLLAND PARK
KENSINGTON
KENSINGTON PALACE
KENSINGTON HIGH ST. STA.
CROMWELL ROAD
EARLS COURT
HAMMERSMITH ROAD
4 MILE CAB RADIUS
Scale of One Mile
Furlongs
Metres
0 1 2 3 4 5 6 7 8
0 400 800 1200 1600
Continue

Continued on Section V

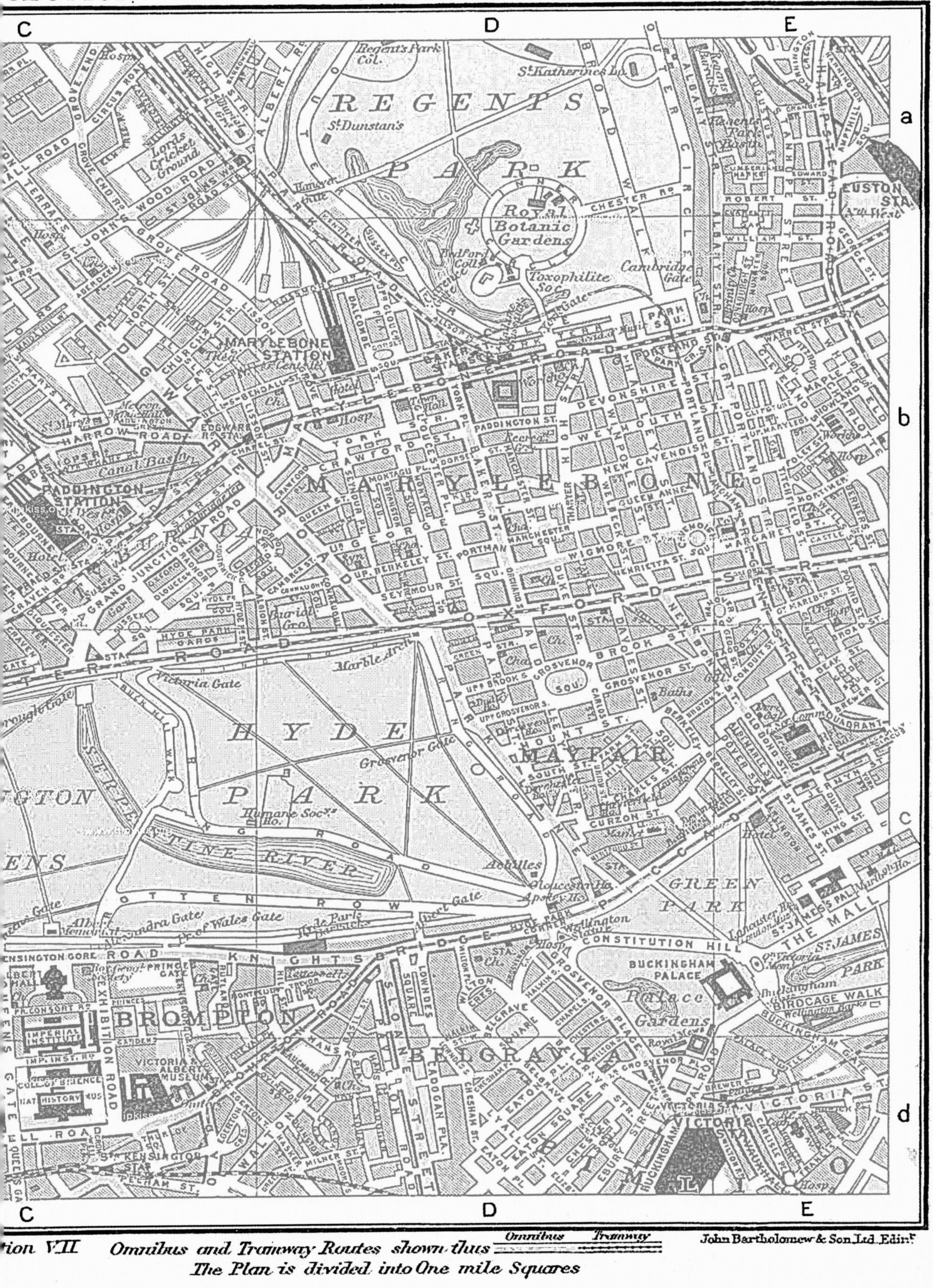
C
D
E
a
b
c
d
REGENTS PARK
Regent's Park Col.
St. Katherine's Ho.
St. Dunstan's
Royal Botanic Gardens
Toxophilite Soc.
Bedford Coll.
Cambridge Gate
Regent's Park Hosp.
EUSTON STA.
Lords Cricket Ground
ST. JOHNS WOOD ROAD
GROVE END RD.
MARYLEBONE STATION
MARYLEBONE
PADDINGTON STATION
Canal Basin
HARROW ROAD
EDGWARE ROAD
MARYLEBONE ROAD
EUSTON ROAD
PARK SQU.
PARK CR.
DEVONSHIRE ST.
WEYMOUTH ST.
NEW CAVENDISH ST.
PORTLAND PL.
GT. PORTLAND ST.
BAKER ST.
GLOUCESTER PL.
YORK PL.
PADDINGTON ST.
CRAWFORD ST.
GEORGE ST.
MANCHESTER SQU.
WIGMORE ST.
QUEEN ANNE ST.
CAVENDISH SQU.
HENRIETTA ST.
MARGARET ST.
PORTMAN SQU.
SEYMOUR ST.
OXFORD ST.
TYBURNIA
GRAND JUNCTION ROAD
HYDE PARK
Marble Arch
Victoria Gate
Grosvenor Gate
Humane Socy. Ho.
SERPENTINE RIVER
ROTTEN ROW
Albert Gate
Alexandra Gate
Pr. of Wales Gate
Achilles
Apsley Ho.
Hyde Park Corner
Wellington Statue
PARK LANE
GROSVENOR SQU.
BROOK ST.
GROSVENOR ST.
MOUNT ST.
MAYFAIR
BERKELEY SQU.
CURZON ST.
PICCADILLY
GREEN PARK
CONSTITUTION HILL
BUCKINGHAM PALACE
Palace Gardens
St. JAMES PARK
THE MALL
BIRDCAGE WALK
St. James's Pal.
Marlboro. Ho.
REGENT ST.
KNIGHTSBRIDGE
BROMPTON
BROMPTON ROAD
IMPERIAL INSTITUTE
VICTORIA & ALBERT MUSEUM
NAT. HISTORY MUS.
EXHIBITION ROAD
ALBERT HALL
KENSINGTON GORE
BELGRAVIA
BELGRAVE SQUARE
EATON SQUARE
LOWNDES SQUARE
SLOANE STREET
CADOGAN PLA.
GROSVENOR PLACE
VICTORIA STA.
VICTORIA ST.
BUCKINGHAM PAL. ROAD
VAUXHALL BRIDGE RD.
EBURY ST.
PELHAM ST.
S. KENSINGTON STA.
PIMLICO

Continued on Sections II, III & VIII

tion VII *Omnibus and Tramway Routes shown thus* Omnibus Tramway
The Plan is divided into One mile Squares

John Bartholomew & Son Ltd. Edinr.

Lewis Trondheim is an award-winning French comics creator and publisher. His books include Poppies of Iraq and Slaloms. Trondheim was made a Knight of the Order of Arts and Literature in 2005. He lives in Paris.

Stéphane Oiry is a comic book artist, animator and children's book author. The creator of a number of graphic novels, he teaches illustration at the Condé School of Art and Design. He lives in Paris.